Animated Encounters

ASIA POP!

Allison Alexy
Series Editor

Animated Encounters: Transnational Movements of Chinese Animation, 1940s–1970s
Daisy Yan Du

Animated Encounters

Transnational Movements of Chinese Animation, 1940s–1970s

Daisy Yan Du

University of Hawai'i Press
Honolulu

Printed in the United States of America

24 23 22 21 20 19 6 5 4 3 2 1

Library of Congress Cataloging-in-Publication Data

Names: Du, Daisy Yan, author.
Title: Animated encounters : transnational movements of Chinese animation, 1940s–1970s / Daisy Yan Du.
Other titles: Asia pop!
Description: Honolulu : University of Hawai‘i Press, [2019] | Series: Asia pop! | Includes bibliographical references and index.
Identifiers: LCCN 2018037381| ISBN 9780824872106 (cloth ; alk. paper) | ISBN 9780824877644 (pbk. ; alk. paper)
Subjects: LCSH: Animated films—China—History and criticism. | Animated television programs—China—History and criticism. | Motion pictures and transnationalism.
Classification: LCC NC1766.C6 D8 2019 | DDC 791.43/340951—dc23
LC record available at https://lccn.loc.gov/2018037381

Cover art: Film still from *Heroic Little Sisters of the Grassland* (1965). Reproduced with permission by the Shanghai Animation Film Studio.

University of Hawai‘i Press books are printed on acid-free paper and meet the guidelines for permanence and durability of the Council on Library Resources.

For Alex, Victor, and Henry

Contents

Series Editor's Preface

It is a distinct pleasure to be able to introduce the first book in Asia Pop! from the University of Hawai'i Press. This new series explores the impact and import of popular culture across myriad perspectives, academic disciplines, time periods, and cultural contexts. With ambitious vision, the series examines how popular culture is created, consumed, critiqued, and subverted in Asia and as it makes its way around the world. Popular culture's wide reach includes a remarkable range of formats and engages an enormous number of fans and not a few critics, including those for whom something as banal as the Hello Kitty mascot can incite gender panic and moral indignation. Popular culture triggers exhilaration and anxiety: It has the power to provoke deeply emotional responses and worm its way into our wallets as well as our psyches. Asia has become a key location for both producing and consuming popular culture and Asian governments continue to nation-brand and wield soft power abroad by exporting TV dramas, pop stars, and video game franchises. This series explores the tremendous energy—positive and negative, transnational and deeply personal—focused on the subject.

Daisy Yan Du's book perfectly embodies the series' most ambitious goals. At first glance, this book might seem to explore a topic familiar within pop culture studies: animation. But Du theorizes and historicizes animation from entirely new cultural and transcultural perspectives, arguing that Chinese animation has been "trivialized or forgotten," and that well before it became a national project it was fundamentally international. In this stirring cultural history of Chinese animation, we find convincing evidence to counter any narrative that situates the development of the genre only in the United States, Europe, Japan, or Taiwan. Moreover, Chinese animation gives Du remarkable perspective from which to theorize trends that occur in other places as well, for instance the use of animals and children within animated stories. Pinning the sudden disappearance of anthropomorphic animals in animated films to the beginning of the Cultural Revolution, Du argues that these characters were critical tools in defining socialist modernity. Throughout her analysis Du manifests the energy and creativity of popular culture; at the same time she traces its capacity as a political tool. Drawing readers in, this book demonstrates how much can be gained when we pay thoughtful attention to popular culture.

Acknowledgments

The origins of this book lie in the spring of 2008, when I was a graduate student at the University of Wisconsin–Madison. I thank all my mentors at Madison: Nicole Huang, Steve Ridgely, Susan Stanford Friedman, Julia Murray, Louise Young, and Ben Singer all taught me and offered their unfailing support. During my years as a researcher at the University of California–Irvine, Jeffrey Wasserstrom, Ackbar Abbas, and Bert Scruggs provided sympathetic ears and generously hosted me despite their busy schedules.

This supportive intellectual community extended beyond Madison and Irvine, of course. Poshek Fu, Andrew Jones, Haiyan Lee, Paul Clark, and Alex Cook read parts of the manuscript at its early stage and offered constructive feedback for further improvement. I am indebted to Paul Pickowicz, Tani Barlow, Jason McGrath, Tina Mai Chen, Yingjin Zhang, Xiaomei Chen, Ban Wang, and David Wang for their interest and warm encouragement. I am equally grateful to many scholars in the field of Japan studies for their unwavering faith in my project: Thomas Lamarre, Sharalyn Orbaugh, Akira Lippit, Michael Baskett, Douglas Slaymaker, and Michael Raine.

In 2013, I joined the Hong Kong University of Science and Technology as an assistant professor and have since then been surrounded by numerous warm and supportive colleagues. Among them are Wei Shyy, James Lee, Jianhua Chen, Shengqing Wu, Jianmei Liu, and Kenny Ng. I also thank Pascale Fung for introducing me to her animator father, Fung Yuk-song.

It was a great pleasure for me to share my research of this project with all my graduate and undergraduate students. I also thank my research assistants for helping with the technical issues in preparing this manuscript for publication.

I must acknowledge the various intramural grants from the Division of Humanities, the School of Humanities and Social Sciences, and the Hong Kong University of Science and Technology for the research, writing, and publication of this book. This project was also generously funded by the Research Grants Council of Hong Kong (Project Number: ECS 26400114 and GRF 16600417).

I completed the book's final stage of publication at the Harvard-Yenching Institute (2017–2018). I thank Elizabeth Perry and the institute for providing me with generous financial and intellectual support. I am indebted to Jie Li and Alex Zahlten for their hospitality and for commenting on portions of the manuscript. My thanks also go to Karen Thornber and the Harvard Asia Center for inviting me to share my research and to Susan Napier for her thoughtful feedback.

I am deeply indebted to many animators and their descendants or friends for their interviews, shared materials, and moral support: Duan Xiaoxuan; Yan Dingxian and his wife, Lin Wenxiao; Zhou Keqin; Qian Shanzhu; Deng Hu; Xu Zuming; Liu Jian; Mochinaga Noriko; and Sumi Kazuhiro.

As the Shanghai Animation Film Studio celebrated its sixtieth anniversary, I organized the Animators' Roundtable Forum, titled Chinese Animation and (Post)Socialism, held on our campus on April 27 and 28, 2017. Almost all the veteran animators from the Shanghai Animation Film Studio came and discussed Chinese animation between the 1940s and the 1980s from their insiders' perspectives. At the forum, I was also able to discuss with Chang Guangxi, Pu Jiaxiang, Yan Shanchun, Jin Fuzai, and Ono Kōsei. Dai Tielang, although unable to attend the forum, shared by telephone his experience of making television animation series in the 1980s. Pu Yong and Yin Xiyong also kindly shared their experiences at the Shanghai Animation Film Studio.

During my field studies in Hong Kong, Shanghai, Beijing, Tokyo, San Diego, Cambridge, and Montreal, the libraries and archives were crucial to my project. I thank Wan Shan Wong at the library of Hong Kong University of Science and Technology; Angel Ok Shing and Winnie Fu at the Hong Kong Film Archive; Liu Wenning at the China Film Archive in Beijing; Tochigi Akira, chief curator of the National Film Center of Japan; Xi Chen, the Chinese studies librarian at the University of California–San Diego's Geisel Library; Donald McWilliams and Katherine Kasirer at the National Film Board of Canada; and Xiaohe Ma and James Cheng at the Harvard-Yenching Library. I also thank the many other librarians and staff at the Shanghai Library, the Shanghai Municipal Archive, the National Library of China, the National Diet Library in Tokyo, and the Tsubouchi Memorial Theatre Museum (Enpaku) of Waseda University.

I thank Lee Kyung Hwa, the programmer and manager of the 19th Seoul International Cartoon & Animation Festival, for inviting me to serve on an international jury in May 2015. My experience with this film festival helped me better understand the black crow incident in the context of the history of Chinese animation.

The project reinforced in me the importance of sharing and community support and led me to establish the Association for Chinese Animation Studies to introduce and promote Chinese animation to the English-speaking world. (Animated films discussed in this book can be accessed at http://acas.ust.hk/category

/films/films-database/mainland-china/1947-1979.) This project is workable in Hong Kong, long considered a dynamic in-between place where the East encounters the West. I thank my colleagues for their enthusiastic support: John Crespi, Rolf Giesen, John Lent, Hua Li, Sean Macdonald, Paola Voci, Hongmei Sun, Li Guo, Gigi Tze-yue Hu, and many others.

I thank many young scholars and friends for their interest in and support for this book project along the way: Paola Iovene, Weihong Bao, Yiman Wang, Ling Zhang, Karen Fang, Liang Luo, Hui Faye Xiao, Jessica Chan, and Lanjun Xu.

The publication team at the University of Hawai'i Press has been invaluable, acquisitions editor Stephanie Chun and Asia Pop! series editor Allison Alexy in particular, but not least the two anonymous reviewers of the press for their compliments, encouragement, and insightful suggestions for further improvements. I also thank my copyeditor, Helen Glenn Court, for her professional and timely work.

Finally, I extend my sincere thanks to my husband, Alex Jianzhong Chen, whose love and understanding have animated my academic life. The arrival of our sons, Victor and Henry, brought us tremendous joy, pleasant distractions, and a strong sense of responsibility. This book is then dedicated to these three men, the backbone of my life.

Animated Encounters

Introduction

Animated Encounters: Chinese Animation in Motion

The international success and global popularity of *Kung Fu Panda* (2008), an animated feature film by DreamWorks, triggered heated discussion in scholarship and public discourse around the world. Some scholars and intellectuals argue that in transforming the panda into an American icon the film erases China and its ethnic traces.[1] Others maintain that the film highlights China's inability to appropriate its culture and produce a global blockbuster.[2] In these discussions, scholars and intellectuals position China as an invisible, silent, passive, and even victimized object of this Sino-US encounter, underscoring China's incapacity to safeguard its national treasure or produce an animated film that attracts a global audience. Few commentators attend sympathetically to China's animation industry and to its interactions with the rest of the world. With China missing from the international network of animated filmmaking, our knowledge is confined to and shaped by the hegemonic discourse of Hollywood and Japanese animations.

Chinese animation has played a vital and indispensable role in the world history of animation, but a role that has been either trivialized or forgotten. This book introduces readers to the early history of Chinese animation to map the place of China in world animation. Through historical study of Chinese animation and its active engagement with international forces during its formative period, it focuses on how Japan, the Soviet Union, the capitalist West (the United States in particular), Taiwan, and ethnic minorities in China were involved, at sociohistorical or representational levels, in Chinese animated filmmaking from the 1940s through the 1970s. It argues that the history of Chinese animation was international before it became national, and that these transnational border-crossing movements shaped the Chineseness of Chinese animation—and consequently transformed the history of animation across the world. The historical trajectory of Chinese animation epitomizes the general process in modernity and reflects the constant tension between transnational cultural production and national identity formation in China and beyond. Reanimating still images that were relegated to dark and dusty film archives, the book brings dead stories back to life by writing a cultural history of early Chinese animation and locating it in modernity's international context.

Shanghai Animation Film Studio and Socialist Collectivism

Western, especially American, animated films such as the *Out of the Inkwell* series (1918–1929) were introduced to Shanghai as a foreign medium in the late 1910s and early 1920s. In Republican China under the Nationalist Party (1912–1949), the Chinese called animated films *katong* or *katong pian,* a transcription of the English word "cartoon." After the end of the eight-year Sino-Japanese War (1937–1945), the Nationalist Party and the Communist Party fought a three-year civil war (1946–1949). The Communist Party ultimately seized political power and forced the Nationalist Party and its government, under the leadership of Jiang Jieshi (Chiang Kai-shek), to relocate to Taiwan in 1949. To welcome the new political regime, Chinese animators replaced the English word "cartoon" with a new term for the artistic form: fine arts film (*meishu dianying,* or *meishu pian*), which was endorsed by the socialist government. The Shanghai Animation Film Studio (Shanghai meishu dianying zhipianchang) was established in 1957 as the sole state-owned animation studio. It centralized animated film production in socialist China (1949–1976) and continues to use "fine arts film" in its name and in reference to its animated films to this day. The new name implies that Chinese animated film was indigenized as it increasingly became associated with traditional Chinese fine arts rather than with international cinema. During the socialist decades, many animators, especially senior animators with a background in fine arts, considered themselves more artists than filmmakers. This name change has historical significance because it demonstrates nationwide attempts to institutionalize and nationalize Chinese animation. Even when Chinese animation was the most nationalized—that is, during the socialist decades—international undercurrents loomed large and called into question the pure and essentialist Chineseness of Chinese animation.

After the introduction of Western animated films, Chinese artists began to experiment with the art of animation in Republican Shanghai. The Wan brothers—Wan Laiming (1899–1997), the eldest; his twin, Wan Guchan (1899–1995); and his two younger brothers, Wan Chaochen (1906–1992) and Wan Dihuan (1907–present)—were born in Nanjing and became the forefathers of Chinese animation.[3] They produced many animated shorts in Shanghai beginning in the 1920s. In wartime Shanghai, the twins created *Princess Iron Fan* (*Tieshan gongzhu,* 1941), the first animated feature film in China and Asia. Because the majority of these early animated shorts no longer exist, this discussion begins with *Princess Iron Fan* and ends with animated films made by the Shanghai Animation Film Studio in the late 1970s. The book thus mainly covers the fine arts films produced by socialist China. The rise of television and then computer animation in the 1980s and 1990s gradually plunged fine arts film into crisis and transformed the subsequent history of Chinese animation. After 1980, animated films became much more diversified in form, content, (intended) audience, production or screening venue, and technique or technology; they deserve their own book-length study of the postsocialist context.

In its examination of animated films, this volume concentrates on the socialist era under the leadership of Mao Zedong (Mao Tse-tung), that is, on films made from the 1940s through the 1970s. It has long been believed that due to ongoing war and revolution in China and widespread Cold War ideologies, the period from the 1940s through the 1970s is defined by a cultural separatism that ended with the death of Mao in 1976 and China's gradual opening to the world. This book calls attention to cultural contact and infiltration in Chinese animated filmmaking to demonstrate that these apparently closed decades were more open and fluid than previously depicted. Despite wartime blockades, *Princess Iron Fan* traveled to Japan, Singapore, Indonesia, Hong Kong, America, and Canada. The Shanghai Animation Film Studio frequently held film exhibitions in other Chinese cities and Hong Kong in the early 1960s.[4] Animators during the socialist era actively drew on international resources from Japan, the Soviet Union, America, Taiwan, ethnic minorities in China, and others, on the material level (the border-crossing movements of animators, technologies, techniques, films, studios) or on the representational level (themes, motifs, images, styles). Major animated shorts and features of the period frequently traveled abroad and won awards at prominent venues, including the Venice International Children's Film Festival, the Cannes International Film Festival, the Annecy International Animated Film Festival, the Ottawa International Animation Festival, and the Locarno International Film Festival. It is estimated that between 1950 and June 1964, approximately sixty-five Chinese animated films traveled to nearly sixty-four countries and regions, including Europe, Asia, Africa, Latin America, Australia, and America.[5] Some Chinese animated films continued to travel abroad and were active at international film festivals during the Cultural Revolution (1966–1976). These successes occurred decades before the fifth-generation filmmakers, such as Zhang Yimou and Chen Kaige, appeared on the global stage at international film festivals of the 1980s.[6]

In analyzing the animated films produced during this period, this study challenges the reified myth that art and literature during the Mao era were no more than political propaganda that slavishly served the government. Overemphasis on politics can be traced to Mao's 1942 Yan'an Talks, during which he stipulated that literature and the arts should be subordinate to politics. Mao's totalitarian impulse to nationalize and unify all literature and arts encouraged the critical perception that literature and arts at that time were political propaganda devoid of artistic value and subtlety. According to conventional studies of Chinese cinema, it was only with the rise of the fifth-generation filmmakers in the 1980s that the totalitarian and didactic cinema witnessed a breakthrough in terms of artistic style and content—an innovation and elevation enabled, in part, by the transnational mobility and popularity of these films.[7]

However, a close study of the animated films produced in the socialist era reveals a different story. The totalitarian era coincided with a golden age of Chinese animation, during which many masterpieces were produced. When fifth-generation live-action films began to flourish in the 1980s, animated filmmaking began to face unprecedented challenges resulting from decollectivization, the rise of a free market economy, and the emergence of new media and new technology such as television and computers. In addition, animated film was less affected than live-action film by politics and ideology, probably because it was considered a minor artistic and cinematic form for children, and therefore received less critical attention and inspection from above. At that time, it was easy for live-action films to make political missteps and then be subject to severe censorship and persecution. In retrospect, some senior animators felt lucky because animated films were not as politically sensitive as their live-action counterparts, and missteps made in animation would be considered moral or educational rather than political.[8] During the socialist era, when live-action films were severely restricted, censored, or prohibited from traveling to foreign countries, animated films frequently traveled abroad and won prizes at international film festivals in socialist and capitalist countries.[9] It comes as no surprise that many animated films with great artistic value were distanced, if not completely divorced, from totalitarian politics during the socialist era.

This book focuses primarily on the Maoist era, destabilizing the rigid political periodization of Mao's China by drawing attention to the early 1940s and the late 1970s. It is almost impossible to discuss socialist animated films without examining animated filmmaking before 1949. From the perspective of animators and the animation industry, animated filmmaking before the regime change of 1949 and filmmaking after the Communist takeover were continuous. For instance, the Wan brothers had been fascinated with the character of Monkey King since they were young and enjoyed making animated films featuring the mythic hero. *Uproar in Heaven* (*Danao tiangong,* 1961–1964), a masterpiece of the socialist era, was actually a continuation and perfection of *Princess Iron Fan*, which they had made in wartime Shanghai. Also, animated filmmaking in early socialist China had a connection with the Manchukuo Film Association (Man'ei), which flourished during the wartime era (discussed in chapter 2). Furthermore, the Cultural Revolution did not come to a complete and immediate stop in 1976. Instead, it lingered in various ways in animated filmmaking until the late 1970s. Despite regime changes, culture flowed across rigid political divides established by politicians. For many years, studies on the literature and arts of the Mao era followed their rigid political periodization of 1949 through 1976 because the era was usually interpreted as a rupture and aberration in political and cultural histories. Looming over these political and temporal divides is a binary between propaganda films produced in the Mao era and the commercial films made during the times of the Republicans and Deng Xiaoping. This book draws attention to the movement of animated films across arbitrary temporal boundaries demarcated by politics and regime changes and highlights the disjuncture between politics and aesthetics in the sense that politics cannot fully control arts.

In terms of location, this discussion revolves around the Shanghai Animation Film Studio. Republican China had no separate and independent animation studio and therefore animated filmmaking depended on live-action film production. At that time, the Wan brothers made animated films for live-action film studios such as Great Wall (Changcheng), Great China (Da Zhonghua), United China Productions (Lianhua), Star Productions (Mingxing), Denton Film Company (Diantong), Central Film Studio (Zhongdian), and New China Productions (Xinhua). In the late 1940s and early 1950s, animated filmmaking in China was first affiliated with Man'ei, then the Northeast Film Studio, and later Shanghai Film Studio (chapter 2). On April 1, 1957, the animation division of the Shanghai Film Studio declared independence and became the Shanghai Animation Film Studio, the first and the only separate (state-owned) animation studio in the country at that time. The studio had approximately twenty staff in the beginning and around five hundred at its peak.[10]

Live-action film studios also established animation groups or workshops involved in small-scale animated filmmaking during the period. Changchun Film Studio, which was called Northeast Film Studio until February 28, 1955, established its animation group in 1958. It produced two puppet animated films entitled *The Little Donkey Wiseacre* (*Zizuo congming de xiaolü*, 1958) and *The Ginseng Girl* (*Renshen guniang*, April 1961), as well as a cel-animated propaganda film titled *Expelling the God of Plague in Anger* (*Nu song wenshen*, September 1961). It produced no other animated films until 1984. When the Shanghai Science and Education Film Studio was established on February 2, 1952, it also built an animation workshop and mainly produced science and educational films. Not until 1992 did it produce animated films with narratives. The Beijing Science and Education Film Studio was founded with an animation workshop on March 2, 1960, and worked primarily on science and educational films until 1980. The animation workshop at August First Film Studio was established in 1952 and focused on military educational films before 1987. Nanjing Film Studio established its animation group in 1972 but did not produce an animated film until 1983. During the socialist era, about 90 percent of Chinese animated films were produced by the Shanghai Animation Film Studio. Most of these animation groups or workshops were shuttered during the Cultural Revolution and did not reopen until the 1980s.[11]

At the Shanghai Animation Film Studio, the socialist state was in charge of almost everything, from script writing to film production, distribution, screening, and even collective viewing. The majority of the animated films were shorts and a few exceptional animated feature-length films.[12] Mainly targeting children, they were often screened in children's theaters (*ertong yingyuan*), special screenings for children (*ertong zhuanchang*), arranged by ordinary theaters on Sunday mornings and sometimes on the afternoons of weekdays, and early screenings for children (*ertong zaozaochang*), usually scheduled on early Sunday mornings before the official opening hours of theaters. Some were also screened at children's film weeks (*shaonian ertong dianying zhou*), a film festival that had daytime and night screenings.

It is reasonable to assume that because it was controlled by the state, the Shanghai Animation Film Studio was likely to be the mouthpiece of the Communist Party, capable of producing only communist propaganda devoid of artistic value. The studio, however, was dynamic and creative, producing hundreds of animated films of high artistic quality, most of which are extant and remain popular today. Quantity aside, the studio also made groundbreaking innovations in animation technology, artistic styles, genres, and subject matter. The Mao era, conventionally associated with literary and artistic oppression and stagnation, ironically witnessed the golden age of the Shanghai Animation Film Studio, which began to decline in the late 1980s.

Socialist collectivism, which was reinforced by totalitarian politics and centralized state control, contributed to the prosperity of the Shanghai Animation Film Studio during the socialist decades. Adopting the system of planned economy during the socialist decades, the state—in the form of the State Bureau of Radio, Film, and Television—only required the studio to produce a certain number of films (around thirty to forty films, ten minutes per film, altogether three hundred to four hundred minutes, around CN¥3 million annual output value) per year; the state took care of all other matters, including distribution (by China Film Distribution and Exhibition Corporation) and even screening and viewing (organized by schools, work units, communities, and so on). The studio focused on production and did not worry about the market and profits.

The socialist state was also generous in financially supporting big-budget animated films and, in the early 1960s, costly ink-painting animated films as well (discussed in chapter 3). For the production of *Uproar in Heaven* (first and second episodes, 110 minutes), the socialist state invested more than CN¥1 million, a sky-high price in the early 1960s, without thinking much about its market and profits.[13] Animators received their fixed salaries from the state on time and did not have any opportunities to work outside and earn extra wages, which was regarded as a capitalist practice and a severe crime.[14] The salaries of animators of the same rank were almost all the same given the egalitarian practice at that time, which eliminated comparison and peer competition. In this way, animators could concentrate on animated filmmaking without being distracted by material pursuits. Zhou Keqin was hired as a recent graduate by the Shanghai Animation Film Studio in the 1960s with a monthly salary of CN¥54; directors were paid CN¥89 to CN¥103, more than the average salary in Shanghai at the time.[15] Thus the salary of animators at the Shanghai Animation Film Studio enabled them to live more comfortably than many other workers. Because the socialist state took care of most daily needs, Chinese animators at the studio enjoyed ivory-tower privileges, enjoying abundant funding, time, and energy to pursue their artistic goals without being burdened by concerns about the market, consumers, and profit. Totalitarian political control carved out a space within which a certain degree of artistic creativity was not simply allowed but even encouraged.

Animated filmmaking is a collective endeavor, involving different types of professionals, such as key animators, in-betweeners, inkers, and painters, as well as a range of industries and social sectors. In his discussion of Japanese animation, Ian Condry argues that it is "collaborative creativity" across industries and fan communities that has contributed to the global success of anime. He calls this collective social energy the "soul" of anime.[16] Collective social energy was equally important in Chinese animated filmmaking during the socialist era, but in a totally different sociohistorical context. When Te Wei, the first president of the Shanghai Animation Film Studio, whose tenure lasted from 1957 to 1984, gave up his cartoon (*manhua*) career and joined the animation industry at the Northeast Film Studio in early socialist China, he already realized that the difference between the two art forms was that the cartoon was about the creativity of an individual and that animation was a collective enterprise involving a group of excellent animators.[17] As the socialist state tightened its control over the film industry, Chinese animated filmmaking was subjected to increased collectivization and centralization. Many film scholars today criticize the totalitarian state's control of cinema and usually celebrate the rise of fifth-generation filmmaking in the 1980s as a break from the state-centered mode of film production. However, this period affected animated filmmaking differently. It is ironic that by strengthening the collective energy of animated filmmaking, the totalitarian state unexpectedly brought about the golden age of Chinese animation.

As the only animation studio at that time, the Shanghai Animation Film Studio adhered to the principles of collective enterprise and followed a meticulous division of labor despite a seemingly unified style. Almost all of the country's talented animators joined the studio and worked collectively. Many of the masterpieces made at the time, such as *Little Tadpoles Look for Mama* (*Xiao kedou zhao mama,* 1960), acknowledged this collective effort with phrases like "collectively created" (*jiti biandao* or *jiti chuangzuo*) in the credit sequences. The chickens in the film were drawn by Tang Cheng and Pu Jiaxiang, the golden fish and shrimp by Wu Qiang and Dai Tielang, and the tadpoles by Lin Wenxiao.[18] In addition to animators, numerous nameless inkers, painters, and clean-up artists worked on the films as well. Although an individual animator was given credit as director of a particular film, he or she acknowledged the collective effort of the studio's entire staff. For many years, Wan Laiming was credited as the only director of *Uproar in Heaven.* In recent DVDs (first and second episodes together) released by the studio, Tang Cheng is included on the director credits along with Wan Laiming, having worked as the vice director and taken charge of the practical duties for the making of the film.[19] As was true of the studio's other animated films, the production of *Uproar in Heaven* involved a meticulous division of labor and the collective efforts of the entire studio.

To cultivate the collective spirit among the younger generation of Chinese animators, the Shanghai Animation Film Studio established the Youth Creative Collective (Qingnian chuangzuo jiti) in 1958. Young animators without directing experience were organized into groups that worked collectively under the supervision of a senior animator to write film scripts, direct films, and design the drawings. Following this model, the groups produced many animated films, which used "collective" (*jiti*) as the director and erased individual names in credit sequences.[20]

With concentrated intervention and the support of the totalitarian state, the Shanghai Animation Film Studio collaborated with other industrial sectors, such as the Shanghai Film Studio Orchestra, on sound production. Even audiences were centralized because animated films were screened in theaters and occasionally on television for collective viewing, education, and entertainment, which were organized by schools, work units, and street communities. Group cohesiveness and social bonding were thus reinforced by socialist collectivism. Their disintegration began during the late 1970s and gradually contributed to the decline of the Shanghai Animation Film Studio in the late 1980s.

Totalitarian Politics, Childish Mimicry, and the Double Marginality/Power of Chinese Animation

Lu Xun, one of modern Chinese literature's greatest writers, published the influential short story *A Madman's Diary* (*Kuangren riji*) in 1918. In it, a madman thinks his family members and villagers are cannibals who are eating each other. The story was often interpreted as a protest against the rapacious practices of traditional culture and society and a call for a new culture and societal reform. The story ends with the famous sentence "save the children," which triggered heated discussion in China about the relationship between children and nation. From then on, children and children's literature and arts were co-opted into the national and nationalist agenda and imbued with intense political significance. Andrew Jones analyzes the important and precarious role of children in development programs of the nation and civilization in Republican China and asks who, in a society in which everyone has eaten human flesh, can be in a morally superior position to save the children?[21] Lu Xun's call seemed an impossible task, given its implication that children are passive victims waiting for adults to save them.

In reality, children were never as politicized as they were in Mao's revolutionary era, particularly during the radicalism of the Cultural Revolution, which has been demonized by scholars at home and abroad as totalitarian, extremist, terroristic, and suffocating for literature and the arts (see chapter 4).[22] For these reasons, Stephanie Donald regards children as "political messengers" in her studies of Maoist posters of the 1960s and 1970s.[23] Mary Ann Farquhar sees children's literature in Mao's China as a "battlefield" full of militant and ideological meanings, and that it was not until the death of Mao in 1976 that children's literature was transformed into a depoliticized "garden."[24] Donald and Farquhar are insightful in capturing the big picture of the Mao era: children were appropriated by adults as political and ideological tools and symbols. I do not challenge their arguments here. Instead, I reveal the discontent and even resistance of children against the ideological meanings imposed on them by adults in authoritarian China.

In her analysis of Chen Kaige's film *The King of the Children* (1987), Rey Chow points out that the child and the peasant were the two crucial figures used by Chinese intellectuals to reflect on issues of revolution, nationalism, and cultural regeneration. One feature they share is their powerlessness.[25] It is precisely because they are powerless and cannot speak for themselves that they are easily co-opted into cultural, political, and nationalist projects. However, as Ann Anagnost points out, despite their presumed powerlessness and silence, both the child and the peasant have "a performativity" that is difficult to control. Children, like peasants rebelling against authority, can subvert state ideology with unruly and aberrant behavior.[26]

I contend that in highly politicized socialist China, children could mock and subvert the totalizing state ideology through what I call childish mimicry, a term inspired by Homi Bhabha's "colonial mimicry" and Luce Irigary's "feminine mimicry."[27] Used in different contexts, postcolonial studies and feminist studies respectively, Bhabha and Irigary make similar arguments for the subversive power of mimicry of the colonized or the female against the power center, the colonizer or patriarchy. This argument can be extended to the power relationship between children and adults as well. A typical feature of socialist China was that the division between children and adults was blurred to the extent that children were expected to think and behave like adults armed with communist ideology that was often incomprehensible to them, and adults were expected to be as naive as children to believe in whatever the Communist Party said. By pretending to accept, appropriate, and even abuse the contradictory roles assigned to them by authoritative adults, children could masquerade and transform the prescribed roles into their own, challenging politicized adult discourse and causing it to backfire. By imitating, repeating, exaggerating, and distorting adult thought and behavior through models from real life and media representations, children could deviate from the original political message imposed on them by authoritarian adults. Functioning as a category of difference, children could pose a threat to the hegemony of adults and stage forms of childish mimicry that are playful, mischievous, recalcitrant, and subversive, beyond the control of adult authorities.

News and reports about childish mimicry during the socialist decades unsettled the nerves of the Communist government. For example, the revolutionary animated film *The Rooster Crows at Midnight* (*Banye jijiao*, 1964) is about the strike by a small group of peasants against a greedy landlord who forces them to wake up and begin to work early in the morning by making the roosters crow even earlier. Rather than appreciating and accepting the message of class struggle, audiences of children criticized the peasants for being lazy and "not loving labor."[28] They invoked the language that the Communist Party used to indoctrinate them with socialist ideology. During the Korean War, when American fighter aircraft appeared on film, children clapped their hands happily and never showed a sign of hatred against American imperialism, despite the politically correct message conveyed by adult propagandists immediately before the screenings.[29] To deal with these issues, adult authorities such as teachers, film propagandists, and party secretaries had to work out ways to intensify the ideological indoctrination before and after the film screenings.[30]

Children in socialist China might assume subversive power through childish mimicry, yet they remained marginalized subjects. In fact, their subversive power came from their marginalization. Ann Anagnost points out that the child and the peasant did not always assume equal significance in history, observing that "where one appears, the other recedes from view." During the Republican era, the child was idealized as the representation of the unmediated real and assumed vital importance in national projects; during the socialist era, the peasant displaced the child and attracted most of the attention in projects of revolution and nation building.[31] It was precisely this invisibility and marginality that made children relatively less if not completely depoliticized in socialist China when compared with adults—particularly peasants.

The marginalized status of children had a tremendous impact on animation, which mainly targeted children during the period. As an art form for children, animation too was marginalized and assumed a status inferior to other established art forms such as live-action film and literature. Animation was regarded as childish and funny, and thus not a serious art form for mature adults. I call this characteristic the double marginality of animation, in the sense that animation was a minor artistic form for minors (children). Just as children as marginalized subjects could assume subversive power through childish mimicry, double marginality afforded animation increased power and possibilities beyond subordination and victimhood, possibilities that those in the center might not enjoy. The double marginality of animation can thus be transformed into double subversiveness and even double power, enabled by the marginalized statuses of both children and animation. In the context of socialist China, animation could toy with totalitarian politics and enjoy more freedom and fluidity because political attention was riveted on live-action film revolving around the peasant as well as the worker and the soldier. Of course, the double power did not overtly and directly counter state power but could at least play with it strategically in being subversive. The double power enabled by the double marginality of animation, I maintain, partly protected Chinese animation from political turmoil, helped it escape the government's censorship and people's critical attention, and granted it temporary immunity from politics that other art forms, such as live-action feature film, did not enjoy.

This double power contributed to the prosperity, mobility, and fluidity of Chinese animation in wartime and the socialist decades. For instance, people paid less attention to *Princess Iron Fan*'s connections with Japan than they did to other live-action feature films in wartime Shanghai (discussed in chapter 1). Reflecting on animated filmmaking in the socialist era, some senior animators felt lucky that animated films received less strict censorship and critical attention than live-action films, allowing them to engage in more audacious experimentation in terms of animation techniques, technology, artistic style, and subject matter.[32]

The difference between the double marginality and power of animation and the normality and vulnerability of live-action film is well illustrated by the controversy over the animated film *Catching Fish through Collectivity* (*Jiti youyu*, 1963). In the film, an individualistic old peasant tries to catch a big fish but fails. A collective effort finally enables him to catch the big fish. The film's theme emphasizes collectivity, which was a key political principle at that time. However, the film was severely censored and criticized to such an extent that production was suspended in the middle of filming—an uncommon response. When talking today about the fate of this film, senior animators are still confused by the severe criticism it received.[33] In my view, the major reason for the response is the film's critical portrayal of an adult peasant—a highly sensitive political subject—and targeting of an adult audience. In doing so, it ventured into the realm of live-action film, making it vulnerable to harsher censorship. The film might not have been criticized so vehemently had it portrayed instead a selfish child or an anthropomorphic animal. Indeed, other animated films with similar themes—such as *Three Neighbors* (*Sange linju,* 1956) and *Plucking the Big Radish* (*Ba luobo,* 1957)—did not attract the same level of critical attention precisely because they revolved around children and talking animals.[34] Dramatizing the complicated and delicate relationship among peasant, child, and totalitarian politics, *Catching Fish through Collectivity* illustrates the double marginality and power of animation during the socialist decades.

Examining animation from this more positive perspective does not imply that animation is free from politics. On the contrary, animated filmmaking was never as politicized as it was during the socialist era, especially during the Cultural Revolution (discussed in chapter 4), when animated films were criticized and animators persecuted. My point here is based on a relative comparison between animation and other art forms produced for adults during the period. Even strict political control left space for artistic creativity and potentially audacious transgression, which could find its fullest expression in animation. After all, people tend to be more tolerant of children and childish art forms, which can more easily be laughed off and forgiven. This partly explains why Chinese animation continued to flourish during the socialist decades, an era commonly decried for its stagnation and even suppression of literature and arts due to countless wars, campaigns, and revolutions.[35]

Soviet animation under Stalin sheds further light on the double marginality and power of animation and the consequent ambiguous relationship between animation and totalitarian politics. Early Soviet animated films were highly politicized propaganda intended for adults. For instance, *China in Flames* (1925), the Soviet Union's first animated feature film, vehemently criticizes American imperialism and eulogizes international communism. Soviet animation underwent a dramatic transformation when ideological control tightened and socialist realism became a state policy between 1934 and 1953. Beginning in 1934, animation in the Soviet Union changed its direction by targeting children. Almost all artistic forms under Stalin's rule (1934–1953), such as literature and live-action film, conformed to socialist doctrines by dramatizing the protagonists' achievement of socialist consciousness. Children's literature was no exception.[36] It is ironic that under such tight ideological control, animation distanced itself from totalitarian politics by portraying a fairy-tale world for children full of princesses, cute anthropomorphic animals, demons, and spirits, in films such as *The Little Humpbacked Horse* (1947), *The Flower with Seven Colors* (1948), and *The Fisherman and the Goldfish*

(1950). These fantasy films were produced by Soiuzdetmultfilm, an animation studio established in 1936 that changed its name to Soiuzmultfilm in 1937 to centralize animated filmmaking in the Soviet Union.[37] Like the Shanghai Animation Film Studio, Soiuzmultfilm was not simply a government mouthpiece for political propaganda. On the contrary, it eagerly learned from American animation and produced films that were close to Disney in terms of both form (roundness and realism) and content (fairy tale and fantasy). It is unexpected that the well-known boundary between socialism and capitalism during the Cold War era collapsed in animation.[38] I hold that double marginality granted animation the double power to play around with and even eschew totalitarian politics.

A Bite of Ethnic Taste: The National Style Complex

Although Chinese animation boasts a long and complex history, the topic has attracted little research in English despite a recent surge of studies on Western and Japanese animation. Other than a few dissertations, articles, and chapters, the books by Sean Macdonald, Weihua Wu, and Rolf Giesen are the only pioneering works on the subject in English so far.[39] All of them examine Chinese animation mainly from a national rather than a transnational perspective.[40]

Much on animation is written in Chinese, however.[41] Most adopt a linear narrative and provide a comprehensive history of Chinese animation from its inception to the present. These studies are descriptive, written in a review style without in-depth discussion of conceptual issues concerning medium specificity, modernity, visual culture, mobility, gender, children, and animals. In addition, they are characterized by a preoccupation with the national style, which refers to the use of authentic Chinese materials, techniques, aesthetics, and culture (such as Peking opera, papercutting and paperfolding, ink painting, folklore, and traditional Chinese literature) to represent a pure Chinese identity in animated filmmaking. Emphasizing Chineseness, the national style is an artistic marker used to differentiate Chinese animation from its Japanese and Western counterparts for the sake of constructing a distinctive Chinese identity on the global stage. The national style has become the yardstick by which to measure the success of a Chinese animated film. The majority of these studies concentrate their analyses on national style films, neglecting other films that do not fit into the paradigm.

Similar assertions of national essence and identity are made in academic research in Japan and the United States. Japanese artists such as Takahata Isao and Murakami Takashi argue for historical continuity and cultural resonance by tracing the roots of contemporary anime to ancient art forms. A similar theory of national uniqueness is evident in studies of American animation. According to it, Disney films epitomize American culture at large.[42] Although both of these cases work within a national framework, neither is as dominant and influential as China's national style discourse, an institutionalized public and official discourse guiding both animated filmmaking and academic research.

The scholarly preoccupation with national style and national identity in animated filmmaking in China must be understood in its larger cultural context. The consequence of globalization is not only homogenization, but also the assertion of differences and national identities at a time when national borders seem to become more and more porous in the global village. Globalization goes hand in hand with localization, generating a form of "glocalization," in which the global and the local coexist. Anxiety was tremendous over the potential loss of Chinese culture and national identity in the late 1970s and early 1980s, when China officially opened up to the world and embarked on a process of globalization. Cultural nationalism arose. Chinese intellectuals promoted the idea of a national cinema in response to the influence of foreign film cultures. This in turn provoked heated debate over films' nationality and internationality in mainland China. Some people welcomed globalization and celebrated the prospect of integrating Chinese cinema into global networks of film production and viewing. However, others advocated for the nationalization of Chinese cinema with a focus on representing Chinese culture and authenticity.[43]

The preoccupation with the national style is more intense in the field of animated film than in live-action feature film. The pervasive view is that if live-action feature film has to be inevitably influenced by foreign films, then animated film, because of its association with drawings and paintings that can be readily taken from the repertoire of traditional Chinese art, should function as the last fortress defending Chineseness in national cinema.

Beginning in the late 1970s and early 1980s, Chinese animators and intellectuals, anxious about the inevitable influence of anime and Disney, committed themselves to upholding the national style and to promoting what they referred to as the Chinese School of Animation. Tracing the origin of this term is difficult, but it first appeared in print in a 1988 article by Yin Yan to refer to Chinese animated films made in the national style.[44] The Chinese School of Animation became the most powerful discourse guiding the mainstream animated filmmaking industry and dominating the language of animators, film critics, fans, intellectuals, and researchers. Because of a fascination with national style artistic forms and content, films from the Chinese School of Animation were considered categorically different from both Western and Japanese animation. The school argues that the formal and thematic uniqueness of Chinese animated film should stand for a monolithic and timeless Chinese identity, an assertion that makes Chinese animated film popular and well recognized on the global stage. The catchphrase of this school is "the more national, the more international."[45] In James Clifford's words, the "roots" of Chinese art present in animated films paradoxically grant them the "routes" to travel abroad and gain international recognition.[46]

Since the early 1980s, national style has been regarded as the best and probably the only way to revitalize Chinese animation and to gain an international market and recognition in the face of unprecedented challenges, downturns, and fierce competition from anime, Disney, and other foreign animations.

This strategy contrasts sharply with the success stories of Japanese animation. Critics have pointed out that although anime is regarded as a cultural product of Japan, Japanese identity is problematized in anime, which itself exists in a world that transcends any singular national framework. These critics often use the word *mukokuseki,* which means stateless or without a national identity, to refer to anime. Human characters in anime, with their blond hair, blue eyes, and elongated figures, are often de-Japanized and seem to belong to a different world that cannot be located anywhere on earth. In terms of their transnational mobility, many anime films were first de-Japanized and became what Koichi Iwabuchi calls "culturally odorless" before they were exported to foreign countries. The erasure of Japaneseness became a prerequisite for anime to win international recognition, especially from the United States.[47] Furthermore, anime's stateless world is often created by animators who are also "stateless." In fact, anime is not necessarily made by Japanese animators in Japan. It is commonly created by non-Japanese animators and outsourced and produced in China, Korea, Taiwan, and other regions or countries. Susan Napier proposes the concept of "postethnic identities" in the "stateless fantasy space" of anime.[48] However, this stateless world is exactly what made Japanese animation recognizably Japanese.

Chinese animators and intellectuals of the fine arts film generation are reluctant to turn to anime for inspiration today. Rather, they look inward to find strength and inspiration within traditional Chinese culture of the past.[49] One major reason for the strong desire to distinguish Chinese animation from Japanese art forms might be the long-standing cultural and political rivalry between the two countries more recently evidenced in the two Sino-Japanese Wars (1894–1895 and 1937–1945).

The discourse of the national style was further reinforced in the 2000s when it intersected with the Chinese government's framework of "soft power." The concept of soft power was proposed by Joseph Nye in 1990 to describe the power of culture to attract, persuade, and co-opt people, in contrast to the hard power generated by economic and military forces.[50] Since the early 2000s, the discourse of soft power has become popular among East Asian governments, and the emphasis on the national identity of culture itself becomes a transnational phenomenon. Hu Jintao, then president of China, first advocated the promotion of the soft power of Chinese culture in a meeting with authors and artists on November 10, 2006. From then on, revitalizing the domestic animation industry and Chinese culture at large, such as creating Confucius Institutes around the world, became important goals. The Chinese government formulated policies to protect and promote the domestic animation industry, such as by establishing domestic animation bases, promoting animation film festivals and exhibitions, waiving taxes for domestic animation studios, and banning foreign animation. Central to all these practices is the assertion that Chinese animation should be rooted in traditional Chinese culture and should disseminate Chinese values and spirit. According to Beijing, even the international coproduction of animated films should focus on Chinese traditions and national style. Coproduced animated films with "Chinese features, Chinese stories, Chinese images, Chinese styles, Chinese manner, and Chinese spirit" could be treated as domestic animation and enjoy all the financial and promotional benefits offered by the government.[51] With the government's involvement, the national style became an official and institutionalized discourse that dominated the animation industry and academia in mainland China.

The contemporary discourse of the national style is relevant to the older history of animation. Throughout the history of Chinese animation, animators never ceased in their efforts to pursue and establish a national style. In the Republican era, the Wan brothers advocated that "Chinese animated films should portray Chinese-style protagonists."[52] They thus struggled to portray an "authentic" Chinese princess (Princess Iron Fan) and to distinguish her from Disney's Snow White. They were conscious of Chineseness in animated filmmaking though they did not use the term national style.

The discourse of the national style was not institutionalized until the Communist Party took over the film industry and nationalized cinemas. This process began in 1949 with the adoption of the term "fine arts film" for Chinese animation, but it was not until what I call the black crow incident in 1956 that the national style was official. In 1956, China received the first international award for animated film at the Venice International Children's Film Festival for *Why Is the Crow Black* (*Wuya weishenme shi hei de*, 1955), proclaiming it to be the country's first color cel-animated film. Some international jurors, however, initially regarded the film as a production of the Soviet Union. Traumatized and humiliated by this misidentification, Chinese animators felt compelled to seek a national style that would make their films' Chineseness clear.[53] At that time, the Sino-Soviet relationship was deteriorating and nationalism was surging. Beset with these aesthetic and political crises and supported by the government, Chinese animators soon launched their artistic experimentation and produced *The Conceited General* (*Jiaoao de jiangjun*, 1956), which was regarded as the beginning of the grand exploration of the national style. Animators then turned to traditional arts such as ink painting, papercutting, Peking opera, and folklore to make national style films in the late 1950s and early 1960s. However, the widespread story about the birth of the national style in the late 1950s was probably invented, thus calling into question conventional narratives about its origin (discussed in chapter 3).

Although the discourse of the national style began in the context of the Sino-Soviet relationship during the Cold War, it was revived, systematized, and empowered in response to a new set of national and international crises that began in the early 1980s: the decline of the monopoly status of the Shanghai Animation Film Studio and the infiltration of foreign animated films into the domestic market. The infiltration was not only in animated filmmaking, but also in live-action filmmaking and other forms of production. Throughout history, the search for a national style was always the most intense and urgent when China encountered its powerful Other or experienced either a national or a cultural crisis. Under such circumstances, the Chinese government became involved in promoting this type of aesthetic movement. The discourse of the national style and national identity is thus a product and symptom of what Rey Chow calls "the logic of the wound," which justifies the radical assertion of Chineseness as the necessary reaction to foreign aggression and humiliation.[54] It is a self-defense mechanism that responds to external crises.

In this book, I use national style and national identity to refer to this institutionalized discourse that originated in the late 1950s and was revived during the 1980s to dominate animated filmmaking and academic studies. Although proposed with good intentions and effects in the late 1950s, the national style discourse has gradually become misunderstood and misinterpreted. It is seen as a rigid, timeless, exclusive, and even xenophobic standard, one suppressing other national and international styles said to be tainted with foreignness (*yang*) that does not fit well with the pure and idealized framework of the national style. Such a view neglects the fact that the concept of the national style changes as the Chinese society changes, and that there should be many national styles—even the most international style can be a form of national style. This volume destabilizes the singular notion of the national style and contends that national style is not one, but many. The national style should not be used for xenophobism, because many national cultures are (trans)formed through interacting and absorbing foreign ones. Foreign traces do not necessarily dilute the authenticity of the national style, but more often than not make it more national and original.

Unexpectedly, the pure national style argument is complicit with Orientalist discourses in the West. First, animated films produced in the national style cater to a Western audience's desire to watch "authentic" Chinese films. Their curiosity and interest is understandable given that they have watched few if any Chinese animated films. In addition, the Western demand for authenticity fuels the domestic desire to produce animated films with the national style to win international recognition. In this respect, these films are similar to the successful model of the fifth-generation films made by Zhang Yimou and Chen Kaige, which are questioned by some scholars for essentializing Chinese culture to cater to the Orientalist tastes of Westerners. This self-Orientalizing and self-essentializing tendency proved highly successful at international film festivals from the 1950s to the 1980s. It did not grant Chinese animation access to the lucrative international market for mass consumption, however, which the "culturally odorless" anime did. In other words, (over)emphasis on the national style privileged the artistic and local rather than the commercial value and universal appeal of Chinese animated film. Despite critical recognition from international film festivals and their audiences, in the end Chinese animated films are consumed primarily by domestic viewers.

The national-nationalist argument of national style has its rationale, but it unexpectedly results in a static and ossified approach to animated filmmaking and academic research. One common practice in animated filmmaking is to go to ancient and remote China to revive traditional artistic forms, classical literature, and folklore to exemplify the unique identity of Chinese animation and by extension the nation. As a result, Chinese animated films, especially those made in the spirit of the national style, tend to look like paintings, drawings, and handicrafts and to focus on the past in terms of their content. In academic research, scholars tend to concentrate on the formal features of canonical films that best represent the authenticity of national essence and neglect and even devalue the majority and variety of other Chinese films as being tinged by foreign influences or distanced from the orthodox national style.[55] They also tend to break down a classic national style film into stills to analyze their unique formal features rooted in tradition and folk art. In other words, everything about Chinese animation can be found and explained in traditional Chinese art, aesthetics, and culture, distanced from the contemporary modern world. With this methodology, Chinese animation is painterly and artistically beautiful but loses its movement and dynamism and is reduced and flattened into an isolated, still, seamless, and pure image that contains national essence and identity. The multiple layers within the image and the movement within and across media, space, and time are pushed aside. The overemphasis on traditional art and art history neglects the cinematic and technological mediation of animated film, overlooking the fact that the modern technology of animation, as well as cinema, was initially a foreign and international medium, despite the idea of animation (making images move) being present in the optical toys of ancient China.

Preoccupation with capturing Chinese essence and identity in turn marginalizes animation's movement and mobility. Animation is mobile in the sense that it travels across media (such as painting, photography, cinematography, and toy production) and genres (such as women, children, and animals). It also travels between different sites of media production, both temporal and spatial. Transnational dimensions and cross-cultural interactions outside the national space were deliberately ignored by scholars and became the repressed or even demonized side of the history of Chinese animation. Ironically, this occurs as transnational cinema studies are on the rise in an age characterized by accelerating transnational flows of culture. In some circles, discussion of the transnational dimension and the contamination or hybridization of national identities in live-action films might seem cliché now.[56] It remains taboo in Chinese discussions of Chinese animation.

Chinese animation thus remains stubbornly and overly national. Too little attention has been paid to Chinese animation's travel, reception, and afterlife in other spaces and times. For example, *Princess Iron Fan* was far more influential in wartime Japan than in wartime China (see chapter 1). However, any foreign influence or connection in Chinese animated filmmaking had to be disavowed and rejected. For example, the roles of Mochinaga Tadahito and Man'ei were ignored in the history of Chinese animation (see chapter 2).[57] The controversy over the alleged Soviet connection with *Why Is the Crow Black* is another example (see chapter 3). The television broadcast of *Police Chief Black Cat* (*Heimao jingzhang*, five episodes, 1984–1987), a popular series, was suspended soon after release because an expert criticized it for departing from the national style.[58] In 1988, the Shanghai Animation Film Studio refused to work on *Journey to the West* (*Saiyūki*, one hundred episodes), a project outsourced by NHK (Nippon hōsō kyōkai/Japan Broadcasting Corporation), because the image of Monkey King in the Japanese animated television series deviated from the Chinese national style.[59] *Pleasant Goat and Big Big Wolf* (2005–present), a popular animated television series, was regarded as unsuitable for export because it was not Chinese enough.[60] *Monkey King: Hero Is Back* (2015), an animated feature film that broke box office records in China for animated film, was obviously influenced by Hollywood despite disavowals by its director Tian Xiaopeng.[61]

Foregrounding the transnational movements of culture, this volume aims to jump out of the pure national space to see mobility, encounters, and entanglements between different cultures, media, peoples, and theoretical concepts in animated filmmaking. It thus positions travel, movement, and mobility as prerequisites of Chinese animation.

Animated Encounters: The Mobility and Diplomacy of Animation

Animated film, which is usually regarded as subsequent and subordinate to live-action film, actually preceded it. The concept of animation can be traced to pre-cinematic optical toys, such as the magic lantern, flip book, zoetrope, mutoscope, and praxinoscope, many of which date to ancient times. It is fair to say that cinema is in fact based on the idea of animation—the animation of photographs with slight variations. Although cinema can be regarded as a descendant of animation, it severed its ties to animation after it gained artistic legitimacy, making animation its "bastard relative, its supplement, its shadow."[62]

Despite their close kinship, animation has its own medium specificity, or special features that distinguish it from live-action film. Here we begin with Sergei Eisenstein's classic concept of plasmaticness, which refers to the elasticity and fluidity of drawings in animated filmmaking. The outlines of characters in animated film, unlike those in live-action film, can stretch, elongate, inflate, deflate, and fluctuate, embodying "a rejection of once-and-forever allotted form, freedom from ossification, the ability to dynamically assume any form."[63] Echoing Eisenstein, Thomas Lamarre renames plasmaticness as plasmaticity to discuss the fluidity of drawings, namely, how "the deformation and reformation of characters—stretching, bending, flattening, inflating, shattering—becomes a source of pleasure in itself."[64]

The plasmaticness or plasmaticity of the fluid outlines and other formal features of animation extend to its subject matter and theme. For Eisenstein, formal plasmaticity goes hand in hand with fluidity and mobility of content, theme, and subject matter: an unstable character can become a hero and vice versa.[65] The notion of plasmaticness and plasmaticity focuses on the form and content of animated film that are visible and self-evident to the audience. In other words, they look at the images drawn by an invisible hand on different frames.

Departing from an approach that focuses on images drawn by an invisible hand, some scholars look at the invisible cinematic mechanism and technology that make drawings move, proposing that movement defines the medium specificity of animation. Norman McLaren sees animation as an art of movements rather than an art of drawings. For him, drawings on individual frames are less important than the invisible gaps and interstices between drawings or frames—the in-between sites that generate movements: "Animation is not the art of drawings that move but the art of movements that are drawn; what happens between each frame is much more important than what exists on each frame."[66] In animated film, the invisible interstice between frames generates the movement. Without these intervals, individual frames are drawings devoid of movement, life, and energy.

Focusing on the multiplanar camera in anime, Thomas Lamarre further looks inside the cinematic mechanism by arguing that the invisible interstices between layers, rather than those between frames, generate the force of the moving image.[67] He calls the invisible interstices between layers the "animetic interval," which generates movement and the life force of anime.[68] Despite their different perspectives, these studies all agree that movement defines the medium specificity of animation.

I am more interested, however, in larger sociohistorical formations—that is, modernity. But, as Lamarre points out, the medium-specificity thesis (microaesthetic analysis) and the modernity thesis (macrohistorical paradigms) in animation studies are not diametrically opposed. Rather, dialogue can take place between them.[69] I contend that movement is the bridge in animation studies connecting the specificity thesis and the modernity thesis. Animation is plasmatic, mobile, fluid, and migratory not only in terms of production by hands (Eisenstein) and animation machines (McLaren and Lamarre) from the perspective of medium specificity, but also in terms of circulation, transmission, and reception in the larger sociohistorical context of modernity. Taking a cue from the invisible interstice and the animetic interval in medium-specificity theses, I maintain that in the global history of animation, the invisible interstices between demarcated national borders, understood as both geopolitical (state territoriality evident on maps) and historical nationhoods (imagined communities shaped by shared history and culture), are more significant than the animated film produced within a single national, cultural, or territorial space. This invisible yet animated middle ground generates the movement and life force of animation as a whole art form across national, cultural, spatial, and temporal borders in multiple directions, and subsequently (trans)forms the histories of world animation. I call this interstice the animated contact zone, the in-between space of dynamic encounters, in material sociohistorical and representational terms, that generate the ceaseless play, transformation, and entanglement of animation histories around the world.[70] The movement or life force of animation resides not only inside the animation machine (medium specificity), but outside it as well, to reach and animate other places and times (modernity).

Animated encounters in the contact zone might register suspicion, confrontation, misunderstanding, and even hostility at the personal and collective (cultural and political) levels, generating what Samuel Huntington calls the clash of civilizations.[71] However, more often than not it also triggers outbursts of artistic creativity during the process of contact, friction, and reconciliation. In other words, encounters lead to the "animation" of cultures on both sides of the border, literally in the sense of animation as an art form, and metaphorically in the sense of animation understood as cultural revitalization. Furthermore, this volume demonstrates that animated movements across geopolitical borders do not necessarily follow the hegemonic and diffusionist mode of modernity, flowing from center to periphery. Instead, they flow in multiple directions with unexpected turns, detours, and entanglements.

In crossing geopolitical borders, be they material or symbolic, animation demonstrates fluidity and smartness, what I call the diplomacy of animation. That is, the form and content of animation is plasmatic and fluid, as Eisenstein noted, as is its ideology. First, the content of animation has plasmatic ideology, which often results in fluid ideological interpretations. The nonpolitical animated films can be highly politicized, even as the highly politicized can be depoliticized. Second, animation is plasmatic in terms of its relationship with ideology, understood as external forces specific to certain sociohistorical context, such as the totalitarian ideology in socialist China. Animation plays with serious ideologies with innate levity yet remains politically elusive, which enables it to cross ideological and geospatial borders at home and abroad, as demonstrated by animation's ambiguous and even benign relationship with totalitarian politics in socialist China (as well as the Soviet Union) and the travel of *Princess Iron Fan* across wartime Sino-Japanese borders.

With a form as amorphous as water and content and ideology as slippery as ice, animation is not readily pinned down. Yet it has the potential to become everything by transforming itself, adapting to new environments, and squeezing into and out of any political framework, as does a malleable animation character. In addition, as an artistic form of double marginality, animation does not attract the same critical attention directed at art forms for adult audiences and can transgress boundaries without detection. All these features grant animation the diplomatic ability to travel in multiple dimensions, across ideological and geospatial borders at home and abroad, as well as representational, media, and other divides.[72]

Because of animation's mobility and diplomacy, the history of Chinese animation is replete with animated encounters, entanglements, and creative frictions. *Uproar in an Art Studio* (*Danao huashi,* 1926), proclaimed as the first animated film short in Chinese history, was produced by Great Wall Film Company, a studio founded by the Chinese-American Mei Xuechou in New York in 1921 and relocated to Shanghai in 1924. Hollywood animations, such as those featuring Koko the Clown, Felix the Cat, Mickey Mouse, Popeye, and Betty Boop, were popular in Republican Shanghai. *Snow White,* the first Disney animated feature film, premiered in Los Angeles on December 21, 1937, and in Shanghai in the summer of 1938. Its release in Shanghai triggered the creation of *Princess Iron Fan*, the production of which would have been impossible without financial capital and film stock from Japan. Upon completion, *Princess Iron Fan* traveled to Japan, Singapore, and Indonesia—despite wartime blockades. The beginning of the animation industry in socialist China would have been difficult without the involvement of Japanese animators such as Mochinaga Tadahito. During the socialist decades, animated films featured representations of external (the West and the United States in particular) and internal (Taiwan and ethnic minorities) Others.

Although the socialist era was regarded as a period of closure, animated films traveled to foreign countries such as Italy, Canada, France, England, Denmark, Switzerland, the Soviet Union, Poland, Yugoslavia, Australia, Germany, Indonesia, Syrian Arab Republic, and Czechoslovakia and won international awards.[73] Animated films made in postsocialist China traveled abroad even more frequently, thanks to the opening-up policy of the late 1970s. The mobility and diplomacy of animated film today is reinforced by the media democratization resulting from the rise of the internet and other media technologies. We can watch animated films from any country by visiting YouTube, Youku, and other websites. An extreme example of animation's mobility and diplomacy is the fact that contemporary anime was introduced to China largely through the media practices of copying and piracy, which led Laikwan Pang to argue that "among other forms of representation, animation might be the one most resistant to claims of essentialist cultural roots."[74]

Chinese Animation in Motion

The aim of this book is to move beyond the reified national style approach that centers on roots and static images and to unveil the multidirectional routes, encounters, and movements disavowed in the master narrative of national-nationalist cinema. This aim does not deny the role of national identity, because in writing about Chinese animation, I acknowledge the subtle differences between this artistic form and animation in other countries, such as Disney and anime. Rather, my purpose is to foreground previously invisible movements in the formation of national cultures. Thus, I approach Chinese animation as an artistic form in motion and examine visuality and national identity, which are constantly (trans)formed in movements, journeys, and travels across artistic, geopolitical, temporal, and cultural borders.

Destabilizing the notion of national and transnational as fixed binaries, this volume focuses on interstitial movements between the two polarities. This focus teases out how these polarities constitute, enable, and subsume each other in the (trans)formation of national cultures and national identities. The national is not constructed in a vacuum; it is never free from the infiltration of the transnational. Transnational movements do not necessarily lead to a demise of the nation and loss of national identity. Rather, the transnational is usually an indispensable part of and sometimes even triggers the formation of the national and nationalism, as exemplified by the rise of the national style in the late 1950s. On the other hand, the national is a prerequisite for the transnational, because without it, the transnational has nothing to cross and thus ceases to exist. In other words, the transnational is as much enmeshed in the national as the national in the transnational.

The implied slash in the word "trans/national" indicates both separation and connection. It marks an interstitial zone of contact between two contested sides. It is the in-between site that generates the moving force of animation as an art form that crosses multiple borders. Furthermore, this volume does not merely look outward and examine transnational flows of culture. It also looks inward, moving into the core of what constitutes the national, with an analysis of ethnic minorities and other marginalized groups, to explicate how national identity is (trans)formed through the interplay between national and regional flows of culture.

The theme of movement is central to this discussion. At the medium-specificity level, it refers to movement of images on the screen, which is generated by the interstices between frames and layers. Movement gives anima and life to the otherwise still drawings.[75] At the intermedial, aesthetic, and imaginative levels, movement suggests the travel of images and styles in animated film across media, space, and time—an imaginative shift that leaves traces, symptoms, and the textual unconscious on film. By tracking these migrating images, we uncover the mechanism of compositing images and cultural encounters that otherwise may remain hidden in the history of Chinese animation.

On a larger sociohistorical level, movement is defined by multidirectional rather than unidirectional (from center to periphery) flows of films, technology, labor, people, studios, ideologies, and cultures across rigid national, spatial, and temporal borders. These flows of culture, as Arjun Appadurai argues in his analyses of ethnoscapes, mediascapes, technoscapes, financescapes, and ideoscapes, are incongruous with each other. Disjunctures rather than conjunctures always take place among them.[76] From the methodological perspective, movement refers to the fluidity of approaches adopted in this volume. Rather than limiting myself to a singular approach and framework that focuses on the pure image of the national style, I move within and between different disciplines: (transnational) film studies, animation studies, travel and migration studies, art history research, women, children, and animal studies.

In brief, my aim is to track these multifaceted movements on both textual and contextual levels and to explore the contested relationship between national identity and animated aesthetics from the 1940s through the late 1970s. This transformative historical period was fraught with radical artistic movements, political revolutions, and national crises. The discussion moves synchronically and diachronically, each chapter revolving around certain movements across spatial and temporal borders.

The formal structure involves movement from the transnational (chapters 1 and 2) to the national (chapter 3) to the subnational (chapter 4). Chapter 1 looks from the inside out, voyaging out of the national to examine how Chinese animated film was appropriated by and embedded in other national cultures.

Chapter 2 looks from the outside in, exploring how other animated national cultures were part and parcel of Chinese animation. Chapter 3 looks sideways at the national and draws attention to the international context during the Cold War, in which Chinese national culture emerged and was interpreted in response to international and national crises; it also explores how traditional art traveled from the past and was appropriated for nationalist agendas in the socialist present. Chapter 4 looks further into the core of what constitutes the national by highlighting internal border-crossing movements (ethnic minorities and villains) that repeatedly transgress the boundaries of national identity represented in Chinese animation.

Overview of the Chapters

Chapter 1 focuses on the role of *Princess Iron Fan*, the first animated feature film produced in China and indeed in Asia, in the formation of early Japanese animation. Given the global popularity of Japanese animation today, Chinese animation is widely believed to have been influenced by its Japanese counterpart. It is thought that this would be true particularly during the wartime era, when China was semi-colonized by Japan, because it is widely assumed that culture is transmitted from the hegemonic center (the colonizer) to the periphery (the colonized). Chapter 1 challenges these conventional views. It maps an alternative route by examining the transmission, reception, and integration of *Princess Iron Fan* in early Japanese animation. First, it examines the role of *Princess Iron Fan* in the making of *Momotarō's Sea Eagles* (*Momotarō no umiwashi,* 1943) and *Momotarō's Divine Sea Warriors* (*Momotarō umi no shinpei,* 1945), the first animated feature film produced in Japan. Second, it explores the postwar impact of *Princess Iron Fan* on Tezuka Osamu, known as "the god" of modern Japanese manga and anime. Focusing on *Princess Iron Fan*'s entanglement in early Japanese animation, this chapter demonstrates that Chinese animation is enmeshed with other national cultures and that transnational journeys change national identity.

Chapter 2 moves in the opposite direction to examine the role of Japan in animated filmmaking in early socialist China (1945–1953). It further challenges the national essence and Chineseness argument prominent in national style discourse by demonstrating that, from the very beginning, animated filmmaking in socialist China involved Japanese animators. This chapter focuses on Mochinaga Tadahito, a Japanese animator who worked on *Momotarō's Sea Eagles* with Seo Mitsuyo in wartime Tokyo. Mochinaga migrated to Manchuria and worked for the Manchukuo Film Association just before the end of the war. He later became one of the important animators establishing the animation industry in socialist Shanghai in the early 1950s and was known as a pioneer of Chinese and Japanese puppet animation. Tracking the movements of Mochinaga across wartime and postwar Sino-Japanese borders, this chapter focuses on the indispensable role of transnational flows of culture, which are so often disavowed in national cultural histories about the formation of Chinese animation.

Chapter 3 discusses the rise of the national style in the context of international relationships during the Cold War in the late 1950s and further explores the ups and downs of ink-painting animation in the early 1960s, a prime example of the national style. Chinese animation was influenced heavily in the 1950s by the Soviet style. Chinese cultural nationalism surged after the Sino-Soviet split in the late 1950s. Chinese animators, supported by the government, were determined to make Chinese animation look distinctively Chinese. They resorted to traditional Chinese art and culture to create the national style. Despite the domination of the national style, however, an international style emerged in response to the capitalist West. It coexisted with the national style and destabilized its dominant status in animated filmmaking in the late 1950s and early 1960s, the so-called golden age of national style, which I reframe as the golden era of the inter/national style. After examining the national style synchronically in relation to the Soviet Union and the capitalist West, the second part of this chapter continues to analyze the national style diachronically, focusing on the rise and fall of the first two ink-painting animated films made in the early 1960s. It demonstrates that national style and national identity are not fixed or timeless concepts, but instead are fluid, shifting, and historically contingent.

Chapter 4 focuses on the role of internal border-crossing movements in animated filmmaking during the Cultural Revolution. It examines this topic through the perspective of animals. Like the fairy tale, animated film is an artistic form of fantasy full of anthropomorphic animals. Such animals, however, disappeared from animated films produced during the Cultural Revolution and were replaced by positive revolutionary heroes, who were used to embody national identity in animated filmmaking at that time. Animals, however, did not vanish entirely; instead, they assumed spectral metonymic and metaphorical forms as ethnic minorities and villains. Anthropomorphic animals temporarily found shelter in animalized human bodies while waiting for opportunities to return, avenge, and talk back. Focusing on animalized subnational forces, this chapter demonstrates that the construction of national identity through positive heroes during this decade was not solid because it was constantly in tension with racialized Others attempting to transgress and redefine national borders.

Taken together, chapters 1 through 4 demonstrate that the history of Chinese animation was international before it became national and subnational. Even the national, as represented by ink-painting animation, was created in an international context during the Cold War. Although the Chinese School of Animation might proclaim "the more national, the more international," this slogan can be reversed by asserting that in the history of Chinese animation, the more international, the more national. In conclusion, national identity constructed through Chinese animation did not emerge from a vacuum of cultural purity; it was never stable, unchanging, homogenous, or impermeable. Instead, it continuously contested multidirectional flows of culture. It emerged from animated encounters and movements across nationhoods, media, genre, space, and time—encounters and movements that made Chinese animation Chinese and transformed the histories of world animation.

1 An Animated Wartime Encounter

Princess Iron Fan and the Chinese Connection in Early Japanese Animation

Japanese animation, commonly and reductively called anime, is a global phenomenon, popular in the West and elsewhere in Asia, including South Korea, mainland China, Hong Kong, and Taiwan. It has had a distinctive influence in mainland China, where it has shaped the aesthetic taste, thinking, behavior, and culture of today's younger generations. Because of this, it is commonly assumed that anime influenced Chinese animated filmmaking. Indeed, with the introduction and dominance of Japanese animated films in mainland China, Chinese animated films are heavily influenced by the anime style. Although Japanese influence might be said to prevail in China today, this was not always the case. The earliest Sino-Japanese encounter can be traced to Manchuria, where Japanese filmmakers produced animated segments in northeast China in the 1930s and early 1940s.[1] Japan began to be thematized in patriotic Chinese animated films after Japan attacked Shanghai on January 28, 1932. In semi-occupied Shanghai in the early 1940s, Chinese animation had a far-reaching influence on its Japanese counterpart. In China after the war, Japanese animators such as Mochinaga Tadahito played an important role in animated filmmaking (1945–1953). At the same time, they brought the technology and techniques of Chinese puppet animation back to Japan and inaugurated Japanese puppet animation in the early 1950s.[2] Encounters between Sino and Japanese animators were few in socialist China, but after the country opened and the reform policies were adopted in the late 1970s, Japanese animated films began to flood the Chinese market and many Chinese animation studios began working on animated projects outsourced from Japan. These trends resulted in the dominance of anime in contemporary China since the mid-1980s.

Focusing on the hidden history of the encounter of Sino-Japanese animation in semi-occupied Shanghai during World War II, this chapter challenges assumptions about the hegemonic power of anime by documenting the Chinese influence on early Japanese animation. Many studies of wartime transnational cultural flows in Asia examine how Japanese culture influenced other parts of

Asia through military conquest and how colonized or subjugated countries and regions assimilated Japanese culture. Such studies reinforce assumptions that culture moves from a hegemonic center to its periphery, and this diffusionist view is not groundless. As the military, political, and cultural center in Asia during World War II, Japan disseminated its culture in China using military aggression. Even before the early 1940s, Western technology and ways of thinking often were transmitted to China through Japanese mediation. At the same time, Chinese professionals and intellectuals, such as Lu Xun, went to Japan to learn about its advanced technology, political system, literature, and culture and returned to China with this knowledge.[3]

Exploring how animated filmmaking in semi-occupied Shanghai transformed the history of early Japanese animation complicates the model of unidirectional cultural transmission. Specifically, I focus on *Princess Iron Fan* (*Tieshan gongzhu,* 1941), the first animated feature film made in China and Asia, and how its wartime travel to Japan gave rise to the birth of *Momotarō's Sea Eagles* (*Momotarō no umiwashi,* 1943) and *Momotarō's Divine Sea Warriors* (*Momotarō umi no shinpei,* 1945), the first animated feature film in Japan. *Princess Iron Fan* also had an impact on Tezuka Osamu (1928–1989), the so-called god of modern Japanese manga and anime. Suffering from the anxiety of Chinese influence, Tezuka's works, such as the serialized manga *My Sun Wukong* (*Boku no Son Gokū,* 1953–1961), *Alakazam the Great* (anime, 1960), and *I Am Sun Wukong* (*Boku wa Son Gokū,* anime, 1989), were shadowed by *Princess Iron Fan* from the beginning to the end of his career.

Princess Iron Fan transformed the early history of Japanese animation, yet its national identity was changed by the journey. That is, the Chinese film's original anti-Japanese sentiment became ambiguous after it traveled to Japan and was assimilated into Japanese film culture. The promiscuous travel of *Princess Iron Fan* was intertwined with wartime gender politics because Chinese women and films about Chinese women assumed more mobility than men in crossing the Sino-Japanese border. The Japanese assimilation of the film was a masculinization process in that Japanese animators created numerous heroic male protagonists in response to the animated Chinese princess. The travel of *Princess Iron Fan* and its animated afterlife in Japan demonstrate that, contrary to expectations, Chinese animation is deeply enmeshed in other national cultures. Chinese national identity as represented in animation became particularly amorphous after transnational journeys and contact with Japanese cultural forms, even during the highly politicized wartime era, when geopolitical and cultural borders between self and Other were clearly defined.

Women, Films, and Wartime Travels

After the Marco Polo Bridge incident on July 7, 1937, Japan's forces extended their control into northern China and the Sino-Japanese war escalated. On November 12, the Japanese took Shanghai and occupied the city apart from the International Settlement (governed by Britain, America, and Japan) and the French Concession, making these places into an "isolated island" (known in historical narratives as Orphan Island or Solitary Island) surrounded by Japanese-occupied areas. A month later, after Japanese soldiers took over Nanjing, then capital of China, on December 13, the Nationalist government under the leadership of Jiang Jieshi (1887–1975) relocated its capital to Chongqing, in the hinterland, where it established film studios such as Central Film Studio (Zhongdian) and China Productions (Zhongzhi) to produce patriotic anti-Japanese films. On December 8, 1941, the day Pearl Harbor was bombed, Japanese soldiers in Shanghai took over the International Settlement and French Concession as well, occupying the whole of the city until 1945, when Japan surrendered and the war ended.

Wartime Shanghai was not a cultural desert. Instead, it witnessed the rise of a vibrant local film industry. Old film studios had been all but destroyed in the outbreak of war. Star Productions (Mingxing), a well-known studio established in Shanghai in 1922, was reduced to ashes in 1937 because its leader, Zhang Shichuan (1890–1954), refused to cooperate with the Japanese. United China Productions (Lianhua), a renowned studio established in 1930, was closed in 1937 after its factory was destroyed by Japan's bombing. The Shaw Brothers relocated their Unique Film Productions (Tianyi, established in 1925) to Hong Kong in 1934.[4] Taking advantage of the temporary vacuum in the city's film industry, Zhang Shankun (1905–1957), the most influential film tycoon in wartime Shanghai, established New China Productions (Xinhua), and later China New (Huaxin) and China Success (Huacheng) in 1938. In 1940, Zhang Shankun established China United Film Company (Zhongguo lianhe, including New China, China New, and China Success), which was registered as an American-sponsored company to avoid harassment by Japan. Zhang Shankun could no longer avoid Japanese involvement when the Japanese Army Press Bureau selected Kawakita Nagamasa (1903–1981) to head the China Movie Company (Zhonghua dianying gongsi), which was formed in Shanghai in 1939 to make propaganda shorts and to distribute Japanese and Chinese films in occupied areas. Kawakita had been educated in Beijing and was therefore fluent in Chinese. Adopting a policy of cooperation rather than coercion, he gradually befriended Zhang Shankun. In April 1942, with Kawakita's involvement, Zhang Shankun brought together the eleven Shanghai film companies to form China United Film Company (Zhonghua lianhe zhipian gufen gongsi) and became its CEO, half of its capital coming from Kawakita's China Movie

Company. In these circumstances, Zhang Shankun could by no means sponsor overtly nationalist films that might offend the Japanese authorities. To survive, he produced innocuous popular entertainment that could pass Japanese censorship and sell tickets, a strategy that led to the production of many entertaining costume films set in ancient times.[5] Neither anti- nor pro-Japanese, these films were criticized by mainstream wartime critics as decadent and traitorous, in sharp contrast to the patriotic resistance films produced in China's wartime capital of Chongqing.

On January 27, 1940, the costume feature film *Mulan Joins the Army* (*Mulan congjun,* 1939) premiered in Chongqing. The film was directed by Bu Wancang and produced by Zhang Shankun's New China Productions. During its screening, a young man climbed on stage and condemned both the film and the company for collaborating with the Japanese. Echoing his patriotic speech, another man urged the audience to take immediate action. The now-angry crowd then rushed into the projection room, snatched portions of the film print, and burned them outside the theater.

The burning triggered vigorous scholarly discussions. Poshek Fu argues that the incident demonstrates the wartime geopolitical bifurcation between entertainment cinema in semi-occupied Shanghai and anti-Japanese propaganda films in Chongqing, the wartime capital of China. It showcased the widespread anger of people living outside Shanghai toward films produced in Shanghai, which were decried as escapist entertainment and even collaborative.[6] Weihong Bao argues that the film burning was more than a mob action; it was instead an intermedial event between theater and cinema carefully planned, rehearsed, and staged by a coordinated group of agents.[7]

The burning can be reinterpreted using the lens of travel and gender and be seen as a cinematic introspection on film's relationship to women and wartime travel. The plot revolves around Hua Mulan, a female warrior who disguises herself as a man and joins the army in place of her aged father as an act of resistance to the foreign invasion during the Tang dynasty (618–907). The story follows the woman's travels to the frontier and her subsequent gendered transformation in ancient wartime China. As a cultural product, *Mulan Joins the Army* traveled during the war and, in doing so, its Chinese identity was transformed. The film premiered in Shanghai in February 1939. Its themes of national defense, resistance, and patriotism made the film hugely successful and it was regarded as Shanghai's most outspoken resistance film of the wartime era.[8] The move from Shanghai to Chongqing transformed the film's audience, its public space of exhibition, and its interpretative framework. Indeed, travel transformed both the identity of the female protagonist Mulan and the film about her. Thus the burning can be understood as a theatrical act that dramatized the power of travel in destabilizing the fixed identity of the traveler—female characters as well as films about them—and in disrupting the framework of both departure and return home after the perilous journey.

Travel was especially problematic during the war, when the border between the self and the Other was clearly demarcated. Shanghai and Chongqing might represent an internal divide, as the incident of *Mulan Joins the Army* illustrates, but the most prominent line during the war was between China and Japan. Any attempt to cross the border between the two countries would be treacherous.[9] Hu Die, one of the most famous actresses at that time, was invited by the Japanese to travel to Tokyo to make the scenic film *Hu Die's Travel in Tokyo* (*Hu Die you Dongjing*). She protected her reputation by declining the invitation; the film was never made. The Japanese forced the Chinese actress Zi Luolian to go to Tokyo and to make *The Battle of Hong Kong* (*Xianggang gonglüezhan,* 1942). Condemned as a traitor when she returned to Hong Kong, she later fled to mainland China.[10]

Only three Chinese films traveled to Japan during the war, all made in Shanghai: *Camille* (*Chahuanü,* 1938), *Mulan Joins the Army,* and *Princess Iron Fan* (the world's fifth oldest surviving film of its kind).[11] Whatever their content, that these Chinese films traveled to Japan at the time makes them controversial artifacts.

Camille was highly controversial but criticism was less about its traitorous subject matter than about the film's travel to Japan. Primarily an entertainment film, *Camille* focuses on the tragic love between Shanghai courtesan Ma Lili (Yuan Meiyun) and Du Yameng, the son of a middle-class family in Shanghai. Du's father convinces Ma to give up her romance with Du to preserve the reputation and prosperity of his family.[12] *Camille* was not a resistance film, yet it did not express any pro-Japanese sentiments. It was not subject to criticism prior to its screening in Japan and thus its content was not regarded as traitorous. It was the film's border-crossing that fueled the strident criticism—even in Shanghai, the city of "treason" and "decadence" in the wartime, nationalist imagination.[13]

Reactions to the border-crossing offer a context for the burning of *Mulan Joins the Army.* At the time, a variety of reasons were reported for why *Mulan Joins the Army* was burned, but the major concern was its potential connections with Japan. Like *Camille*'s producers, the makers of *Mulan Joins the Army* also were questioned about where the money and film came from for its production, most likely Japan. Furthermore, a song in *Mulan Joins the Army* with the line "Sunlight floods the world when the sun rises" was regarded as pro-Japanese because the rising sun was a popular wartime metaphor for Japan.[14]

The burning aroused sympathy among the Japanese for the film, which was released in Japan in February and early March 1940 without any of the editing and deletions characteristic of Japanese censorship.[15] Tokyo audiences were fascinated by Mulan's beauty and did not regard the female protagonist as a resistance symbol or the film as anti-Japanese.[16]

Princess Iron Fan, the third Shanghai film and first animated feature film to travel to wartime Japan, did not elicit the same indignation as the two live-action films that preceded it. The Shanghai media had not publicized its release in Japan, having learned from reactions to the first two. Since its beginning, animation had been regarded as a genre featuring non-serious, fantastic, and humorous subject matter suitable for children. In wartime China, animation attracted less critical attention than live-action feature films because it was considered a relatively unimportant art form due to its double marginality.

The titles of the three films that traveled to Japan included mention of Chinese women, contributing to the wartime Japanese impression that Shanghai films and the Chinese nation as whole were feminized. Originally, nine films were scheduled by Kawakita's China Movie Company to be introduced to Japan: *Family* (*Jia*), *Princess Iron Fan, Xishi the Beauty* (*Xishi*), *Autumn Rain* (*Xiaoxiang qiuyu*), *Confucius* (*Kongfuzi*), *Modern Youth* (*Xiandai qingnian*), *Waterloo Bridge* (*Hunduan lanqiao*), *Romance of the West Chamber* (*Xixiang ji*), and *The Way of Husband and Wife* (*Fufu zhidao*).[17] All focused on women and romantic love, with the exception of *Confucius,* whose title character was seen as nonmilitarized and thus nonthreatening. An advertisement for the films showed only the film's female protagonists. For unknown reasons, only three of the nine were released in Japan during the war.

Many theories contend that travel is depicted as a masculine activity: men are associated with movement and the world of adventure and conquest; women are associated with home, stasis, and stability.[18] Although the Sino-Japanese war increased the number of men mobilized and the frequency of movement for warfare, it was also the time that the borders between the two countries were the most highly fortified. Such fortifications were made to restrict men's (especially soldiers') potential transgressions of geopolitical borders. Travel by men, dubbed by Eric Leed as "spermatic journey," was associated with sexual and spatial conquest, as evident in the Nanjing Massacre (also known as the Rape of Nanking, December 1937).[19] Spatial movement during the wartime era was ideologically inscribed, yet the war also meant increased mobility for women because their border crossings were seen as less threatening than men's. This is the context in which women featured prominently in wartime Shanghai films, particularly indicated by the titles and posters of the three films that traveled to Japan. The ideological fluidity of these traveling female characters evoked a symbolic parallel with the equivocal and nomadic status of wartime Shanghai films.[20] Nicole Huang observes that Japanese-sponsored magazines deployed images of Chinese women as icons of collaboration.[21] Women seemed to be more mobile and fluid in crossing geopolitical and cultural borders, thus destabilizing the rigid nationalist narrative of resistance that focused on a clear-cut boundary between the self and the Other.

The 1941 short story "When I Was in Xia Village" by communist writer Ding Ling vividly illustrates the sexual, cultural, and political promiscuities associated with travel by women and girls. Zhenzhen is the protagonist, a Chinese peasant girl whose name means chastity. She leaves home and works as a prostitute while spying on Japanese troops. When she returns home, her parents and others treat her with suspicion, making her a stranger in her own village. She believes she has not changed and cannot understand why her family and neighbors shun her. Travel outside the home and village with its associated dangers and harm (prostitution, rape, torture) transformed her identity in the eyes of others—and eventually her self-perception. After her return, she becomes an elusive figure, what Haiyan Lee calls an "insider-turned-stranger," and has to recompose her identity to come to terms with a once familiar yet new reality.[22] The only viable option for her is to leave home and embark on another journey.

Although women can remain elusive in nationalist discourse, the female body is a key embodiment of national identity and contested ideological site. Nationalist discourse, which relied on a clear-cut separation between the wartime self and the enemy Other, never ceased to mobilize and co-opt women into the collective and stereotypically masculine enterprise of resistance. This nationalist attempt at assimilation inflicts new forms of oppression and violence on women in the name of the nation-state, which according to Denize Kandiyoti are as intense and tyrannical as those inflicted by patriarchs of a family, clan, or tribe. Women can become active agents, but they also can become hostage to nationalist projects.[23]

Chang-tai Hung highlights two groups of women captured by nationalist projects and constructed as female symbols of resistance in discursive wartime narratives: patriotic courtesans and female warriors.[24] Hua Mulan was singled out among the female warrior group as the most popular female symbol of resistance. Referring first to the archetype of a modern woman, Hung argues, "If Nora was a symbol of liberated women in the May Fourth era, Hua Mulan was a symbol of resistance in wartime China. And the character Hua Mulan, as a symbol, played an important role in both the political and the military struggles against the Japanese."[25] Highlighting the roles of gender and wartime travel, I ask these questions: if Hua Mulan and other patriotic courtesans (as both women and films) traveled to Japan and were loved by the Japanese during the war, how could they remain nationalist symbols of patriotism and resistance at home? The burning of *Mulan Joins the Army* in Chongqing and its popularity in Japan undermined the image of the female warrior as a national symbol of resistance. Likewise, the character Camille, represented as a virtuous courtesan who sacrificed herself to the interests of her lover's family, and by extension the nation, challenged the image of the virtuous and patriotic courtesan in nationalist discourse. Nationalist identities became ambiguous after the travel of women and films during the wartime era. Given this context, what were the effects of *Princess Iron Fan*'s journey to Japan? Before examining this pivotal film, we must first consider the context of animated filmmaking in which it was produced.

The Wan Brothers and the Early Years

Wan Laiming launched his career as an illustrator and cartoonist in the Fine Arts Department of Shanghai Commercial Press in 1917 and was soon joined by his brothers in Shanghai.[26] He also was chief art designer of *The Young Companion* (*Liangyou huabao*) from 1926 to 1945 and chief editor of *Social Phenomenon Cartoons* (*Xianxiang manhua*) from April 1935 to May 1935. Wan frequently published cartoons and caricatures in renowned cartoon magazines such as *World Pictorial* (*Shijie huabao*) and *Shanghai Sketch* (*Shanghai manhua*).[27] Wan Laiming's brothers later joined him in Shanghai and together they launched their career as animators.

Early animated shorts from the West, such as those featuring Koko the Clown, were introduced to Shanghai in the late 1910s and early 1920s. Fascinated by this new medium, the Wan brothers were determined to produce one in China. The Shanghai Commercial Press, for which the Wan brothers were working, began making films in October 1919 and formally established its film department on July 15, 1920, which became the National Light Film Company (Guoguang yingpian gongsi) in 1926. The Wan brothers began to experiment with the technology of animation in a shabby pavilion room (*tingzi jian*) in Shanghai. After many failures, they finally produced the animated short *Su Zhendong's Chinese Typewriter* (*Su Zhendong de Zhongwen daziji,* 1922), an advertisement for the Shanghai Commercial Press. Some believe that this commercial segment marked the birth of Chinese animation. Others believe that the Wan brothers might in fact not have made the first animated film in China because other animators, such as Yang Zuotao, were active at that time in China. These early shorts are no longer extant, making it impossible to document the first Chinese animation. However, the Wan brothers were the most active and influential animators during the early period.

Their entry into the Shanghai film industry was pivotal in the development of Chinese animation. In 1926, the Wans joined the Great Wall Film Company (Changcheng huapian gongsi), headed by Mei Xuechou, who had received training in animation from the Fleischer brothers in the United States and was greatly interested in the Wan brothers' animation project.[28] Supported by Mei and his company, the Wans produced *Uproar in an Art Studio* (*Danao huashi,* 12 minutes, 1926), commonly considered the first animated film short in China.[29] It combined live action and animation. In it, the artist (played by Wan Guchan) is drawing when a character jumps off the paper and makes a mess in the art studio; the artist finally succeeds in getting the character back onto the paper. This short is highly self-reflexive in that the art of animation is so powerful that an animated character assumes a life of its own. It breaks free of the paper and transgresses the boundary between representation and reality. Despite struggles at the outset, ultimately the animator has the power to control every detail in an animation.

Early Chinese animated shorts are characterized by reflexivity about animation. After the Great Wall Film Company went bankrupt in 1930, the Wan brothers joined the Great China-Lily Film Company (Dazhonghua baihe) and produced two animated shorts combining live action with animation: *The Rebellion of a Paper Man* (*Zhiren daoluan ji*) and *A Delivered Letter Returned* (*Yifeng shuxin ji huilai*). Each film revolves around the rebellion of characters against the artists who created them. This theme draws on the work of American animator Max Fleischer (1883–1972). In his famous *Out of the Inkwell* series (1918–1929), Koko the Clown, an ink man in these films, jumps out of the inkwell and makes trouble for his artist. After many comic twists, the artist puts Koko back into the inkwell and restores peace to the art studio.[30]

After Japan attacked Shanghai on January 28, 1932, the theme of Chinese animated film shifted from artistic self-reflexivity to patriotism. In August 1930, the Great China-Lily Film Company had become part of the United China Productions. During their time at United China Productions, the Wan brothers produced six patriotic animated shorts, including *Compatriots Wake Up* (*Tongbao suxing*), and *Sincere Unification* (*Jingcheng tuanjie*).

From 1933 to 1937, the Wan brothers worked at Star Productions, which had been founded by Zhang Shichuan in March 1922. In April 1922, Star Productions had established its animation department (*katong ke*) with Wan Guchan as its leader, making it China's first specialized film unit devoted to making animated films. While at Star Productions, the Wan brothers produced nine animated shorts charged with a leftist message. These included *Painful Story of a Nation* (*Minzu tongshi,* 1936), which won an award from the Nationalist government and was the first Chinese animated film to receive an award.[31] In 1935, they produced *The Camel Dance* (*Luotuo xian wu*), the first animated talkie made in China.[32] At this time, the Wan brothers were involved with Denton Film Company (Diantong yingye gongsi), which was under the control of underground communist leaders of progressive artists in Shanghai, such as Tian Han and Xia Yan.[33] Under their influence, the Wan brothers participated in anti-Japanese activities. Wan Laiming even became a member of the Anti-Japanese Association within the Chinese film community.

When the Sino-Japanese war broke out after the Marco Polo Bridge incident, many film companies in Shanghai were bombed to ashes or forced to close. The older three Wan brothers left Shanghai for Wuhan and later Chongqing, joining the China Productions sponsored by the Nationalist Army. The fourth brother, Wan Dihuan, stayed in Shanghai, gave up his animation career, and ran a photography studio to support the extended Wan family in Shanghai. Meanwhile, the other brothers produced resistance propaganda shorts, including *Resistance Slogan Cartoons* (*Kangzhan biaoyu katong*) and *Anti-Japanese Songs* (*Kangzhan gequ*). Among the shorts' patriotic songs, "The River Is Red with Blood" ("Man jiang hong") is the most famous. It is based on a poem by Yue Fei (1103–1141), a patriotic general who resisted the foreign invasion during the Song dynasty (960–1279). "The River Is Red with Blood" tells how Yue Fei climbs Mount Fuji and defeats a Japanese samurai. Lyrics appear at the bottom, a white ball bouncing from one character to another indicating the song's rhythm to make it easier for audiences to follow the tune and sing along. Finding it difficult to earn a living in Chongqing, the first two Wan brothers returned to Shanghai in April 1939 via Vietnam and Hong Kong, where they later produced *Princess Iron Fan*, the first feature-length animated film in Asia.[34]

As noted, the Wan brothers were not the only filmmakers in the early history of Chinese animation, but they were the most influential. Other pioneers include Yang Zuotao, Huang Wennong, Mei Xuechou, and Qin Lifan.[35] When the Wan brothers were making *Princess Iron Fan* in Shanghai, Qian Jiajun was experimenting with animation at the Spirit Encouragement Society (Lizhishe), a military club organized by Jiang Jieshi in Nanjing in 1929 that moved to Chongqing after late 1938. Although a graduate of Suzhou Fine Arts Academy, Qian Jiajun felt that fine arts were less powerful than film for disseminating anti-Japanese messages. Qian Jiajun and his colleagues, after much trial and error, completed *The Happiness of a Village* (*Nongjia le*) in November 1940. This black-and-white sound animated film about anti-Japanese activities in a village was released in domestic theaters with the live-action film *A Tour of Tibet* (*Xizang xunli*, 1940). In the spring of 1941, it traveled to Singapore and other Asian countries along with a documentary film about war orphans directed by Pan Zinong.[36]

Early Chinese animation had a symbiotic relationship with live-action film. The Wan brothers used live action in their self-reflexive animated shorts, a strategy that saved on the increased time and expense required for animation. They used animation for special effects in feature-length live-action films, achieving with animation what they could not with live action. For instance, in *The Burning of the Red-Lotus Temple* (*Huoshao Honglian si*, 1928–1931), animation portrayed swords, without anyone holding them, automatically fighting with each other in the sky. Live-action feature films such as *Vanilla Beauty* (*Xiangcao meiren*, 1935), *The Urban Scene* (*Dushi fengguang*, 1935), and *Parents and Children* (*Fumu zinü*,

1936) included brief animated sequences. In addition, feature films used animation more subtly in credit sequences and sing-along songs. For instance, the Wan brothers used stop-motion animation to transform a string of pearls into the Chinese character disaster (*huo*) in *A String of Pearls* (*Yichuan zhenzhu,* 1926) and for the credits for the Great Wall Film Company. They also used animated bouncing balls to indicate the rhythm of the on-screen songs for sing-alongs in *Street Angel* (*Malu tianshi,* 1935), probably the earliest form of karaoke in China. This usage recalls work by the Fleischers, who introduced the bouncing ball in 1924 and made it a feature of their animated films.[37] The Fleischers' sing-along films were popular in 1920s' Shanghai, and they may have inspired the Wan brothers to use the bouncing ball too.

Cinemas usually screened animated shorts with live-action films. Eileen Chang, an avid fan of animated cartoons, wrote about this in an essay in 1937:

> Usually animated shorts are screened after newsreels and before a live-action feature film. Occupying a short period of time of entertainment, animated films are especially designed to please children. They need to be humorous and fantastic, but should not be long, because the audience will feel dizzy if they keep watching these moving pictures for a long time.[38]

Chang's remarks not only reveal how animated films were screened in the 1930s, but also highlight the status of animation as dependent on live-action film. Only after the birth of *Princess Iron Fan* did Chinese animation assert itself as an autonomous artistic form whose production and screening were independent of live-action film.

The Birth of *Princess Iron Fan* in Wartime Shanghai

Wartime Shanghai was not the Orphan Island cut off from the outside world that it was popularly characterized as being. In fact, wartime barricades and blockades increased transnational flows of culture and people. Shanghai had never been as eager to know the outside world. Hollywood films continued to flood Shanghai theaters. For example, Disney's first animated feature film *Snow White* premiered in Los Angeles on December 21, 1937, and was released in Shanghai six months later to popular acclaim. Audiences in Shanghai were familiar with animated shorts such as *Mickey Mouse, Popeye,* and *Betty Boop,* but *Snow White* was their first opportunity to see a feature-length animated film. *Snow White* premiered simultaneously in Nanking (Nanjing) and at the Metropol (Da Shanghai) Theater. This was atypical at that time, because usually only masterpieces, such as the works of Charlie Chaplin, premiered simultaneously in these two renowned theaters.[39] *Snow White* also premiered in Hong Kong on January 16, 1941. The Chinese audience totaled four hundred thousand: more than two hundred thousand in Shanghai and another two hundred thousand in Tianjin and Hong Kong.[40]

Snow White's travel to wartime Shanghai transformed the history of Chinese animation. Encouraged by the success of *Snow White,* film mogul Zhang Shankun invited the Wan brothers, who had returned to Shanghai in April 1939, to join New China Productions and produce the first animated feature film in Asia.[41] Wan Laiming and Wan Guchan soon established the animation department (*katong bu*) with Wan Guchan as its headman, hired 250 artists, and embarked on the project on April 25, 1940, in their animation studio located in Dingxiang Garden.[42] Because *Snow White* was translated into *Princess Snow White* (*Baixue gongzhu*) in Chinese, the Wan brothers decided to feature a Chinese princess and ride on the petticoat of *Snow White*'s fame. They turned to *Journey to the West* (*Xiyouji,* by Wu Cheng'en, 1522–1566), their favorite childhood story, and adapted one of its well-known episodes into the animated feature film *Princess Iron Fan.*[43]

In the story's animated version, when the young monk Tripitaka and his three disciples (Monkey, Pigsy, and Sandy) are en route to India, a mountain covered in flames blocks their way. To extinguish the fire, they need to borrow a magic banana-leaf fan from Princess Iron Fan, who is under the protection of her husband, Bull Demon King. With the help of the villagers, Tripitaka and his disciples subdue Bull Demon King, obtain the fan, extinguish the fire, and continue their journey to the west. To make the movement of the characters appear lifelike, as Disney had in *Snow White,* the Wan brothers adopted rotoscoping and based the characters' movements on a live-action film, actress Bai Hong posing for Princess Iron Fan and the popular comedian Han Lan'gen playing the role of Monkey.[44] The film's music and songs were composed and recorded by Zhang Zhengfan, Lu Zhongren, and others from National Music Institute (Guoli Yinzhuan), which is now the Shanghai Conservatory of Music.[45] Two of the film's songs, "Obtaining the Treasure" ("Debao ge") and "Delicious Chicken and Duck" ("Jixiang yamei"), were sung by Han Lan'gen, Yin Xiuqin, and others.[46] Just as the production reached a critical stage, New China Productions faced a financial crisis and was unable to pay the animators or other production costs. Sheng Pihua, the head of Shangyuanyin Company, made a deal with Zhang Shankun that Sheng's company would pay the remaining costs of *Princess Iron Fan* on the condition that the film premiere in theaters owned by Sheng's company, including the Metropol Theater, Astor Theater (Huguang), and Strand Theater (Xinguang). With Sheng's financial support, *Princess Iron Fan* (80 minutes) premiered in three Shanghai theaters on November 19, 1941, and immediately became a hit (see figures 1.1 and 1.2). The film cost around CN¥600,000, by far the most expensive in the history of Chinese animation.[47]

Figure 1.1. Film poster for release of *Princess Iron Fan* in Shanghai, *Shenbao,* November 19, 1941.

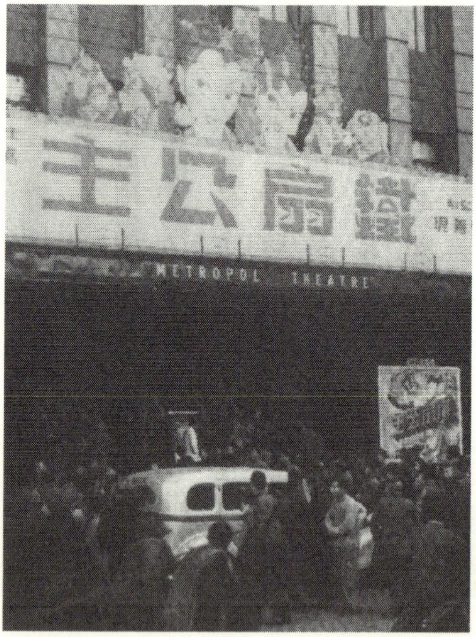

Figure 1.2. Crowd waiting outside the Metropol Theater when *Princess Iron Fan* premiered in Shanghai in November 1941. From Tsuji Hisakazu, *Chūka den'ei shiwa: Ippeisotsu no nitchū eiga kaisō-ki* 1939–1945 (Tokyo: Gaifūsha, 1998), 147.

Princess Iron Fan marked the emergence of animation as an autonomous artistic form in China. From its inception, animation depended on live-action films in terms of both production and screening. Animation accomplished special effects that live action could not. Even when studios established animation departments and moved away from using live-action films to create animated shorts ten to twenty minutes long, cinemas still screened the animated shorts as appetizers before a live-action film. *Princess Iron Fan* changed this by inviting the audience to watch an animated film for its own sake rather than as merely an opener for a live-action feature film. When *Princess Iron Fan* was released, a comic live-action short was even screened as an opener for it, thus reversing the conventional screening relationship. This short was directed by Li Pingqian and featured Han Lan'gen and Yin Xiuqin. Titled *Filial Children* (*Hao zisun*) or *Father and Stones* (*Laozi yu shizi*), it was a satire about three unfilial sons.[48] *Princess Iron Fan* thus reversed the long-established relationship between animated and live-action films in terms of both production and screening in Chinese film history.

Gendered Wartime Speciesism: Princess Iron Fan as an Exotic-Erotic Mediator

As John Dower points out, World War II was a race war in which racialized images of the Other, usually represented by animals, were prevalent. Wartime American media was full of racialized animal images intended to humiliate, insult, and denigrate its enemy Japan.[49] After the attack on Pearl Harbor, American media often portrayed Japan as a monstrous and aggressive King Kong figure. Thomas Lamarre calls this "wartime speciesism," and defines it as "a displacement of race and racism (relations between humans as imagined in racial terms) onto relations between humans and animals."[50] In contrast to American speciesism, which was characterized by a clear-cut boundary between the self and the enemy, Japanese speciesism was nuanced and layered. Japanese media emphasized the elevation of the pure self rather than the denigration of the Other. Many wartime Japanese live-action films have no obvious enemies at all. When enemies are portrayed, it is done with images such as a passing plane or the sound of a machine gun.[51]

If Japanese live-action films did not denigrate enemies, other forms of propaganda such as cartoons and animated films disseminated the hate-the-enemy message more directly.[52] Unlike its American counterpart, Japanese speciesism did not overtly animalize and dehumanize its American enemy. On the contrary, the American enemy, often figured as humans with demons' horns in wartime cartoons and animated films, was portrayed with awe, respect, and dignity. Colonized countries were often represented as cute and happy companion animals, a representation freighted with its own ideological implications. However, it is difficult to identify which animal stands for which race or nation. Japanese speciesism thus tended to be fluid at the levels of form and referent.[53]

Chinese speciesism was closer to its American counterpart. In resistance cartoons, the Sino-Japanese war is a life or death issue without any gray area. The Chinese represented Japanese soldiers as pigs, dogs, venomous snakes, and apes; Chinese soldiers were depicted as lions or tigers, symbols of power, courage, pride, dignity, and steadfastness. The meaning was direct and immediate and connoted the opposition between good and evil, leaving no room for uncertainty. The play of moral polarities achieved a powerful effect, as Hung Chang-tai writes:

> Such an approach set up an opposition of subhuman and human, evil and good, in which the viewer was clearly aligned with the latter . . . it is psychological warfare that is meant to be cruel and to hurt . . . The hate shines through, uncontrolled and slightly insane.[54]

Building on these theories, I argue further that wartime speciesism was coded in masculine terms. In violent speciesism and nationalism, the animals used to portray the wartime Other were usually (hyper)masculine figures embodying threat and hatred that needed to be exterminated. For instance, Bull Demon King, with his enormous and bestial body, has been regarded as representing Japan.[55] In his memoir, Wan Laiming also acknowledged that they intended to allegorize Bull Demon King despite Zhang Shankun's entertainment and escapist strategy: "We purposefully and indirectly used Bull Demon King's defeat as a trope to suggest the theme of this film. That is, all Chinese people should unite and resist Japanese invaders for the final victory in war against Japan."[56] Wan Laiming even tried to make the theme of resistance more evident by adding an anti-Japanese slogan at the end of the film, which was censored by the Japanese. He explained in his autobiography:

> Considering the situation within Orphan Island, we were taking quite a risk by expressing a resistance theme. During the whole process, I was anxious because I would have been killed if the Japanese had noticed it. When *Princess Iron Fan* was close to completion and ready for its soundtrack, the Japanese invaders were about to take over the International Settlement and French Concession [figure 1.3]. The situation was tenuous and rumors were widespread. We had to delete the slogan "to strive for the final victory in the anti-Japanese War" from the film.[57]

The film's resistance message is conveyed through the war between Tripitaka's group and Bull Demon King. For this reason, *Princess Iron Fan* conventionally has been interpreted as a wartime resistance film. Weihong Bao regards the film as a

Figure 1.3. Japanese soldiers marching in front of the poster of *Princess Iron Fan* at Shanghai's Metropol Theatre during their takeover of the International Settlement and French Concession on December 8, 1941. From Takatsuna Hirofumi, *Senji Shanhai 1937–45 nen* (Tokyo: Kenbunshuppan, 2009), 165.

mixture of genres—martial arts, god-spirit, leftist, and resistance. She points out that the representation of the villagers in black silhouettes at the end of this film is reminiscent of the endings of national defense films made between 1936 and 1937 and of the wartime resistance cartoons and propaganda posters, including those created by the Wan brothers in their *Resistance Slogan Cartoons.*[58] In fact, Wan Laiming stated clearly that the mission of Chinese animation is national salvation: "Our animation went beyond entertainment the moment it was born. From the very beginning, it served the needs of national salvation in real life . . . and, as our country was in national crisis, I really did not want to produce animated films just for entertainment."[59]

When considered as a resistance film, the female protagonist Princess Iron Fan is an anomaly. Wartime speciesism and nationalism are masculinist discourses that lose traction when they intersect with gender. Princess Iron Fan, a human princess who marries the animal Bull Demon King, is similar to the Chinese woman (played by Li Xianglan in *China Night* [*Shina no yoru*], 1940) who marries a Japanese soldier in wartime films.[60] Princess Iron Fan sympathizes with the villagers and uses her magic fan to bring about rain and harvests, but she also identifies with her husband, which puts her at the margins of the human world. She lives alone in her Palm Leaf Cave, spatially isolated from both the human villagers and her animal husband, who lives in another cave with his mistress Fox Spirit. Princess Iron Fan is therefore a liminal woman situated between humans and animals in a wartime discourse of speciesism.

Princess Iron Fan is also an in-between figure during the war between Bull Demon King and Tripitaka. As a woman and a wife, she is part of and apart from the war between the males. She supports Bull Demon King but does not participate in the final battle. In several skirmishes between Princess Iron Fan and the three disciples that appear at the beginning of the film, the fighting is humorous and even erotic. For instance, Monkey metamorphoses into a tiny bug and worms his way into Princess Iron Fan's stomach as she drinks tea. He wreaks havoc in her stomach until she unconditionally surrenders her fan to him. Pigsy disguises himself as Bull Demon King and flirts with her to steal her magic fan. Bull Demon King is the undisputed enemy of Tripitaka and his followers, but Princess Iron Fan is always associated with the personal and is trivialized by them. She will not lend her fan to Monkey because he had once subdued her son Red Boy, who became a servant of the Goddess of Mercy and lost contact with his mother. Unlike her husband, Princess Iron Fan is not regarded as a dangerous and unredeemable enemy by Tripitaka's forces. She is a comic character whose naiveté borders on foolishness.

Princess Iron Fan's spatial movement is decisive in the war between the two parties. A liminal figure associated with the feminine and the personal, Princess Iron Fan belongs to the sphere of domesticity. She lives in her Palm Leaf Cave and seldom goes out, but Monkey and Pigsy continuously infiltrate her body and even struggle with her physically in attempts to wrest the fan from her. When the war between the two masculine parties is drawing to an end, Princess Iron Fan leaves her cave and travels to the frontier to make peace between them by surrendering her magic fan to Monkey. She resembles the princess in ancient times who served as an erotic and exotic mediator by traveling to the frontier to marry the invading king and ensure peace for her country (*heqin*). In a patriarchal society, girls and women are used as a gift to build and repair political and social ties between men, making them "a conduit of a relationship rather than a partner of it."[61] The difference with Princess Iron Fan is that rather than offering her body, she offers her treasured fan, which is hidden in her mouth and operates as an extension of her corporeal self.

The female body is therefore the site of equivocality and contested meanings. The image of Princess Iron Fan in this film is a female warrior who looks like Hua Mulan but subverts Hua Mulan's image as a resistance symbol in nationalist discourse. Tripitaka's journey to India is a sacred and nationalist mission. The Buddhist sutras he brings back from India will enable him to save his people. Yet Tripitaka cannot fulfill his mission without the assistance of Monkey, his most capable disciple. Monkey, rather than Tripitaka, is often represented as a national and nationalist symbol in Chinese culture. Haiyan Lee therefore interprets Monkey as a "greater-than-human figure" who assumes a "priestly role" on the way to India.[62] To achieve this lofty goal, Monkey transforms into a bug and enters Princess Iron Fan's stomach, where he creates havoc and thereby forces her to give up her fan. This scenario can be interpreted as a symbolic rape in the sense that, wartime Chinese women, like Princess Iron Fan, were co-opted and forced to participate in the nationalist project against the Japanese. Nationalist discourse, no matter how sacred it was made to seem, perpetrated violence on female bodies in its drive for assimilation, cooptation, and domination. Princess Iron Fan is unwilling to assist Tripitaka by relinquishing her magic fan. She refuses to be co-opted into his nationalist mission and instead highlights the personal suffering she endures when she loses contact with her only child. Princess Iron Fan resists the mainstream wartime narrative of yielding to the collective and transgresses the borders between private and public, humans and animals, and self and Other.

Princess Iron Fan is not given a major role in the film's story, yet she and Fox Spirit are given visual and textual prominence in the film's title and posters. On Chinese and Japanese posters, the film's male characters recede so far into the background that they are barely visible (see figures 1.1 and 1.4). In this way, the film's message was softened and sweetened by its association with feminine qualities, thus increasing both its ambiguity and capacity to cross entrenched Sino-Japanese borders. Princess Iron Fan subverts the image of Hua Mulan as a resistance symbol and Fox Spirit subverts the nationalist ideal of the virtuous and patriotic courtesan. Fox Spirit is a female fox who metamorphoses into a girl. She and Bull Demon King live together in Emerald Cloud Cave. As the seductive mistress of Bull Demon King, Fox Spirit takes pains about her clothing and toilette. She becomes angry and jealous when Bull Demon King has contact with his wife, Princess Iron Fan. Lacking in patriotism and selflessness, Fox Spirit resembles the fallen courtesans in wartime Shanghai, who were known as fox spirits for their coquetry and wiles. Unlike Lady Camille's renunciation of personal desire for the sake of the patriarchal family and by extension the nation, Fox Spirit is a vain and selfish pleasure-seeker.

Assuming heightened visuality in the posters, the character Princess Iron Fan functions as an allegory for the indeterminate status of the film *Princess Iron Fan.* The Wan brothers made *Princess Iron Fan* ambiguous so that it could withstand turbulent political waters and censorship. *Princess Iron Fan*'s seemingly innocuous setting, like that of other wartime Shanghai films, is a remote and imagined past devoid of direct reference to the present. In sharp contrast to the resistance films in Chongqing, *Princess Iron Fan* is entertainment oriented, despite the Wan brothers' claim of an indirect message of resistance. The love triangle between Bull Demon King, Princess Iron Fan, and Fox Spirit would have been amusing for petty urbanites in Shanghai. Princess Iron Fan's dancing and singing, Fox Spirit's flirtation, and the appearance of a naked woman (her clothes are blown away by the strong wind caused by Princess Iron Fan's fanning of her fan) in this film are charged with eroticism, while the playful banter, slapstick, and gags add humor.

Figure 1.4. Film poster for release of *Princess Iron Fan* in Tokyo.

The film's vague politics enabled it not only to elude censorship but also to travel in multiple directions during World War II.

Turbulence: *Princess Iron Fan*'s Journey to Japan

With its ambiguous themes, *Princess Iron Fan* negotiated a variety of symbolic and geopolitical borders, traveling to Chongqing, Hong Kong, Japan, Singapore, Indonesia, Canada, and the United States.[63] Before it arrived in Japan, the film was released in the Shanghai International Theater, a Japanese theater in occupied Shanghai, on February 13, 1942. During its six-day run, the film became an immediate hit with the Japanese audience in Shanghai.[64] It then traveled to Japan and was dubbed by Japanese film stars Tokugawa Musei (voice for Monkey), Yamano Ichirō, Makino Shūichi, and Maruyama Shōji. The film was released in Tokyo on September 10 the same year under the title *Journey to the West: The Episode of Princess Iron Fan* (*Saiyūki: Tessen Kōshu no maki*) (see figure 1.4). Japanese theaters were designated white line (*hakkei*) or red line (*kurenai-kei*), in reference to a distribution system designed to maximize the use of the limited amount of film stock in wartime Japan.[65] *Princess Iron Fan* was released exclusively in white-line theaters. How did *Princess Iron Fan* manage to travel to Japan in such a highly politicized context when the geopolitical borders between the two countries were so strictly delineated?

The production and release of *Princess Iron Fan* in Japan was a joint Chinese and Japanese venture. Zhang Shankun had dealings with both the Nationalists and Japanese in Shanghai; that he was eventually arrested by both political parties attests to his double-dealing. Zhang collaborated with Kawakita Nagamasa, head of the China Movie Company, which Japan supported. Kawakita advocated cooperation rather than Japanese domination in the film world of Shanghai. From Kawakita, Zhang ensured a steady flow of funding and film stock, which were both scarce at the time.[66] Kawakita also assisted in the production of *Princess Iron Fan*. Furthermore, Kawakita's China Movie Company released *Princess Iron Fan* in Japan.

Although the film was extremely popular in Japan, some among the Japanese audience regarded *Princess Iron Fan* as anti-Japanese. For example, Tezuka Osamu recalled that

> The people who, while sneering at Chinese animation, went to see this film were so surprised by its quality and humor that they were speechless. I also hoped for an opportunity to get a hold of a copy of this film, but when I watched it I knew for certain that this is a work of resistance. It is clearly a

> satire, saying that if the Chinese people work together they can overcome the Japanese Army that has invaded and attacked their country.[67]

Despite its anti-Japanese sentiment, mainstream Japanese film magazines deliberately watered down the Chinese identity of *Princess Iron Fan*. In 1942 issues of *Movie Times* (*Eiga junpō*), *Princess Iron Fan* was treated as having a broader Asian identity and being symbolic of the victory of Greater East Asian cinema over Hollywood.[68] Traveling films were then associated with wartime's pan-Asian discourse. Advertisements in the *Movie Times* appropriated *Princess Iron Fan* for Japanese film history: "The Wan brothers' names should be recorded in the history of Greater East Asian cinema! They are lucky dogs who turned their dreams into realities! *Princess Iron Fan* is a great gift dedicated to Japanese moviedom!"[69] These reviews conform to the ideology of the Greater East Asian Film Sphere, created around 1941, which called for the unification of Asian countries to protect Asian cinema from Western influence. Films in this sphere were intended to represent the purportedly pure "Oriental Spirit," which in fact was wholly Japanese. Thus, a Japanese identity was imposed on *Princess Iron Fan* as it was celebrated as exemplifying the Greater East Asian Film Sphere.

Even Wan Laiming and Wan Guchan, who proclaimed their nationalist position in Shanghai, were ambiguous about the film's political message after its release in Tokyo. In their letter to the Japanese film critic Shimizu Akira in *Film Review* (*Eiga hyōron*) in December 1942, they not only avoided mentioning the film's resistance message, but also toned down its specific Chineseness by positioning the film within the larger East Asian history of animation. They particularly distinguished their work from Hollywood:

> We believe that in order to create a unique cinematic art of the East, we need to endow films with an Eastern personality characterized by Eastern color and Eastern taste. We can by no means achieve this goal by simply imitating classical Hollywood films. Our purpose is not imitation, so our guiding principle is to use traditional Chinese art to delineate the characters' demeanor, costumes, and gestures in *Princess Iron Fan*.[70]

However, *Princess Iron Fan* and animated shorts in Republican Shanghai were heavily influenced by Hollywood: Monkey looks like Mickey Mouse and Fox Spirit is a Chinese version of Betty Boop. The plasmaticness, the squash and stretch, gags, slapstick, and humorous twists in this film also follow Disney's style. Highlighting the Asianness of *Princess Iron Fan* in defiance of Hollywood, the Wan brothers echoed the pan-Asian ideology of the Greater East Asian Film Sphere. Without reference to the original letter in Chinese, it is not known whether its meaning was reshaped when the letter was translated into Japanese. However, such reshaping is a possibility given the long-standing interest in Japan in having the Wan brothers work for the Japanese.

Essays published in wartime Japanese film magazines also attempted to co-opt the Wan brothers into Japan's Greater East Asian Film Sphere. According to an essay in *Film Review,* December 8, 1942, marked a new chapter in East Asian Film history because on that day Chinese animators and film studios discarded the impurities of the past (Western and Hollywood influences) and made new plans under the aegis of Japanese leadership. The Wan brothers published their plan for their second animated feature film, *The Domesticated Duck of the Yangtze River* (*Chōkō no ahiru*), which would be made by Kawakita Nagamasa's China Movie Company. It would be an animated propaganda film made for the Japanese army and feature a domesticated duck. As envisioned, the duck would travel downstream along the Yangtze River from Sichuan province, an allusion to the wartime capital Chongqing, before stopping in Nanjing to visit the Mausoleum of Sun Zhongshan and to meet President Wang Jingwei, who founded the wartime puppet regime in Nanjing with support from Japan—and was regarded as a traitor by the Nationalist government in Chongqing. The duck would finally arrive in Shanghai, just "liberated" from the invasion by the United States and UK to become the site of Greater East Asian construction projects. The purpose of this film was to encourage Jiang Jieshi and his government in Chongqing to abandon their military resistance and collaborate peacefully with Japan.[71] Although the film was mentioned again and again in Japanese materials, it never appeared in Wan Laiming's biography and other materials in Chinese. It was in fact never produced. Instead, it marks Japan's failed attempt to co-opt the Wan brothers and Chinese animation for its political and military goals in China.

Princess Iron Fan was not the only film whose nationalist character was distorted after arrival in Japan. Two earlier films, both live-action features, that traveled to Japan were also assimilated into the Greater East Asian Film Sphere. The transformation of *Princess Iron Fan* should not be understood only in terms of this wartime context. The benefit of hindsight allows us to see that *Princess Iron Fan* also became enmeshed in the history of Japanese animation.

Peach Boy and the Rise of Japanese Animated Feature Film

The Ministry of Home Affairs and the Media Section of the Imperial Army controlled the Japanese film industry from 1937 to 1945. The 1939 Film Law forced the film industry to disseminate Japan's imperialist ideology and tightened Japanese government censorship. The Home Ministry issued more detailed regulations about filmmaking in 1940 as the war intensified and censorship increased. The regulations banned urban romances, the most profitable genre, and resulted in the exclusive production of what were called national policy films.[72] However, under the military government's tight control, these films seldom portrayed the violence of war and rarely referred to wartime enemies. Other forms of propaganda, such as animated films and cartoons, represented the war and Japan's enemies more explicitly and violently.

The forceful appearance of Momotarō the Peach Boy in Japanese cartoons and animated films to propagandize military and imperialist ideology demonstrates the close relationship between revivals of legends and folklore and the rise of nationalism and patriotism.[73] Animated films based on the Peach Boy include *Momotarō the Undefeated* (1928), *Momotarō's Sky Adventure* (1931), *Momotarō's Underwater Adventure* (1932), among others. Klaus Antoni observes that these films played a vital role in promoting Japan's imperialist ideology and nationalist spirit around the world: "with the fairy tale of the 'Peach Boy' the gate to 'Japanese spirit' was opened."[74] *Princess Iron Fan* was introduced to Japan in the context of this wartime animated film culture. Considering the widespread fascination with Momotarō stories, it is no surprise that Japanese animators later made an animated feature film about him in response to *Princess Iron Fan.*

The release of *Princess Iron Fan* in wartime Tokyo shocked Japanese audiences because it was the first animated feature film ever viewed in a public theater in Japan. The Japanese were familiar with Western animated films such as Mickey Mouse, Betty Boop, Felix the Cat, and Popeye because they had been screened in public theaters before the war. However, after war broke out, the Japanese government banned Western films to protect the people from the harmful influence of Western culture. Only a few prints of American animated films circulated in Japanese-occupied Shanghai and Singapore.[75] Consequently, *Snow White* and other Western animated films were not released in Japan until after the war. *Snow White* premiered in Japan on September 26, 1950. The release of *Princess Iron Fan* in public theaters in wartime Japan was therefore an eye-opener for Japanese audiences. Despite Japan's military domination of China, *Princess Iron Fan* made the Japanese people—and especially animators—awed and envious.

Reviews were published in Japanese film periodicals and screening seminars were held to watch and then discuss *Princess Iron Fan.* Japanese film critics and animators acknowledged it as a substantial accomplishment: it was almost miraculous for Chinese animators to make such a high-quality animated feature film when its animation technology and facilities were so much less advanced than Japan's. Even with China's limited resources, *Princess Iron Fan* was much better than the animated shorts and live-action films featuring Monkey King that had been made in Japan.[76] They also thought that although *Princess Iron Fan* emulated Disney's style by using gags and slapstick, it was an excellent creative work that effectively embodied China's national style. Its drawings were much better than Japanese ones and the flexibility of Monkey's facial expressions and physical movements was impressive.[77] The characterization of Pigsy made him most attractive and successful, and the final battle scene was especially praiseworthy because it displayed the essential characteristics of animation. According to these critics, the film was especially impressive because, unlike Japanese animated films that included repetitive elements in order to reduce labor and costs, *Princess Iron Fan* did not reuse frames as frequently. Of course, *Princess Iron Fan* had shortcomings, such as an unstable soundtrack probably resulting from incorrect positioning of microphones and defects of the electric motors, and the use of a single still picture rather than several dynamic successive pictures to portray Tripitaka's final speech to the gathered villagers.[78] As a whole, though, Japanese critics and animators lavished praise on *Princess Iron Fan,* suggesting that it should be a "reference for Japanese animators."[79]

Its release triggered profound self-reflection and self-criticism within Japanese animation circles. Most animators maintained that Japanese artists should learn from the excellent narrative skills and animation of details in *Princess Iron Fan.* Japanese film critic Ueno Kōzō compared *Princess Iron Fan* with Seo Mitsuyo's *Ant Boy* (*Arichan,* 1941) and argued that *Princess Iron Fan* was much better in terms of storytelling and detail than Japanese animated shorts. He suggested that Japanese animators learn from *Princess Iron Fan* and come to terms with rather than try to escape the challenges of animated filmmaking.[80] Ueno's view was shared by Seo Mitsuyo, who admitted that Japanese animated films at that time were slow because of their tedious narration and endless detail. He advocated for Japanese animators to be more serious about animating details, down to a single blade of grass.[81] This difference in the way detail was handled was also evident in their different treatments of character movement. *Princess Iron Fan* strictly adhered to the procedure of rotoscoping and meticulously drew the movements of characters, Japanese animators skipped steps and did not fully follow the process of movement decomposition.[82] This difference can be explained by the different practices in the two countries: Chinese animators drew in reference to a live-action film and analyzed character movement frame by frame for accuracy; Japanese animators made rough sketches based on the action of live performers on stage, which resulted in less accurate and less detailed character movement.[83] Seo regretted that although Japan had excellent animators, Japanese animated films remained simple and coarse because animation was dismissed as entertainment for children and little funding supported it.[84] In contrast, *Princess Iron Fan* targeted adults as well as children and was well supported by investors. Seo and others continued to discuss the major reasons why Japan could not produce as successful an animated feature film at the time: the lack of passion and perseverance of Japanese animators, the extremely low salaries for script writers and animators, the lack of traditional Japanese stories as compelling as the *Journey to the West*, the small scale of animated filmmaking in Japan (the number of animators involved in the making of *Princess Iron Fan* was thirteen times larger than Seo's animation team), and the lack of substantial, long-term investment necessary for such a labor-intensive project.[85] In a seminar held later, Seo, Masaoka Kenzō, and other Japanese animators highlighted the lack of talented animators. They considered the biggest problem for Japanese animation was its organization as a family-based handicraft industry, and animators were unwilling to pass on their ancestors' secret formulas to the younger generation not in the family. This led to a lack of talented animators and restricted the scale of animated filmmaking. The first task for developing the industry in Japan, they concluded, was to train as many animators as possible.[86]

By this time, the Japanese Imperial Navy had realized the potential of animation as a media for propaganda in occupied areas where local people did not understand the Japanese language.[87] Motivated by this practical reason and the nationalist competition, it ordered Seo Mitsuyo to experiment with making Japan's first animated feature film and allocated funds for its production, which would not have been financially feasible without the state's generous support. The outcome of Japan's rivalry with China for animation supremacy was the birth of *Momotarō's Sea Eagles* (Art Film Company/Geijutsu eigasha/GES), released in Japanese white-line theaters on March 25, 1943. About ten animators, including Mochinaga Tadahito, drew forty thousand pictures and worked intensively on the film for ten months.[88] Seo tried to make *Momotarō's Sea Eagles* as long as possible to rival the eighty-minute *Princess Iron Fan*, but ended up with only thirty-seven minutes.

The film was based on the well-known Japanese folk tale about Momotarō, the standard version of which focuses on a childless couple. The wife finds a peach floating on the river and brings it home. A baby boy is born from the peach. The couple adopts him and names him Momotarō. Demons on Devil's Island had long terrorized the family's village. As soon as Momotarō grows up, he embarks on a sacred journey to conquer the demons. En route, he first befriends a hungry dog, to whom he gives the best dumplings he is carrying and explains his mission to conquer the demons. The dog eats the dumplings and then happily follows him. Momotarō similarly befriends a monkey and a pheasant. With the help of his three animal companions, Momotarō subdues the demons and returns home with treasure.[89]

The popular Japanese tale of Momotarō has its roots in the sixteenth-century Chinese novel *Journey to the West*. As early as 1758, the Japanese novelist Nishida

Korenori translated *Journey to the West* and the novel became popular in Japan, giving rise to the tale of Momotarō.[90] The two stories have several similarities, including the motif of a human (Tripitaka and Momotarō) leading three animals on a quest. According to Nakata Senpo, Momotarō originated from the character of Monkey in *Journey to the West:*

> The Japanese people, inspired by *Journey to the West,* created the story of Momotarō in line with the image of Monkey and made Monkey a companion animal of Momotarō. The protagonists in Momotarō stories and *Journey to the West* are wise heroes who embark on a journey as a sacred mission. Their followers are each three animals.[91]

The commonalities between the two stories are even more apparent in the modern Japanese manga interpretation of *Journey to the West* drawn by Tezuka Osamu. In it, Monkey travels to Japan, where a Japanese couple mistakes him for Momotarō. When Monkey finally meets Momotarō, he becomes Momotarō's companion animal and helps him conquer the demons on Devil's Island.[92] The couple's mistake shows how misrecognition is used in modern manga as a subtle motif that continues the connection between these Chinese and Japanese folk tales.

The legend of Momotarō was revived and became a popular mode of articulating nationalism within the political ideology that supported imperial expansion in wartime Japan. When Seo began to produce Japan's first animated feature film, the central theater of war had already shifted from continental Asia to the South Seas. This shift propelled Japan to modify its strategy for propaganda. As early as mid-1939, it was favoring a new direction: the construction of the Greater East Asian Co-Prosperity Sphere.[93] At the center of an ideology of hierarchy and domination, it presented Japan as the benevolent elder brother leading his younger—and subordinate—Asian brothers in the war against Western imperialism. Japanese films thus began to depict pan-Asian amicability and cooperation under Japan's leadership and to dramatize the enmity between the East and West. As mentioned, the term Greater East Asian Film Sphere was coined around 1941 to complement the ideology of the co-prosperity sphere. The film sphere called for a unified Asian film market against "corrosive Western influences" through the establishment of a new order.[94]

Consistent with wartime speciesism, Momotarō embodied Japan's position within the pan-Asian community. Just as Momotarō leads his companion animals to vanquish demons, Japan leads assimilated Asian countries in the fight against the West (demons). In *Momotarō's Sea Eagles,* for instance, Momotarō becomes a Japanese general and leads his troop of animals in a successful surprise attack on the demons in Pearl Harbor, the wartime Devil's Island. To realistically portray the battle, Seo and other animators visited Japanese Air Force bases in Tsuchiura and Kasumigaura and studied military aircraft taking off, flying, and landing. This allowed the animation to depict accurately details such as the rotational speed of the propellers.[95] This documentary-like approach injected realism into the film.

Wartime Japanese audiences welcomed *Momotarō's Sea Eagles* as the first animated feature film made in Japan. The film marked an important turning point in history of Japanese animation, despite its alleged shortcomings, such as a mediocre soundtrack and the erratic movement of Momotarō's hair. Animated shorts had previously been screened in small news theaters (*nyūsu gekijō*), but beginning with the screening of *Momotarō's Sea Eagles,* animated films came to be shown in large cinemas and were thus available to larger audiences. Unlike animated shorts, which had not generated enough revenue to cover production costs, *Momotarō's Sea Eagles* was a box office success. Released with the documentary film *War Convoy System* (*Tatakafu gosōsen dan,* 1943), it made around JP¥650,000 in box office receipts in the premier screenings in Japan, the majority of which came from ticket sales for *Momotarō's Sea Eagles.*[96] This commercial success demonstrated that an animated feature film could be popular and profitable—as well as impressively well made. *Momotarō's Sea Eagles* rose above the prevailing characterization of Japanese animated films as a national disgrace (*kokujoku*) and inspired hope for animation's future.[97] It was heralded as an accomplishment meriting national pride and paved the way for the imminent arrival of the commercial and artistic prosperity of Japanese animation on the global stage.[98]

Momotarō's Sea Eagles was first released in 1943 in the Roxy Theater (Dahua) in Shanghai between January 24 and 29, two months prior to its premiere in Japan. The Roxy had screened mostly American films but was transformed into a Japanese theater after Wang Jingwei's puppet government in Nanjing declared war against the United States and the UK on January 9. The following day, Kawakita Nagamasa's China Movie Company ordered a ban on all US and UK films. The premiere of *Momotarō's Sea Eagles* in the Roxy was a direct challenge to American films, portraying American soldiers as Hollywood animation characters such as Bluto from the *Popeye* cartoon and comic. The film's title in Chinese, *The Flying Prince Bombs Pearl Harbor* (*Fei taizi kongxi Zhenzhugang*), celebrated Japan's successful attack on Pearl Harbor. The Shanghai premiere of *Momotarō's Sea Eagles* was also meant to be a triumphant response to the shame incurred by *Princess Iron Fan.* The use of "Prince" in the Chinese title was a retort to the feminine titles of *Princess Iron Fan* and *Snow White.* Although *Momotarō's Sea Eagles* was a hit in Japan, it failed at the box office in Shanghai. *Momotarō's Sea Eagles* was released together with *Divine Sky Warriors* (*Sora no shinpei,* 1942) for nearly a week in the Roxy Theater, and the total audience was only 2,441, of whom 80 percent were Chinese and 20 percent Japanese. Chinese audiences found it boring and compared it unfavorably with American animated films, making comments such as "Has Japan ever made an animated film like *Mickey Mouse* and *Popeye?*" During the Lunar New Year festival in January 1944, *Momotarō's Sea Eagles* and *Princess Iron Fan* were screened together in a special program of animation at the Capital Theater (Guanglu), a theater that screened Disney films in the past and was transformed by the Japanese into the Culture Theater (Wenhua) on March 25, 1943 (see figure 1.5).[99] They were first screened together on January 29, 1944. The showing lasted for five days. The goal of the pairing was to exclude American animation and set the stage for *Momotarō's Sea Eagles* and *Princess Iron Fan* to compete with each other in wartime Shanghai.

Because *Momotarō's Sea Eagles* was so much shorter than *Princess Iron Fan,* the Japanese Navy ordered Seo to work on *Momotarō's Divine Sea Warriors*. The purpose of both was to inspire more young men to enlist in the Japanese military. Its production cost was JP¥270,000, a large budget for the time.[100] Seo left the Art Film Company to make this film and joined Shochiku for its larger-scale production facilities. The substantial funding from the Japanese Imperial Navy enabled Seo to hire fifty animators, giving *Momotarō's Divine Sea Warriors* the biggest team of animators to date in the history of Japanese animation.[101] The Navy protected Seo and other animators from being drafted into military service and sent into combat. It also provided crucial information for animators. For example, it arranged for Seo and other animators to stay with its paratrooper forces for a week to observe the aircraft and paratroopers.

Figure 1.5. Chinese poster for *Princess Iron Fan* and *Momotarō's Sea Eagles* in *Shenbao,* Shanghai, January 29, 1944.

Although banned in wartime Japan, the Imperial Navy arranged special screenings of Disney films such as *Fantasia* (1940, officially released in Japan in 1955), which had been intercepted by the Japanese Navy from American transport ships before the Pacific War broke out, for Seo and other animators so that they could learn from Disney's advanced animation techniques.[102] Thus the generous funding from the Imperial Navy made possible the production of Japan's first animated feature film, *Momotarō's Divine Sea Warriors* (74 minutes),[103] as well as its precursor, *Momotarō's Sea Eagles.*

Momotarō's Divine Sea Warriors tells the story of the general Momotarō and his troop of animals as they land on a colonized South Sea Island and conquer another island occupied by demons who turn out to be British soldiers. The conquest alludes to the fall of Singapore to Japan on February 15, 1942, which resulted in the war's largest surrender of British-led forces.[104] Seo and his team began work in January 1944 and finished in February 1945. The film premiered in Tokyo and Osaka on April 12. Tezuka Osamu was among the small audience who saw the film during the three-day premiere in Osaka. The audience for the premieres was small because Japanese children had been evacuated from cities and many theaters had been destroyed during the war. Few Japanese saw the film in 1945. All prints of *Momotarō's Divine Sea Warriors* were believed to have been destroyed by the war until a copy was recovered from the Shochiku Studio in 1982, restored, and publicly screened in 1984.[105]

Given the links between *Princess Iron Fan* and the two wartime Momotarō films, their common elements are hardly a surprise. All three turned to folklore as the vehicle to convey contemporary nationalist messages. *Princess Iron Fan* was set in the ancient past and referred indirectly to current politics. The two Momotarō films, however, were military propaganda; their wartime setting and nationalist messages were explicitly contemporary. *Princess Iron Fan* and the two Momotarō films used wartime speciesism to arouse nationalist sentiments. Tripitaka, the only human in the group of characters in *Princess Iron Fan,* is symbolic of the Chinese nation. In the Momotarō films, the only human in the group on the quest is Momotarō, who is symbolic of Japan, a modern and young nation rising to dominance in Asia. Tripitaka's quest for Buddhist sutras exemplifies the spiritual and pacifist tendencies of the Chinese, unlike the militarist and imperialist Japanese, as symbolized by Momotarō's sword and conquest of demons. The Bull Demon King represents Japan in *Princess Iron Fan,* yet the two Momotarō films depict China as a friendly companion animal assisting Momotarō in eliminating Western demons from the Greater East Asian Co-Prosperity Sphere. Wartime China and Japan are figured in masculine terms in both cases, albeit using literati (*wen*) and military (*wu*) traditions respectively. The most striking difference between them is that the character of Princess Iron Fan, an elusive female figure in wartime speciesism and nationalism, has no equivalent in the two Momotarō films. Unlike

Princess Iron Fan, the two Japanese films are about a highly masculine military leader who embodies clear-cut boundaries between the self and the Other. The strategic foregrounding of female protagonists in the posters and titles of *Princess Iron Fan* was transformed into male homosocial bonding of soldiers in wartime Momotarō films.

After *Princess Iron Fan* traveled to Japan, its visual style also was appropriated and rendered harmless. The Bull Demon King in *Princess Iron Fan* represents Japan, as evidenced by the sun insignia on his chest. This insignia was not an invention of the Wan brothers; it was common for artists in wartime resistance cartoons to use it on the chest of an animal or monster to symbolize the nation.[106] Japanese animators appropriated the symbols while transforming their meanings. Tokugawa Musei, the Japanese voice of Monkey, pointed out that the way Bull Demon King struts across the sky resembles the style of Japanese Kabuki.[107] In *Momotarō's Divine Sea Warriors,* Momotarō is the only human who leads the companion animals in their war against Western demons. The second generation of these companion animals, such as Monkey's younger brother and the Pheasant's children, bear a sun insignia on their chest, symbolizing their loyalty to Japan. Such symbolism exhorted the second generation of people colonized by Japan to be loyal to the Empire of the Rising Sun. Thus the creators of *Momotarō's Divine Sea Warriors* transformed a symbol of resistance in *Princess Iron Fan* into an icon of Japanese nationalism and collaboration.

The two films also share a silhouette style. The final battle scene in which the villagers pull down a tree is portrayed in silhouette in *Princess Iron Fan.* This style reflected Wan Laiming's talent for silhouette papercutting, which had been publicized in *The Young Companion* and other popular magazines. The Wan brothers had incorporated this style into *Princess Iron Fan.* A similar style is used in *Momotarō's Divine Sea Warriors* for the historical flashback that narrates conventional Japanese explanations for the war and the enemy's inherent weakness by portraying Europeans and South Sea Islanders in silhouette. Although this may be the influence of *Princess Iron Fan,* it may also relate to the style of animated filmmaking indigenous to Japan. Ōfuji Noburō (1900–1961), for instance, made papercutting silhouette animated films, including *The Whale* (*Kujira,* 1927) and *National Anthem* (*Kokka Kimigayo,* 1931). He continued to do so into the 1940s. Other early Japanese animated films such as *The Tale of the Crab Temple* (*Kanimanji engi,* 1924) and *Madame Butterfly's Fantasy* (*Ochōfujin no gensō,* 1940), used the silhouette style as well.[108] This style can be traced back to the German animation *The Adventures of Prince Achmed* (1926). The importance of the silhouette style in Japanese animation may relate to the high value given to the play of light and shadow in Japanese aesthetics, which was evident in Tanizaki Jun'ichirō's influential *In Praise of Shadows* (*In'ei raisan*, 1933). By the early 1940s, the "aesthetics of shadow" was popular among Japanese filmmakers.[109] Cultural transmission is complex and it is probable that the silhouette sequence in *Momotarō's Divine Sea Warriors* draws on domestic as well as foreign influences.

The Rebirth of the Monkey King in Postwar Japanese Manga and Animation

When *Princess Iron Fan* was released in Tokyo in 1942, fourteen-year-old Tezuka Osamu watched the film several times and was deeply impressed by it. His works from the beginning of his career to the end of his life are haunted by *Princess Iron Fan*. From 1953 to 1961, Tezuka's serialized manga *My Sun Wukong* appeared in the magazine *King of Manga* (*Manga-ō*), which was published by Akita Shoten. *My Sun Wukong* features Monkey, who is born from a stone. Monkey learns magic powers from a Daoist master and challenges the authority of heaven in his quest to become a respectable human. Buddha then imprisons him under a mountain for five hundred years as punishment for his arrogance until Tripitaka arrives and frees him. As repayment, Monkey follows Tripitaka as his bodyguard on the journey to India. In this telling, the story of Princess Iron Fan and Bull Demon King is just one of many challenges Tripitaka and his three disciples encounter en route to India.

My Sun Wukong was an adaptation of *Princess Iron Fan*. In the postscript to the complete version of *My Sun Wukong*, Tezuka acknowledges the impact that *Princess Iron Fan* had on his creation of this Japanese manga:

> I embarked on the project of *My Sun Wukong* after Akita Shoten invited me to create a work of humor. During the wartime era, there were few manga to read. The illustrated works of *Son Gokū*, drawn by Mr. Miyao Shigeo and published by Kōdansha, at one time satisfied my thirst for manga. However, what really opened my eyes, impressed me deeply, and sparked my desire to create today was *Princess Iron Fan*, the first Chinese animated feature film, which premiered in Japan in 1942. Even now I possess a worn-out slice of this film print. At that time, Disney's *Snow White* had just been released; it was really amazing that China could create an animated feature film with such rich content and stunning special effects. The Japanese version was dubbed by Mr. Tokugawa Musei and Kishii Akira. It was really a masterpiece for its humor and magnificent scale. *My Sun Wukong* was heavily influenced by *Princess Iron Fan*. When I was working on the end of the chapter about Fiery Mountain and Bull

> Demon King, the images of *Princess Iron Fan* kept assaulting me, and I could not get rid of it out of my mind. *Princess Iron Fan* possessed me and forced me to imitate its style to such a degree that now whenever I read this chapter, I really feel ashamed of my imitation.[110]

Tezuka's fascination with Monkey King was understandable. In addition to the mangas drawn by Miyao Shigeo, many Japanese animated and live-action films featured the stories of *Journey to the West,* which had long been popular in Japan. The earliest live-action feature film can be traced to *Saiyūki* (1911), in which Kinoshita Kichinosuke starred as the protagonist. In 1926, Ōfuji Noburō made the animated film *Journey to the West: The Story of Sun Wukong* (*Saiyū-ki Songokū monogatari*). Whether living or symbolic, monkeys have such a long history in Japanese culture that at times they become a metaphor for the Japanese people.[111] Thus, both Chinese and Japanese cultures could be involved in Tezuka's fascination with Monkey King.

As Tezuka acknowledged, the chapter "The Battle of the Fiery Mountain" ("Kaenzan no tatakai") in *My Sun Wukong* imitates the style of *Princess Iron Fan.* In the Chinese film and Tezuka's manga, for instance, fire is portrayed as a human-like monster. Tezuka's images of Bull Demon King and his vehicle, a dinosaur-like beast, are similar to those in *Princess Iron Fan,* and although the Bull Demon King does not have the sun insignia on his chest, it appears on the chest of a bear and several monkeys. Much of the visual style of Tezuka's manga resembles *Princess Iron Fan.* A major difference, however, is the angular, edged, and spiked style of *Princess Iron Fan*; the style of *My Sun Wukong* is more rounded and cute. The cute style functioned to attract modern manga readers, and the angular aimed at symbolically attacking the wartime Other.[112]

Suffering from an anxiety of influence, Tezuka did attempt to make "The Battle of the Fiery Mountain" noticeably different from *Princess Iron Fan* by changing details of the story. Rather than casting Princess Iron Fan as the wife of Bull Demon King, Tezuka depicts her as a fairy sent from heaven to extinguish the fire and save the villagers. However, just when she is about to extinguish the fire with her magic fan, the Bull Demon King captures, bribes, and seduces her. Because he is married to Fox Spirit, he takes Princess Iron Fan as his mistress. Bull Demon King promises the villagers and animals that if they pay the requisite tribute, he and Princess Iron Fan will extinguish the fire. They can never pay enough tribute, however, and the villagers continue to suffer from the Fiery Mountain until Tripitaka and his disciples appear. After this point, the story is much the same as *Princess Iron Fan.* Monkey subdues Bull Demon King in the final battle and then forces Princess Iron Fan to extinguish the fire with her fan. After this is accomplished,

Tripitaka and his disciples continue their journey to India and Princess Iron Fan flies back to heaven.

Tezuka's most radical strategy for distancing *My Sun Wukong* from *Princess Iron Fan* is historical anachronism and the use of modern elements, which create moments of unexpected humor. For example, after Bull Demon King persuades Princess Iron Fan to work for him, he invites her to accompany him home: "My home is not far from here. It's just JP¥2,000 by taxi."[113] Similarly, when Monkey is burned by the Fiery Mountain, Pigsy transforms himself into an ambulance and whisks him away. The most striking moment occurs in the final battle scene: after Bull Demon King reveals his original form, Monkey poses as a Spanish bullfighter and uses a red cape to provoke Bull Demon King. Tezuka's strategy of combining ancient and modern elements consciously targets contemporary manga readers.

Tezuka not only disrupts the temporal order by adding modern elements to this ancient story, he also self-reflexively blurs the boundary between ancient characters and modern manga readers. After Tripitaka and his disciples arrive, they meet two villagers and ask them about Fiery Mountain. Tripitaka introduces his disciples to the villagers: "They are my disciples. You would know them if you read the first episode of this manga." The villagers reply, "Oh, really? If you read from page 35 of this volume, you would know the story of Fiery Mountain."[114] This self-reflexivity draws attention to the experience of reading modern manga and distinguishes Tezuka's style from *Princess Iron Fan.*

This creative adaptation evidenced in *My Sun Wukong* attracted the attention of Tōei Animation. Known as the Disney of the East, Tōei Animation was founded in 1956 as the first production company in Japan dedicated to animation. Its first two feature films were *The Tale of the White Serpent* (*Hakujaden,* 1958) and *Magic Boy* (*Shōnen Sarutobi Sasuke,* 1959), the first Japanese animated films to travel to the United States. The first was released in the United States on March 5, 1961, and the second on July 8, 1961. Tōei Animation was interested in the story of Monkey and invited Tezuka to produce its third feature film, *Journey to the West* (*Saiyūki,* 1960), adapted from Tezuka's manga *My Sun Wukong.* This film about Monkey was released in Japan on August 14, 1960, and in the United States as *Alakazam the Great* on July 26, 1961.[115]

When the story of *Princess Iron Fan* was reincarnated in *My Sun Wukong* and *Alakazam the Great,* the role of Monkey was enhanced and that of Princess Iron Fan was diminished. Princess Iron Fan is a minor character with only a handful of appearances in *Alakazam the Great.* She is eclipsed by DeeDee, a new female character who is Monkey's childhood sweetheart. DeeDee allows Monkey to assert his heterosexual masculinity in the same way that Princess Iron Fan does for Bull Demon King. More important, DeeDee's presence radically redefines the meaning of Monkey's journey to the West. In the beginning of the film, Monkey and DeeDee live peacefully in his realm. After he is crowned king of the monkeys, his desire to be the world's most powerful creature causes him to become increasingly self-centered and arrogant. To gain supremacy, he decides to leave his island to learn magic powers from a Daoist master. DeeDee asks to accompany him, but Monkey dismissively replies, "It is no place for girls." Monkey then leaves to study with a Daoist master living on a mountain, where DeeDee later visits him. As soon as she arrives at the Daoist's mountain retreat, Monkey shows off his magical powers and flies to heaven. He wreaks havoc and offends Buddha, who imprisons him under a mountain. DeeDee feeds him fruit every day until Tripitaka arrives and frees him. Monkey again leaves DeeDee and sets off with Tripitaka on their journey to India. The rest of the story is about Bull Demon King and the Fiery Mountain. In this version, the impetus for Monkey's journeys is escape from DeeDee, who symbolizes stability and home, the point of departure and return. When Monkey returns home, now enlightened by Buddha, he marries DeeDee and lives with her happily ever after in his monkey kingdom.

From Monkey King to Astro Boy: Japanese Animation for Television

Alakazam the Great was Tezuka's first foray into animated filmmaking. He was excited when he received the invitation from Tōei because "Japan finally would be able to render *Journey to the West* into an animated feature film as China had."[116] Tezuka expanded his experience as an animator while working at Tōei and cultivated a taste for the auteur style. It was difficult, he felt, to maintain his artistic sensibility in a big studio with its emphasis on efficiency and profits. For instance, Tōei Animation vetoed his proposal to make Monkey and DeeDee's love story into a tragedy by having her die and insisted that its ending be happy like a Disney romance. Despite some uneasiness about the final result, Tezuka regarded *Alakazam the Great* as a crucial step in his animation career. He writes in his afterword to the manga *My Sun Wukong,*

> *Alakazam the Great* reaped high box office revenues. Although some people regarded it as vulgar and worthless, it did enter the American market. More importantly, it opened the door to my career in animation. Therefore, *Alakazam the Great,* or more precisely *My Sun Wukong,* had a profound and far-reaching significance on my life and career.[117]

Encouraged by the international success of *Alakazam the Great,* Tezuka founded his own animation studio Bug Productions (Mushi purodakushon) in 1961 and continued making animated films. Television was expanding in Japan, which had begun its own broadcasting in 1956 with the debut of the public network NHK and the private network TBS.[118] More networks followed later in the decade, such as Nihon TV (1957), Fuji TV (1959), and TV Asahi (1959). American animated film series such as *Popeye, Mighty Mouse,* and *Woody Woodpecker* were broadcast on television in Japan from 1959 onward.[119] In addition, the number of animated television commercials was increasing in the 1950s, providing opportunities for a new generation of animators and fostering the television animation industry in the 1960s.[120] It was in this local and international context that Tezuka's animation studio produced its first animated film, *Mighty Atom* (*Tetsuwan Atomu,* 1963), a black-and-white television anime with 193 episodes.[121] *Mighty Atomu,* the first weekly television animated series made in Japan, was broadcast on the Fuji TV channel starting January 1, 1963. The popular program was broadcast for four consecutive years in Japan.

In this television series, Tezuka initiated the style of "limited animation" in Japan. In full animation, the style of Disney's productions, animators usually use twenty-four drawings per second that show slight variations of movement. In limited animation, eight or fewer drawings are each used three times or more per second.[122] Limited animation is less time consuming and less expensive, but the movement is not as smooth as full animation. In the 1970s, anime, the abbreviated Japanese pronunciation of *animēshon,* became the common term for Japanese limited animation. Although the first Japanese animated film predates the 1970s, anime as limited animation attained worldwide popularity during the 1980s and can be traced to Tezuka's *Mighty Atom* of the early 1960s. Anime originally signified difference from manga film (*manga eiga*), the form of full animation prominent in Tōei and Miyazaki Hayao's works. However, the meaning of anime later expanded and became a generic term for Japanese animation as a whole. In this sense, *Alakazam the Great,* or *My Sun Wukong,* paved the way for the rise of Japanese anime on the global stage, Astro Boy becoming a Japanese national icon.[123]

The release of *Mighty Atom* triggered the worldwide popularity of modern anime. In May 1963, NBC Films signed a contract with Tezuka to broadcast fifty-two episodes in the United States. On September 7, 1963, *Mighty Atom* was broadcast as *Astro Boy* by New York's WNEW station. It was the first Japanese television anime shown to American audiences and became so popular that an English comic book version was published in 1965.[124] *Mighty Atom* was later rendered in color and continues to be popular across the world.

Scholars have highlighted the international context of Astro Boy's creation by emphasizing the influence of Western animation on Tezuka, pointing out Astro Boy's connections to Pinocchio, Mickey Mouse, Mighty Mouse, and Superman.[125] In his autobiography, Tezuka acknowledges the influence of Mickey Mouse on Astro Boy. When Tezuka was an elementary school student, his father used his camera and projector for home screenings of animated films featuring Mickey Mouse. Astro Boy's hair looks very much like Mickey Mouse's ears, a similarity made more obvious because, like Mickey's two ears, the two crests of Astro Boy's hair can be seen simultaneously from almost any angle. The upper body of both Mickey Mouse and Astro Boy is naked.[126] Like Pinocchio, Astro Boy is sold to a circus, and, like Mighty Mouse and Superman, Astro Boy flies and helps people in distress.

This assessment of international influences on Astro Boy, however, neglects the impact of *Princess Iron Fan* on Tezuka's career. Humanism is one of Astro Boy's most prominent characteristics. Astro Boy is a robot who desperately wants to become human. This humanistic theme also is found in Tezuka's adaptations of *Princess Iron Fan.* In his recreation of the Chinese story, Monkey is an animal born from a stone whose desperate hope to become a human compels him to set off on his journey to the West. Astro Boy shares key characteristics with Monkey and has similar powers: Monkey flies with the help of his magic somersaulting cloud; Astro Boy, created in a postwar Japan that was embarking on a journey of modernization and reconstruction, has atomic-powered engines in his boots that propel him across the sky like a rocket. Chinese animation was not Tezuka's sole influence. Nevertheless, the "international context" in which modern Japanese animation emerged certainly needs to encompass the influence of Chinese animation.

The encounter between Tezuka Osamu and *Princess Iron Fan* is often celebrated by Chinese animators and intellectuals because it represents not only a highpoint in the history of Chinese animation, but also the friendship between Chinese and Japanese animators, who were devoted to the same artistic form. To recognize the achievements of Chinese animation, the Association of Japanese Animation (AJA) organized an exhibition of Chinese animation in Tokyo in April 1981. Tezuka Osamu, then president of AJA, was one of the members who initiated this exhibition. Japanese animators, scholars, intellectuals, and fans attended the exhibition and watched Chinese animated films such as *Uproar in Heaven* (*Danao tiangong,* 1961–1964). Three representatives from China attended the exhibition: Te Wei, president of the Shanghai Animation Film Studio; Yan Dingxian, a director; and Duan Xiaoxuan, a camerawoman. Tezuka spoke publicly about the influence of *Princess Iron Fan* and Chinese animation in general on his career. At the farewell banquet, Tezuka Osamu and Yan Dingxian, who succeeded Te Wei as president of the studio and who worked as the key animation designer for *Uproar in Heaven,* drew a picture together to celebrate their kinship as animators. The picture shows Monkey shaking hands with Astro Boy. It was published in 1981 in *Sun Wukong,* the film pictorial of Shanghai Animation Film Studio (see figures 1.6 and 1.7).[127]

Although Astro Boy's kinship with Monkey was largely forgotten in Japan, a few Japanese observers acknowledge it. A 2006 exhibition of Tezuka's films at the Suginami Animation Museum in Tokyo between August 29 and November 26 featured an exhibit titled "Tezuka Osamu's Atom and Son Gokū Exhibition—Were Atom's Roots in Chinese Animation?" The exhibition's poster illustrates the historical entanglements between Monkey and Astro Boy.[128] The man wearing glasses on the bottom of the poster is Tezuka, who looks at a frame of Monkey from the film *Princess Iron Fan*. The poster depicts the connection between *Princess Iron Fan* and Tezuka, a connection that resulted in Tezuka's creating two of the most important characters in his career: Astro Boy and (Japanized) Monkey, who are shown at the top of the poster. Without *Princess Iron Fan* and the success of *Alakazam the Great*, Tezuka's animation career and the history of modern Japanese animation would have been different.

Figure 1.6. Tezuka Osamu and Yan Dingxian in 1981, courtesy of Yan Dingxian.

Figure 1.7. Astro Boy and Monkey in 1981, courtesy of Yan Dingxian.

Tezuka Osamu Encounters Monkey King

Tezuka's animation career both began and concluded with Monkey King. Only a few months before his death in 1989, Tezuka began to work on one of his last animated films, *I Am Sun Wukong,* which was released posthumously on August 27, 1989. *I Am Sun Wukong* is an autobiographical film that illustrates the impact of *Princess Iron Fan* on Tezuka's life and career. It begins with Tezuka's childhood. He wears thick eyeglasses and is portrayed as a fragile and vulnerable boy living in his own imaginative world. He is obsessed with insects. Other boys regard him as a freak and bully him. One summer day, his mother takes him to a movie theater where he watches *Princess Iron Fan* with wonder and admiration. Black-and-white "footage" of the final battle scene between Monkey and Bull Demon King from *Princess Iron Fan* appears in Tezuka's film. Yet this footage is not the same as the original Chinese film, but rather is reconstructed through drawings Tezuka made from memory. In Tezuka's memory, the fire was red because the Wan brothers dyed it in the original black-and-white film prints. After the young Tezuka character finishes watching *Princess Iron Fan,* he becomes curious about the art of animation and enters the projection room. The projectionist, moved by Tezuka's enthusiasm for animation, gives him the Japanese poster of *Princess Iron Fan* and a film fragment that shows Monkey.

After his encounter with Monkey in the cinema, young Tezuka tries to figure out how to animate pictures. He hangs the poster of *Princess Iron Fan* in his bedroom and carefully examines the movement of Monkey on the fragment of film. He draws many pictures of Monkey with slight variations of movement and makes a flip book to animate them. Monkey then steps off the paper, comes to life, and becomes Tezuka's interlocutor. The animated Monkey encourages Tezuka as he survives the bullies (dubbing them Bull Demon Kings) and the war, grows up, and becomes a professional animator. Monkey interacts not only with Tezuka in the film's story, but also with the audience in the role of the film's narrator. As narrator, he relates the impact of *Princess Iron Fan* on Tezuka's career, telling the audience how the film inspired Tezuka to establish his own animation studio and create *Astro Boy.* In Tezuka's previous works, such as *My Sun Wukong* and *Alakazam the Great,* Monkey is just one of Tezuka's characters. In *I Am Sun Wukong,* Monkey and Tezuka merge and at certain moments Tezuka transforms into Monkey. The transition from "My Sun Wukong" to "I Am Sun Wukong" illustrates the intimate and symbiotic relationship between Monkey and Tezuka.

The climax of *I Am Sun Wukong* occurs when Tezuka meets Wan Laiming on the Great Wall of China. By this time, the Tezuka character has established himself as a successful animator. Overwhelmed with joy, excitement, and admiration, he tells Wan about the impact of *Princess Iron Fan* on his life and career, and he promises to produce a film about Monkey to pay homage to Wan Laiming. The rest of the film tells a new story about Monkey, one that is dedicated to Wan Laiming.[129] Tezuka visited China five times during his life.[130] On his second visit, in December 1981, Tezuka met Wan Laiming for the first time. On his last visit, in November 1988 to attend the first International Animation Festival in Shanghai, he met Wan Laiming again. When he returned to Japan he began to work on *I Am Sun Wukong*. Tezuka died on February 9, 1989, before seeing his last film screened in a theater.

The Return of Monkey King

Tezuka's animation career had its ups and downs. He founded Bug Productions in 1961 and became president of the studio, resigning in 1971 when 119 employees formed a union. He then established Tezuka Productions, continuing his animation career until his death in 1989.[131] The original Bug Productions went bankrupt in 1973, and the union established a new studio of the same name in 1977 without Tezuka. Throughout his career, Tezuka was fascinated with animating Monkey. One of his posthumous works, *My Sun Wukong*, was released by Tezuka Productions on July 12, 2003, to memorialize Tezuka and to celebrate the birth of Astro Boy. The year 2003 is significant in the history of Japanese animation: the fictional birthdate of Astro Boy in Tezuka's original story is April 7, 2003, and 2003 was the fortieth anniversary of the release of *Mighty Atom*. This celebration of the birth of Astro Boy with the release of a film about Monkey further demonstrates the historical ties between the two characters.[132]

My Sun Wukong was released in China under the name of *Sun Wukong* on November 6, 2004, to commemorate Wan Laiming's death on October 7, 1997.[133] Wan Laiming not only produced *Princess Iron Fan* but also created *Uproar in Heaven*, a highly popular animated film featuring Monkey. As a tribute to Wan's achievements in animating this beloved character, his tomb is engraved with an image of Monkey. The year 2004 was the fortieth anniversary of the production of *Uproar in Heaven* as well as the year of the monkey in the Chinese zodiac.[134]

Matsutani Takayuki, president of both Tezuka Productions and the AJA, delivered a speech at the premiere of *My Sun Wukong*: "Mr. Wan is the person Mr. Tezuka admired and respected the most. Many people think that Tezuka was heavily influenced by Disney animation. In fact, the influence from Chinese animation, especially Mr. Wan's animated films, was much greater and more profound." He then added, with a touch of sadness, "Tezuka knew that he was going to leave the world after he visited Mr. Wan in 1988, so he finished the draft of *My Sun*

Wukong. He wanted to use his work to bid farewell to Mr. Wan, telling him that 'I am gone.'"[135] The release of *My Sun Wukong* in China was therefore an homage to Wan Laiming specifically and Chinese animation more generally. It also completed the trip of Monkey from China to Japan and back to China. The wartime journey of *Princess Iron Fan* returned to where it had started.

2 Mochinaga Tadahito and Animated Filmmaking in Early Socialist China

Mochinaga Tadahito (1919–1999) was a Japanese animator who flourished in wartime Tokyo and lived in China from 1945 to 1953, where he was prominent among the group of animators who established the industry in early socialist China. His role in the history of China is ignored or downplayed, however, because of a prevailing scholastic preoccupation about national identity and pure Chineseness. Mochinaga is obscure in histories of Japanese animation simply because he is considered less influential than Tezuka Osamu and Miyazaki Hayao but also because of the relative belittling of puppet animation. This chapter discusses hidden histories associated with Mochinaga and tracks the movements across the borders of Japan and China that constituted his career, and in so doing demonstrates that from the beginning of socialist China, the Chineseness of Chinese animation was tinged by Japanese animation, which was an indispensable stage for the development of Chinese animation at the time of regime change in the late 1940s and early 1950s.

From Fantasy to Propaganda: Wartime Japanese Animation

Mochinaga was born in Tokyo on March 3, 1919, and spent his childhood in Manchuria, where his father worked for the South Manchuria Railway Company, or Mantetsu, which ran from 1906 to 1945.[1] Mochinaga and his family traveled back and forth between Japan and Manchuria during his childhood. After the Manchurian Incident (a staged event engineered by the Japanese military as a pretext for invasion) on September 18, 1931, he returned to Japan and finished middle school in Tokyo. Inspired and moved by Western animated films such as Disney's *Water Babies* (1935), Mochinaga decided to become an animator. He learned how to make animated films during his three years at the Applied Arts Department of Japan Art School (Nippon bijutsu gakkō ōyō bijutsu-ka) in Tokyo. His final art school project was the short film *Until an Animated Film Is Made* (*Manga eiga no dekiru made*, 1938).

Mochinaga's career as an animator was launched when Seo Mitsuyo hired him to work at the Art Film Company (GES) in 1939. Seo and Mochinaga worked primarily on animated films for children. Their first film, *The Marine Corps of Ducks* (*Ahiru rikusentai,* 1940) was commissioned by the Ministry of Education. Seo and Mochinaga later produced *Ant Boy* (*Ari-chan,* 1941) for which Mochinaga built a four-level multiplanar camera, the first to be used in Japan.[2] *The Marine Corps of Ducks* and *Ant Boy* are fairy tales that feature anthropomorphic animals and evoke a lyrical tranquility.

As World War II broke out in the Pacific, Mochinaga began to produce animated propaganda films for the Japanese Navy. As discussed earlier, Mochinaga and Seo Mitsuyo at the Art Film Company produced *Momotarō's Sea Eagles* (*Momotarō no umiwashi,* 1943) in response to the Chinese animated feature film *Princess Iron Fan* (*Tieshan gongzhu,* 1941), a preview of which they had seen, and which they then watched repeatedly in theaters to learn from (see chapter 1).[3] In *Momotarō's Sea Eagles,* Mochinaga was responsible for backgrounds, special effects, and photography. The goal of the film was to propagate militarist ideals and encourage young Japanese men to join the Japanese Air Force. According to his memoir, Mochinaga later was filled with remorse by the fact that many young men who watched it identified with Momotarō, joined the Japanese Air Force, and died.[4]

In 1943, the Art Film Company dissolved and was reincorporated into Asahi Film Company (Asahi eigasha). Seo left for Shōchiku Production Company and later produced *Momotarō's Divine Sea Warriors* (*Momotarō umi no shinpei*) in 1945.[5] Mochinaga stayed at Asahi Film and produced *Fuku-chan's Submarine* (*Fuku-chan no sensuikan,* 1944), his first solo effort. A propaganda film sponsored by the Japanese Navy, *Fuku-chan's Submarine* tells the story of a Japanese submarine attacking an enemy ship. To make the film, Mochinaga visited the naval base in Kure and was permitted as a passenger on a submarine (No. 157). Mochinaga drew on this experience when he animated *Fuku-chan's Submarine.*[6]

Man'ei, Northeast Film Studio, and Shanghai Animation Film Studio

Japan exerted its colonial control over northeast China from the beginning of the twentieth century through the South Manchuria Railway Company, which was founded in Japan in 1906 and relocated to Dalian in Liaoning province of China in 1907. Given its monopoly over railways, coal mines, and the industrial sector, the company controlled much of Manchuria's formal economy. In 1923, it established a film unit to produce travel films to advertise Manchuria to potential passengers, investors, and businessmen. After Akutagawa Kōzō became the unit's head in 1928, the unit expanded and produced numerous propaganda documentaries supporting Japanese imperialism in Manchuria. After the Manchurian Incident, Japan quickly occupied northeast China. The puppet state of Manchukuo was established in 1932 with the aim of advancing Japan's imperialist agenda in China. Puyi, the last emperor of China, was invited by the Japanese to become emperor of Manchukuo. Its capital was today's Changchun (named Xinjing, new capital, by the Japanese), and the areas under Manchukuo rule were commonly called Manchuria.

To better disseminate Manchukuo's "national policy" and advocate the ideology of the Greater East Asian Co-Prosperity Sphere, the Manchukuo Film Association (Man'ei/Manying) was established in Changchun in 1937. Given its large scale of film production, Man'ei assimilated the film unit of Mantetsu in the early 1940s. Its primary purpose was to educate "uncultured" local Manchurians rather than Japanese people. It produced documentaries, live-action feature films, and newsreels, which were categorized into enlightenment films (*keimin eiga*), entertainment films (*gomin eiga*), and newsreels (*jiji eiga*). To better disseminate its film culture, Man'ei began publishing Japanese and Chinese versions of the magazine *Manchuria Film* (*Manshū eiga*) in December 1937 and renamed it *Film Pictorial* (*Dianying huabao*) in June 1941. Amakasu Masahiko ruled Man'ei with an iron fist from 1939 until it was closed in 1945.[7]

After Mochinaga finished *Fuku-chan's Submarine* in Tokyo in 1944, he suffered not only from overwork and physical exhaustion, but also from malnutrition due to food shortages in Japan. The production of animated film halted during the war, making it difficult for Mochinaga and other filmmakers to find employment in Japan.[8] Mochinaga's house was destroyed in Allied bombings. Having endured enough from what he described as a refugee-like lifestyle, Mochinaga migrated to Manchuria in June 1945.[9] This decision proved right. His wartime colleague Seo Mitsuyo, who co-created the propaganda films for the Japanese Navy, stayed in Japan, saw his career decline, and was forced to leave animation altogether.

Mochinaga's move had a reasonable basis, in part his personal connection with Manchuria, having lived there as a child. Furthermore, in Japanese popular imagination, Manchuria was a peaceful haven with abundant food and jobs at a time when Japan was besieged by war and food shortages. Man'ei films had popularized an image of Manchuria as prosperous, idyllic, and democratic. As Michael Baskett points out, "Man'ei's representation of self-sufficiency, relatively stable food supplies, and high salaries, tapped into the Taishō era (1912–1926) fantasies of a romantic Manchuria that was a haven for film personnel seeking to escape widespread industry downsizing and massive food rationing in Japan."[10]

Manchuria and Man'ei thus attracted Japanese filmmakers who felt economically and politically displaced in wartime Japan.

After Mochinaga settled in Manchuria, a former colleague at the Art Film Company who was working for Man'ei in Changchun introduced him to Man'ei director Kimura Sotoji. Kimura then invited Mochinaga to join the Man'ei art department. At the time, Kimura was working on *Little Sister Su* (*Su shaomei,* 1945), which combined live action with animation, and Kimura hoped that Mochinaga could contribute to its production. Mochinaga was officially put on the Man'ei payroll on July 15, 1945. He anticipated working on *Little Sister Su,* but received no further news from Kimura. Instead, he was assigned to produce *The Agriculture of Northern Manchuria* (*Kita Man no nōgyō*), using animation as a special effect to portray the growth of beans, sorghum, sweet potatoes, and other crops. However, as World War II came to an end the following month, Man'ei underwent a radical transformation and Mochinaga ended up producing no animated films during his stay.[11]

On August 15, 1945, Japan surrendered, and by August 19 the Soviet army controlled Changchun. Man'ei's head, Amakasu Masahiko, committed suicide on August 20. Without their charismatic leader, Man'ei was rudderless.[12] The Chinese Communist Party (CCP) capitalized on the city's turmoil and endeavored to take control of Man'ei. It wanted to develop its own film industry in Communist-controlled areas but had neither advanced filmmaking equipment nor skilled technicians. Man'ei was the largest film studio in East Asia and had the most advanced technological facilities, leading technicians, plentiful celluloid, and talented filmmakers.[13] The CCP thus felt that taking control of Man'ei was an important step for establishing its own film industry.

The Party kept a close eye on a Chinese man by the name of Zhang Xinshi. In 1936, Zhang had gone to Japan to earn a degree in film studies. While in Japan, he helped establish the magazine *Friends of Film and Literature* (*Yingyi zhi you*), modeled on Guo Moruo's *Creative Society* (*Chuangzao she*) in China. This left-leaning magazine attracted the attention of the Japanese government, and many of those associated with it were arrested and Zhang was blacklisted. When Zhang returned to China in 1939, he joined Man'ei as a script writer. Frequently investigated by the Japanese authorities, he was imprisoned in 1944 on the basis of a progressive left-leaning film script he had written. He was released shortly before the end of the war.[14] In late August 1945, Liu Jianmin, a CCP representative, approached Zhang and persuaded him to work for the Party to take over Man'ei. Through its informant Zhang, the CCP organized several of Man'ei's more progressive left-leaning staff, including Chinese and Japanese personnel, and launched its mobilization campaign. With the support of the CCP, progressive left-leaning Man'ei staff members transformed Man'ei into the Northeast Film Company (Dongbei dianying gongsi) in Changchun on October 1, 1945.[15] The company mainly worked on Chinese, Japanese, and Korean versions of Soviet films, and Mochinaga was responsible for adding animation sequences to these Asian versions and for supplying handwritten subtitles.[16]

The CCP's rival, the Nationalist Party, also attempted to control Man'ei. As an agent of the Nationalist Party, Jiang Xueqian studied in Japan before joining Man'ei. When Amakasu became the head of Man'ei, he felt obliged to hire Chinese people to supervise Chinese employees. Jiang was the first of these he hired.[17] In late November 1945, Jiang collaborated with the Nationalist Party, arrested Zhang Xinshi and other pro-Communist members, and imprisoned them in the Public Security Bureau. They planned to replace Zhang with their own agents.[18] Although the Soviet Union's official position was neutral, it covertly supported the CCP and, as early as November 11, had transferred the Public Security Bureau to it.[19] Zhang and others were then released. Jiang Xueqian committed suicide.

To avoid further antagonism with the Nationalist Party, the Soviet Union appointed a Soviet whose Chinese name was Guo Xizhen as director of Northeast Film and Zhang Xinshi as vice director. In sum, the Nationalist Party did not want to offend the Soviet Union and made every effort to avoid a hostile takeover of the company.[20] On April 14, 1946, the Soviet army withdrew from Changchun. The Eighth Route Army led by the CCP soon launched an attack on Nationalist Party troops and took control of the entire Changchun region for the first time. Several days later, the Soviet Union transferred the Northeast Film Company to the CCP with Shu Qun as its director and Zhang Xinshi as vice director.[21]

During the following month, however, the Nationalist armies, equipped with advanced American weapons, launched a large-scale attack on Changchun. To prevent the annihilation of Northeast Film, the CCP ordered that the company's staff and equipment be moved to Harbin as soon as possible.[22] It wanted the Japanese filmmakers and technicians to go with them, so it sent its representative Shu Qun to mobilize the Japanese. Shu's humble uniform and his mild, friendly demeanor impressed Mochinaga. Other renowned Japanese filmmakers, such as Kimura Sotoji and Uchida Tomu, agreed to the move.[23] This encouraged Mochinaga and other Japanese members to move as well.[24] On May 13, 1946, almost all of the machinery, costumes, and other equipment were loaded onto thirty trucks and moved north to Harbin. According to Mochinaga's memoir, on May 18, when Mochinaga learned that the animation stand was not loaded with the other equipment, he anxiously inquired about its absence. No one, he discovered, knew how to dismantle and reassemble it. Because Mochinaga had some experience from working at the Art Film Company when he was in Tokyo, he was able to dismantle it himself and have it moved; it was going to be the only animation stand available at the Northeast Film Company.[25] On May 18, four hundred staff members boarded trains and traveled north. On May 23, as the Nationalist Air Force bombed Changchun, Shu Qun and Zhang Xinshi caught the last train heading north, while some Japanese staff members missed the train and were arrested by the Nationalist Party.[26]

The staff of Northeast Film Company traveled to Harbin with the intention of settling there. However, because of the political instability in Harbin, the CCP ordered them to continue to move northward to Jiamusi. When the staff arrived in Jiamusi, they discovered that Japanese armies had burned numerous homes, and therefore no housing was available for them. They traveled farther north until they arrived at Xingshan (renamed Hegang in 1951), which they reached on June 1, 1946, ending their exodus. On October 1, the company celebrated its first anniversary and changed its name to Northeast Film Studio (Dongbei dianying zhipianchang), appointing Shu Qun as its director and Zhang Xinshi as vice director.[27] Soon thereafter it established its animation group (*katong zu*), with Mochinaga Tadahito as its head. In the beginning, the staff numbered only three and none were Chinese: Mochinaga Tadahito and Sei Mitsuo (Shi Manxiong) were Japanese, and Jo Ming (Zhao Ming) was Korean. In June 1948, the animation group expanded and became the animation branch (*katong gu*), Mochinaga again serving as head. Other members included Sei Mitsuo, Jo Ming, Li Lianqing, Lu Xipeng, Shu Chang, Cui Yongquan, and Ma Yanqiu.[28] They worked on animated war maps, animated shorts, and credits for live-action films.

When the Northeast Film Company had moved out of Changchun, among the four hundred employees were approximately one hundred Japanese and their ten family members. When the company arrived in Harbin, nearly one hundred Chinese employees stayed there, leaving more than three hundred staff to travel on to Xingshan. Some Japanese employees joined the company but later did not relocate to Xingshan; other Japanese joined just as the company was about to move northward. In June 1946, Wang Yang, the leader of the North China Film Team (Huabei dianyingdui) came to the Northeast Film Company and asked for personnel and infrastructural support. The company dispatched seventeen technicians, including three Japanese. In August 1946, many Japanese refugees in Northeast China returned to Japan, including some of the Japanese staff at Northeast Film.

By the end of 1946, eighty-four Japanese experts (sixty-one men and twenty-three women), not including their family members, were working at Northeast Film (see figures 2.1 and 2.2). These included nineteen in the art department, thirty-nine in the technology department, and twenty-six in the administrative department.[29] By the end of May 1949, only fifty-three remained. Morikawa Kazuyo and Mochinaga Tadahito returned to Japan in May and August of 1953 respectively. By October 1953, almost all remaining Japanese at the studio had returned to Japan, including Uchida Tomu.[30]

Figure 2.1. Japanese staff at Northeast Film Studio, 1947, courtesy of Mochinaga Noriko.

Figure 2.2. Japanese families at Northeast Film Studio, 1948, courtesy of Mochinaga Noriko.

Approximately thirty thousand Japanese doctors, nurses, railway technicians, film technicians, coal workers, and soldiers remained in China after the end of World War II. They made important contributions to the construction of early socialist China, filling a role similar to that of foreign experts during the Meiji Restoration in Japan. For instance, the fourth Air Force branch of the Japanese Kwantung Army in Manchuria helped the People's Liberation Army (PLA) establish its own air force. Kimura Sotoji helped the CCP design postage stamps to commemorate the liberation of the Northeast and Mochinaga Tadahito, together with other Japanese and Chinese animators, contributed to the establishment of the animation industry in early socialist China.[31]

Northeast Film was reorganized when filmmakers from the Yan'an Film Troupe (Yan'an dianyingtuan), which was officially established in Yan'an in 1938 to mark the beginning of the communist film industry, and the Northwest Film Team (Xibei dianyingdui) came to Xingshan under the command of the CCP.[32] Shortly after returning from the Soviet Union, the Yan'an Film Troupe's founder, Yuan Muzhi, became the director in the spring of 1947, Zhang Xinshi and Wu Yinxian became vice directors, and Chen Bo'er (from the Yan'an Film Troupe) became Party secretary of the studio.[33]

In April 1949, shortly after the Communist takeover of the city, Northeast Film Studio moved back to Changchun and changed its name to Changchun Film Studio in 1955. In the autumn of 1949, it established its animation group (*meishu-pian zu*), naming Te Wei as its new director, succeeding Mochinaga Tadahito. Te Wei stayed in Hong Kong between 1947 and March 1949 and arrived in Changchun in July 1949. Jin Xi was appointed as vice director and Mochinaga as technical supervisor. Jin Jing, a well-known children's author, also joined the animation group. The number of animation staff increased from eight to twenty-two. To further develop the animation industry in socialist China, Te Wei appealed to top Communist Party leaders and expressed the hope of moving the animation group to Shanghai. Ultimately, the Cultural Bureau under the leadership of Xia Yan and the Film Bureau under the leadership of Yuan Muzhi supported his proposal. In late March 1950, the animation group of Northeast Film Studio moved its staff of twenty-two to Shanghai and became a division of Shanghai Film Studio, which was founded in Shanghai in November 1949 immediately after the Communist takeover of the city in May 1949. Mochinaga and other Japanese animators moved to Shanghai with the division. Morikawa Kazuyo, a young Japanese woman whose Chinese name was He Dai, soon became the director of the inking and painting department in 1950 at the age of twenty-one, leading more than thirty staff.[34] On April 1, 1957, Shanghai Film Studio was divided into several studios, including the Shanghai Animation Film Studio, the only state-owned animation studio in socialist China.[35] Te Wei served as its first president until 1984 and continued working for the studio as a consultant until 1988.[36]

Plasmatic Empire: Animated Filmmaking in Man'ei

Although Mochinaga produced no animated films during his stay in Man'ei, animated films were being produced there before his arrival. Little research has been done on this topic, however, given inadequate primary sources and limited access to Man'ei films, which were long considered as lost. However, in 1989, Yamaguchi Takeshi and other Japanese researchers discovered the Man'ei films in Moscow at the Russian State Film Archive. When the Soviet army left Changchun after the war, they learned, it had taken many Man'ei films to Moscow. Yamaguchi and others brought the prints back to Japan in 1994 and converted selected films to VHS in 1995. With the good will of "giving the people in China who helped make these films a second chance to see them," Yamaguchi Takeshi presented the videos to the Chinese government, who reluctantly accepted them in 1995, declaring the films to be solid evidence of Japanese imperialism.[37] The Chinese government regarded them as pure Japanese propaganda films. Although Man'ei films were indeed produced by Japanese filmmakers, many Chinese had played important roles in Man'ei. The films were made within Chinese territory, and for this reason, Chinese scholars such as Hu Chang and Gu Quan regarded them as Chinese films.[38] Rather than viewing them as either Chinese or Japanese products, I approach Man'ei films, and animation in particular, as an interstitial product that ensued from the animated encounter between wartime China and Japan.

Recent studies demonstrate that the puppet state of Manchukuo existed more like an imagined rather than a material and sociohistorical country. Even historians such as Louise Young and Prasenjit Duara noted the role of imagination in constructing Manchukuo.[39] Highlighting the essential role films played in constructing the imagined empire of Manchukuo, Jie Li uses the term "phantasmagoric" to describe the illusionary and ephemeral nature of Manchukuo and argues that, rather than being imagined retrospectively a là Benedict Anderson, Manchukuo was imagined prospectively and invented beforehand through the documentary films produced by the South Manchuria Railway Company.[40] Manchukuo and Manchuria were imagined into being, retrospectively and prospectively, films functioning as centripetal forces. Different from the documentaries, animation, renowned for its wild imagination, demonstrated a more centrifugal force that diverted the imagination away from Manchukuo and Manchuria, creating an interstitial, plasmatic, fluid, and fantastic empire located in another space and another time—distanced, if not completely detached from wartime Manchuria, China, and Japan. Manchukuo and animation thus share a fundamental connection in that both of them can be regarded as imagined constructs.

The film unit of the South Manchuria Railway Company produced many documentaries, in which animation was used as special effects for what live-action film was unable to achieve in the 1930s. Since the mid-1930s, the term "culture film" (*bunka eiga*) was used to refer to nonfictional documentaries that were not blatantly political, such as travel, science, and ethnographic films.[41] Many of these documentaries were an introduction to Manchuria and its geography. A map of China appears first, and then animated outlines demarcating and foregrounding the territory of Manchuria. A male voiceover describes a particular location in

Manchuria as a map of Manchuria appears, an animated arrow pointing to it on the map. In some travel films, the movement of people on trains, which sometimes was suggested merely by the noise of wheels and whistles, are accompanied by the movement of animated lines or arrows across a hand-drawn map. The physical experience of Manchuria was transcribed into a fantastic spectacle in which Manchukuo and Manchuria were composed of fluid and permeable outlines, dots, arrows, and shapes. As a hand-drawn plasmatic empire, Manchukuo had the potential of expanding and contracting, a fantasy land par excellence.

In addition to its use for plasmatic maps, animation was used for charts, tables, and diagrams. In the documentary *The Construction of a Model Village* (*Mofan xiang zhi jianshe,* 1935), animation depicts the idea of collaboration between peasants and the government. Two semicircles, one containing the Chinese character for peasants (*nongmin*) and the other for government (*zhengfu*), appear on the left and right side of the screen. They move toward each other until they merge into a single circle, with the Chinese characters for agricultural cooperative (*nongshi hezuoshe*) inside. Animation was also used for special effects to explain scientific information. In the science documentary *The Expressions of Water* (*Mizu no hyōjō,* 1941), animation portrays snowfall in winter and evaporation of water in spring in Manchuria, creating a vaporous world that could not be represented by live-action film.

Rather than being rooted in the concrete political realities of Manchuria, animated segments transported the audience to a plasmatic world distanced from the geographical territory of Manchuria. Animation and documentary films typically are regarded as opposites, animation being highly fantastic and documentary highly realistic. The juxtaposition of documentary and animation within these films reflect the Janus-faced nature of Manchuria: a highly politicized entity on the one side and a fantasyland on the other. Animation and documentary films continued to have such a kinship at the Northeast Film Studio in the late 1940s.

Man'ei went beyond merely using animation for special effects in documentaries. Its animation equipment was more advanced than that at the film unit of the South Manchuria Railway Company. Man'ei had several Bell & Howell sound animation machines.[42] Its animation stand was the same as the one Mochinaga Tadahito had used at the Art Film Company in Tokyo.[43] Man'ei even offered courses teaching the art of animation to its specialized staff.[44] In the late 1930s and early 1940s, discussions of animated filmmaking frequently appeared in *Manchuria Film,* a Japanese and Chinese film magazine affiliated with Man'ei. In the article "The Secret of Animated Film" ("Manhua dianying de mimi/Manga eiga wa dōshite dekiruka"), Asada Isamu describes in detail the process of animated filmmaking in Man'ei and illustrates it with a series of cartoons (see figure 2.3).[45]

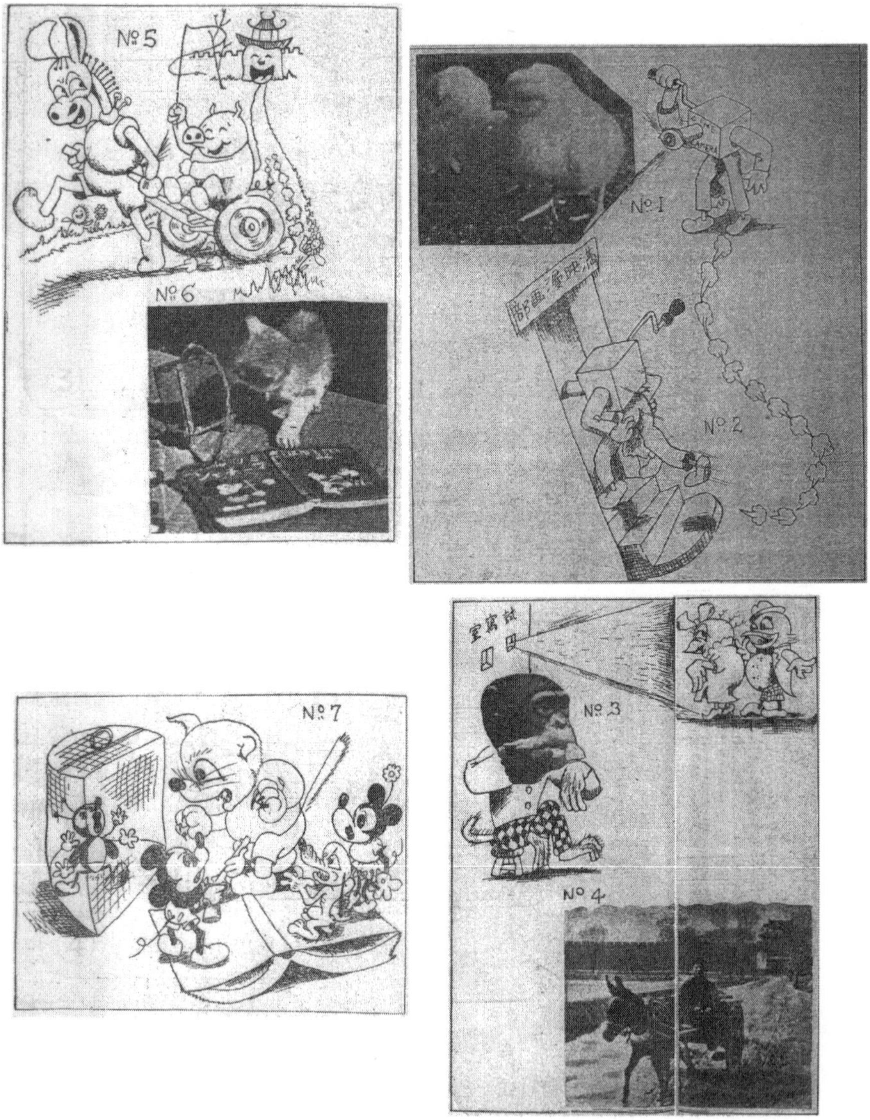

Figure 2.3. "The Secret of Animated Film," *Manchuria Film,* 1939, courtesy of Yumani Shobo Publishers Inc.

These illustrations show that the cartoon department (*manhua bu*) of Man'ei was responsible for animated filmmaking, in addition to its role of producing illustrations and cartoons for *Manchuria Film*. According to Asada, "photography" was the first step in animated filmmaking at Man'ei. Animators needed a special "camera" to "photograph" the objects to be animated. He jokingly wrote that this special camera was the eyes of the animator. The animator needed to use his "eyes" to observe and "record" the movements of the objects to be animated, such as the two chickens illustrated in Cartoon No. 1. Although Asada highlighted the importance of the animator's eyes, the reference might also pertain to a live-action camera, which records the movements of objects to be rotoscoped or partially referenced by the animator. The animator in Cartoon No. 1 is a cyborg creature with a camera head, two human hands, and three human legs, which looks like a tripod. The camera is labeled "cine camera," which refers to a live-action film camera that can take sequential photos with slight variations. It is possible that the animator uses both a real camera and his eyes to make an animated film that partially draws on, if not solely depends on, the method of rotoscoping.

With the "recorded" materials in hand, the animator then goes back to the cartoon department of Man'ei and uses cels to make an animated film (Cartoon No. 2). When the film is made, it will be screened and tested in the Trial Writing Room (Shixieshi) of the cartoon department. In a joking manner, Asada said that an ape named Chen Wanqi was in charge of the trial screening of animated films that have animal protagonists (Cartoon No. 3). His facial expressions indicate whether the animated film is good or bad. Chen Wanqi might be one of the many Chinese staff working in Man'ei and he was caricatured as an ape here. The two chickens were animated and talking in human language: "I love you." "Oh, really?" Chen Wanqi lavished his praises on the film: "Good! Really good!"

Cartoon No. 4 shows a photograph of a man driving a donkey cart away from a gate in a city wall. An animated film was made based on this, with a clothed donkey pulling the cart and a pig whipping the donkey (Cartoon No. 5). The next photo shows a cat playing around a cage and several books. This scenario was animated, the cat trying to grab and eat a firefly in the cage. With a gun in hand, Mickey Mouse, together with several other Disney characters such as Minnie and Goofy, appear to stop the vicious cat (Cartoon No. 7). The appearance of Disney characters here is intriguing, given that they were banned in wartime Japan. Also, these Disney characters were represented as positive heroes in line with the Hollywood gangster film style, in sharp contrast to the negative representations of American cartoon characters (such as Betty Boop, Popeye, and Bluto) in *Momotarō's Sea Eagles* and its posters. Man'ei was often regarded as a Japanese propaganda machine for its "national policy" films, but these positive Disney characters as well as the humorous and depoliticized animated films suggest that

Man'ei was more fluid than previously thought. The plasmatic empire constructed by Man'ei animation seemed to have a life of its own, distanced if not completely detached from wartime realities.

Because only a small portion of Man'ei films can be accessed by researchers today, I was unable to view most of the animated films mentioned in Asada's essay and cartoons. However, experimental, if not active, animated filmmaking certainly took place at Man'ei. In another essay, Asada declared that the cartoon department at Man'ei was working around the clock to produce animated films, which would be released soon. He warned readers that they would laugh convulsively from watching the animated films produced by Man'ei. He suggested that to protect oneself from possible bodily harm from laughing too violently, the reader should acquire the skill of not laughing and practice it diligently until the release of Man'ei's animated films.[46] In this plasmatic world of humor and laughter, politics was pushed to the background.

Man'ei emphasized the importance and urgency of animated filmmaking because it symbolized a country's advanced development of film art. An author named Li Lei published "The Process of Making an Animated Film" ("Manhua yingpian zhizuo guocheng") in the April 1940 issue of *Manchuria Film*. He cited Lin Yutang, a well-known Chinese writer and intellectual, as evidence that animation was extremely important. A staunch supporter of humorous literature, Lin Yutang said, "When a country's literature attained a very high level, humorous literature will appear." Li Lei borrowed Lin Yutang's words and claimed that "when a country's film art advanced to a very high level, animation will surely appear." In this sense, animation was not an inferior successor of live-action film, but rather a higher level of a country's achievement in film art. Because Manchukuo had only recently been established, the rapid appearance of animation by Man'ei would not only lead to pride in higher artistic achievements, but also signal the new country's maturity, solidarity, and steadfast development. The implication was that animation was not a minor or lightweight art form, but instead a crucial product of—and also a defining agent—in empire building and the historical and artistic development of Manchukuo.[47]

Manchuria Film mentioned the "sound cartoon" (*yousheng manhua*) *Purchasing Oil* (*Maiyou,* 1940) in the same issue in which Li Lei's article appeared. This sound cartoon was probably an animated film, given that the Man'ei cartoon department was working hard to produce animated films at that time, as Asada Isamu mentioned in December 1939. In a short essay written in the 1930s, the term "sound moving cartoon" (*yousheng huodong manhua*) was used to refer to animated films with sound.[48] Although the middle word "moving" (*huodong*) was missing in the term "sound cartoon," it is probable that *Purchasing Oil* was an animated film with sound. Or at a minimum, it might be situated between an

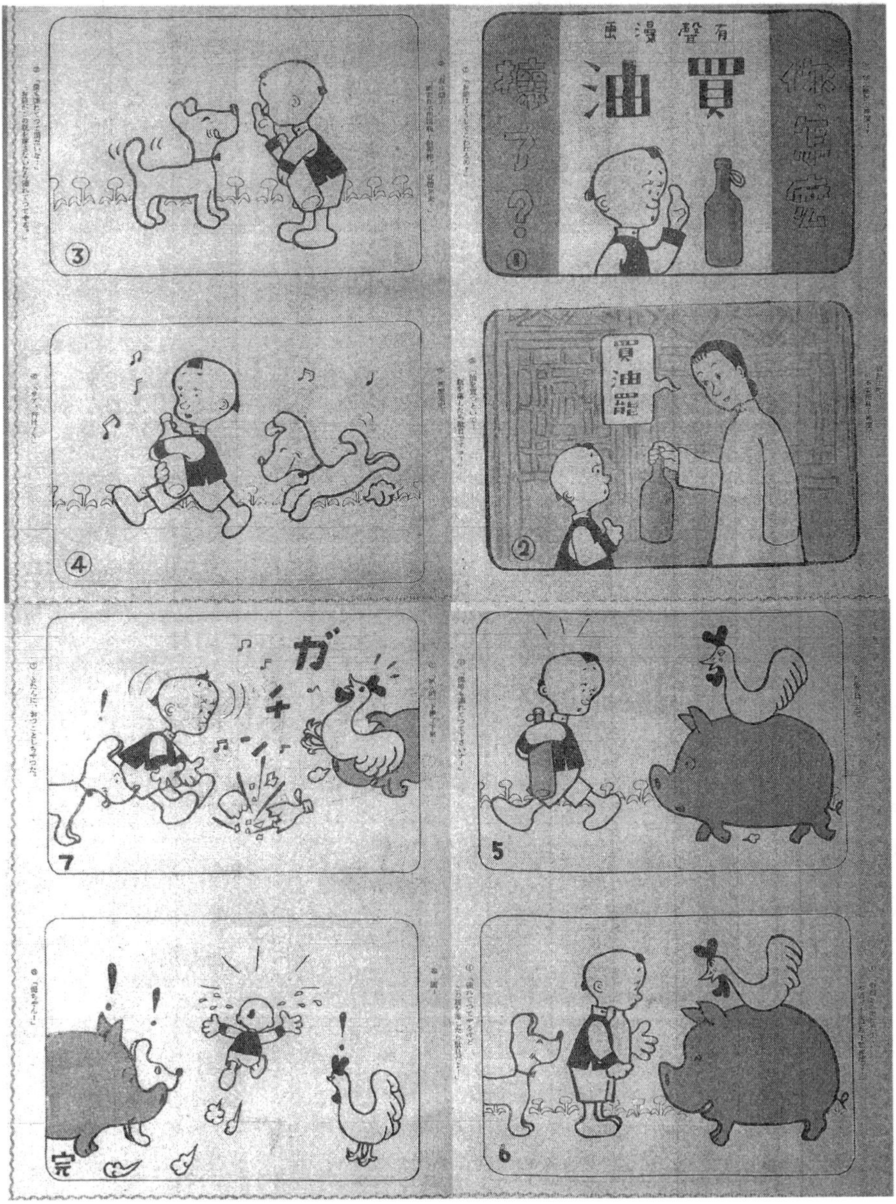

Figure 2.4. "Purchasing Oil," from *Manchuria Film,* 1940, courtesy of Yumani Shobo Publishers Inc.

animated film and still cartoons, which were screened in theaters like a film with sound, but with less or without the movement typical of an animated film, rendering it a cinematic version of "paper play" (*kamishibai*), a traditional form of storytelling accompanied by illustrated cards.[49]

In *Purchasing Oil,* the drawings of characters are simplistic and the background is almost empty, except a few lines suggesting a door at home or a grassland outside (see figure 2.4). The hairstyle and the clothes of the mother and the boy, as well as the Chinese in the mother's speech bubble connote the characters are native Chinese (or Manchurians) living in northeast China. The film's protagonist is a little boy whose mother gives him an empty bottle and asks him to go to the market to purchase oil. The boy sets off with the empty bottle in hand. A dog wants to go with him, and the boy agrees when the dog promises not to break the bottle. Then a pig and rooster ask to go with him, and the boy says that they too can follow him as long as they do not break the bottle. On their way to the market, the boy accidentally drops the bottle and breaks it. Crying "mother," the boy runs back home, leaving the three companion animals dumfounded.[50]

The boy is an antihero to Momotarō. *Purchasing Oil* has similarities with the Japanese films *Momotarō's Sea Eagles* and *Momotarō's Divine Sea Warriors* in terms of the quest motif, boy protagonist, and three animal followers. Unlike the highly motivated Momotarō, who volunteers to embark on a divine journey on behalf of the village-nation to conquer the demons, the boy in this Man'ei film is asked by his mother to run a mundane errand for his family. Unlike Momotarō, who is brave, heroic, independent, determined, and above all militaristic, the boy in *Purchasing Oil* is passive, dependent, incompetent, and vulnerable. If Momotarō is a superman and winner, the boy is a weak child who cannot complete an insignificant task. The three animals are domestic animals, in contrast to the wild animals in Momotarō films, thus further reinforcing the boy's docility. The Momotarō films deal with momentous matters such as Japanese nationalism and patriotism; *Purchasing Oil* is lightweight, humorous, and detached from national politics.

These differences might be explained by the nationality of the protagonist: Momotarō is a Japanese wartime hero, and the boy in the potential Man'ei film is a local Manchurian assigned to an inferior status in the Japanese-led Greater East Asian Co-Prosperity Sphere. These differences could also be read as a reflection of the gap between Man'ei and the national policy film studios in Japan. Rather than being a slavish propaganda machine of Japan producing jingoist films like the Momotarō features, Man'ei's seemingly apolitical animated films constructed a plasmatic empire that kept its distance from wartime Japan.

This plasmatic empire seemed to be distanced from wartime China as well. Chinese films made by the Wan brothers in Chongqing were highly nationalistic and patriotic, like the Momotarō films. Despite its Japanese connections, *Princess*

Iron Fan had hidden anti-Japanese messages and thus remained ambiguous. *Purchasing Oil* and other potential films at Man'ei did not include any hidden messages or ambiguity. They were apolitical, humorous, and entertaining, thus differentiating themselves from Chinese animation in Chongqing and Shanghai.

Man'ei was experimenting with puppet animation and produced the puppet performance film *The Legend of the Luminous Pearl* (*Yemingzhu zhuan*) in 1942. The film opens with a shot from a high angle showing a woman dancing gracefully. She is attired in ancient Chinese costume. A dragon appears and eats a large luminous pearl. A marionette performance comes next. Although it is not stop-motion puppet animation, it is a precursor to puppet animation. The marionettes are roughly made, and their strings are visible on-screen.

Although the setting suggests ancient northeast China, it is an imaginary place and shows a fascination for Arabian culture. The story is about a village couple and their sick child. The husband goes to the mountain in search of ginseng to cure the child. He helps a wounded tiger, and to show its appreciation, the tiger gives him a luminous pearl. The pearl has the power to replicate whatever it sees. The husband shows the pearl a drawing of ginseng, but the pearl makes a tree in their yard, which resembles the ginseng in the picture. Two Arabian merchants pass by and witness the pearl's magic power. They offer their treasure and camels in exchange for the pearl, but the husband is reluctant. However, when the Arabians give him the ginseng that cures his child, the husband happily gives the pearl to them. The couple and their recovered child bid farewell to the Arabians, who ride away on their camels and into the desert. Like the films discussed, *The Legend of the Luminous Pearl,* set in ancient times with exotic content, had little connection with wartime Japan and China.

However, another Man'ei film, *Terrible Lice* (*Kepa de shizi,* 1943), was indeed set in the context of wartime politics. It originally had Chinese and Japanese versions, but only the Chinese version survives. *Terrible Lice* is a live-action film in which animation is used for special effects to portray the actions of lice on human bodies. At that time, such actions could not be represented by live-action filmmaking because of the limitations of film technology. It was one of Man'ei's many "enlightenment" films to educate and civilize the local Manchurians. Katō Taitsū (1916–1985) directed the film, Sasaya Iwao and Morikawa Nobuhide did the animations, Yoshida Sadaji was the cameraman, and Imai Shin was the scriptwriter. The film takes place in a residential area for coolies working at the Fushun coal mines, which were developed by the South Manchuria Railway Company. Most of the coolies were from Shandong province.[51]

The beginning of the film shows a Japanese man with glasses who wears a doctor's white gown and an army cap and boots. He runs through the neighborhood, his voice booming through a handheld loudspeaker, "Typhus is spreading!

We must kill the lice that carry the germs. Let's do a deep cleaning now!" His message meets the resistance of the local Chinese residents, who were played by coolies living there. A man wearing a hat, the human protagonist of the film, complains that he would rather sleep more in the morning than waste his time on deep cleaning. He says to his friends, "Typhus? I've never experienced it. Without lice, I'll feel lonely!" When he is speaking, an animated louse, who claims himself to be from Shandong, lands on his pants and replies, "You are right! Without you I will be very lonely. You are our good friends and our blood supply. Other people say that you are dirty men, but for us, you are our ideal home, a good place for us to multiply our descendants." This newcomer louse, the animal protagonist of the film, climbs up the man's pants until he arrives at his waist and joins the lice already there. The subsequent animation sequence shows the lice's activities on the man's body. They bite, drink blood, excrete, multiply, and spread germs on the man's skin. The man in the hat falls sick with typhus and dies; other dirty workers die after him. Shocked by the deaths, the local residents finally realize the importance of deep cleaning. They launch a campaign to boil, steam, and wash their dirty clothes, to shower, and to do a deep cleaning. Their efforts kill the lice and the residents come to appear healthy, clean, and happy.

Terrible Lice seems to be a national policy film that portrays how the Japanese colonizers, equipped with more advanced medical knowledge and technology, care for the Chinese, educate them, and protect them from disease, as is the duty of the elder brother in Greater East Asian Co-Prosperity Sphere's family. Although highlighting the fraternity between China and Japan, the film also hints at the enemy of East Asia. In the middle of the film, a poster of a Fushun coal mine appears quickly with the text, "The lice are just like the United States and the UK, and we must kill them." In this way, the lice are symbols following the rhetoric of wartime speciesism to refer to the biggest enemy of the Greater East Asian Co-Prosperity Sphere. This poster aligns the film with national policy films made in Japan.

The film claims that lice is the cause of typhus. In fact, lice and germs might have been spread among the Chinese by Unit 731, a secret biological and chemical warfare research unit of the Japanese Army. A cameraman from Man'ei was assigned to record human experiments carried out by Unit 731 in a bungalow in the suburbs of Harbin. The experiment's Chinese subjects were infected by germs planted by Unit 731 and were vivisected to examine the medical effects of the germs on human bodies. The appearance of germs, masked military doctors, stretchers, and the panic of the suffering Chinese in the film *Terrible Lice* were reminiscent of the human atrocities caused by Unit 731. When making the film *Terrible Lice,* the cameraman Yoshida Sadaji failed in attempts to shoot a close-up of a louse. He asked Imai Hiroshi, another cameraman, to help him because at that time Imai Hiroshi and other Man'ei filmmakers were shooting a film about the spread of germs among humans and animals in Nong'an, Changchun. In Man'ei, rumor had it that the infection there was caused by Unit 731. When Imai was shooting a close-up of a louse in Nong'an for Yoshida, he was infected with typhus and almost died. His personal experience provided evidence supporting the claim that Unit 731 spread germs and typhus among the Chinese in Nong'an.[52] Taking these historical facts into account, *Terrible Lice* can be seen as glossing over the brutalities of Japanese imperialism and thus functioned as a piece of propaganda. This view was shared by scholars such as Choe Kilsung and Jie Li, the latter of whom interprets the film as an embodiment of the Janus-faced colonial policies, "a government that constructs with one hand and destroys with the other, that heals and infects and that has both a benevolent and monstrous side."[53]

No matter how serious, bloody, grotesque, and heavy-hearted these topics are, the animation sequence in *Terrible Lice* takes the audience away from the violent wartime reality and brings them to a plasmatic world full of humor and fantasy. The aesthetics of cuteness present the animated lice as fat silkworms. They wear white gloves on their four-fingered hands like Mickey Mouse. In their gloves and white boots, the anthropomorphic lice look like gentlemanly businessmen, similar to the well-dressed mosquito in Winsor McCay's *How a Mosquito Operates* (1912). Plasmaticness is still the most prominent feature of this film. When the protagonist newcomer louse meets the other lice, who have been living off the man for a while, he immediately asserts his leadership by demonstrating his physical prowess. He uses two hands to keep pulling out his mouth, until his mouth, originally flat and rounded, becomes sharp and elongated, like the end of a drinking straw. He then plants his mouth into the man's skin and starts to suck blood voraciously. The plasmatic style of this sequence is reminiscent of Disney animated shorts. The animated sequence is juxtaposed with a live-action close-up of a real lice drinking blood from human body, shot by the Man'ei cameraman Imai Hiroshi, who almost died from it. In this case animation and live-action evoke strikingly different emotions. The use of animation here significantly downplays the gravity of the subject matter with its inherent levity. When the coolies start to boil their clothes and take hot showers, animation was used again to portray how the lice suffer and die. They jump and bounce in the air until their bodies suddenly flatten and are lifeless. The humorous twists and comical effects of these animated sequences temporarily dispelled grotesque wartime realities. The plasmaticness and diplomacy of animation made it possible to play with and temporarily suspend wartime politics in both Japan and China.

According to Yamaguchi Takeshi, the film's director, Katō Taitsū, deliberately kept a distance from the imperialist ideologies during his stay at Man'ei. He declined many requests for making overt military films, no matter how good the terms were. That was why he made only two films there, including *Terrible Lice*.

He decided to make *Terrible Lice* probably because the film was primarily for health education and hence less political. In choosing animation as a form, he further distanced himself from the subject matter. Yamaguchi concludes that *Terrible Lice* did not reflect the ideology of the state, and that Katō Taitsū did not become deeply involved in wartime politics and thus remained true to himself as an artist.[54] The poster that compares the lice with the United States and the UK might make the film guilty of jingoism, but it appeared so briefly that it was unnoticeable and could not achieve any propaganda function. It is entirely possible that Katō Taitsū strategically inserted this poster to get permission to shoot this film. In 1940, Man'ei formed mobile projection teams and built many new theaters. Its animated films and more politicized live-action films reached almost every corner of Manchuria, bringing laughter and fantasy together with propaganda and brutal realities to the local Manchurians.[55]

Man'ei extended its plasmatic empire to north China. In July 1937, Japan moved to fully occupy north China, using Peking (Beijing) as its center. In February 1938, Man'ei established its branch of the New People Film Association (Xinmin yinghua xiehui) in Beijing, which monopolized production, screening, distribution, importation, and exportation of films in north China. In December 1939, the New People Film Association established the North China Film Company (Huabei dianying gongsi), which was an extension of Man'ei. In 1943, the same year *Terrible Lice* was made, North China Film Company produced the silent animated short *The Kite* (*Fengzheng,* 1943). The animator was Liang Jin, a cartoonist and illustrator in Beijing. The villain of the film is a dragon. As the personification of winter, the dragon appears in the sky above a dormant earth covered with fallen leaves and snow. The protagonist is a Chinese boy, who is shown flying a kite. A boy god, aloft on the mythical Chinese creature Kirin, slides down the kite string and possesses the boy. Empowered by the spirit of the god, the boy and his kite battle the dragon and win. A goddess appears and places a flower garland on the kite and scatters flowers in the sky. Flowers begin to bloom with smiling faces, trees bud, and birds start singing. Spring has been restored to earth, and the boy happily returns to flying his kite. Set in a celestial and mythical world, *The Kite,* like other Man'ei animated films, was distanced from the reality of wartime politics.

The legacy of Man'ei split in China and Japan after the war. Many of its animators, such as Sasaya Iwao, returned to Japan and worked for Tokyo-Yokohama Films (Tōyoko eiga), which was founded in 1938 and later transformed into Tōei Company (Tōei kabushiki-gaisha) in 1951. In China, Man'ei had laid a solid technological and infrastructural foundation for Mochinaga Tadahito and other Japanese and Chinese pioneers to help establish the animation industry in postwar China.

Mochinaga Tadahito and Transnational Leftism

In histories of Chinese animation, Mochinaga Tadahito is sometimes mentioned briefly as a "Japanese leftist and member of the Japanese Communist Party."[56] These leftist connections can be traced to December 1939, when he joined the Art Film Company, which was founded in 1937 by Ōmura Einosuke, a Communist who later became head of culture for the Japanese Communist Party. While affiliated with the Art Film Company, Mochinaga worked closely with established animator Seo Mitsuyo. Seo was a leftist and member of the Proletarian Film League of Japan, or Purokino (Nippon puroretaria eiga dōmei), a communist documentary film movement that originated in 1927 and was suppressed by the government in 1934. Pressured by the Japanese government, many Purokino members submitted to political conversion or apostasy (*tenkō*) and officially denounced their communist beliefs. After denouncing their past, these filmmakers joined Photo Chemical Laboratories, or PCL (Shashin kagaku kenkyūjo), Man'ei, and other mainstream film studios. Seo and talented Purokino members joined the Art Film Company during this period. According to Peter High, "The very act of moving into the company . . . seemed to inspire a form of *tenkō*, causing them to renounce their old leftism and embrace progovernment positions."[57] The Art Film Company produced films commissioned by government agencies. Accordingly, filmmakers had to work for the government once they joined the Art Film Company. Thus Seo and Mochinaga entered mainstream film production (a quiet *tenkō*) in the 1930s and produced animated films for the Ministry of Education and the Japanese Navy.

Mochinaga's exposure to leftism increased when he joined Man'ei, which was a haven for purged Japanese leftist filmmakers. In mainstream Chinese film history, Man'ei is usually portrayed as a mouthpiece of the Japanese government who disseminated imperialist ideology. However, as Michael Baskett points out, Man'ei was independent of Japan and comprised filmmakers from different political backgrounds:

> Ironically, many left-wing filmmakers purged from the Japanese film industry after the anti-Communist crackdowns in the early 1930s not only found a home at Man'ei but by all accounts appeared to have a free hand in their work. Man'ei created an unlikely space where former Communists produced films side-by-side with right-wing ultranationalists.[58]

Uchida Tomu, for instance, was one of the many progressive Japanese filmmakers who fled to Manchuria and became a Communist there.

It was not until the CCP took over Man'ei in 1945 that Mochinaga was fully exposed to Chinese communism. Although he did not declare himself a

Communist at the time, he sympathized with the CCP. After the civil war broke out between the Communist Party and the Nationalist Party on April 14, 1946, Mochinaga was arrested twice by Nationalist Party agents. The CCP rescued him after both arrests. The first arrest occurred at his office. The CCP-controlled Public Security Bureau later had him released. The second arrest took place at Mochinaga's home. Nationalist Party soldiers searched the home, took him away, and hauled him into an underground bathroom, accusing him of possessing guns and espionage. He was later rescued by the Eighth Route Army and was escorted home by a teenaged soldier.[59]

Mochinaga went through the CCP's ideological campaign at Northeast Film Studio in Xingshan. He was in fact the first Japanese who made a public self-criticism there. He revealed that he listened to Japanese news on the radio and disseminated the news to his colleagues—a counterrevolutionary act according to CCP policy. He was also accused of being too bourgeois, because during a gathering at his home he used a Japanese hotpot and borrowed some tatami mats to add Japanese flavor to the party. He explained these things in the self-criticism meetings launched by the Party, but was criticized even more severely by others. Although Mochinaga did not reveal the identity of the people who criticized him, they were most likely hard-liners from Yan'an. According to Zhang Xinshi's memoir, conflict between the people from Man'ei and Yan'an was conspicuous during the early stages of the Northeast Film Studio. People from Man'ei had more advanced filmmaking technology, but not the political consciousness their counterparts from Yan'an. It was therefore imperative for the CCP to elevate the ideological consciousness of Man'ei employees while improving the technological proficiency of the Yan'an staff.[60] The criticism of Mochinaga was due, in part, to this conflict between Man'ei and Yan'an. In terms of his political ideals at the time, Mochinaga later explained in his memoir written in Japanese:

> As a member of the team constructing a new China, undoubtedly I had great shortcomings in terms of ideological consciousness. Things that were taken for granted in capitalist Japan were regarded as politically incorrect in this society. The final conclusion they made about me was: I had heroic individualism.[61]

Despite its skepticism, the CCP still regarded Mochinaga as a progressive Japanese filmmaker during his stay in China. He came to bridge Chinese and Japanese filmmakers within the international community of communism. Mochinaga's role as the middleman was evident in two official letters published in March 1951. The first letter, "Let Us Clasp Hands and Fight against American imperialism" ("Women he nimen jinjin woshou, gongtong wei fandui meidi er douzheng ba"), was written in Chinese by the Animation Division of Shanghai Film Studio to Japanese progressive filmmakers during the Korean War. It criticized American imperialism and called for joint efforts by China and Japan to resist Hollywood films.[62] Japanese progressive filmmakers wrote their reply, "We Will Never Bend Our Knees" ("Women shi buhui quxi de"). Dated January 31, 1951, this letter was addressed to Mochinaga and other Shanghai filmmakers. It praised the theory of Mao Zedong, criticized the dominance of American films in postwar Japan, and condemned the Japanese government's suppression of proletarian magazines and films. This letter's alarmist message claimed that Japanese film was on the verge of extinction and called for a unified effort to "oust American films from Japan."[63]

The suppression of proletarian workers and magazines by the Japanese government refers to the so-called Red Purge of the late 1940s and early 1950s. According to John Dower, this purge began with the firing of eleven thousand progressive union members in industrial circles from the end of 1949 to the beginning of the Korean War on June 25, 1950. After the Korean War broke out, the Red Purge was expanded to the private sector, paying particular attention to potentially subversive or left-leaning people working in mass media. Between ten thousand and eleven thousand leftists were fired by the end of the 1950s. The Japanese Communist Party leaders, such as Nosaka Sanzō and Tokuda Kyūichi, went underground or fled to China during the occupation era.[64]

Mochinaga continued to sympathize with communism after he returned to Japan in 1953. He lived in what was called the Red Residential Area, which was reserved for Japanese nationals who had returned from Communist China. Japanese Communists frequently visited Mochinaga's home to convert him; during these visits, they showed him editions of their Party newspaper *Red Flag* (*Akahata*) and invited him to participate in distributing it.[65] Mochinaga, not a Japanese Communist Party member at that time, volunteered to distribute the paper in the Tanashi district of western Tokyo. He woke up at four o'clock every morning to deliver the papers using a German bicycle he acquired in Shanghai. Unlike when he distributed other newspapers, Mochinaga had to keep the readers' identity secret. This was especially important because policemen were always following Mochinaga on the basis of his involvement with the Japanese Communist Party.[66]

Mochinaga had mixed feelings about his political commitments. As a result, he did not declare that he was a Communist in his autobiography. He did, however, officially join the Japanese Communist Party in the mid-1950s after he returned to Japan from China.[67] His case was not unique. Many Japanese filmmakers, such as Morikawa Kazuyo, who had worked at Northeast Film Studio joined the Communist Party when they returned to Japan.[68] In a letter addressed to the Cultural Bureau of China in November 1978, Mochinaga and other Japanese filmmakers who had worked at Northeast Film acknowledged the role of Chinese communism in shaping their political thinking and commitments:

> In the past, Japanese militarism manipulated our view of life, albeit it was not our intention. It was China, Marxism, Leninism, and Maoism that changed our view of life and directed us on the right track. It was a result of the efforts of our Chinese comrades . . . Because of this connection, we call China, which changed our mindset, our second motherland.[69]

However, in 1966, when the Cultural Revolution was launched in China, Mochinaga became disillusioned and withdrew from the Japanese Communist Party, probably because he abhorred the atrocities caused by ultra-leftists in China. Despite his ambivalence, he was invited to visit China and was received as a representative of Japan by Chairman Mao on October 1, 1967, which was the source of great pride for him. After Mochinaga died in 1999, the *Red Flag Newspaper* identified Mochinaga in his obituary as a Communist Party member.[70]

Mochinaga's involvement with the CCP took place in the larger context of the flow of leftism and communism between China and Japan in the postwar era. The Japanese Communist Party had a close and long-standing relationship with its Chinese counterpart. Nosaka Sanzō, a founder of the Japanese Communist Party, left the Soviet Union for Yan'an and stayed there from 1940 to 1945. While in Yan'an, he developed a close relationship with Mao. During the war, the two parties had similar guerrilla statuses, and both looked to the Soviet Union for guidance. After the People's Republic of China was established after the war, the relationship between the parties changed. Now the Japanese Communist Party turned to the CCP for inspiration and leadership. As Rodger Swearingen and Paul Langer point out, "What was once a relation between equals has developed in the postwar period into one of master and disciple."[71] Nosaka hoped to establish a similar "people's government" in postwar Japan, believing that Japan's defeat in the war would create many opportunities for the Party. Thus, in January 1946, he returned to Japan to pursue his political goals. Nosaka's predictions rang true. During the US occupation, it promoted ideals such as democratization and freedom of speech, which, ironically, gave rise to communist movements. In John Dower's words, the communists and socialists "became the country's most articulate critics of acquiescence in U.S. Cold War policy—and (no small irony) the staunchest defenders, for decades to come, of the initial occupation ideals of demilitarization and democratization."[72] However, as the movements intensified, the US and Japanese governments regressed to conservatism and launched the Red Purge to crack down on communists.

Animating China: From Propaganda in the Northeast to Fantasy in Shanghai

Mochinaga bridged a crucial gap in the history of Chinese animation. It is likely that he was one of the few animators making animated films in mainland China in the late 1940s and early 1950s. At the time, from 1947 to 1956, Wan Laiming and Wan Guchan (the Wan brothers) were in Hong Kong after fleeing the mainland to avoid the civil war between the Chinese Communist Party and the Nationalist Party.[73] When World War II ended in 1945, Qian Jiajun left Chongqing and returned to Nanjing to continue working for the Nationalist Party. He made the animated short *The Kingdom of Bees* (*Mifeng guo,* 1947) and two educational shorts commissioned by the United Nations Educational, Scientific and Cultural Organization in 1947 and 1948. He helped establish the animation department in Suzhou Fine Arts Academy in October 1950 and taught there regularly until the department closed and his team joined the animation division of the Shanghai Film Studio in 1953.[74] Te Wei, a young illustrator and cartoonist, also went to Hong Kong in 1947 and did not enter the animation industry at Northeast Film Studio in Changchun until late 1949. Mochinaga was a key animator at Northeast, the first studio owned by the new socialist government.

The animation stand Mochinaga dismantled and loaded on the train before the exodus to Xingshan became the only one at Northeast. It was not shipped to Shanghai because Wan Chaochen had brought with him a more advanced model. Wan Chaochen worked at China Productions (Zhongguo dianying zhipian chang) in Chongqing and was sent by the Nationalist Party to the United States to learn animation technology in 1946. When he returned to China in 1948, he went to Shanghai. Wan had worked as an intern at United Productions and Disney, where he learned how to make color animated films in Technicolor. He purchased an animation camera during his stay in the United States and took it back to Shanghai when he returned.[75] Because the multiplane camera stand was too large and expensive, he drew a blueprint and took it home with him instead. He gave the drawing to Dashen Machinery Factory, which then produced the stand. The Nationalists tried to ship Wan's camera and stand to Taiwan during the regime change but were intercepted by the PLA. In the early 1950s, Wan's was the only animation equipment in Shanghai.[76]

In the late 1940s, Northeast Film Studio favored films such as documentaries and propaganda messages that addressed political realities. Live-action feature films were assigned a low priority as the civil war intensified and the studio's resources became more constrained. On February 20, 1947, numerous live-action feature filmmakers and other staff were laid off. A total of forty-three Japanese employees and their family members were sent to work in a remote coal mine in Shuangyashan.[77] Among those laid off were Uchida Tomu, Kimura Sotoji, and Morikawa Kazuyo. They did not return to Northeast Film until October 1948. Mochinaga did not suffer this fate, however, because he was needed to draw portraits of Communist leaders such as Mao Zedong and Zhu De and to animate battlefield maps for documentary films such as *Democratic Northeast* (*Minzhu dongbei,* 1947–1949).[78] Made under the leadership of Chen Bo'er, *Democratic Northeast* is the first documentary film of socialist China and includes seventeen episodes. When Northeast Film was under Yan'an leadership, the only animated films it produced were propaganda pieces. The two animated shorts Mochinaga made were included in the fourth and ninth episode of *Democratic Northeast.* Their affinity with documentary films demonstrates the studio's preference for political and realistic films.

The first animated film Mochinaga made was *Dreaming to Be Emperor* (*Huangdi meng,* 20 minutes, November 1947), and it was the first puppet-animated film of socialist China.[79] It originated from a series of cartoons drawn by Hua Junwu, who worked on propaganda cartoons for CCP newspapers in Harbin. In the fall of 1947, Hua Junwu sent a cartoon to Northeast Film Studio. The cartoon was about how George Marshall, with the aid of an array of weapons, manipulates a puppet that turns out to be Jiang Jieshi (Chiang Kai-shek). The top leaders of the CCP ordered that this cartoon be animated and incorporated into documentary films to criticize the Marshall Plan.

In early 1947, prior to making *Dreaming to Be Emperor,* Mochinaga and his colleagues made trial shorts. One such film, the puppet-animated *The Year of Liberation* (*Fanshen nian*), revolves around the collaboration between Jiang Jieshi and Marshall. Included in the third episode of *Democratic Northeast,* this short paved the way for *Dreaming to Be Emperor.*[80] Chen Bo'er wrote the script for *Dreaming to Be Emperor,* and Mochinaga himself made the puppets of Marshall and Jiang Jieshi. A French puppet owned by Mochinaga's colleague Kimura Sotoji was the inspiration for the puppet of Jiang Jieshi. Mochinaga also drew on Jiří Trnka's puppet of the Chinese emperor, which had been given to a representative of Northeast Film Studio who attended the first World Festival of Youth and Students held in Prague in Czechoslovakia in 1947. Jiří Trnka, the most prominent puppet animator in Czechoslovakia, gave a puppet to the Chinese representative as a gift. Trnka used the puppet in *The Chinese Emperor's Nightingale* (1948), which was adapted from a fairy tale by Hans Christian Andersen. The representative brought this puppet to Northeast Film Studio and gave it to Mochinaga. Mochinaga carefully examined the puppet's joints and decided that it would be better to use silver wires. The puppets' heads were made from wet pulp of old newspapers. Because the puppets could not stand upright unsupported, nails were inserted into the bottom of their feet so that the puppets could be affixed to the ground.[81]

Mochinaga's interest in making three-dimensional puppets stemmed from work experience he had before entering the film industry at the Art Film Company in December 1939. As a high school student, Mochinaga experimented with puppets made from papier-mâché.[82] After graduating from the art school in March 1938, he received medical treatment for arthritis at East Asian Medical Institute (Tōa ikagaku kenkyūjo). The head of the institute invited him to work there while receiving medical treatment. During his stay, Mochinaga made artificial hands for wounded Japanese soldiers. He studied x-rays and anatomy, and learned how to use metalworking and leatherworking tools to make and seal artificial hands. Mochinaga also learned how to polish and color artificial hands with different pigments. After he recovered from arthritis, Mochinaga quit this job and lectured on leathersmith design and woodcarving at Tokyo Women's School of Art and Design (Tōkyō joshi bijutsu-kōgei gakkō). Mochinaga also was interested in stage lighting and color and later worked on stage design at Tokyo Takarazuka Theatre (Tōkyō takarazuka gekijō). His work at the theater involved the creation of pigments. Later he became responsible for the entire stage design, including lighting and sets.[83]

Mochinaga's experience working in the theater from March 1938 to December 1939 contributed to the creation of the puppet-animated film *Dreaming to Be Emperor* in November 1947. Chen Bo'er worked on the script and Yu Yanfu and Xu Wei were also involved in production. The foreigners working on this film included Mochinaga Tadahito (under the sinicized name Chi Yong), Sei Mitsuo, Murata Kōkichi, Oda Kenzaburō, Kiga Yasushiware, and the Korean Jo Ming (see figure 2.5). Chen Bo'er insisted that Chinese animation should have Chinese characteristics. Accordingly, Mochinaga and his colleagues decided to use the form of Peking opera for the film. Because Mochinaga was unfamiliar with the art form, they invited an expert to perform the acts for them (figure 2.6). This provided Mochinaga with a sense of character movement, personality, and aesthetic sensibility. They transcribed his performance into the puppet-animated film (figure 2.7). Later animators at the Shanghai Animation Film Studio continued with the practice of experiencing performances and sketching from life, even when making fantasy films featuring gods, spirits, and anthropomorphic animals. *Dreaming to Be Emperor* was officially proclaimed the first animated film in socialist China. Its Peking opera style made it the earliest attempt at exploring a national style, thus marking the beginning of a discourse of animation nationalism in socialist China. However, some Japanese audiences interpreted the Peking opera style in terms of Japanese Kabuki, thus attenuating the film's Chineseness.[84]

Dreaming to Be Emperor is a satire of Jiang Jieshi and George Marshall. Structured as a self-reflexive play within a play, it is set in a puppet theater. Its Peking

Figure 2.5. Mochinaga Tadahito (right) and a fellow animator, 1947, courtesy of Mochinaga Noriko.

Figure 2.6. Peking opera performer, 1947, courtesy of Mochinaga Noriko.

Figure 2.7. Still from *Dreaming to Be Emperor,* 1947, courtesy of Mochinaga Noriko.

opera style makes the characters appear more theatrical. Jiang Jieshi trades China's sovereignty for Marshall's planes and cannons. Thereafter, Jiang steps to the front stage and performs four acts. The first, "Dancing and Praying for Promotion" ("Tiaojiaguan"), takes the form of the prelude in traditional Chinese operas, which is associated with ritualized prayers for wealth and promotion. The performer usually wears a mask, dons the attire of a high official, holds a gigantic gold ingot, and displays banners with auspicious phrases such as "promotion and wealth" (*jiaguan jinlu*). Jiang's prayer is to become emperor of China. The second act, in traditional opera, "Beggar Picks Up a Gold Ingot" ("Huazi shi jin"), provides a way for the clown to express himself after he accidentally obtains a gold ingot. The film parallels this with Jiang Jieshi expressing himself and justifying the civil war. The third act, "Ascending the Throne" ("Da dundian"), is a Peking opera depicting a peasant named Xue Pinggui becoming an emperor in the later years of the Tang dynasty. At this point in the film, Jiang Jieshi is almost ready to ascend to the throne. His officials and relatives come to the court to extend their congratulations, but fight with each other over a bone for dogs. The last act, "Besieged from All Sides" ("Simian chuge"), alludes to the defeat of Xiang Yu in the Qin dynasty. Essentially, the people revolt against Jiang Jieshi. Albert Coady Wedemeyer, a US agent, comes to his rescue but his efforts are futile. Jiang Jieshi has become a cornered beast and fails to realize his dream of becoming an emperor.

Using the Chinese pseudonym Fang Ming, Mochinaga made his second animated short *Capturing the Turtle in the Jar* (*Wengzhong zhuobie,* 10 minutes, December 1948). It is the first hand-drawn cel-animated short made in socialist China. At the time, they used expensive cels imported from the Soviet Union because China was unable to produce them. They recycled the cels after use by erasing the existing paintings with water, drying them, and painting on them again for the next use.[85] Zhu Dan wrote the script, and Hua Junwu participated in the production. Jiang Jieshi in this film is backed by the United States and wages civil war. He is defeated by the PLA, transformed into a turtle, and captured in a jar (figure 2.8). This cel-animation film was more plasmatic—with more squash and stretch techniques and fluid metamorphosis of body forms—than the puppet-animated film *Dreaming to Be Emperor.* When Jiang Jieshi and his army are about to be defeated, an American general in military uniform takes off a badge from his cap and throws it into the sky, which is soon transformed into a flying eagle and then a fighting airplane to drop military supplies to the Nationalist Army. The eagle looks quite similar to those in *Momotarō's Sea Eagles.* The two animated films were more politicized than Man'ei animation, demonstrating the plasmaticness or flexibility of animation, be it cel or puppet, in quickly fitting into a new political framework.

Northeast Film Studio established a mobile projection team and screened its animated films to mobilize peasants and PLA soldiers during the civil war.[86] Chen Bo'er allowed Mochinaga to join the projection team because she hoped that his observation of the audience's response would help him improve his animation techniques. The team would first convene the peasants and teach them revolutionary songs, with Mochinaga in charge, and then screen documentary and animated films. Peasants often felt joyful watching animated films because they had never seen anything like them.[87] The PLA soldiers were also inspired by watching these animated films. It is said that after they watched *Capturing the Turtle in the Jar,* they burst into laughter and loudly applauded. The soldiers asked to see the film again and again and saw it four times in a row.[88] To rally their fighting spirit

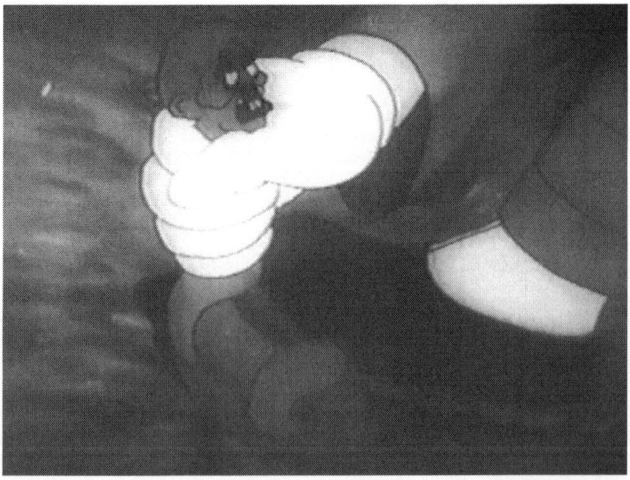

Figure 2.8. Jiang Jieshi captured alive as a turtle by a PLA soldier in *Capturing the Turtle in the Jar,* 1948.

against the Nationalist Army, the film was screened for PLA soldiers just before they crossed the Yangtze River and entered battle against Jiang Jieshi.[89]

On March 17, 1950, the Animation Division of Northeast Film Studio moved to Shanghai and joined the Shanghai Film Studio on March 24. This merger paralleled with a stylistic and thematic shift in Chinese animation. After the establishment of the People's Republic of China in 1949, Xia Yan, then minister of the Cultural Bureau, stated that animated films should serve children and reflect children's lives.[90] During his stay in Shanghai, Mochinaga and his colleagues produced four cel-animated films: *Thank You Kitty* (*Xiexie xiaohuamao,* 1950), *Little Iron Pillar* (*Xiao Tiezhu,* 1951), *Kitty Goes Fishing* (*Xiaomao diaoyu,* 1952), and *Picking Mushrooms* (*Cai mogu,* 1953). Unlike the previous films targeting adults, animated films in the early 1950s were children's entertainment. Although animated films in the northeast were concerned with the demonized Other, those in Shanghai were characterized by adorable animals in a fantastic world. In addition, the angular lines and shapes in previous animations became curvier lines and more rounded forms. Thus the relocation of animators from Changchun to Shanghai paralleled with the "cutification" and gradual depoliticization of Chinese animation in the early 1950s.

The first film Mochinaga made in Shanghai was titled *Thank You Kitty.* It is also the first animated film based on a fairy tale in socialist China. Jin Jin, a children's novelist, wrote the script for this film. The story takes place in a rural village whose tranquility is disrupted by four mice that rob the villagers of their grain. Kitty is a peasant soldier tasked with protecting the village. With the help of Rooster, Kitty sets a trap for the thieving mice and captures them, restoring peace to the village.

The film's overt political message is diluted compared with earlier propaganda films produced by Northeast Film. However, it had a didactic message that targeted children. Because the animation for this film began at Northeast Film and was completed in Shanghai, it is not surprising that this film had traces of Northeast Film's propaganda films. The good and bad characters in this film are clearly distinguished. The virtuous animals include Kitty as protector of the village, and Rooster as the steward of agriculture. The villains are four mice who steal eggs and grain from the village's hardworking animals. The lyrics of the film's theme song convey an unambiguous message: "You help me, and I help you. Together we exterminate the reactionaries and guard against traitors and thieves." The four mice embody the reactionaries, traitors, and thieves who attempt to disrupt the established order. This message was meant to arouse sympathy for the CCP, which had recently founded the People's Republic of China and was on guard against saboteurs. Because Mochinaga was not familiar with the Chinese countryside, he and his animation team went to examine rural conditions outside Changchun to help in preparing to make the film. This was a dangerous undertaking because saboteurs lurked in "newly liberated" areas recently won back from Nationalist control. The visiting animators carried guns for their protection.[91] These violent conditions were conveyed in *Thank You Kitty* by the good animals' tireless pursuit and destruction of bad animals. Conversely, *Little Iron Pillar* shows a cruel leopard devouring weaker animals, a scene that was too shocking for children. These types of violent scenes were gradually watered down as the CCP consolidated its rule in rural China. From then on, it became standard practice for Chinese animators to visit real-life locations and make sketches on-site before making an animated film, even for fantastic films like fairy tales and legends.

Kitty Goes Fishing was another well-known animated film with Jin Jin again as the scriptwriter. In this film, Mother Cat, sister Miaomiao, and younger brother Mimi live in a village in the countryside. When they go fishing together, Miaomiao follows her mother's instructions and catches a big fish. Mimi is restless and distracted. He does not catch anything. The family goes home for lunch. On their return, Mother Cat patiently tells Mimi that fishing requires concentration. Mimi realizes the error of his ways and is determined to redeem himself. When he goes fishing again in the afternoon, he catches a big fish. In the same scene the song's repetitive lyrics, "labor is glorious," extol one of the grand CCP narratives. The political message of this animated film is considerably weaker than *Thank You Kitty*. Yet its moral for children is unambiguous: concentration on one's work is rewarded with success.

Mochinaga and his colleagues combine fantasy with the aesthetics of cuteness in *Kitty Goes Fishing*. Its cats are more attractive than the cat in *Thank You Kitty*. That is, in *Thank You Kitty*, Kitty is an adult male cat whose aggressive masculinity evokes a tiger. Of particular importance is the artist's attention to physical characteristics. Some of Kitty's facial features, such as his slanted eyes, flat nose, and fat lips, were modeled on the angular features of Jiang Jieshi in *Capturing the Turtle in the Jar*.[92] The three cats in *Kitty Goes Fishing* resemble Kitty the soldier but have a different emphasis. The three cats have white patches of beards just like Kitty. However, their eyes are larger, and their noses and mouths are minimally depicted with a few lines and dots. Their faces thus look smoother and more refined than Kitty's. The hairstyles of the three cats also contribute to their cuteness. Mother Cat combs her hair into a bun at the back of her head—a typical hairstyle for married women in northern China. Miaomiao has two small braids, decorated with bows like a young girl. Mimi has the bowl-shaped haircut popular among young boys in northern China. In addition, unlike Kitty, who only wears a leather belt, the three cats are fully dressed and more humanlike. The absence of Father Cat or other adult masculine figures in the film further demonstrates the association between the aesthetics of cuteness and infantility and femininity.

Despite its success, viewers criticized the image of the cute cats in *Kitty Goes Fishing.* An article by the renowned writer and literary critic He Yi points out that the three cats look too much alike: their faces are basically the same; only their hairstyles and clothes set them apart. He contrasts them with Disney's seven dwarfs, each of which has distinctive physical features and personalities. He Yi also observes that the three cats have lost their feline quality and appear overly humanlike. If the white spots of beards on their faces were removed, the cats could be mistaken for a fisherman's family members. He criticizes this approach on the grounds that "we expect to see anthropomorphic animals, not humans mechanically wearing animal masks."[93]

He Yi further argues that the animators of *Kitty Goes Fishing* are unsuccessful in their use of the national style. According to him, the national style in films depends not on the physical environment, such as landscape, homes, clothing, hairstyle, but on the character's personality and the spirit of the society. *Kitty Goes Fishing* pays attention to the material dimension of the national style, but ignores the underlying spirit of Chinese people and society. He concludes that *Kitty Goes Fishing* smacks of Western animated film.[94] His criticism was not unfounded; these films were indeed made in the context of transnational flows of images and aesthetics. However, Japanese animators had more influence than He Yi describes. Given the involvement of Mochinaga and other Japanese in the film, it was not strictly speaking a "pure Chinese" film. So why was it expected to articulate the authentic national style of Chinese animation?

Traveling Images and the Textual Unconscious

Once Mochinaga began to make animated films for socialist China, he was required to use a Chinese pseudonym in the credits so that the films appeared to be wholly Chinese. For example, in *Dreaming to Be Emperor,* the first propaganda short Mochinaga made at Northeast Film Studio, his pseudonym in the credit sequence was Chi Yong, a Chinese homophone for the first two characters of his Japanese name (Chi yong zhi ren). As party secretary of the studio, Chen Bo'er later gave Mochinaga the Chinese name Fang Ming (*ming* means bright; *fang* means direction). She also gave Mochinaga's wife Ayako, who was Mochinaga's animation assistant, the Chinese name Li Guang (*guang* means light). The couple's Chinese names read together create the word *guangming,* which means bright light. Chen Bo'er gave the couple these names to signify her hope that the future and direction of Chinese animation would be very bright. In the late 1940s and early 1950s, it was a common practice for Japanese filmmakers to adopt Chinese names because the memory of the Sino-Japanese war was still vivid and Chinese audiences might feel offended if they saw these Japanese names on Chinese films. As a result, Japanese filmmakers either used their Chinese names in the credit sequence or did not display their names at all.[95]

Despite the apparent Chineseness achieved through pseudonyms, certain stylistic features in these films betray their Japanese connections. As the earliest animated films made in socialist China, Chinese audience would not associate them with the Momotarō-animated wartime propaganda films. However, some stylistic features from *Momotarō's Sea Eagles* appear in early socialist animated films. The eagle in *Capturing the Turtle in the Jar* resembles the eagles in *Momotarō's Sea Eagles,* although it was portrayed as fiercer and more sinister in the Chinese film. Some stylistic features from *Momotarō's Sea Eagles* also appeared in *Thank You Kitty.* For example, the most conspicuous feature of Kitty is his leather belt, which resembles those worn by Momotarō and the animals in *Momotarō's Sea Eagles.* Leather belts in *Momotarō's Sea Eagles* announce that the animals are Japanese soldiers. In *Thank You Kitty,* Kitty wears a similar leather belt because a village policeman is associated with the military. Rooster wears a knotted cotton waistband that resembles the dress of peasants in the northeast. Rooster's peasant identity is further evident in his wife's clothing. She wears the scarf and upper garment typical of peasant women in northeastern China. Kitty's leather belt denotes he has higher status and more authority than Rooster. The belt on an otherwise unclothed animal was taken from Japanese animation, but it resembled the currently fashionable belted Mao jacket, which symbolized elevated status at that time.[96] Kitty enacts the role of leader while trapping and killing the mice. Important characters wear clothes and have anthropomorphic qualities. In contrast, minor characters such as the mice are unclothed and mute. They are presented naturalistically rather than anthropomorphically. When the mice are stealing food from the hen house, one mouse tears down a curtain and wraps it around his body like a cloak. He admires himself in a mirror only to realize it makes him appear even less humanlike. He smashes the mirror in rage, revealing his longing for a humanlike appearance and the futility to hope that clothing could elevate him from his animal status.

Rotating objects are prominent in *Momotarō's Sea Eagles* and also appear in *Thank You Kitty.* The first rotating object is the airplane propeller. When Momotarō orders the animal soldiers to depart for Pearl Harbor, their airplane propellers start to spin. After a five-second close-up of a single rotating propeller, the camera cuts to six-second shot of a group of rotating propellers. In another scene, when the monkey swims to capture the torpedo, his two hands strike the water until they simulate propellers. The rotating propeller is the film's most prominent symbol, symbolizing militarism and war for general audiences.

The second rotating object in *Momotarō's Sea Eagles,* a windmill attached to a carp banner, reinforces the propeller's militarist associations. The tradition of the

Japanese carp banner originated in a Chinese legend in which a carp becomes a dragon after it jumps over the Dragon Gate. On the fifth day of May in the lunar calendar, Japanese families decorate their homes with carp banners in the hope that their sons grow up and become successful "dragons." Another shot shows both rotating objects. A windmill rotates in the foreground in sharp focus as a propeller rotates in the background out of focus. This shot juxtaposes the national with the familial, emphasizing boyhood bravery and loyalty. Throughout the film, the fate of the windmill is linked to that of the propeller. According to Japanese film critic Mori Takuya, these rotating objects were animated independently by Mochinaga during his stay at the Art Film Company. Such animation became part of Mochinaga's signature style.[97]

In *Thank You Kitty,* the rotating object is a spinning wheel. The militarist connotation is replaced with that of the domestic life of a peasant housewife. In *Thank You Kitty,* when the rooster goes to the field to attend to the crop, the hen stays at home to weave. This is followed by a shot of the hen with her spinning wheel's shuttle rotating like a propeller. This shot lasts for nine seconds and the camera cuts to a close-up of the spinning wheel, which lasts for another nine seconds until the hen stops weaving. The revolving spinning wheel is the only inanimate object in the film that receives such significant attention. The transformation of the rotating object from *Momotarō's Sea Eagles* to *Thank You Kitty* marked the sociohistorical transition from militarism in wartime Japan to rural life in postwar China.

Kitty Goes Fishing was considerably more popular than *Thank You Kitty.* Indeed, *Kitty Goes Fishing* was so popular that it was later incorporated into textbooks for elementary schoolchildren and circulated so widely that it approached becoming national lore for Chinese children. Its theme songs also became hits. In his autobiography, Mochinaga mentioned how Disney's *Water Babies* had inspired him to become an animator. He especially noted the film's use of sunlight: "The changing sunlight transforms the color of the natural environment. The beauty is beyond description."[98] *Water Babies* begins with a still picture of a pond in the early morning. Everything is asleep, including the lilies in the pond and two birds perched symmetrically in a tree. When the sun rises, its light brightens the colors and awakens the scene. The birds wake up and the lilies begin to blossom.

Mochinaga's fascination with Disney's use of sunlight is evident in *Kitty Goes Fishing,* which also begins with an early morning sequence. The camera pans from right to left and presents a panoramic view of a rural village before dawn. Thereafter, the camera cuts to a pond. As sunlight gradually penetrates the pond, lilies blossom one by one. The shape and movement of the lilies are analogous to those in *Water Babies.* The two red birds in *Water Babies* are replaced by ducks in *Kitty Goes Fishing.* A mother duck and her three ducklings sleep near the edge of the pond. As the sunlight becomes brighter, the mother duck opens her eyes and wakes her ducklings, just as the two red birds in *Water Babies* awaken the lilies and water babies. The mother duck leading her ducklings in *Kitty Goes Fishing* parallels the film's protagonists, Mother Cat and her two children. This reinforces the ties between femininity, infantility, and the aesthetics of cuteness.

Mochinaga's fascination with sunlight is also evident in *Thank You Kitty*. The film opens with a scene of a rural village before dawn. Stars twinkle in a dark sky. As the sun rises, the village is gradually illuminated and a new day begins. Rooster crows and village animals go about their day. Throughout the film, Mochinaga pays meticulous attention to light and shade. When Kitty hides in the dark at the hen's house and captures two mice, Rooster comes to his aid and opens the door. As the door opens, the sunlight floods in and transforms the tonality of Kitty. These stylistic traces disclose some of the connections between these Chinese films and the Japanese and Disney animated films that featured similar transitions.

The Rise of Japanese Puppet Animation

Young animators in the early 1950s such as Te Wei successfully transitioned from drawing cartoons and illustrations to animated filmmaking. Veteran animators, including Qian Jiajun and his students, joined the animation division of Shanghai Film Studio in July 1953. Between 1950 and 1953, the division recruited approximately one hundred recent graduates from Suzhou Fine Arts Academy, the animation class of Beijing Film Academy, Central Academy of Fine Arts, Lu Xun Academy of Fine Arts, and others. It organized part-time animation and fine arts classes and other activities to educate the younger generation. Wan Laiming and Wan Guchan left Hong Kong and joined the animation division, in 1954 and 1956, respectively, shortly before the Shanghai Animation Film Studio was established in 1957.[99] By the end of 1956, the animation staff at the Shanghai Film Studio gradually increased from twenty-two to 208.[100] Meanwhile, Mochinaga had returned to Japan in mid-August 1953, shortly before the animation industry in socialist China began to flourish, because he felt that Chinese animators should produce their own animated films.[101] Separately, the Chinese and Japanese governments, after several rounds of negotiations, reached an agreement to transfer the diasporic Japanese back to Japan in January 1953. On March 22, 1953, Japan sent its first ship to China. The transfer involved rounds in all, returning 29,040 Japanese home to Japan in the early 1950s.[102] Mochinaga was one of them.

Mochinaga was the first major puppet animator in the history of Japanese cinema.[103] In 1950, Iizawa Tadashi, Hijikata Shigemi, Sumida Yūjirō, and Kawamoto Kihachirō established a Puppet Animation Company. On his return to Japan in August 1953, Mochinaga was invited by Iizawa Tadashi to join his company. He and Kawamoto Kihachirō later made the puppet-animated advertisement *Mr. Bitter Beer's Magician* (*Horoniga-kun no majutsushi*, 1953) for Asahi Beer Company, which marked the birth of three-dimensional puppet animation in Japan (figure 2.9).[104] In August 1955 in Tokyo, Mochinaga and Inamura Yoshikazu established the Puppet Animation Film Studio (Ningyō eiga seisakusho), which focused on independent puppet animation and used Dentsu Film Company (Dentsu eigasha) as its distributor. Films produced by Puppet Animation Film Studio were supported by the Ministry of Education and targeted elementary school children.

The Puppet Animation Film Studio produced nine independent puppet-animated films from 1955 to 1960. The first, *The Melon Princess and the Demon* (*Uriko-hime to amanojaku*, 1956), is based on a Japanese legend and regarded as the first of its kind. The studio spent two and a half months and JP¥780,000 in production costs on it. Upon completion, Ōmura Einosuke, then minister of culture of the Japanese Communist Party, brought the film to China during an official visit. Mochinaga continued to export his films to China to expand the market there until May 2, 1958, the day that right-wing Japanese groups in Nagasaki destroyed China's national flag and demonstrated their contempt for the newly established socialist China, which retaliated by suspending Sino-Japanese commercial and cultural exchanges.[105]

The release of the second puppet-animated film, *Five Little Monkeys* (*Gohiki no kozaru-tachi*, 1956), which draws on a Chinese legend, caught the attention of Tōei Animation (Tōei animēshon kabushiki-gaisha).[106] Interested in three-dimensional puppet animation, which was still nascent in Japan, the president of Tōei Animation asked Uchida Tomu to invite Mochinaga and his independent studio to join Tōei Animation. Mochinaga declined the invitation, claiming that

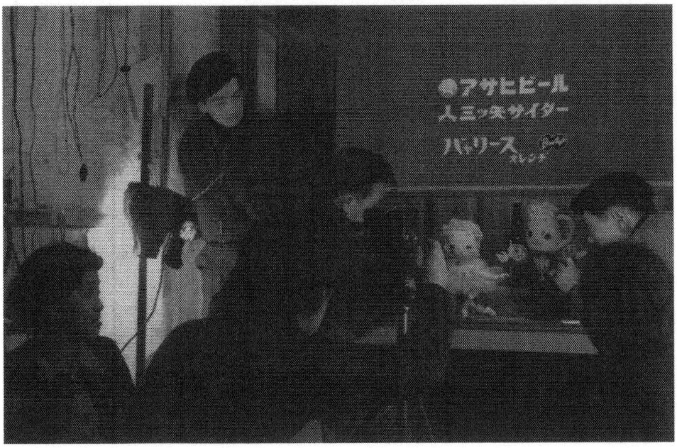

Figure 2.9. The making of *Mr. Bitter Beer's Magician*, 1953, courtesy of Mochinaga Noriko.

he wanted to preserve his artistic autonomy as an independent auteur. Given that Tōei Animation emphasized the strict division of labor and teamwork also characteristic of Disney, Mochinaga worried that he would lose creative control over his work.[107] In contrast, Tezuka Osamu and Miyazaki Hayao had worked at Tōei for some time and gained firsthand experience before they started their own studios.

The approach Mochinaga adopted for his puppet-animated filmmaking in the 1950s was similar to the national style at the Shanghai Animation Film Studio. Because children were the intended audience, most of Mochinaga's puppet-animated films drew on folklore and legends rooted in traditional Japanese culture. These films were released in Japan and occasionally won awards at international film festivals. Unlike the labor-intensive and individuality-erasing cel animation, puppet animation requires a less fragmented labor process and is more conducive to an auteur style. These films were essentially art and educational films for children, like the classic films produced by the Shanghai Animation Film Studio during the socialist decades.

Sympathetic to Chinese and Soviet filmmaking, Mochinaga was critical of American filmmaking. Hundreds of American films were imported to postwar Japan every year, and were very popular among Japanese audiences. For Mochinaga, most of the imported American films were about imperialism, war, police, crime, gangsters, and racism. They emphasized individual heroism and competitiveness, featuring lone individuals triumphing over their opponents to succeed. Full of irrationality, madness, killing, and sex, Mochinaga called American films "sugar-coated bullets and bombs," a term borrowed from Chairman Mao. He thought American films were exploding and harming people in Japan. Mochinaga advocated the erasure of American influence in postwar Japan, as in China after the Korean War. According to him, Japanese cinema would flourish only if progressive Soviet and Chinese films were introduced to Japan.[108]

Mochinaga specifically criticized Disney's global influence and advocated that any conscientious animator should produce work that reflected their national or ethnic style. For him, postwar Disney films no longer served children because they emphasized individual heroism and adventurism without teaching children to help others. He praised French animation for its stress on national characteristics and the collective power of the masses. Soviet animation was praiseworthy because it served children well. For instance, he advocated that Japanese children should learn from the boy protagonist in the Soviet animated film *The Golden Antelope* (1954), who selflessly helps others in need while remaining brave and intelligent.[109] For Mochinaga, national or ethnic style (which should be different from Disney) and the political or educational function of animation (for children) were the most important factors for conscientious animators anywhere in the world. Mochinaga's efforts to export his puppet-animated films to the commercial markets of North America were unsuccessful partly because their Japanese ethnic flavor was too strong for international audiences.

Mochinaga's approach in the 1950s differed from Tōei Animation and Tezuka Osamu, who created a more de-Japanized world and successfully brought their products to lucrative international markets during the late 1950s and 1960s. They charted two courses for the future of Japanese animation: cel or two-dimensional animation follows the commercial and international approaches of Tōei Animation, Tezuka Osamu, and later Miyazaki Hayao; puppet animation largely remains a domestic art (sometimes popular at international film festivals) and continues to struggle for survival in Japan. Cel animation can be organized using a strict division of labor and mass production, whereas puppet animation calls for a smaller and tighter production team. Cel-animated film tends to erase the animator's individuality and represent a studio's particular style, whereas puppet animation tends to foster the auteur style of a specific animator.

Without financial support from the state, such as that received by the Shanghai Animation Film Studio, and international markets, such as enjoyed by Tezuka Osamu's Bug Productions, Mochinaga's Puppet Animation Film Studio gradually declined. Its major supporter was Inamura, who successfully secured funds for the studio until he died suddenly in 1960 shortly after the release of the ninth and last independent puppet-animated film, *The Fox That Became the King* (*Ōsama ni natta kitsune*, 1959). After his death, Puppet Animation Film Studio faced severe financial crises and closed within the year (1960).

The closure reflects the larger difficulties facing puppet-animated filmmaking in Japan. Mochinaga's work in puppet animation resulted in the conventional thinking that the form was for children's education and entertainment, and that cel animation was oriented to adults as well as children. Puppet animators and studios inspired by Mochinaga supported this thinking. In 1959, Gakken Film Bureau (Gakken eiga kyoku) officially established a puppet animation studio under the leadership of Jinbo Matsue, with Mochinaga as its technology supervisor. Following Mochinaga's approach, Gakken also focused on educational puppet animation films for children by drawing on folklore, legends, and fairy tales. Given high costs and the lack of a profitable market, Jinbo Matsue gave up puppet animation and began to work on two-dimensional animation for television in the 1980s. Another example is Kawamoto Kihachirō, who was Mochinaga Tadahito's student and probably the best-known Japanese puppet animator. His films targeted adults and were highly praised at international film festivals as art films, but there was no market for them in Japan and overseas and his studio struggled to recover production costs.[110]

The fate of Mochinaga's Puppet Animation Film Studio is not only a particular Japanese case, but also a window to understanding the puppet animation industry around the world during the Cold War. Commenting on it in 1959, Iizawa Tadashi argued that puppet animation was labor intensive and time consuming. Because of its high production costs, puppet animation did not succeed in the United States because it was not profitable. It flourished in communist countries such as Czechoslovakia and the Soviet Union, however, where it was a generously supported state-owned industry.[111] Ivo Caprino, a Norwegian puppet animator, lamented that in Norway they struggled every day for funding, whereas Czech puppet animators such as Jiří Trnka received the equivalent of approximately JP¥400 million from the state.[112] Without state support, Mochinaga had to raise funds to produce educational puppet-animated films for children that were not profitable in capitalist Japan. His studio had to make commercials to generate funds, yet they were not enough to support the studio.

MOM and the Early Outsourcing Industry in 1960s Japan

Mochinaga's *Little Black Sambo Subdues the Tiger* (1956) won the Best Film award for the category of the Films for Children at the first Vancouver International Film Festival in 1958. Arthur Rankin, who founded Videocraft International in New York in 1960 (renamed Rankin/Bass Productions in 1968), was deeply impressed by this film. At that time, a Japanese delegation seeking to expand international trade visited Washington, DC. Delegation member Kawamoto Minoru met Rankin there and invited him to visit Japan. Rankin visited Tōei Animation, Bug Productions, and other small animation studios. Kawamoto Minoru asked Rankin about exporting Japanese animated films to the United States. During his visit to Mochinaga's Puppet Animation Film Studio, Rankin remarked, "the storylines and subjects were solely for Japan and not suitable for export but the technique, based on the Japanese puppet art of Bunraku, was good."[113] Rankin and his team then designed a character and storyline that would appeal to the international audience and later outsourced the project to MOM Productions (MOM purodakushon), established by Mochinaga, Ōmura, and others in 1960 after the disintegration of Puppet Animation Film Studio. The goal for MOM Productions was to produce animated commercials, the revenue from which would fund the revitalization of independent Japanese puppet animation. The first project outsourced by Videocraft International to MOM became *The New Adventures of Pinocchio* (1960).

Mochinaga Tadahito opposed taking this outsourced project. *The New Adventures of Pinocchio* was a puppet-animated TV series with 130 five-minute episodes. To finish the project on time, MOM's entire staff had to work around the clock. As a result, MOM had neither the means nor labor to produce its own creative works, forcing it to cut ties with its established audience of children in Japan.

This heavy workload also made it impossible for the studio to produce animated commercials. MOM's entire dependence on projects outsourced from the United States made the studio vulnerable. MOM's film producer, whose name remained anonymous in Mochinaga's autobiography, wanted to take outsourced projects to earn money and pay off the debts incurred from independent puppet-animated filmmaking. He argued that the profits from outsourced projects could revive their independent puppet animation. He even urged Mochinaga's wife to persuade her husband to take the project. Mochinaga agreed on the condition that he would take no more outsourced projects after finishing *The New Adventures of Pinocchio.* When the staff of MOM was working on the last ten episodes, the studio caught fire, damaging the facilities and destroying the negatives of twenty-eight episodes. With only two months left before the deadline, MOM had to complete the final episodes and remake those lost to the fire. Although they completed the work on time, the studio suffered a huge financial loss, which meant accepting more outsourced projects. MOM ended up only producing projects for Videocraft International.[114]

In addition to *The New Adventures of Pinocchio*, MOM produced five features and television series: *Willy McBean & His Magic Machine* (1963), *Rudolph the Red-Nosed Reindeer* (1964), *Andersen's Fairy Tales / The Daydreamer* (1966), *The Ballad of Smokey the Bear* (1966), and *Mad Monster Party* (1967). Most of these were specials made for Christmas, Halloween, Thanksgiving, Easter, and other holidays. Videocraft International named the stop-motion puppet animation technique Animagic. Mochinaga's name appeared as animation supervisor or Animagic Technician: Tad Mochinaga in the credits.[115] These films were well known in the United States and the English-speaking world, but scarcely known in Japan because officially they were not "Japanese" animation.

The most well-known Animagic film was probably *Rudolph the Red-Nosed Reindeer*. Videocraft International prepared the storyboards and pre-recorded voices and sounds and sent them to MOM animators, who made puppets and animated them in Tokyo. Rankin flew to Tokyo to supervise the production. Each puppet character cost approximately $5,000. Mochinaga had used silver wire inside the puppets in China, but lead and copper wire for *Rudolph the Red-Nosed Reindeer.* The prop department made the costumes by hand and when it was difficult to find suitable fabric, they wove it themselves, as they did for the vest of Snowman Sam. Before they animated the reindeer puppets, they went to a park to observe the movements of deer. They also invited performers such as Danny Kaye, Jerry Lewis, and Romeo Muller to act out the scenes so that animators could observe their movements and personalities. Sometimes the performance was filmed to be referred to later during the animation process.[116] This practice of live performance and sketching from it was popular in animated filmmaking during Mochinaga's stay in China.

At the outset, the studio had ten staff, that number growing to 130 at the peak of MOM's activity. Lighting supervisors received between JP¥50,000 to JP¥70,000 per month, ordinary staff between JP¥20,000 to JP¥30,000, and assistants around JP¥10,000. The working hours were so long that animators slept at night in the studio near the puppets. To save time and cost, each puppet character had several duplicates so that different animators could work on different scenes with the same characters simultaneously.[117] A single animator ideally would be in charge of a single character to ensure consistency of movement and style of puppet animation, as Mochinaga did for his independent animated films, an approach that is even more time consuming. MOM developed a style of "limited" puppet animation for American television productions in the 1960s, the same time that Tezuka Osamu introduced limited cel animation to television in Japan. Both artists hoped to earn profits from less expensive limited animation on television to support their experimental and independent animated filmmaking, which was not profitable.

When *Rudolph the Red-Nosed Reindeer* was finalized in New York and premiered on December 6, 1964, it attracted so much public attention that "the phone literally jumped off the hook," and within a few years Videocraft International "controlled that particular market."[118] General Electric provided the financial backing for the production of *Rudolph,* which was released as a segment of the program *General Electric Fantasy Hour.* When *Rudolph* was on air, many commercials for General Electric products featured characters from the series. MOM animators featured minor characters in these commercials, probably because the major protagonists had a lot of screen time and were occupied with making the series and thus unavailable for the commercials.[119]

The production of *Rudolph* as well as other Animagic works took place in a transnational network that went beyond New York and Tokyo. In early 1964, the cast at RCA Victor recording studios in Toronto, Canada, began to record the soundtrack. Rudolph was voiced by Billie Mae Richards and Hermey by Paul Soles. Burl Ives played the voice of Sam the Snowman and sang many songs that became hits. Videocraft International, always based in New York, outsourced so much of its early production work to Canada that books and magazines frequently misidentified it as a Canadian studio.[120]

MOM was probably the earliest Japanese studio working on projects outsourced from the United States, and it marked the beginning of the outsourcing industry in Japan. In 1966, Tōei Animation began to work on an outsourced television series, *The King Kong Show,* for Videocraft International. In 1969, Tezuka Osamu's Bug Productions also began to work on an outsourced TV movie, *Frosty the Snowman*, for Rankin/Bass. During the 1960s, 1970s, and up to the 1980s, many Japanese animation studios worked on outsourced US projects.[121] It marked the beginning of animation as a global industry and suggested the relatively disadvantaged status of Japan in the global network of animated filmmaking. As Japan gradually became an animation power from the late 1970s onward, it began to outsource its animation projects to the Shanghai Animation Film Studio and other studios in mainland China, Taiwan, and South Korea.[122] These invisible studios and nameless animators contributed to the global success of Japanese animation since the late 1980s, much as MOM and other Japanese studios did in the success of American animation in the 1960s, 1970s, and 1980s. Interestingly, Mochinaga's experience with MOM in the 1960s presaged the fate of the Shanghai Animation Film Studio in the 1980s. Both focused on art and educational films for children before they were forced to accept outsourced projects to generate the revenue necessary to keep the studios in operation.

MOM was criticized by some Japanese scholars for sapping the creativity and energy of Japanese animators and hampering the development of the creative industry locally, thus having a negative impact on Japanese animation.[123] Mochinaga felt guilty for being unable to produce original work at MOM.[124] When he visited China in October 1978, he warned Chinese animators interested in taking projects outsourced from abroad by listing the disadvantages he had experienced. First, working on outsourced projects cut off the animator's and studio's ties with Japanese children. Second, because the profits from outsourced projects tripled the creative work, animators' salaries working for outsourced projects were much higher than those working on creative animated films, putting tremendous financial pressure on domestic creative animated filmmaking. Third, working on projects outsourced from America led Japanese animators to imitate American gags and styles.[125] Fourth, no matter how hardworking local animators were and no matter how wonderful outsourced films might look, domestic audiences could not watch them.[126] However, from a longer-term and more positive perspective, working on outsourced projects trained many talented young Japanese animators and earned revenue that kept the studios and the entire animation industry alive, which contributed to the rise of Japanese animation on the global stage in the late 1980s and 1990s.

Mochinaga ended his animation career at MOM in April 1967 to work for the China News Service (Chūgoku tsūshinsha), a company endorsed by the Xinhua News Service and the Beijing TV Station. His job was to introduce Japanese newsreels to China and Chinese newsreels to Japan on topics related to Sino-Japanese friendship. To shoot newsreels, Mochinaga traveled to China several times. He worked for the China News Service until 1978.[127]

The Return of Kitty/Mochinaga in Postsocialist Shanghai

In 1979, the Shanghai Animation Film Studio invited Mochinaga to make a puppet-animated film. The film *Who Meowed?* (*Miaowu shi shei jiao de,* 1979) is one of the last animated films he made for China. Mochinaga's Chinese name, Fang Ming, still appeared in the film's credits because his colleagues regarded him as half Chinese. Like the previous animated films made in the early 1950s, *Who Meowed?* takes place in a rural village. A small dog chained to a house is eager to see the outside world, so he breaks free and runs into the field for the first time. The dog hears a disembodied meow. Everything in the field is new and curious to him and he sets out to discover the source of the meow. On his way, he meets a rooster, a pig, two mice, a lamb, and other animals. The dog finally learns that the cat is the source of the meow at the end of the film.

Absent Kitty represents the origin of meaning, namely, the source of the mysterious meow, a revelation deferred until the end of the film. Kitty's absence leaves room for multiple narrative possibilities for the rooster, pig, mice, and others. The meow uttered by Kitty at the end of the film is a return to that original mysterious sound and a reassertion of its authorship after a long period of absence. Kitty can be seen as symbolizing Mochinaga's place in the history of Chinese animation. Mochinaga enjoyed animating adorable cats and made *Thank You Kitty* and *Kitty Goes Fishing* in early socialist China. After he returned to Japan, Chinese animators continued to animate cute animals, but films rarely featured a cat as protagonist.[128] Because Mochinaga was no longer in China, the protagonist Kitty was absent for two decades in the history of Chinese animated film. His departure gave rise to other animation possibilities, such as the rise of the national style in the late 1950s and early 1960s and the depiction of political heroes during the years of the Cultural Revolution. In this sense, Mochinaga is the returned Kitty who uttered the meow in Chinese animation.

Who Meowed? was probably inspired by a Soviet puppet-animated film under the same title *Who Meowed?* It was directed by Vladimir Degtyarev (1916–1974) and released in 1962. Degtyarev received his education at the Leningrad Art School. After he was wounded in World War II, he pursued further education at the All-Union State Institute of Cinematography, graduating in 1948, after which he began working at the Soiuzmultfilm Studio as an art director. From 1953 onward, he worked as a director of cel- and puppet-animated films that targeted children. The best-known of his films is *The Ugly Duckling* (1957). *Who Meowed?* won an international award at the IV International Film Festival in Annecy, France.[129] The protagonist, a puppy, hears a disembodied meow and tries to find the source of the sound. In his quest for an answer, he meets a rooster, a bee, a frog, and other animals. In the end, he discovers that a cat had made the meow sound.

Mochinaga's story closely resembles Degtyarev's *Who Meowed?* Even the images of the puppy, cat, and other animals look similar. It is possible that the Soviet film had influenced Mochinaga's version made in Shanghai in 1979. This Soviet influence is not surprising given his leftist tendency, his criticism of postwar Disney films, and his preference for films with their own national or ethnic style. In fact, during his stay in early socialist China, Mochinaga learned the art of puppet animation from Soviet and Czech films.[130] Soviet animation indeed had a profound impact on Mochinaga's puppet animation.

Mochinaga's bond with China was reinforced when he worked with Hu Jinqing and produced a fourteen-minute educational film using papercutting, *Twin Lotuses* (*Shuanglian*) in 1992. It was a coproduction of Shanghai Animation Film Studio and Sakura Motion Pictures (Sakura eiga-sha) in Tokyo. The film's production was sponsored by the Japanese Organization for International Cooperation in Family Planning (JOICFP), a nongovernmental organization active in family planning and maternal health since 1968. JOICFP began its collaboration with China in 1984. The film's goal is to educate women about healthful habits.[131] It was broadcast on television for collective viewing by peasants. The film's title is highly symbolic, the lotus flower representing virtue in Chinese culture because it emerges from the mud yet is pure and beautiful; Lian is a popular Chinese name for girls, giving the title a feminine connotation; and last, lotus seeds are a traditional herbal medicine for women and symbolize female fertility. The twin lotuses refer to the film's characters, an open-minded wife, who pursues a healthy and independent life, and her caring husband. More important, the title evokes the expression "even when the lotus root breaks, the fibers still hold together" (*ou duan si lian*), that referred to the friendship between China and Japan, two Asian countries separated by the sea yet connected by culture.[132]

Mochinaga's art of puppet animation spread in Japan through his students. The first and most talented of them, Kawamoto Kihachirō (1925–2010), participated in the production of the first puppet-animated advertisement, *Mr. Bitter Beer's Magician.*[133] Kawamoto went on to study puppet animation techniques from Jiří Trnka in Prague from 1963 to 1964. After Kawamoto returned from Prague, he launched his own career and became Japan's most influential puppet animator.[134]

Mochinaga's connections with Chinese animation continued through Kawamoto's career. In 1988, Kawamoto made the puppet-animated film *To Shoot without Shooting* (*Bu she zhi she*) for Shanghai Animation Film Studio. The original was adapted from the Chinese classic *Master Lie* (*Liezi*). Nakajima Atsushi (1909–1942), a Japanese writer and sinologist, rewrote this classical Chinese legend and titled it "The Story of a Celebrity" ("Meijinden," published on December 1, 1942). Kawamoto adapted "The Story of a Celebrity" for the puppet-animated film *To Shoot without Shooting* for China.

The journey of the story in *To Shoot without Shooting* parallels the travel of the artistic form of puppet animation. In 1947, Mochinaga made *Dreaming to Be Emperor,* the first puppet-animated film in socialist China. In 1953 he then brought the art of puppet animation to Japan and passed on his knowledge to Kawamoto. In 1988, Kawamoto brought the art back to China in the film *To Shoot without Shooting.* Unlike films in the late 1940s and early 1950s in China, *To Shoot without Shooting* directly acknowledged its complicated connections with Japan. The film's opening sequence celebrates the film as "a landmark in the time-honored history of Sino-Japanese friendship." Kawamoto's Japanese name appears in the credits. Thus the connections of Chinese animation with Japan resurfaced.

To Shoot without Shooting demonstrates the process of adaptation and supplementation in the cultural flows between China and Japan. In the original Chinese legend, Jichang learns archery from Feiwei, who passes on his knowledge to Jichang without reservation. Jichang wants to be the world's best archer. After learning everything Feiwei could teach him, Jichang sets out to kill his teacher. The two archers meet in the wilderness and stage a duel. Each time they shoot at each other, their arrows meet halfway and break into two halves. Feiwei runs out of arrows first, but he picks up a branch and uses it to fend off Jichang's last arrow shot. Jichang realizes that he cannot defeat his master, so he reconciles with Feiwei. The two men weep. The Chinese legend ends here, but the Japanese version, as demonstrated in the puppet-animated film, goes further. After their reconciliation, Feiwei tells Jichang that if he really wants to be the world's best archer, he needs to learn archery from a master in E'mei Mountain in Sichuan province. Jichang travels there, finds the mysterious Daoist master Ganying, and becomes Ganying's disciple. Ganying teaches Jichang the art of shooting without using bows and arrows. Jichang's aggressive nature is gradually tamed by learning a philosophy and form of archery that embrace humility, withdrawal, and solitude. By the time Jichang returns to the city as the world's best archer, he does not even remember what a bow is. As a result, people in the city abandon their bows and arrows. Peace and harmony are restored to the world.

To Shoot without Shooting thematizes the complicated love-hate relationship between China and Japan. Japan emulated China before the Meiji period, but tried to supplant China and become the most powerful nation in the world—or at least in East Asia. Japan's ambition culminated during World War II, a time when Japan considered China inferior. When *Princess Iron Fan* was released in wartime Tokyo, Japan developed a strong sense of competition with China in the field of animation. The protagonist Jichang in *To Shoot without Shooting* is portrayed as having exceptional perseverance, stamina, and ambition, the characteristics of a samurai (a figure often used to represent Japan). Jichang suffers from the anxiety of influence and tries to kill his master to prove that he is the better archer. Paradoxically,

Jichang becomes the best archer in the world only when he gives up competition. The film ends with a vision of utopian cosmopolitanism as everyone in the city abandons bows and arrows to ensure peace and harmony. This ending gestures toward the conclusion of the long-standing rivalry between China and Japan that began with the transnational reception of *Princess Iron Fan* during World War II. The film's ending also foreshadows the destiny of Japanese animation. After reconciling with China after the war, Japanese animation gradually became the most influential and popular in East Asia, if not the entire world.

3 Inter/National Style and National Identity

Ink-Painting Animation in the Early 1960s

National style, as explained earlier, is prominent in Chinese animated films that use traditional Chinese artistic, literary, and cultural forms, materials, and techniques (such as Peking opera, papercutting and paperfolding, ink painting, folklore, classical literature) to construct a putatively pure, authentic, and unique Chinese national identity. This identity distinguishes Chinese animation from its counterparts in other countries—Japan and the United States in particular—and, more important, articulates nationalistic sentiments and national pride in defiance of foreign influence and dominance.

With its emphasis on national identity, Chinese essence, and Chineseness, the national style—promoted by mainstream animators, intellectuals, scholars, and the government—became the dominant metric for judging the merits of animated films in China beginning in the late 1950s and early 1960s. Many mainstream Chinese animators, often encouraged by the state, are preoccupied with creating national style films, believing that the unique style of Chinese animated film represents a monolithic and timeless Chinese national identity and asserting that this Chineseness brings Chinese animated film global recognition. In addition, researchers and scholars often lavish attention on "pure" national style films and analyze their formal and thematic uniqueness, neglecting and even denigrating the vast majority of animated films that do not conform to its conventions. Thus the discourse of the national style is dominant in the mainstream animated filmmaking industry and academia.

Conventional academic approaches to the national style are essentialist, static, and ahistorical in that they deploy formal or thematic uniqueness to represent a monolithic, timeless, and transcendental national identity. In *Uproar in Heaven* (*Danao tiangong*, 1961–1964), the legend of Monkey King marks the Chineseness of the story and the made-up face associated with Peking opera asserts the Chineseness of the animation's formal style. Ink-painting animation is another example of the formal uniqueness exemplified by the national style. To construct a distinct Chinese identity for international audiences, ink-painting animated film sequences were exhibited in the China Pavilion of the Shanghai World Expo in

2010. Zheng Dasheng, director of *A Harmonious China* (*Hexie Zhongguo*), the leitmotif film of the China Pavilion, uses computer-generated ink-painting animation to represent the nation and to accompany the film's narrative about China's rapid development. The use of ink-painting animation in the China Pavilion culminated in *Along the River during the Qingming Festival* (*Qingming shanghe tu*), in which animators adopted computer ink-painting techniques and animated a traditional painting by Zhang Zeduan from the Northern Song dynasty (960–1127). The conflation of national style and national identity may have its logic. However, it positions the national style in a timeless nation-bound vacuum and neglects the spatial-international and temporal-historical contingencies that gave rise to it.

Here I trace the origin of the national style in Chinese animation to the late 1950s and early 1960s, and situate its rise in its international and historical context. The national style was in sum a product of the Cold War. In the 1950s, Chinese animation and other literary and artistic forms were influenced by the Soviet style, which, of course, was far from the only international influence.[1] As Sino-Soviet relations began to deteriorate in the late 1950s, rising cultural nationalism was accompanied by calls to turn inward to Chinese tradition. In response to this shifting sociohistorical context, the national style was proposed as a guiding principle for Chinese animated filmmaking. Yet an alternative style of animation emerged at the same time, which I call the international style. International style films adopted more universal artistic forms such as cartoon and caricature, and featured content associated with the capitalist West, in particular the United States. The international style and the national style were born at the same time and coexisted during the late 1950s and early 1960s. However, the discourse of the national style came to overshadow the international in Chinese animation. By highlighting the coexistence and even contestation between the two styles in the late 1950s and early 1960s, this discussion expands the horizon of the national style, previously examined in isolation as the autonomous sine qua non of Chinese animation. The international and national styles, however, were not necessarily in opposition to each other and no clear-cut boundary separated them, In fact, the international style is arguably one of several national styles in Chinese animated filmmaking. National style is after all not one, but many.

A synchronic approach repositions the national style in the international context of the Cold War. A diachronic approach examines the evolution of the national style within socialist China. This chapter adopts a diachronic approach to demonstrate that the national style was neither stable nor fixed, that, over time, its definition changed in response to sociohistorical and political forces. For this discussion, I use the rise and fall of the first two ink-painting animated films produced in the early 1960s to illustrate the instability of the national style in socialist China. When the first, *Little Tadpoles Look for Mama* (*Xiao kedou zhao mama*), was released in 1960, it was praised, celebrated, and considered as a perfect representation of the national style and a source of national pride. However, when the second, *The Herd Boy's Flute* (*Mudi*), was made in late 1963, it was criticized and banned. By this time, just three years later, the artistic form of ink painting was no longer considered representative of the national style. Exploring the rise and fall of the first two ink-painting animated films in the early 1960s, I argue that the conventional conflation between national style and national identity is problematic: concepts of national identity and national style, far from being fixed essential and timeless categories, are fluid, ever-changing, and historically contingent. This is especially true during the 1960s, a period of rapid change in the international and historical milieus.

Socialist Film Culture in the 1950s

The Chinese film industry underwent a drastic transformation in the late 1940s. After Beijing was taken over by the Chinese Communist Party (CCP) in January 1949, the Northeast Film Studio, the first film studio under the control of the Communist Party and located in Changchun, sent Tian Fang and others to Beijing to take over the film industry that was controlled by the Nationalists. On April 20, 1949, they established Peking Film Studio, which was renamed Beijing Film Studio on October 1, 1949. In a similar vein, after the CCP took control of Nanjing and Shanghai in April and May of 1949, the Northeast Film Studio sent Zhong Jingzhi and others to take over its film industries that had been under Nationalist control. In November 1949, the CCP established the Shanghai Film Studio.[2]

The early 1950s witnessed the nationalization of private studios. After 1949, the socialist state tolerated private film studios and even financially supported them and provided them with film stocks. These studios—such as Kunlun, Wenhua, Datong, and Guotai—also received loans from the People's Bank of Shanghai. They were, however, under much tighter state surveillance after the Korean War broke out in 1950 and during the Three and Five Anti-Campaigns, reform movements against "bourgeois habits" in 1951 and 1952. A campaign was soon launched to denounce *The Life of Wu Xun* (*Wu Xun zhuan*, 1950), a controversial film produced by Kunlun studio. Yan'an-spirited hard-liners called on the public to close down or take over Kunlun because of its ideological "mistakes." This inaugurated the nationalization of private film studios. In 1953, the last private studios were assimilated into the state-run Shanghai Film Studio. By 1953, the state and Yan'an hard-liners, who were inspired by the Soviet model, controlled all film production in mainland China.[3] Consequently, socialist realism, borrowed from the Soviet Union, was adopted as the dominant principle for cultural production in the 1950s.

From approximately 1956 to 1965, controls over the cultural scene eased, allowing it to diversify as socialist realism gave way to greater variety and flexibility. As a modest modification of the Yan'an dogma, in 1956 Chairman Mao proposed the slogan "Let a hundred flowers bloom, let a hundred schools of thought contend" to encourage debate and criticism of socialist culture and politics. Writers, filmmakers, and intellectuals were suspicious at first, but quickly responded with harsh condemnation of the new regime, which finally caused Mao and the government to crack down on the emerging dissidents. The CCP launched the Anti-Rightist Campaign in 1957, which labeled the Hundred Flowers critics as rightists and persecuted them.[4]

In 1958, Mao and the CCP launched the Great Leap Forward (1958–1960), which encouraged rapid production and technological innovation across a wide range of industries. Many films were produced to answer the call, but quality was inconsistent. With the deterioration of the Sino-Soviet relationship in the late 1950s, the CCP steered a course away from socialist realism. By 1958, it was advocating for "combining revolutionary realism and revolutionary romanticism." The two slogans coexisted for a while until socialist realism declined and disappeared from critical discourse by 1960. The slogan "combining revolutionary realism and revolutionary romanticism" enjoyed dominance during the 1960s and 1970s until it lost favor in 1979.[5] With the introduction of "combining revolutionary realism and revolutionary romanticism" in 1958, filmmakers were encouraged to go beyond the rigid dogma of socialist realism and experiment with new techniques and technologies to explore new modes of representation. Elements of "revolutionary romanticism," such as myth, folklore, legend, and fantasy, were allowed during this period. When the Great Leap Forward's disastrous effects on Chinese economy gave rise to the Great Famine (1959–1961), Mao temporarily retreated from center stage and loosened his ideological grip on arts and artists. As a result, the cultural scene was relatively relaxed in the early 1960s, giving rise to a diversity of arts and literature that did not follow the rigid doctrine of socialist realism.

The Revival of Traditional Art in the Early 1960s

The late 1950s and early 1960s witnessed a revival in traditional art related to the "elevation of (artistic) standards" under Mao. In his Yan'an Talks in 1942, Mao proposed the two concepts: "popularization of art" and "elevation of standards." "Popularization of art" meant that art should serve the needs of peasants, workers, and soldiers. Thus, art should not be elitist or abstract. "Elevation of standards" involved artists, including amateur peasant artists, improving their level of artistic taste and accomplishment. According to Mao, these two concepts were inextricable:

elevation of standards should be based on popularization of art, and popularization of art should lead to elevation of standards. Although Mao maintained that the two concepts were equally important, the historical record indicates that he valued popularization of art over elevation of standards.

In his book *Painting in the People's Republic of China,* Arnold Chang proposes three distinct periods: 1949 to 1956 as a period of popularization, 1958 to 1965 as a period of elevation of standards, and 1966 to 1971 as an era of popularization. According to Chang, popularization and elevation of standards centered on issues such as choice of artistic styles and the status of professional artists. Professional artists included ink-painting artists who were educated before 1949 and found it more difficult than younger artists to adapt to the style that the Communist Party advocated. During the period of popularization, the Party encouraged realistic styles, such as Soviet socialist realism, as well as figure painting, and amateur folk art. Furthermore, it disparaged landscape and bird-and-flower painting, criticizing and even persecuting professional artists (see also discussion in chapter 4). However, during the elevation of standards period, landscape and bird-and-flower paintings enjoyed a notable comeback, along with improvement in the status of professional artists.[6]

Elevation of standards and the revival of traditional art between 1958 and 1965 began with Mao's Hundred Flowers Campaign in January 1956, which encouraged artistic and intellectual diversity. Soviet socialist realism, which was the dominant model after Mao's Yan'an Talks, acceded to a more sinicized style. Consequently, traditional art forms flourished, including traditional ink painting (*guohua*). In the fall of 1956, a *People's Daily* editorial titled "Develop the Art of *Guohua*" announced the Communist Party's new policy concerning traditional ink painting: "*Guohua* is part of the precious heritage of our country's national arts; it has a long history and rich tradition. Over time, painters have expressed the magnificence of the rivers and mountains of our motherland and the living conditions of the people during each period."[7]

Under this new policy, opponents of traditional ink painting were considered enemies of the nation. Detractors were criticized, and even persecuted during the Anti-Rightist Campaign in 1957 and 1958. For example, Jiang Feng (1910–1982), an influential artist and leader in China's art world, was a staunch opponent of traditional ink painting and strong advocate for Soviet and Western arts instead in accordance with the Yan'an tradition. He was denounced by his political and artistic rival Cai Ruohong (1910–2002), a proponent of traditional ink painting. With Mao's acquiescence, Jiang Feng was labeled a rightist and purged from the art world in 1958. Cai Ruohong remained China's most influential art leader until he was ousted in 1967, when Yan'an hard-liners returned to power.[8]

Besides the revival of traditional ink painting, the late 1950s also saw a similar quest for tradition, past, and Chineseness in the field of film. In the 1961 article

"Elevating Chinese Film Art to a Higher Level" ("Ba woguo dianying yishu tigao dao yige gengxin de shuiping"), Minister of the Bureau of Culture Xia Yan (1900–1995) argued that contemporary filmmaking lacked both artistic excellence and range in subject matter, genre, and style. He emphasized the importance of artistic forms:

> For the past twelve years, we have produced many good films loved by the masses. However, among these films, only a few were excellent, and most of them were just mediocre. The main problem for these mediocre films was that they did not have a high artistic level. Although they had politically correct content, they did not have "a perfect artistic form" to transmit political messages to the masses.[9]

Because Xia Yan advocated the elevation of standards, films from the late 1950s broke with the Soviet model of socialist realism. Filmmakers began to explore a wider range of artistic forms that were regarded as genuinely Chinese, such as musicals, ethnic minority films, and traditional heritage.

According to Paul Clark, the early 1960s, which he calls the period of "cultural thaw," witnessed the Communist Party's relaxation of ideological control on filmmaking. This gave rise to a greater variety of film styles and subject matter. Clark notes, "The general relaxation in Chinese political life was paralleled in a wider range of film subjects and a more ready recognition that films not only educated, but also entertained."[10] In other words, films were more than ideological tools; they had the potential to be entertaining. In a 1962 essay, Qu Baiyin argued that Chinese films were constrained by three gods: theme, structure, and struggle. He highlighted the need to cater to different audiences and their tastes, rather than being limited by the principle of popularization's exclusive focus on workers, peasants, and soldiers. Qu wrote: "This magic power of the god of structure has the unexpected effect that the blind can understand [the films] by listening and the deaf by looking, but those who are neither blind nor deaf find them totally uninteresting."[11] Filmmakers went beyond the norm of serving workers, peasants, and soldiers, and began to consider more sophisticated audiences.

The Black Crow Incident: Animated Sino-Soviet Encounter and National Style and Identity

China's deteriorating relationship with the Soviet Union and the responding surge of nationalism partially contributed to the inward turn and revival of traditional arts in the late 1950s and early 1960s. After 1957, Mao demonstrated an implicit rejection of Soviet literary models.[12] Border disputes with the Soviet Union led Mao to officially part with Soviet doctrines in 1960. At the same time, border clashes with India and Mao's war in Tibet in 1959 increased China's international isolation. International crises fostered the rise of nationalism in China and encouraged the people to seek out their national heritage and assert their national identity in the field of representation. Traditional artistic forms, such as ink painting, were considered politically correct on the grounds that they were "essentially" Chinese. In addition, the disastrous Great Leap Forward and subsequent Great Famine resulted in internal agricultural and economic crises, which led to criticism of Mao. Occupied with these international and domestic crises, Mao temporarily retreated and loosened his control over intellectuals and artists.

The development of Chinese animation did not take place in a vacuum, but was always closely related to the international context. Before 1949, Chinese animated films were influenced by the West, as demonstrated by the Wan brothers' animated films. During the 1950s, Chinese animated films had a kinship with the Soviet Union. In the 1950s, the Shanghai Animation Film Studio sent young animators Wang Shuchen, He Yumen, and Hu Jinqing to the Soviet Union to learn animation techniques and discuss the possibility of a Sino-Soviet coproduction of the animated film *Nezha Makes Havoc in the Sea* (*Nezha naohai,* 1959).[13] At the same time, Soviet animated films, such as *The Fisherman and the Goldfish* (1950), *The Grandfather and His Grandson* (1950), *The Story of the Yellow Crane* (1950), and *Christmas Eve* (1951), were dubbed into Chinese and released in China.[14] Chinese animators even considered Soviet animated films such as *The Golden Antelope* (1954) the "animation bible" of the Shanghai Animation Film Studio and encouraged emulation of such films.[15] Soviet animated films at that time were renowned for realism in that they integrated Disney's verisimilitude style with Russian folk culture and the use of rotoscoping.

In many mainstream histories of Chinese animation, it is said that in 1956, China received its first international award for animation at the Venice International Children's Film Festival for *Why Is the Crow Black* (*Wuya weishenme shi hei de,* 1955), the first Chinese color cel-animated film. However, some international judges initially regarded it as a product of the Soviet Union rather than China. Extremely frustrated and ashamed, Chinese animators felt the need to establish a uniquely Chinese national style. At that time, the Sino-Soviet relationship was already deteriorating and nationalism was on the rise. Thus, the creation of a national style was not only an aesthetic issue, but also a political one. Having learned a lesson from the black crow incident, Te Wei, then president of the Shanghai Animation Film Studio, proposed to develop a national style in Chinese animated filmmaking. He and his colleagues began their artistic experimentation and produced the cel-animated film *The Conceited General* (*Jiaoao de jiangjun,* 1956), which is regarded as inaugurating the grand exploration of the national style in Chinese animation.[16]

Why Is the Crow Black was regarded as a negative example in history of Chinese animation due to its alleged Soviet connection. It was accused of imitating Soviet animated films such as *The Little Gray Neck* (1956) and widely demonized by the artistic community at that time. Qian Jiajun, director of *Why Is the Crow Black*, felt humiliated after he was told that the international jurors mistook the film for a Soviet production. Domestic criticism soon followed: *Why Is the Crow Black* was a failure because it imitated Soviet animation and was not characteristically Chinese.[17] The fate of this film illustrates Chinese animation's obsession with evincing a pure national style and identity. In this case, a national aesthetic style was closely associated with nationalism and political conformity. Decades have since passed and Cold War ideology has waned, but the stigma associated with this film persists today in Chinese articles, books, and websites. The historical record decries *Why Is the Crow Black* as the contaminated past and prehistory of Chinese animation that needed to be overcome. They celebrate *The Conceited General* for initiating "authentic" Chinese animation and for serving as a model for the future of Chinese animation. This argument about the rise of the national style in the late 1950s is a widely accepted "truth" in historical accounts of Chinese animation.

However, the background story behind the allegation about the Soviet connection in the reception of *Why Is the Crow Black* was probably fabricated. Such a fabrication could undermine the entire mainstream narrative of the birth of the national style. To begin with, the allegation was based on a rumor. It was said that the international jury members' remarks were reported to the Shanghai Animation Film Studio through the Chinese Embassy in Venice.[18] It is unprofessional and unlikely that a juror for such a prominent international film festival would comment publicly like this. Even if they spoke privately about the film, it is questionable that what they said would be overheard, transmitted to the Chinese Embassy in an official manner, and then communicated to the Shanghai Animation Film Studio with so much fanfare.

Sean Macdonald checked the database at the Historical Archive of the Foundation for the Venice Biennale and found that *Why Is the Crow Black* did not win an award at the Venice International Children's Film Festival. The Chinese film that did win an award was the puppet-animated *The Magic Brush* (*Shenbi*, 1955).[19] I emailed the Historical Archives of Contemporary Arts about this in early July 2017. Elena Oselladore, the person in charge, replied that *Why Is the Crow Black* was presented at the Venice International Children's Film Festival under the Italian title *Perché il corvo è nero* on August 16, 1956. From what they could find in their archive, the film did not win any award there. She also provided me with a document of the international jurors that year: M. Jean Bonoit-Lévy (France),

Professor Antonin M. Brousil (Czech), Dr. Luciano Emmer (Italy), and Mrs. Mary Field (Great Britain). I tried to locate these people, with the hope of conducting interviews with them about the alleged Soviet connection of the film, but they have passed away. These new findings, although they still need to be further verified, challenge the foundational myth of the mainstream narratives about the birth of the national style.

Additionally, *The Conceited General* is depicted in the national style discourse as a prompt response to the disgrace of *Why Is the Crow Black.* It was claimed as a triumph of an authentic Chinese film over a contaminated Soviet production. However, according to senior animator Pu Jiaxiang (1932–), director Te Wei and his colleagues started the production of *The Conceited General* in early 1955. When the preparation work was almost finished, Te Wei fell ill and the film's production was suspended. To fulfill the state's annual production quota (approximately thirty to forty films, each ten minutes long), the Shanghai Animation Film Studio ordered the team of *The Conceited General* to work on a new project titled *Why Is the Crow Black,* which was designed and directed by Qian Jiajun.

By the time *Why Is the Crow Black* was completed in 1955, Te Wei had recovered and resumed the production of *The Conceited General.* Because the film was based on the well-known Chinese expression "to sharpen the spear just before battle," or "making last-minute preparations that are too late" (*linzhen moqiang*), Te Wei proposed to "explore national style" in producing this film, but the slogan was not proposed specifically in response to the alleged national humiliation of *Why Is the Crow Black.* To highlight the Chineseness of *The Conceited General,* Peking opera masks and makeup were used to portray the human characters. *Why Is the Crow Black* was said to have received the international award from Venice in August 1956, and *The Conceited General* was almost completed by late 1956. It is obvious that the making of the film *The Conceited General* and Te Wei's advocacy for a national style had no obvious connection with the allegation that *Why Is the Crow Black* had Soviet connections.[20] The film *Why Is the Crow Black* was probably used by some as a straw man and a demonized Other to construct the grand narrative of the rise of the national style in the late 1950s.

In fact, both films were indebted to the Soviet Union for their animation techniques. Soviet animated films were renowned for their realism and rotoscoping, which created very smooth character movement on film. The two Chinese films adopted a realist approach for animating the movement of characters. When the project of *The Conceited General* began in early 1955, animators invited actors and actresses to make a live-action film to which they could refer. Their use of sophisticated, detailed, and realistic backgrounds was also reminiscent of Soviet style at the time. Both films drew on traditional Chinese stories, *Why Is the Crow Black* on the tale of *hanhao niao* (a bird too lazy to build its nest who ends up homeless and frozen in the winter) and *The Conceited General* on the proverb *linzhen moqiang*. The difference between them is that whereas *The Conceited General* features human characters that can easily be identified as Chinese (Peking opera masks, costumes, buildings), *Why Is the Crow Black* revolves around unclothed animals living in a forest, which cannot be easily represented or identified as Chinese. Precisely because it did not look specifically Chinese, the film was then charged with Soviet influence. The reliance on folklore for motif, the meticulous realist style, and the smooth movement all made some people suspect that Soviet influence was prominent in this film.

The on-screen and off-screen story of *Why Is the Crow Black* ironically became an allegory for the status of the film itself in history of Chinese animation. The plot is about a conceited crow who is very beautiful and has a sweet voice. She becomes overly proud of herself and distances herself from other birds. When the other birds are busy building their nests, the crow laughs at them and shows off her beauty and golden voice. When winter arrives, the crow has no place to stay. Suddenly she sees a fire and flies close to it to warm herself. The fire burns her and turns her colorful feathers black and her sweet voice husky. Off-screen, the film itself experiences the same downward trajectory. At first it was considered a beautiful film worthy of international recognition, but it catches fire from nowhere and turns into a denigrated "black crow" due to alleged Soviet influence. No matter how beautiful and great an animated film may be, it will become a black crow if it fails to represent properly the essence of (red) China. The black crow functions as a metaphor for marginalized animated films that do not conform to the national or nationalistic paradigm.[21]

Defending the national elements in *Why Is the Crow Black,* Pu Jiaxiang points out that the image of the crow is based on the phoenix, a legendary bird in Chinese tradition. The pink breast of the crow draws inspiration from *dudou,* a kind of traditional underwear for Chinese women and children. Also, the crow's dancing around the bonfire is based on the traditional bonfire dance of Yi ethnic minorities in China. The landscape stems from the "mountains and rivers" (*shanshui*) style and the trees depicted are the pine trees popular in traditional Chinese painting rather than the silver birch trees characteristic of Russia. The use of warm colors, which Chinese tradition considers auspicious, also adds to the Chineseness of this film.[22] Pu Jiaxiang thus forcefully argues that *Why Is the Crow Black* is an authentic Chinese animated film, rather than broaching the possibility and legitimacy of cross-cultural influence: even if *Why Is the Crow Black* was influenced by the Soviet style, what is the fuss about it? Pu's argument reflects a preoccupation in Chinese animation with a pure national style that marginalizes and even demonizes the international dimension, a view that continues to prevail. This view makes it shameful for Chinese animators to produce an inauthentic Chinese film "contaminated" by foreign influences.

In the Soviet Union in the 1940s and early 1950s, Soviet animators produced many animated films that did not necessarily represent Soviet identity. For example, China was the subject of *China in Flames* (1925), the first animated feature film in Soviet Union. *The Story of the Yellow Crane* (1950), *The Three Brothers of the Liu Family* (1953), and *The Royal Sword that Slaughters the Dragon* (1953) were all based on Chinese legends and portrayed Chinese characters in recognizable Chinese landscapes. *The Golden Antelope*, the so-called Soviet animation bible for Chinese animators, was based on an Indian legend and exuberant with Indian flavor. These films did not incite the Soviet people to accuse Soviet animation of being inauthentically Soviet. All this cultural borrowing and appropriation did not damage the identity or reputation of Soviet animation, but rather made it more Soviet. In addition, in terms of its realist style, Soviet animation was heavily influenced by Disney, despite the ideological barriers between the socialist and capitalist camps. The Disney influence did not undermine the credibility and national identity of Soviet animation, nor did it cause a fanfare among the Soviet people such as that of the black crow incident in China.

In 1962, Chinese animators produced the film *The Little Stream* (*Xiao xiliu*), which is about an anthropomorphic stream's journey to the sea. One year later, the Soviets released the animated film *Flow, Little Stream* (1963), which looked almost identical to the Chinese film. How do we explain such similarities when the two countries had parted ways? Were Soviet animators guilty of "imitating" a Chinese animated film?[23] Animation is an international art form, and great artistic works can absorb and indigenize other cultures, transcend national boundaries, and appeal to audiences around the world. Coevality and cross-referencing, rather than influence and indebtedness, exist in artistic and cultural production throughout the world.

The controversy over national identity and *Why Is the Crow Black* illustrates the overwhelming importance of the idea of a pure national style in Chinese animation. The film functioned as the demonized Other that Chinese animation needed to negate and overcome. Many mainstream narratives say that shortly after the black crow incident, animators turned to traditional art forms and legends and produced cel animation, papercutting animation, paperfolding animation, puppet animation, ink-painting animation, and other kinds of national style films, such as *The Conceited General* (cel), *Peacock Princess* (puppet, 1963), *Pigsy Eats Watermelon* (*Zhu Bajie chi xigua*, papercutting, 1958), *The Fishing Boy* (*Yutong*, papercutting, 1959), and *Uproar in Heaven* (cel).

In this context, Te Wei published in 1960 the influential essay "Creating National Animated Films" ("Chuangzao minzu de meishu dianying"), in which he denounced the practice of following a single (Soviet) model and encouraged animators to make a national style out of an originally foreign and modern medium. Te Wei stressed the importance of ink-painting animated films for developing a national style: "Ink-painting as well as papercutting animated films are the touchstone for our success in creating a national style animation."[24] It comes as no surprise that the Shanghai Animation Film Studio produced two ink-painting animated films, the pinnacle of national style according to Te Wei.[25] In addition to ink-painting animation, Chinese animators experimented with other traditional artistic forms such as papercutting, paperfolding, puppet, and Peking opera. The late 1950s and early 1960s witnessed the rise of the national style in Chinese animated filmmaking. Animation was not alone in this artistic movement; the national style was also advocated for live-action filmmaking and other artistic productions at the time.

Animated Sino-West Encounter: Recontextualizing the Rise of the Inter/National Style

If *The Conceited General* represents the beginning of the national style, *Why Is the Crow Black* marks the end of the international style (the Soviet style in particular) in conventional histories of Chinese animation. In light of the massive production of national style films since 1956, the national style seemed to have triumphed over the international style once and for all and dominated the animated scene in the late 1950s and early 1960s. There is no denying that the Soviet style lost its influence after the black crow incident, but the national style was not the sole guiding principle and did not have a monopoly on animated filmmaking activities at the time. As the national style was rising from the ashes of Soviet influence, another international style came into being, coexisted with, and competed with the national style. Of course, this iteration of the international style was no longer a product of Sino-Soviet cultural exchange, but rather an outcome of the imagined Sino-West encounter during the Cold War. In any case, the international style was not eliminated. It simply fell under the shadow of the national style.

As the biggest enemy of communist countries, the capitalist West and the United States in particular were regarded as absent from social reality and cinematic representation in socialist China due to presumed Cold War isolationism. Michael Berry points out that the practical reason for this cinematic absence was that Chinese filmmakers could not afford to hire American actors and travel abroad to shoot on location in the United States. The main reason, however, was ideological: America was regarded as China's principal enemy, and representations of capitalist America were unacceptable in socialist China.[26]

When live-action film failed to represent the Other, animation seized the opportunity to overrepresent the capitalist West on screen. Never in the history of Chinese animation have as many animated films directly portraying the capitalist West been produced as during the late 1950s and early 1960s. The era of the national style featuring the apparent Chinese past and artistic tradition across temporal borders ironically turned out to be the golden age of international-motif animation (*guoji ticai pian*) featuring the capitalist West across geopolitical and ideological borders. Although national style films conventionally turned to traditional Chinese literature, folklore, and legend for content and subject matter, international-motif films focused on current events unfolding in the capitalist West. National style films were supposed to use traditional Chinese art forms such as ink painting, papercutting, paperfolding, and Peking opera, whereas international-motif animated films deployed a more de-sinicized, international, and even modernist style to mark the exoticness and Otherness of the form. In other words, national style films were characterized by an emphasis on prescribed Chineseness, and international-motif films demonstrated a distance from, if not a complete erasure of, conventional Chineseness in terms of form and content. These were the two poles on the spectrum of Chinese animation during the late 1950s and early 1960s. Foregrounding the (co)existence of international-motif animation during these years expands the horizon of the national style, which is routinely treated as a timeless, static, and pure image isolated from the specific international and domestic contexts in which it emerged.

International-motif films became prominent as a new genre of animation during the Great Leap Forward. Animated filmmaking is labor-intensive and time-consuming, because animators need to make thousands of drawings, which are photographed and animated frame by frame. Accordingly, animation is often regarded by Chinese animators as unsuitable for portraying news and current events: hot events cool off before an animated film can be completed. Given the temporal requirements of animated filmmaking, Chinese animated films often revolve around folklore, legends, fables, and fairy tales, which are fantastic and timeless stories rooted in the past. To answer the needs of the Great Leap Forward, Chinese animators began making animated films more quickly so that they could respond to domestic and international events, the goal being to mobilize the masses to participate in political campaigns and indoctrinate them in Communist ideology and principles.

Catching up with the United Kingdom (*Gan Yingguo*, 1958) was made in response to the Communist Party's slogan of "catching up with the United Kingdom in fifteen years" and was seen to announce the arrival of the new genre.[27] These films adopted a minimalist style featuring simplified outlines and backgrounds to expedite their production and rapidly respond to political demands. They frequently drew on the visual style of cartoons, caricature, and posters, and used still pictures, photos, and even tables to save time. Passionate voiceover narration, slogans, and mood music reinforced explicit political messages. Unlike ordinary animated films that targeted children only, these films were aimed at both children and adults who could understand the sophisticated political messages.

The golden age of the national style during the late 1950s and early 1960s also witnessed a boom in international-motif animation. *Lobsters* (*Longxia,* 1959), a puppet-animated film, was about the persecution of communists in the United States. *Who Sings the Best* (*Shei chang de zuihao,* 1958) featured the miserable lives of two orphaned white children in the United States. *The Pigeon* (*Gezi,* 1960) revolved around American military bases in Italy. *The Little Guests of the Sun* (*Taiyang de xiao keren,* 1961) contrasted the dreary lives of American children with the happy lives of children in socialist countries. *The Dream of Gold* (*Huangjin meng,* 1963) delineated the greed and evils of capitalist countries in the West. The early 1960s in particular witnessed the rise of international-motif animation that revolved around American imperialism.[28] In these films, Western adults were demonized as evil imperialists, but children, whether white or black, were represented sympathetically and positively as victims of or rebels against capitalism and imperialism, yearning for the sunny made-in-China socialist paradise that welcomes all children around the world.

Set in the "decadent" capitalist West, these international-motif animated films demonstrated an international and even modernist style that was radically different from the national style. In terms of form, they adopted a more universal style that deemphasized national identity and downplayed Chineseness. Take, for instance, the cel-animated film *The Dream of Gold,* in which caricature was used to portray the protagonists without any ethnic markers. Its minimalist style had a blank background and several characters made of simple lines, reminiscent of UPA's (United Productions of America) modernist style during the 1950s. Fast motion and movement, squash and stretch techniques, and plasmatic and violent transformations of body forms between humans and nonhuman objects, which were characteristic of early Disney shorts and the Fleischers, were used prominently in this and other international-motif films.[29] In sharp contrast, national style films, best represented by ink-painting animation, demonstrated stillness and stiffness, with minimal or no plasmatic movement or change of body forms. Due to the national style's kinship with traditional Chinese arts, the films represent an idealized image of pure Chineseness. With Western landscapes, buildings, costumes, and characters, international-motif films conveyed an exoticness and Otherness that were intensified by their difference from the Chinese settings seen in national style films. Western music, such as jazz, reinforced exoticness.

International motif (content) and international style (form) work together to mark the distinctiveness of this new genre from the national style.

I use international style, which includes both form (nontraditional Chinese and more universal art forms) and content (international motif), to refer to this new genre of animation that differed from the national style. Chineseness was out of the question in international style films, because they demonstrated foreignness and exoticness (*yang*) in contrast to the seemingly indigenousness (*tu*) of national style films. Ironically, although national style films won international awards abroad at international film festivals, international style films targeted the domestic Chinese audience with their ideological messages. The cliché storylines about the evils of imperialism and the wretched life of ordinary people (especially children) living in the capitalist West made it obvious to audiences that the films were communist propaganda. In this sense, the international style films, no matter how international they are, are still Chinese and can even be regarded as an alternative national style at that time. I therefore reframe the late 1950s and early 1960s as the era of the inter/national style. The slash connects and separates the two styles at the same time, suggesting that the two styles overlapped even as they differed.

Unlike the collective criticism and abandonment of the Soviet style in the wake of the black crow incident, during the late 1950s and early 1960s, the international style (in relation to the West) was not the object of criticism or attack. Animators and critics welcomed the international style as a new genre of animation for portraying one particular subject matter. To better criticize the capitalist West, unusual and even transgressive artistic forms, such as the modernist style as opposed to the realism favored by the CCP, representational modes (plasmaticness and the transformation of body forms characteristic of early Disney shorts and the Fleischers), and forbidden content (the capitalist West) were tolerated, sanctioned, and approved.[30] Despite the lack of controversy similar to the black crow incident, competition between the national style and the international style took place on the discursive level. I now demonstrate how the two styles contended with each other, with the former triumphing over the latter, through a close reading of *The Fishing Boy*, a film long regarded as exemplary of the pure national style.

The Textual Exorcism of the International Style: Rereading *The Fishing Boy*

The Fishing Boy takes place in a northern fishing village on the eve of the Boxer Rebellion, a peasant uprising in 1900 that aimed to erase foreign influences in China during the last years of the Qing dynasty (1644–1912). When an old fisherman is at sea fishing on a stormy night, he retrieves a white jade fish pot decorated with the images of a fishing boy, a lotus flower, and a pair of golden fish. At night, the images on the pot come to life. When the boy on the pot goes fishing in the pot, the golden fish splashes drops of water onto the table that are magically transformed into luminous pearls. The next morning the old fisherman sells the pearls in the marketplace and shares the secret with other villagers. The foreign priest from a church passes by and overhears the secret. He conspires with a local Chinese magistrate, arrests the old fisherman, and tries to take the pot from him. In a fit of fury, the old fisherman smashes the pot on the ground so that it will not fall into the hands of foreign devils and their collaborators. The fishing boy comes back to life, creates havoc in the court, and throws the priest into the sea. The pieces of the broken pot gather themselves back together and the pot becomes whole again.

As a film commemorating the tenth anniversary of the founding of socialist China, *The Fishing Boy* has long been regarded as a canonical national style film. Its director Wan Guchan used the traditional Chinese art form of papercutting to animate the characters. In order to create an authentic image of a Chinese fisher boy, the animators went to Mount Putuo and drew inspiration from the "golden boy and jade girl" (*jintong yunü*), who appear in Buddhist stories as immortal children in-waiting at a divine mansion. Chinese animators went fishing with fishermen on Ant Island on stormy days. They also visited nursing homes and talked to fishermen in their seventies and eighties to learn about life in the "old" society.[31] The image of the fishing boy also was based on the *bunt takefu* style in Peking opera (*duanda wusheng*), in which a male actor playing a martial role wears shorts, carries weapons, and is exceptionally agile. The old fisherman in the animated film was inspired by the image of underground heroes (*jianghu haohan*) in the Chinese martial arts tradition. Chinese animators and critics lavished praise on the authentic Chineseness of the images of the fishing boy and old fisherman.

Rather than celebrating the film as pure national style, I reread it as an allegory of the contestation between the national style and the international style. It features two oppositional groups of characters in the film: the magic fishing boy and the old fisherman (positive) are pitted against the foreign priest and the local Chinese magistrate (negative). The positive characters are portrayed in accordance with principles of the national style, but the negative ones closer to the international style, which charges them with exoticness and Otherness. The priest is portrayed as a typical foreign devil, with an exaggerated aquiline nose and thick beard. The local magistrate is snobbish, slavish to the foreign priest, and does not resemble his Chinese compatriots. With his downward slanting eyebrows, extremely small eyes, well-trimmed mustache, and gaunt and distorted face, he resembles the Fu Manchu caricature of a Chinese man that appears in orientalist narratives. He is de-sinicized and exoticized. The conflict and fight between the two groups, which is conventionally interpreted from the perspective of nationalism and anti-imperialism, can be reread as a power struggle and rivalry between the national style and the international style.

The fishing boy is a figure of animation. In the beginning, he is a static image decorating the fishing pot. At night he comes to life and goes fishing, which requires that he be literally animated. The old fisherman and the foreign priest's fight over the fishing pot is not simply about the precious pearls it produces. It is also about the magical power of animation that brings static images to life. If the old fisherman represents the principle of the national style and the foreign priest the international style, their fight over the ownership of the pot and the fishing boy can be reread as an allegory of the power struggle between the national style and the international style for dominance in animation.

By the end of the film, the national style triumphs and the international style is exorcized. In rebutting the foreign priest's claim that the magic pot was made in his country, the old fisherman declares that the image of the fishing boy is an authentic Chinese boy and thus the pot must have been made in China. The old fisherman's justification is strikingly similar to the rationale about the national style. That is, the image should be a unique marker of national identity, and in line with this theory, the pot only could have been produced in China because it features an image of an authentic Chinese boy. Defending the pure Chineseness of the image, the fisherman's reasoning eliminates the possibility of cross-cultural imagination and representation. Thus, it is impossible for the West to produce an authentic image of a Chinese fishing boy. For the image to be authentic, it must be created by the Chinese in China.

The fisherman's argument, however, is challenged by the image of the foreign priest himself. If China can produce an image of a foreign priest, other countries might produce an image of a Chinese fishing boy. When the old fisherman smashes the pot, the fishing boy emerges from the broken pieces and returns to life. It is up to him to choose a side and his true master. He uses his fishing tackle to disrupt the court and punish the negative characters. He hooks the magistrate's cap and places it on the head of a dog, insulting the magistrate as being a dog official (*gouguan*). The fishing boy's act of throwing the priest into the sea is not simply a colonial patricide, it is also an artistic exorcism of the international style as embodied by the priest. Here animation assumes a life of its own and chooses the national style as its true master. It comes as no surprise because the fishing boy, a figure of animation, originates from a static image rooted in traditional Chinese art, just like the kinship between the national style in film and traditional Chinese art and culture.

The film's textual exorcism of the international style epitomizes institutional and official discourses that espoused the national style and suppressed the international. Of course, oppositional voices questioning the validity of the national style remained, but they were soon marginalized in mainstream animated filmmaking.[32] Although attacks on the international style never reached the level of the black crow incident, there was no collective or official advocacy for it either. The international style was tolerated, slighted, and ignored, yet it coexisted with the national style as an undercurrent that interrupted its monopoly and dominance.

Having done so synchronically, I now examine the national style diachronically to analyze its unstable and changing definition over time. I use the first two ink-painting animated films as a case study because ink-painting animation was one of the highest achievements of the national style in the early 1960s. First, however, background information about ink-painting animation and its unique aesthetic contribution to the national style is in order.

Aesthetics of Absence: Theorizing Chinese Ink-Painting Animation

The most common way to make animated films is "single line and flat color" (*danxian pingtu*) in cel animation, which allows for separate pictures to be matched perfectly with each other by controlling outlines and colors. Animators usually draw images with slight variations on transparent celluloid. The transparency of cels makes it easier for animators to match the outlines on different cels to create smooth movement. Animators also can draw the background on a separate cel and superimpose other cels onto it, so the background on every single cel does not have to be redrawn. This method creates an exceedingly flat and well-controlled visual effect, which contrasts dramatically with ink-painting animation.

Unlike traditional cel animation, ink-painting animated film features a visual style based on what I call the aesthetics of absence. This characterization relates to the fact that ink-painting animated film does not have the typical single-line-and-flat-color form, due to the ink wash or splashing, graded ink tonalities, and ink diffusion. Ink-painting animation usually adopts a minimalist style and significant use of empty space (*liubai*), which therefore becomes the visual focus. This technique of empty space differs from traditional Western oil painting that relies "presence" that builds up layers of oil on the canvas. Chinese animators and intellectuals thus use ink-painting animation to specify Chinese identity in film, an art form typically recognized as imported from the West.

Aesthetics of absence refers not only to formal characteristics, but also to themes and motifs of representative works. The concept of absence defines the origin of Chinese ink-painting animation. The first ink-painting animated film in history, *Little Tadpoles Look for Mama*, drew its inspiration from a well-known

Qi Baishi (1864–1957) ink painting called *Frogs Croaking out of a Spring for Ten Miles* (*Wa sheng shili chu shanquan*), which revolves around the theme of absence and negative inference (see figure 3.1). At a dinner, the renowned author Lao She asked Qi Baishi whether he could paint something that was invisible in the painting but whose presence could still be perceived. Qi Baishi thought for three days and finally worked out this painting, which was mounted as a hanging scroll and done entirely in ink monochrome. A mountain spring is flanked by rocks, and tadpoles are positioned on the surface of water. The exaggerated size of the tadpoles increases their prominence. Given their tadpole state, this prominence implies the proximity of parent frogs. Thus, the parent frogs may be absent from the painting, but they are suggested by the tadpoles swimming downstream toward the viewer.

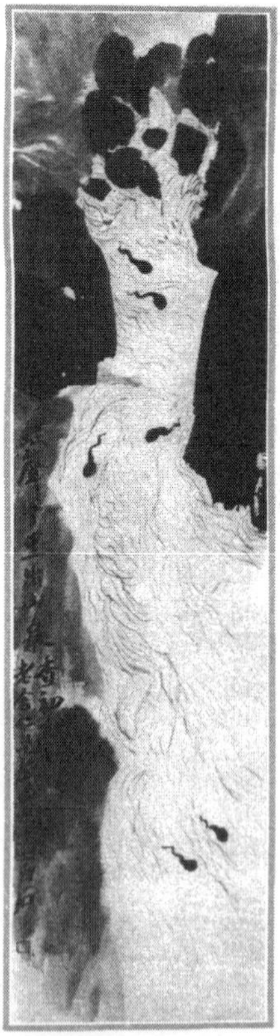

Figure 3.1. Absent frogs in *Frogs Croaking out of a Spring for Ten Miles*, Qi Baishi, 1951.

Little Tadpoles Look for Mama highlights the theme of absent parent frogs in featuring a group of newborn tadpoles who are looking for their absent mother. During their journey, they make friends with chickens and shrimp and mistakenly call the animals "mother." The mother frog's absence triggers the movement of narration and animation. When the tadpoles first meet a golden fish and take her as their mother, the movement of narration and animation almost stops. Because the mother frog is still absent, however, the tadpoles continue their journey and the narration and animation continue their movement. These repeated cycles of stop-motion allow the tadpoles to find their mother, the ultimate source of power that bestows them with the life-anima demonstrated by their movement. Only after the tadpoles do find her does the movement of narration and animation draw to a close.

Thus the mother frog is central despite her absence. That she is absent opens up the space of signification, because the tadpoles are searching not only for their physical mother but also for the meaning of the word "frog," that is, who they are. After the shrimp tells them that their mother has big eyes and then they see a golden fish, they think it is their mother. The fish explains that their mother has a white belly. The tadpoles then meet a crab with a white belly and again think they have found their mother. After the crab tells them that their mother has four legs, the tadpoles turn to a turtle and call it mother, and the story repeats itself. The movement of the tadpoles is therefore a chain of signification in which the meaning of the absent frog is constantly differed and deferred. This chain of iterative difference and deferment leads the tadpoles finally to construct the meaning of the word "frog."

Four ink-painting animated films were made and each one revolves around the theme of absence and loss. The second, *The Herd Boy's Flute,* is about a herd boy's anxiety about loss, which his dream about losing his beloved water buffalo makes evident. The third, *The Deer Bell* (*Lu ling,* 1982), recounts how a girl loses a fawn. A girl living in the forest rescues a fawn that is escaping from an animal predator. They become friends and spend time together. The girl hangs a bell around the fawn's neck so she knows where it is. In the end, she suffers a painful loss when the fawn returns to its parents. The fourth film, *Feelings of Mountain and River* (*Shanshui qing,* 1988), involve a boy's loss of his music teacher when the master chooses to depart from the boy's world.

Reinforcing the theme of absence and loss is the erasure of speech and dialogue in ink-painting animated film. In typical cel-animated films at that time, dialogue and speech are an integral part of the work. Music also features prominently to advance the narrative. In ink-painting animated film, however, absence of speech is the norm. In these four films, no characters in the diegesis or film's story speak. *Little Tadpoles Look for Mama* has a female voiceover but its characters do not speak.[33] Given the characters' silence, music and musical sounds play a pivotal role in these films: flute music in *The Herd Boy's Flute,* the bell in *Deer Bell,* and zither music in *Feelings of Mountain and River.* Music provides clues for tracing the absent love object. In Qi Baishi's *Frogs Croaking out of a Spring for Ten Miles,* from which *Little Tadpoles Look for Mama* originates, it is also the croaking of the frogs, inaudible but evoked by the painting, that provides traces of frogs who are under the water and hence unseen.

Although the method of ink painting by handheld brush is widely known, the actual technique of ink-painting animation has been a national secret since then. Relying on spontaneous ink wash or splashing, graded ink tonalities, and ink diffusion on absorbent mulberry paper, Chinese ink paintings are difficult to control and almost impossible to reproduce. This raises the question of how to reproduce the saturation of ink on film without outlines and flat color. According to Mochinaga Tadahito's speculation, the secret of Chinese ink-painting animation might be in the use of photography, for which China's first animation camerawoman Duan Xiaoxuan was responsible.[34] Animators still needed pencils and cels to draw several duplicates of the object to be animated, probably with the help of stencils to control the edges. Each duplicate would have had different ink gradations. The animation photographer Duan Xiaoxuan and her colleagues first shot these pictures one by one, and then superimposed them to create the effect of ink diffusion. They also might have adjusted the lens to take out-of-focus photos, which, if properly superimposed with in-focus photos, would resemble the effect of ink diffusion. Finding the best combination of cels and the most appropriate photographic techniques would have been painstaking work that required considerable patience. The photographers also must have an artistic sense of pictorial qualities and composition. Usually only a still background such as a landscape was an authentic ink painting unmediated by photography, because animators superimposed it onto other cels and did not need to animate it.

It is said that the process of producing an ink-painting animated film was so complex and time-consuming that in the same amount of time animators could have produced four to five single-line-and-flat-color works of the same length. In addition to the time required, ink-painting animated films are costly. Few animators and studios today are interested in making them because they are no longer profitable. Ink-painting animation has become nearly extinct as an art form in China. The current fervor for using this form to construct a distinct national identity, such as the use of computer ink-painting animation in the China Pavilion of the Shanghai Expo in 2010, brought it to the center of attention. However, the computer-generated hypervisibility of ink-painting animation belies the very absence of this form, much like the role of the panda, an animal threatened with extinction, in promoting Chinese identity on the global stage.

The fourth ink-painting animated film, *Feelings of Mountain and River*, marked the final splendor of this form. With a touch of sadness, this film takes an introspective look into the fate of ink-painting animation. In the film, a retired musician travels through mountains and along rivers. When he falls sick, a young boy who operates a ferry boat takes care of him. During his recovery, the musician teaches the boy how to play the zither. When the old man departs, he gives his treasured zither to the boy, hoping that his disciple will pass on his music. The film expresses the hope of its director Te Wei and his colleagues that the art of ink-painting animation will be handed down from generation to generation, especially as the masters were aging out of the artistic scene. No ink-painting animated films followed *Feelings of Mountain and River*, however.[35] The theme of absence and loss that pervaded ink-painting animated film became the fate of the form itself.

From Ink Painting to Ink-Painting Animation

Given its political significance at a time of national and international crises, the production of ink-painting animated films was supported by the government when leaders sympathized with traditional Chinese arts and did not subscribe to the radical Yan'an-Soviet model. At the end of 1959, the Shanghai Animation Film Studio, following the example of many art exhibitions at that time, held its

"Exhibition of Chinese Animated films" in Beijing, Shanghai, and other major cities. On January 31, 1960, Chen Yi (1901–1972), then foreign minister, visited the exhibition and extended his congratulations on behalf of the central government and State Council. He expressed his hope for this artistic form and exclaimed, "It would be great if you could animate Qi Baishi's ink paintings!"[36] These words encouraged Chinese animators to begin their exploration. When Chen Yi later learned that the Shanghai Animation Film Studio had made several experimental ink-painting animation segments, he marveled at its success and encouraged animators to keep up the good work. Chen Yi assured them, "You should continue your experiment. I will use the resources of the whole country to support you."[37] Considering Chen Yi's significant role in political and artistic circles, his interest was important in ensuring government support for ink-painting animated film at that time.

Supported by Chen Yi and the socialist state, animators decided, for political and artistic reasons, to animate the ink paintings of Qi Baishi. Qi Baishi was the only traditional ink-painting artist to be protected and lionized by the Communist Party. In 1953, the Party had awarded him the honorary title Artist of the People. The same year, he became chairman of the Chinese Artists Association. Like Mao, Qi Baishi grew up in Hunan province, born into a poor peasant family and later working as a carpenter. His lower-class background protected him to some extent in socialist China. In his art, he did not focus on the sublime and monumental objects such as mountains, rivers, cliffs, and pines that are prominent in traditional ink paintings. Instead, he modeled his paintings on daily objects in rural life, such as shrimp, crabs, and mice. By sketching from life, Qi Baishi's paintings coincidentally echoed the Party's call for reforming traditional ink painting. Given Qi Baishi's class, artistic, and political status, it is no surprise that animators, encouraged by Chen Yi, decided to model *Little Tadpoles Look for Mama* on his paintings right after Qi's death in 1957.

Several years later, riding on the success of *Little Tadpoles Look for Mama*, Chinese animators decided to animate the paintings of Li Keran (1907–1989). A student of Qi Baishi, Li Keran was from the countryside of Jiangsu province. He began his career by studying Western oil painting under Liu Haisu (1896–1994), a well-known painter, retreating to the wartime capital Chongqing during the war, where he began to paint herd boys and water buffalo. After 1949, he launched his career by teaching at the Central Academy of Fine Arts, where he began to learn ink painting from Qi Baishi and Huang Binhong. During the Anti-Rightist Campaign against Jiang Feng, Li Keran testified against him, having sided with Cai Ruohong. Also, like Qi Baishi's paintings, Li Keran's herd boy paintings were influenced by his observations of rural life, thus providing a perfect example of the CCP's call for "sketching from life." Li Keran consciously adapted his paintings to the Party's message. In echoing the policy, Li Keran maintained that "entering life deeply [*shenru shenghuo*] is the prerequisite for reforming *guohua*."[38]

More important, Li Keran consciously aligned his ink paintings with contemporary thought in order to make them more politically correct. In a poem titled "Self-Mockery" ("Zichao"), Lu Xun expresses his care and devotion for China's children: "head bowed, like a willing ox I serve the children" (*fushou gan wei ruzi niu*). In his Yan'an Talks, Mao used Lu Xun's expression of "willing ox that serves the children" (*ruzi niu*) to urge artists and writers to serve the masses. Echoing Mao, Guo Moruo wrote a poem titled "Ode to the Water Buffalo" ("Shuiniu zan") the same year. While using the water buffalo as subject matter for his paintings during his stay in Chongqing in 1941, Li Keran inscribed the lines of Guo Moruo's ode in his paintings. He also composed poems in praise of the water buffalo and included those poems in his paintings.

Landscape is an indispensable element in Li Keran's water buffalo paintings. Landscape was regarded as one of the Four Olds (*sijiu,* which are Old Customs, Old Culture, Old Habits, and Old Ideas) and was severely criticized during the period of popularization. Li Keran defended his landscape paintings within the framework of national identity: "What does landscape [*shanshui*] mean? It means territory [*jiangshan*], the territory of our motherland . . . We paint landscape to memorialize the land of our motherland. This is why landscape painting has nationalistic meanings."[39] It is no surprise that after the death of Qi Baishi, Li Keran's paintings, partly for their nationalistic sentiment, became the prototype of *The Herd Boy's Flute,* the second ink-painting animated film in China.

Despite a revival of traditional art in the early 1960s in response to the relative relaxation of cultural control, artists were still restricted in their ability to practice it because it was simultaneously revived, reviled, and reformed. Hence, Zhou Yang, an influential writer and Communist leader of writers and artists explains:

> We attach much importance to tradition, but this does not mean that we will go back to ancient times . . . We should inherit and develop our tradition on the basis of a new ideology. Our literature and art should inculcate communism, not feudal or bourgeois thought in our people.[40]

Zhou Yang encouraged artists to adopt new content while adhering to national or traditional forms. Whereas artistic forms "express the style and vigor of the nation," content "expresses the people and thoughts of the new age."[41] In the early 1950s, revolution and class struggle were the new content. Although the cultural thaw of the early 1960s diminished it politically, the Communist Party continued to advocate for political ideals. Furthermore, the Party's split with the Soviet Union did not mean that it abandoned realism. Against pure expressionism and abstraction, it encouraged realism in ink painting, urging artists to imitate real life by adopting the Western technique of "sketching from life." In his discussion of Qi Baishi, for instance, Cai Ruohong opposed the practice of slavishly imitating ancient masters.[42] At the same time, he also denounced the practice of pure and abstract creation detached from real life, such as the literati paintings that inherited the style of Ming loyalists and the Eight Eccentric Painters of Yangzhou. Qi Baishi's paintings, which were based on his observation of daily life, provided a middle ground between the two extremes. Qi Baishi's artistic motto was "between representational and nonrepresentational." Qi Baishi believed that if painting is too representational, it degenerates into mere artifice and, if it is too nonrepresentational, it threatens to deceive the entire world.[43] In glorifying Qi Baishi's propensity for real life, Zhou Yang said that Qi Baishi's paintings were based on realism:

> Qi Baishi is an artist of the people. . . . He is from the people and has "flesh and blood" ties with the people. He has absorbed the essence of folk art. It is because he is from the people that his painting and his artistic principles are based on realism.[44]

The first two ink-painting animated films, *Little Tadpoles Look for Mama* and *The Herd Boy's Flute,* were created in a sociohistorical context of revival of traditional artistic form, construction of national identity, and shifting international and domestic dynamics. This context gave rise to national style, but also limited its development. I now explore the historical contingencies of national style by examining the rise and fall of the two ink-painting animated films in the early 1960s. This discussion substantiates my point that the concepts of national style and national identity are not stable and immutable categories, but are fluid, changing, and historically contingent, especially during the tumultuous decades of socialist China.

Intended Audience: From Children to Adults

The intended audience for animated films was usually children. Immediately after the People's Republic of China was founded in 1949, the Cultural Bureau presented the policy that "animated films should serve children" and "reflect children's life."[45] Animated films were thus regarded as children's films, which were closely related to children's literature, music, art, and drama. Three types of animated films served children and reflected children's life at that time. The first, narrative realism, features children protagonists and truthfully depicts their lives. *Heroic Little Sisters of the Grassland* (*Caoyuan yingxiong xiao jiemei,* 1965), for example, drew on the true story of two Mongolian girls who almost lost their lives trying to save their commune's sheep in 1964. The second typecasts children as protagonists, but also incorporates fantastic elements. In *Ginseng Baby* (*Renshen wawa,* 1961), a ginseng root transforms into a baby and helps a peasant boy in his fight against a landlord. The third type includes fairy tales featuring anthropomorphic animals. In *Little Carp Jump over Dragon Gate* (*Xiao liyu tiao longmen,* 1958), for example, little carp speak and behave like humans. Their grandmother tells them a legend about carp that can jump over dragon gate to become dragons. After hearing it, the little carp are determined to find the dragon gate. They swim upstream and happily jump over what appears to be the gate, but actually turns out to be Dragon Gate Dam (Longmen shuiku), which was built across the Caohe in Hebei province during the Great Leap Forward.

During the Maoist era, the CCP often changed its policies toward animated films. When the Yan'an-Soviet trend dominated the cultural scene during the period of popularization, only the first two film genres survived—narrative realism and child protagonist. When political control tightened with the rise of ultra-leftism, only narrative realism survived. For example, animated films produced from 1964 to 1976 mostly belonged to the narrative realism genre, as I argue in chapter 4.

The third type, fairy tales relying on anthropomorphism, was the most controversial. For many years, few if any dared to state an opinion. In 1964, the Cultural Bureau acknowledged it, but quickly denounced and severely criticized it during the period of popularization.[46] The first and sometimes second type of animation showcased the CCP's general preference for human action and real life over animals and fantasy. This resonates with Arnold Chang's argument that during the period of popularization, figure painting dominated and landscape and bird-and-flower painting appeared only rarely. In addition, the Party preferred animated films in the current political context. Essentially, all three types were influenced by the political themes of the time in which they were produced: the spirit of self-sacrifice and heroism of *Heroic Little Sisters of the Grassland,* class struggle with landlords in *Ginseng Baby,* and China's modernization during the Great Leap Forward in *Little Carp Jump over Dragon Gate.* This served the CCP's interest in not only educating children but also propagating communist ideology.

Little Tadpoles Look for Mama, adapted from a children's fairy tale written by Fang Huizhen and Sheng Lude, belonged to the third film type. In contrast, *The Herd Boy's Flute* appealed to sophisticated adults. In the early 1960s, filmmakers became more concerned with the elevation of standards and extending the range of audiences beyond workers, peasants, and soldiers. Although the norm for animated films was serving children and reflecting their lives, in the relatively relaxed environment of the early 1960s animators began to make animated films for more sophisticated audiences. As animators experimented with a greater variety of artistic forms, such as ink-painting and papercutting animation, their audience gradually diversified.[47] In an essay in 1960, Te Wei wrote, "With the multiplication of forms and subject matter, we widened our audience. Animated film is not only an important instrument to educate our children and bring up communist successors, but also a popular medium loved by both adults and children."[48] In 1984, he reiterated this idea and emphasized the importance of the intended audience:

> Animated films mainly serve children, but we can still make a few films especially for adults. . . . Before making an animated film, we should first decide whether we mainly target children, adults, or both. Otherwise, our films will not be appropriate for both children and adults. Children cannot understand it, and adults will find it too boring.[49]

Te Wei later admitted that *The Herd Boy's Flute* targeted adults rather than children: "Animated films mainly serve children, but we can also make a few animated films especially for adults. In the past we made *The Herd Boy's Flute* and *The Dream of Gold,* but children cannot understand them. They were designed for adults."[50] *The Herd Boy's Flute* was fated to suffer harsher censorship than films targeting children. With an adult audience in mind, it was artistically experimental and even transgressive by the standards of the early 1960s, factors that contributed to its ban in 1964.

Subject Matter: From Politicized Tadpoles to Idealized Herd Boy

The period of elevation of standards and revival of traditional art (1958–1965) may have ended earlier than 1965. Arnold Chang himself is aware of the problem of periodization and points out that he can only loosely categorize the years between 1958 and 1965 as the period of elevation of standards: "it is impossible, of course, to pinpoint, to the precise year, the terminal dates of any given period."[51] Similarly, Paul Clark argues that the categorization of 1966 to 1976 as the Cultural Revolution is based on a political perspective. Clark contends that the culture of the Cultural Revolution actually began in 1964, during the Four Clean-Ups Campaign (Siqing yundong) related to Shanghai films. This campaign targeted leaders in the film industry, Xia Yan and Chen Huangmei, and began with the criticism of several Shanghai films such as *Early Spring in February* (*Zaochun eryue*, 1963). Produced during the elevation of standards period, the films faced difficulties after ideological control tightened during the years of popularization.

In 1964 animation's national style also began a downturn. The CCP fully supported *Little Tadpoles Look for Mama.* By the time it was ready for release in 1960, Beijing had severed ties with Moscow and nationalism was on the rise. Given its so-called national style, *Little Tadpoles Look for Mama* was released in conjunction with the eleventh annual celebration of National Day in Shanghai.

By the time *The Herd Boy's Flute* was released in 1964, national style as represented by the artistic form of ink painting had become the denigrated Other. Shanghai Animation Film Studio had begun production on *The Herd Boy's Flute* in 1961, and thus the film's design was associated with the idea of elevation of standards prominent at that time. By 1964, the Cultural Revolution had begun changing the political circumstances. Thus *The Herd Boy's Flute* faced a new definition of national style and national identity when it was released. Artistic form was no longer the principal constituent, but rather political subject matter and revolutionary action.[52] Therefore, the discussion that follows centers on the subject matter differences between *Little Tadpoles Look for Mama* and *The Herd Boy's Flute.*

Little Tadpoles Look for Mama is a fairy tale about a group of tadpoles looking for their mother and is meant to appeal to children. *The Herd Boy's Flute* targets an adult audience with beautiful flute music played by the boy.[53] While herding his water buffalo, the boy falls asleep and dreams that he loses it. He asks a fisherman, a woodcutter, and other herd boys if they know its whereabouts. It turns out that the sound of a waterfall leads his buffalo astray. Despite the boy's efforts to coax it to return, the water buffalo refuses. The boy grows frustrated and rests in a bamboo grove. Suddenly he hears an exquisite sound coming from a bamboo. He finds the bamboo and makes a flute from it. His flute playing attracts all the animals in the forest. At this moment, the herd boy wakes up. He then plays his flute, and his water buffalo returns to him. He rides the buffalo home, all the while playing his flute. The film is so subtle that children may not understand its nuances. For example, when the herd boy falls asleep, two fallen leaves are transformed into butterflies, alluding to Zhuangzi's dream of becoming a butterfly.[54] Accordingly, *The Herd Boy's Flute* does not belong to any of the three recognized types of animated films for children. With its dreamlike qualities, it belongs to what might be called the fourth type, which further deviates from those types favored by the CCP.

Subject matter played a vital role in ink-painting animated film. Given the specificity of the artistic form, ink-painting animated films called for subject matter different from that of cel-animated films. As veteran female animator Tang Cheng explains,

> Because of the limitations of the form, many subjects are not suitable for ink-painting animated films. To make an ink-painting animated film, we need good subject matter, which is very difficult to obtain, because it calls

for the kind of characters, background, and atmosphere that fit in well with ink paintings.[55]

Accordingly, the subject matter of ink-painting animated films should draw on the themes of ink paintings. Both *Little Tadpoles Look for Mama* and *The Herd Boy's Flute* were successful in choosing subjects suitable for ink painting. How they differed was in the way they related their subject matter to their times. *Little Tadpoles Look for Mama* was grounded in the political reality of the 1960s, and the idealized world of *The Herd Boy's Flute* transcended its contemporary political context.

At first sight, *Little Tadpoles Look for Mama* depicts a fairytale world and makes no political references. Animators first present a lotus pond and then pan the camera from left to right so that spectators can view the full picture, as if viewing a handscroll (from right to left) from an opposite direction. They create a minimalist background with one or two weeds, daffodils, lotus leaves, and undulating lines to suggest the water. Throughout the film, the visual effect of ink painting is prominent, especially compared with animated films made following the principle of a single line and flat color. For example, although animators depict all the tadpoles with dabs of ink, they use gradation of ink tonality within each tadpole, making the tail lighter than the head. Toward the end of each tadpole's tail, the ink tonality becomes lighter, as if melding into the water. One of the tadpoles is red, likely signifying the leader.

Nevertheless, the film's ending accords with the political trend in the early 1960s. When the little tadpoles find their mother and become frogs, the female voiceover gives the children a lesson: "Little frogs are ambitious. They are determined to eat all harmful insects to protect our agricultural plants." This didactic message is propaganda, because agricultural plants became especially important during the Great Famine. Beginning in 1955, animals were politicized and classified as friends or enemies. From 1958 to 1962, Mao launched the Four Pests Campaign to exterminate rats, mosquitoes, flies, and sparrows. Rats and sparrows were included because they ate grain seeds and disrupted agriculture.[56] On the other hand, the campaign regarded other animals as friends and encouraged people to protect them. The frog is a good animal. Science education films (*kejiaopian*) at the time advocated the protection of frogs and tadpoles to safeguard agricultural production.

Furthermore, the female voiceover conveys political authority. Film scholars point out that the disembodied voiceover symbolizes truth, power, and knowledge. According to Mary Ann Doane, "It is precisely because the voice is not localizable, because it cannot be yoked to a body, that it is capable of interpreting the image, producing its truth."[57] In documentary films, the voiceover is usually male, symbolizing the possession of knowledge and the unchallenged authority of interpretation. *Little Tadpoles Look for Mama* adopts a female voiceover because the film is for children, and the female voiceover is associated with a mother or teacher figure who tells (bedtime) stories to children. In this case, the film's female voiceover does not dilute its authority. On the contrary, its authority is reinforced, because the voice is that of Zhang Ruifang, a famous actress who played the revolutionary heroine in live-action feature films. The narrator's gender identity was thus subordinate to her political identity. The female voiceover makes the film less abstract and easier for children to understand. At the same time, the familiar, affirmative, enthusiastic, and high-pitched female voiceover immediately reminded the audience of the popular revolutionary films, thus emphasizing revolutionary sentiments otherwise absent in this film.

Similar to *Little Tadpoles Look for Mama, The Herd Boy's Flute* follows the hand scroll tradition with the camera's panning to suggest the unfolding of the background—a stream flanked by willow trees. All the background frames of the film were drawn by Fang Jizhong, a well-known painter from the Chang'an School of Painting, which was active during the late 1950s and early 1960s. The herd boy is cel-animated with the regular method of single line and flat color, and the water buffalo is made with the ink-painting animation method. Depicted in ink monochrome, the buffalo's horns are indicated by two boldly curved lines that converge to form a crescent, bold vertical lines indicating the horn's grooves. The water buffalo's body displays the effects of ink diffusion, and the area around its mouth and eyes is defined by lighter ink tonality. The depiction of the water buffalo generally follows Li Keran's style (see figures 3.2 and 3.3). However, the more spontaneous appearance of Li Keran's water buffalo is attributable to his working on absorbent mulberry paper with ink, whereas animators used pencils, cels, and photography to create the effect of diffusion.

Unlike *Little Tadpoles Look for Mama, The Herd Boy's Flute* has no voiceover, thus focusing attention on pictorial quality. Whereas *Little Tadpoles Look for Mama* takes place in the enclosed space of the pond, *The Herd Boy's Flute* crosses an expanse of space that includes willow trees, streams, mountains, waterfalls, forests, and bamboo groves. *Little Tadpoles Look for Mama* adopts a linear temporality with an ending that suggests narrative closure. *The Herd Boy's Flute* disrupts such linearity by juxtaposing dream and reality, and draws attention to the fluidity of narration. In terms of compositional complexity, *The Herd Boy's Flute* is more sophisticated than *Little Tadpoles Look for Mama* because it incorporates landscape, bird-and-flower painting, and figures, whereas *Little Tadpoles Look for Mama* features only animals and plants.

Although figure painting during the Mao era was likely to have obvious political connotations related to human action, the political associations of landscape and bird-and-flower paintings were subtler. In an influential article published in

Figure 3.2. A still of boy with flute from *The Herd Boy's Flute,* 1963.

Figure 3.3. Li Keran's painting of water buffalo and herd boys.

1960, Chen Yude contended that landscape and bird-and-flower paintings did not simply represent the objective world, but also suggested the painters' political position. He argued that landscape and bird-and-flower paintings of proletarian artists usually encompassed revolutionary optimism and expressed the artists' love for their motherland and the people. Qi Baishi's paintings, which were based on real life, were such an example. In contrast, bourgeois landscape and bird-and-flower paintings were usually associated with escapism, decadence, and pessimism, and contained a reactionary message.[58] *Little Tadpoles Look for Mama* converged with Chen Yude's argument in a subtle way. Although *The Herd Boy's Flute* had a human character and therefore was more likely to have political connotations than *Little Tadpoles Look for Mama,* it nonetheless deviated from Chen Yude's contention by depicting a transcendental world reminiscent of traditional ox-herding paintings that had no real connection with the political realities of the mid-1960s.

Scarlett Ju-yu Jang dates the beginning of oxen as a subject for painting to Han Huang (723–787) and other Tang dynasty painters. During that time, herd boys were not represented because the emphasis was on form-likeness of animals. In the Song dynasty (960–1279), depictions of ox-herding and a herd boy became popular. Scholar officials began to project their ideal of Confucian eremitism onto ox-herding paintings and to express their desire for "turning away from big cities and from involvement in governmental affairs to live in the mountains or in the countryside."[59] As Richard Barnhart and Catherine Barnhart contend, "From the late eleventh century on, buffalo herd boys exemplify for many scholars and officials the simple life far away from ceremony, ritual, and social obligation."[60] For example, Song dynasty scholar-official Cui Yan (1057–1126) wrote a poem to accompany an ox-herding painting that expresses his longing for a pastoral life:

> High position and fame are unreal after all; where am I to settle for the rest of my life? While the green grass is still long, I am going to herd my oxen and sheep . . . Playing a flute on the back of an ox in the northern wind, I am a hale old man who does not care about worldly affairs.[61]

These ancient ox-herding paintings also influenced Li Keran, who named some of his paintings after them. His *Five Oxen* (*Wuniu tu*) is named after Han Huang's *Five Oxen,* and his *Ox-Herding in the Four Seasons* (*Siji muniu tu*) is named after Yan Ciping's *Ox-Herding in the Four Seasons.* The style and sentiments of ancient ox-herding paintings reappeared in Li Keran's paintings and the ink-painting animated film *The Herd Boy's Flute.*

Before I continue discussing animators' appropriation of ancient paintings to project national identity in *The Herd Boy's Flute,* I need to point out that the ancientness and Chineseness of this film is constructed, that the film is modern and even Western. For instance, it did not wholly follow the method of ink-painting animation, because the herd boy was cel-animated with modern technology. In addition, the film's music combined Chinese flute music with Western orchestra. National style was thus a blend and did not emerge from cultural purity. This film's relation to ancient ox-herding paintings further demonstrates how animators appropriated traditional art from the past to construct national style in the present, an aesthetic practice that was replete with political stakes during the 1960s.

In terms of composition and pictorial qualities, the depiction of the herd boy and his water buffalo in each frame is reminiscent of ox-herding paintings by court artists in the Song dynasty. According to *Xuanhe Painting Catalogue* (*Xuanhe huapu*), these ox-herding paintings have six themes: herd boy playing a flute, ox drinking water, ox bathing and herd boy returning home from ox-herding, oxen fighting, ox and calf, and ox crossing river. *The Herd Boy's Flute* includes all except oxen fighting and ox and calf.

In addition, the composition of the frame is similar to that of ancient ox-herding paintings. Comparing one frame of *The Herd Boy's Flute* with Li Di's *Buffaloes and Herd Boys in Rainstorm*, it appears that the trees in the background occupy half of the frame and form a diagonal across it with the herd boys positioned on that diagonal (see figures 3.4 and 3.5). In both frames, the herd boy and water buffalo are positioned near the bottom of the frame and move horizontally across it. The proportions of the background, herd boy, and water buffalo are similar. In both frames, neither the figures nor the background is dominant. With these balanced proportions, animators and the ancient artist Li Di create a bucolic image in which humans and nature coexist in balance and harmony.

Figure 3.4. Full-frame still of boy, buffalo, and trees from *The Herd Boy's Flute,* 1963.

Figure 3.5. *Buffaloes and Herd Boys in Rainstorm* (hanging scroll; ink and color on silk), by Li Di (ca. 1163–1225).

Furthermore, Song dynasty ox-herding paintings attached much importance to landscape. During the Northern Song dynasty, artists portrayed a "whole world of ox-herding" by depicting a holistic landscape background, whereas those in the Southern Song dynasty represented "small corners of the world in which the motifs of ox-herding are the focus of the composition."[62] Cinematography integrates the two types in *The Herd Boy's Flute*. In the beginning of the film, the camera pans from left to right to show a panorama of the landscape with a stream flanked by willow trees.[63] The camera then zooms in and focuses on a corner of the stream. Next it cuts to a closer view of the herd boy and his water buffalo with a dissolve. The camera continues to cut in more closely until viewers finally have a close-up of the water buffalo and herd boy. Through cinematography, viewers move from "the whole world" to a "smaller corner" of ox-herding paintings.

The Herd Boy's Flute and ancient ox-herding paintings also share lyrical and atmospheric qualities. In *The Herd Boy's Flute*, the water buffalo does not have any rope or halter, as in ancient ox-herding paintings, suggesting the idea of unbridled freedom. The herd boy lives a leisured life, enjoying nature to his heart's content, much like a hermit in the Song dynasty. The appearance of the fisherman and woodcutter in the film further reinforces the notion of eremitism, because in the paintings of the Song dynasty, the herd boy, fisherman, and woodcutter symbolize lofty scholars in "temporary retreats in nature."[64] The herd boy is not simply a child. In the tradition of ox-herding painting, he stands in for adults. He addresses an adult public and conveys disillusionment and disappointment with the adult world. As Richard and Catherine Barnhart point out,

> That the figures in ox-herding pictures need not be children—and as often as not they seem to be at least young adults—suggests, we believe, that childhood itself is not the central concern of ox-herding pictures. Poems about herd boys are often equally ambiguous regarding the age of the "boy."[65]

In terms of storytelling, *The Herd Boy's Flute* can be regarded as animated linked pictures (*lianhuan hua*), making it reminiscent of Chan (or Zen) Buddhist serial paintings of ox-herding. During the twelfth century, Chan monks composed a series of ox-herding pictures to help Chan masters teach their students. The earliest series of twelve ox-herding pictures is attributed to the monk Qingju Haosheng (active in the 1050s). Similar series of ox-herding pictures appeared later, but only two remain: one by Kuoan Shiyuan and the other by Puming (both were active in the 1150s).[66] In the twentieth century, Japanese woodblock artist Tomikichiro Tokuriki (1902–2000) created a set of ten ox-herding pictures (see figure 3.6). The story is simple. The herd boy loses his water buffalo and goes looking for it. First he sees the footprints of the water buffalo and then its body. He captures the water buffalo, tames it, and herds it. Then he rides on it and returns home. He forgets about the water buffalo and then forgets about himself as well. Everything returns to its origin. Finally, the herd boy goes to the marketplace and spreads Buddhist teachings to save his people.

Figure 3.6. Series of ten ox-herding pictures, Tomikichiro Tokuriki (1902–2000).

These ox-herding paintings, which revolve around the loss, recovery, and taming of an ox (with slight variations), impart the Chan ideal of self-cultivation and enlightenment. Ox-herding is an important Chan metaphor that can be traced back to classical Buddhist scriptures. The ox represents the self; the human has Buddha nature within. Self-cultivation is like herding an ox. By taming the ox, the herd boy controls his own wayward animalistic desires and achieves enlightenment.[67]

The Herd Boy's Flute also revolves around the loss and recovery of the water buffalo. The herd boy tames the animal and achieves self-cultivation and enlightenment through flute music, not through ropes and whips characteristic of Chan paintings. In the "bathing" sequence, the buffalo does not want to go into the water—no matter how much the herd boy urges it to move by splashing water on its head. It is only because of the flute music that the water buffalo obeys the boy. In the dream sequence, the water buffalo is attracted by the sound of a waterfall and reluctant to return to the herd boy. Again, the herd boy's flute music tames the water buffalo. *The Herd Boy's Flute* thus represents the hierarchy between art and nature. Art stems from nature—the boy uses bamboo to make a flute—but it is higher than nature, because flute music triumphs over the waterfall's natural music and brings back the water buffalo. The positioning of nature as subordinate to an imagined artistic world resonates with the fundamental tenets of Chan, namely "the unreality of the phenomenal world," which is further suggested by the allusion to Zhuangzi's dream of being a butterfly.[68] In this sense, *The Herd Boy's Flute* suggests a transcendence of reality, a message that is not conveyed through language but by the mood and sentiments generated by visual and aural arts such as painting and music.

The Herd Boy's Flute is associated with Chan ox-herding paintings not only in terms of its story and ambience, but also in terms of formal composition (see figure 3.7). In all these ox-herding paintings, the herd boy rides a water buffalo and plays the flute. Chan artists chose the water buffalo instead of another kind of ox such as the yellow ox, because the Chan master, Changqing Daan, lived for thirty years at Mount Wei (Weishan), where he did nothing but tend water buffalo. Eventually the color of the water buffalo became white, suggesting the achievement of enlightenment.[69] More important, unlike courtly ox-herding paintings that emphasize the landscape background, Chan ox-herding paintings emphasize the story and figures because they began as pedagogical tools. Chan masters depicted the background in a minimalist and sketchy style. In later Chan ox-herding paintings, the background becomes a void. Although landscape plays a vital role throughout *The Herd Boy's Flute*, images are at moments presented similarly to the Chan paintings. For example, in one film still the background disappears when the water buffalo fords the river.

Figure 3.7. One of the ten ox-herding paintings by Kuoan (active in the 1150s).

The depiction of the herd boy in the animated film was closely associated with traditional ox-herding paintings; it came to differ markedly from the typical representation of the Maoist herd boy in the mid-1960s. The typical Maoist herd boy was best exemplified by Wang Erxiao, the protagonist in a children's linked-picture book titled *Wang Erxiao the Herd Boy* (*Wang Erxiao fangniulang,* 1964). Produced in the same year as *The Herd Boy's Flute, Wang Erxiao the Herd Boy* was written by Xing Ye and illustrated by Yang Yonglian. Drawing on a true story, the book features Wang Erxiao, a poor peasant boy and member of the Communist Children's League. He stands sentry for the Eighth Route Army while herding his oxen. Japanese soldiers arrive at Wang's village and ask him to be their guide. Wang leads these Japanese soldiers into the Eighth Route Army's ring of encirclement. The outraged Japanese soldiers kill Wang, but are killed in turn by the Eighth Route Army. Partly because of its propaganda value to the regime, the story became so popular that it was reproduced in *The Story of Wang Erxiao* (*Wang Erxiao de gushi*) in 1965.

On the cover of the 1965 edition, the human figure is dominant and the background is insignificant (see figure 3.8). In the pose of a national hero, Wang Erxiao stands on top of a rock and ferociously gazes into the distance on the lookout for enemies. He holds a red-tasseled spear in his right hand, the weapon of Communist Children's League members. In his left hand, he grabs an ox horn, which functions as an instrument to alert his oxen or fellow Communists. The two

Figure 3.8. Cover picture of *The Story of Wang Erxiao* (1965).

objects indicate Wang's double identity: a herd boy and a little soldier of the Communist Party. The oxen's absence downplays Wang's identity as a herd boy but highlights his political identity as a member of the Communist Children's League. His herd boy identity is thus a mere suggestion of his peasant class background, which allowed for his sanctification by the Party. The absence of a landscape or other background in the cover picture emphasizes the story's human action. The rock in the foreground is a stage prop that functions to lower the level of our view and increase Wang's monumentality. Wang's spear tassel and his vest are red. The characters of the title are also depicted in red, suggesting the story's revolutionary theme. In sharp contrast, revolutionary red seldom appears in *The Herd Boy's Flute,* which is dominated by cool colors, such as green, blue, white, and black. Unlike the soft and relaxed herd boy in the ink-painting animated film, Wang Erxiao is not a melodious flute player, but instead an alert and ferocious soldier who is ready for battle. He is not a fictional figure in an idealized pastoral world but instead inspired by a real person anchored in revolutionary reality.

The portrayal of Wang Erxiao was typical of the style of children's books during the Cultural Revolution. In her studies of children's picture story books (serial-picture books or linked pictures) that were popular in 1973, Eileen Polley Blumenthal observes that in terms of subject matter, fantastic folk tales and legends popular in 1959 were no longer available.[70] Instead, revolutionary people and their life stories dominated in 1973 (see chapter 4). Examining the cover pictures of 230 children's books, Blumenthal concludes,

> It is striking that almost every cover shows people: only 4 of the 230 covers are landscapes or seascapes without human figures. The scenes are from

> everyday life, and they are all realistic in both subject and artistic style. There are no elements of fantasy in these illustrations; the humorous adventures of animals which were popular in old China are not depicted.[71]

She further points out that the majority of these covers depict a single (usually Han) individual. The singling out of a heroic individual demonstrates the pedagogical and ideological function of these books: to provide children with an exemplary model to emulate. Comparing *Wang Erxiao the Herd Boy* with picture books of the early 1970s, it is apparent that *Wang Erxiao the Herd Boy* survived and even flourished when the Cultural Revolution unfolded in the mid-1960s. In sharp contrast, *The Herd Boy's Flute,* which was not like the Maoist depiction of herd boys, was banned in 1964 for its apolitical and escapist tendencies and released again only in 1979.

The rise and fall of the two ink-painting animated films demonstrate the shifting definitions of national identity partly driven by shifting politics. By the mid-1960s, the construction of national identity was no longer associated with traditional artistic forms such as ink painting, but instead more with national heroes rooted in revolutionary sociohistorical realities of the present. As a result, during the height of the Cultural Revolution in the late 1960s and 1970s, political correctness of subject matter became the new norm for articulating national identity. During this period, the so-called national style of the early 1960s became the enemy in the construction of national identity. This is because traditional ink painting, which stood for China's unique essence in the early 1960s, came to be regarded as old, conservative, escapist, feudal, and reactionary. As a result, the form of ink-painting animated film was denounced.[72] Therefore, the conventional conflation of national style and national identity is static and ahistorical because the concepts are fluid, ever-changing, and historically contingent, especially during the tumultuous 1960s and 1970s.

4 Animals, Ethnic Minorities, and Villains in Animated Film during the Cultural Revolution

In the mid-1960s, the concept of national style, understood as a marker of a unique Chinese identity, began to change in animated filmmaking. In the late 1950s and early 1960s, national style was associated with traditional art forms, literature, folklore, and culture rooted in China's past. During the Cultural Revolution, it was characterized by positive heroes and revolutionary content in a contemporary setting. Rather than fixed, static, and timeless, then, national style is historically contingent and thus continuously changing. An examination of subnational forces such as ethnic minorities and villains represented in animated films during this decade provides evidence for the central argument of this book, namely, that national identity constructed through the positive revolutionary heroes in Chinese animated films was not solid, homogeneous, and monolithic. Instead, it was contested and destabilized by racialized and animalized Others who continuously transgressed and redefined national borders. National identity is therefore a fluid concept contested and reformulated by internal border-crossing movements. I address this issue by looking at animals to unravel the convoluted relationships among species, ethnicity, class, and national identity articulated in animated films produced in this period.

Conventional studies of the Cultural Revolution tend to have a human-centered perspective that focuses on politics, revolution, and class struggle as dramatized in well-established art forms. Such an approach draws attention to the most visible and spectacular scenarios. Here we look instead to what was invisible: how animals were represented and underrepresented in a marginalized art form. Like the fairy tale, fable, and parable, animation is suffused with fantasy and populated with talking animals. Before the Cultural Revolution, animated film was replete with anthropomorphic animals, as earlier chapters make clear, from *Princess Iron Fan* (*Tieshan gongzhu,* 1941) (chapter 1) to *Terrible Lice* (*Kepa de shizi,* 1943) and *Kitty Goes Fishing* (*Xiaomao diaoyu,* 1952) (chapter 2) to *Little Tadpoles Look for Mama* (*Xiao kedou zhao mama,* 1960) (chapter 3). As animation began in the mid-1960s to be dominated by positive heroes and politicized human action, animals disappeared for more than a decade. They did not vanish entirely, however. Instead, they became metonyms and metaphors for ethnic minorities and villains. As such, they destabilized the concept of a totalizing and homogeneous national identity. In essence, the disappearance of animals marked the start of the Cultural Revolution and effectively paved the way for its ideological demise.

Film Culture

Political narratives conventionally depict the Cultural Revolution as having been launched by Mao in 1966 and ending when he died in 1976. Given the disastrous consequences resulted from the Great Leap Forward (1958–1960) and the subsequent Great Famine (1959–1961), Mao's authority temporarily declined and advocates of economic development, such as Liu Shaoqi and Deng Xiaoping, gained support (see chapter 3). To consolidate his power and the centrality of political struggle, Mao and the Chinese Communist Party (CCP) Central Committee issued the May 16 Notification in 1966 against bourgeois elements in the government, which is widely regarded as the start of the Cultural Revolution. That autumn, Mao frequently appeared in Tiananmen Square and greeted millions of fanatical members of the Red Guards who had traveled to Beijing from all corners of the country. The decade is regarded as one of tragedy, turmoil, and devastation. Schools and offices were closed. Cultural relics and historic sites were attacked. Colleagues and family members were pitted against each other, and people were persecuted and killed. Traditional Chinese culture, morality, and ethics based on Confucianism were shattered. The tragedy did not end until Mao died in September 1976.[1]

Recently, however, a more fluid periodization has been proposed using a cultural rather than a political perspective. Paul Clark and Yingjin Zhang, for instance, maintain that in film circles the Cultural Revolution began in June 1964, when Mao criticized all forms of socialist cultural production and organization for their serious political problems. Nationwide campaigns were launched in 1964 to criticize "poisonous" films such as *Early Spring in February* (*Zaochun eryue*, 1963) and *The Lin Family Shop* (*Linjia puzi*, 1959). Xia Yan's writings on film and Cheng Jihua's book on film history were also severely criticized. Furthermore, the Cultural Revolution in the cultural sphere did not end with Mao's death in 1976. It lingered in filmmaking until 1978.[2]

The purge in animated filmmaking began in 1964 with the criticism and banning of *The Herd Boy's Flute* (*Mudi*, 1963), *Uproar in Heaven* (*Danao tiangong*, 1961–1964), and other animated films. The aesthetics typical of the period began with *Heroic Little Sisters of the Grassland* (*Caoyuan yingxiong xiao jiemei*) in

December 1965. This rigid style began to loosen with the release of *The Golden Wild Goose* (*Jinse de dayan*) in April 1976, but not until *The Fox Hunts the Hunter* (*Huli da lieren*) in 1978 did animation finally break away entirely from the Cultural Revolution's rigid aesthetics.

Between 1966 and 1970, fictional filmmaking was suspended and no new fictional films were released. Most of the films made during the Seventeen Years (1949–1966) were banned. Given the shortage of films during this period, Chairman Mao's wife, Jiang Qing, and her cohorts modernized Peking opera, ballet, and symphony and made revolutionary model performances (*geming yangbanxi*) with the aim of establishing a new revolutionary aesthetics and culture for the stage. The Beijing Film Studio produced *Taking Tiger Mountain by Strategy* (*Zhiqu Weihushan*), a film adaptation of one of the model performances and released it in October 1970. More model performances were adapted into film, such as *The Red Lantern* (*Hongdeng ji,* 1970), *Shajiabang* (1971), and *On the Docks* (*Haigang,* 1972). These performances were represented in other artistic forms including posters and linked pictures (*lianhuan hua*), which dominated the cultural scene during the Cultural Revolution. A joke at that time quipped, "eight hundred million people watched eight model performances."[3] The initial performances included five modern Peking operas, two ballets, and one symphony. Additional performances followed.

These model opera films emphasized class struggle and revolution. Their guiding principle was the "three prominences" (*santuchu*), namely, the prominence of positive characters, of heroes among all positive characters, and of the most outstanding hero among the heroes. The appearance of the heroes should conform to the convention of being "tall, big, and full" (*gao da quan*) and should be portrayed with the style of "red, light, bright" (*hong guang liang*); negative characters were portrayed with the convention of "far, small, dark" (*yuan xiao hei*) in the background. Cultural Revolution cinema was dominated by the revolutionary aesthetics of these highly stylized model opera works. Encouraged by the success of the opera films, Jiang Qing and the ultra-leftists launched the production of fictional feature films to advance their political goals in 1973. These films, such as *Breaking with Old Ideas* (*Juelie,* 1975), often portrayed the Party's internal struggle. These films shared the aesthetics of model opera films but were less theatrical; model opera films continued to be made when production of fictional feature films resumed in 1973.[4]

When the Cultural Revolution turned its focus on culture itself, animated films produced during the Seventeen Years were—with only a few exceptions—criticized and banned.[5] Shanghai Animation Film Studio, established in 1957 as the sole animation studio in China (see introduction), produced most of the animated films made during the Cultural Revolution. In August of 1966, the Red Guards took over the studio, renamed it Red Guard Film Studio, and established the affiliated film magazine *Red Guard Cinema* (*Hongweibing dianying*) in July 1967. Given the intensification of revolution and class struggle, from 1966 to 1971 the studio's only animated films were *The New Sprouts of a Village* (*Shancun xinmiao,* 1966) and *The Great Declaration* (*Weida de shengming,* 1968). Shanghai Animation Film Studio made several dozen animated films between 1972 when it resumed production and 1976.[6] Like other artistic forms at that time, these films were influenced by the aesthetics of model performances. However, the most prominent and invisible feature of these animated films is the disappearance of animals.

A Double Disappearance

In animation, animals, modernity, and cinema are intertwined in that cinema is a material icon of modernity yet the animal is the antithesis of it. Akira Lippit argues that when humans began to modernize the world and conquer nature with advanced technology, wild animals disappeared: "Modernity can be defined by the disappearance of wildlife from humanity's habitat and by the reappearance of the same in humanity's reflections on itself: in philosophy, psychoanalysis, and technological media such as the telephone, film, and radio."[7] It is no surprise that early cinema frequently featured animals.[8] Drawing on Lippit, I contend that in the context of socialist modernity during China's Cultural Revolution, wild animals not only disappeared significantly in the real world as Mao launched series of wars against nature but also vanished from the silver screen as a result of the radical artistic forms and cultural policies adopted at the time. The Cultural Revolution was thus characterized by a double disappearance.

During the Great Leap Forward, Mao launched a steel-making campaign, ordering trees to be cut down to fire the furnaces. Deforestation destroyed animal habitats and animals disappeared. In February 1958, Mao launched a campaign to eradicate what it identified as the four pests (*chu sihai*): sparrows, rats, flies, and mosquitoes (see also chapter 3). "All people," Mao ordered, "including five-year-old children, must be mobilized to eliminate the four pests."[9] Thousands of people in a particular place rushed outside simultaneously beating drums, pots, and pans, which induced such panic in sparrows that they flew until they died from exhaustion. For several decades after this campaign, sparrows rarely were seen in the countryside.[10] The Great Leap Forward lasted only two years, but the decade-long Cultural Revolution intensified the radical drop in the population of wild animals. After Mao launched the Learning from Dazhai campaign in 1964, peasants continued to cut down trees to clear land for industrial projects and to modernize the countryside. The animal population was decimated. At the time, for example, the tiger was a metaphor for socialist enemies—US imperialists in particular—and was therefore widely despised. These campaigns brought the species close to extinction.

Animals also began to disappear from Chinese films in the 1960s. Model performance films during the period are typically characterized as being about class struggle and the cult of Mao. I assert that the absence of animals is a prominent albeit invisible feature of these films. Model works were usually performed in theaters, where accommodating and controlling live animals on stage is extremely difficult.[11] Furthermore, in line with the Chinese opera tradition, animals are suggested by gestures or props, as in the horse-riding scene in *Taking Tiger Mountain by Strategy* (figure 4.1). The removal of animals clears the space for revolutionary human action rooted in the realist mise-en-scène of these productions. Revolutionary cinema was less a phantom shelter for animals than a representational tomb during China's decade of radical socialist modernity.

The ban on anthropomorphic animals began with the persecution of the famous fairy tale writer Chen Bochui. In the late 1950s, Chen published several essays advocating for children's literature written from the perspective of children's heart (*tongxin*). Fantasy, he argued, distinguished children's literature as a genre and that the task of the children's writer is to create works suitable for children.[12] In 1960, Mao's wife, Jiang Qing, and her cohorts launched various campaigns to criticize this concept, countering it with rationalist and realist arguments: "Can cats speak? Can roosters sing?"[13] Animated films of the Seventeen Years era were belittled as being about "little dogs and cats, gods and spirits" (*xiaomao xiaogou shenxian guiguai*), and most were forbidden.[14]

Figure 4.1. Horse-riding scene, absent the horse, in *Taking Tiger Mountain by Strategy*, 1970.

Jiang Qing's negative view needs to be considered in an international context. The burgeoning popularity and influence of Disney films in the Third World during the Cold War era was equated with Western cultural imperialism. Anthropomorphism and plasticity were regarded as the antithesis of classical mechanics and rationalism. Donald Duck and other Disney animals, for example, were seen as political messengers of capitalist ideology and cultural imperialism in Latin America in the 1970s.[15] The more direct influence on Jiang Qing was likely Nadezhda Krupskaya, the Soviet educator and wife of Lenin, who advocated that children's stories should be based more on reality than on fantasy.[16] Fairy tales were attacked in the Soviet Union during the 1920s but not banned.[17] Numerous animated fairy tales with talking animals were in fact produced during the Stalin era. Although the validity of fairy tales in Republican China was debated in the 1920s and 1930s, the debates did not lead to a ban.[18] The United States had its own sometimes heated Great Fairy Tale Debate about the legitimacy of fantasy between 1929 and 1931, but no ban followed.[19] The double disappearance of animals during the Cultural Revolution, for all its intense and lasting effects, was a unique phenomenon.

Animal, Fantasy, and Realism

The animal in Chinese animation is typically a figure of the fantastic and an antithesis of realism. Most animated films made during the Seventeen Years drew on myth, folklore, fairy tales, and legends set either in a remote past or in an exaggerated and distorted world, as discussed in the film analyses in earlier chapters. The anthropomorphic animal was pivotal.[20] The disappearance of animals during the Cultural Revolution, though, had precedents in films produced during the Seventeen Years. The boundary between fantasy and realism in animated films was blurred by realist moments, even though the embodiment of fantasy in animals was dominant.

The realist entrée in socialist animation came in two propaganda films produced by Northeast Film Studio in the late 1940s: *Dreaming to Be Emperor* (*Huangdi meng,* 1947) and *Capturing the Turtle in the Jar* (*Wengzhong zhuobie,* 1948) (see chapter 2). Both were satires of Jiang Jieshi (Chiang Kai-shek) in the context of China's civil war and his collaboration with the United States. Although the two films had a politically serious motif, they used caricature and humor. In *Capturing the Turtle in the Jar,* for instance, the character of Jiang Jieshi is transformed into an anthropomorphic turtle after he is arrested by the People's Liberation Army. Thus, although the film addressed an actual political conflict, the fantastic element was present in its use of animals. These films were called political satire films (*zhengzhi fengci pian*) and targeted adults.

The second entrée came during the Great Leap Forward. The film *Long Live the Great Leap Forward* (*Dayuejin wansui,* 1959) was a deliberate and direct reference to the campaign. Despite its realist orientation, the film included fantastic elements and drew on fairy tales to recount how peasants, equipped with modern technology, outwit anthropomorphized black clouds and wind that are attempting to conquer the human world. The film *Little Carp Jump over Dragon Gate* (*Xiao liyu tiao longmen,* 1958) adopts a similar style. A group of anthropomorphic carp, after hearing the story that jumping over the legendary dragon gate transforms carp into dragons, are determined to find the gate. They then jump over what they assume is the legendary gate, but is Dragon Gate Dam (Longmen shuiku), which was built during the Great Leap Forward. Substituting the dam for the legendary dragon gate portrays the industrial achievements of socialist China. Films such as this that targeted children and combined contemporary reality with fantastic elements were called new fairy tales (*xin tonghua*) and contemporary fairy tales (*xiandai tonghua*).

Whereas the previous two realist entrées were characterized by a fusion of realism and fantasy (anthropomorphic animals and exaggeration), the third portrayed children's daily lives in a mimetic and verisimilar style and included neither animals nor fantastic elements. This trend began with the film *The Twins* (*Shuangbaotai,* 1957), which revolves around a series of funny stories that result from the mistaken identities of a pair of twins. Another is *A New Football* (*Yige xin zuqiu,* 1957), which recounts how an initially selfish child becomes willing to share his new football with other children. Verisimilitude continued into the mid-1960s with a new twist. Films such as *New Deeds on the Roadside* (*Lubian xinshi,* 1964), *Four and a Half O'Clock* (*Sidianban,* 1964), and *The Little Brothers* (*Xiao gelia,* 1965) revolve around children doing good deeds to emulate the model soldier Lei Feng. The films are light hearted, humorous, and not overtly political, but do not feature animals or fantasy.

The fourth entrance—revolutionary realism—came in the release of the puppet-animated *Red Cloud Cliff* (*Hongyun ya,* 1962).[21] Other films in this category include *The Rooster Crows at Midnight* (*Banye jijiao,* 1964), discussed in the introduction, and *The Red Army Bridge* (*Hongjun qiao,* 1964). Like the third group, *Red Cloud Cliff* adopts a mimetic style and excludes animals and fantastic elements. However, with its serious motif, *Red Cloud Cliff* does not have the humorous and comic twists characteristic of the third set. Thus it is a serious play (*zhengju*). Set in Sichuan province in the late 1940s, *Red Cloud Cliff* features an old stonecarver who sacrifices his life to defend the honor of the Red Army. When Nationalist soldiers learn that the slogan "reddening Sichuan province" (*chihua quanchuan*) is engraved on a cliff, they threaten to kill the stone carver's grandson if he does not remove it. The stone carver agrees and climbs the cliff. Rather than obeying the soldiers' order, however, he changes the slogan to "reddening the whole country" (*chihua quanguo*). The soldiers kill the stone carver—the first human hero killed in the history of Chinese animation. The killing is designed to make viewers feel heavy hearted, saddened, and vengeful—which is exactly the affective function of revolutionary realism, to arouse in audiences a love for heroes and a hatred for enemies.[22]

The release of *Red Cloud Cliff* triggered heated debate in the mid-1960s about realism and fantasy. Sun Yi, a famous editor of children's periodicals, hailed the film as a "successful experiment" that constructs a positive peasant hero and directly inculcates the ideology of class struggle in children.[23] The renowned animator Jin Xi, by contrast, saw exaggeration as

> an indispensable technique in animated filmmaking. There is a reason for this. Animated cartoons, paper cuts, and puppetry cannot represent a real person true to life due to the limitation of the medium. If animated films have to represent persons, the more realistic they are, the more artificial they will become. Animated films are not suitable for realistic representations.[24]

He was echoed by animated film script writer Wu Lun:

> Due to the nature of being flexible, animated films can use exaggeration and fantasy to represent life. Animated film has its limitations in that it cannot represent the subtle psychology and sophisticated facial expressions of real people. Animated film lacks stereoscopy, so it is not suitable for representing real persons and real events.[25]

Wu Lun went on to sum up the genres that fit in well with the medium of animation: myths, fairy tales, comedies, and satires. That is, genres that deal with the past, fantasy, and exaggeration and are distanced from contemporary reality. Within the terms of Jin Xi's and Wu Lun's arguments, *Red Cloud Cliff* was a failure. If animated films have to represent reality, they should incorporate fantastic or exaggerated elements, as in *Little Carp Jump over Dragon Gate* (see chapter 3). The debate about fantasy and realism soon ended, because the revolutionary realism prominent in *Red Cloud Cliff* later became the official standard for animated filmmaking during the Cultural Revolution and was fully established with the release of *Heroic Little Sisters of the Grassland*.[26]

Animals and Model Animation

Heroic Little Sisters of the Grassland has even more realist elements than the puppet-animated *Red Cloud Cliff. Red Cloud Cliff* draws on revolutionary legends set in the near past, and the characters are fictional.[27] *Heroic Little Sisters* is based on a true story of two Mongolian sisters who almost lost their lives trying to protect the sheep of the people's commune during a snowstorm in February 1964 and were immediately promoted as national models for children.[28] The animators began making the film as if it were a timely documentary or news report. It incorporated rotoscoping and was based on a live-action film, which lent smooth movement to the characters. The animation of the sisters was based on photographs of them to enhance corporeal verisimilitude and authenticity.

Accordingly, I identify *Heroic Little Sisters of the Grassland* rather than *Red Cloud Cliff* as the true transitional film between the Seventeen Years and the Cultural Revolution. The first serious play (*zhengju*) in the history of cel-animated film, *Heroic Little Sisters* was also the first to directly portray, praise, and deify Chairman Mao.[29] Mao's portrait appears at the beginning and the end of the film. The film's theme songs directly praised him. In terms of revolutionary content and realist style, *Heroic Little Sisters of the Grassland* served as the model for subsequent animated films during the Cultural Revolution, a decade characterized by repetition of both style and stories.

According to critics at the time, the images of the protagonists in the films of the period departed from the cute Western doll-like (*yang wawa*) style of the past and took on more national characteristics related to contemporary politics and culture.[30] These heroes thus became markers of national style and national identity. Guided by the three prominences, the heroes were portrayed using low angles and bright colors to heighten their monumentality and enemies by using high angles and dark colors.

It was precisely the disappearance of anthropomorphic animals that gave rise to this model of animation. The script of *Heroic Little Sisters of the Grassland* was based on a fairy tale titled "Red Flowers on the Snowy Grassland" ("Xueyuan honghua"). In the original script, the sisters sing, dance, and play with anthropomorphic sheep. The villain is an evil hawk, which snatches the good animals and the sisters into the sky. After the animators went to Inner Mongolia and sketched from life, however, they decided to follow a documentary style to portray the sisters as they had been in the original news reports. They deleted the anthropomorphic animals.[31] The hawk disappeared. The sheep did not talk and were simply animals owned by the commune (figure 4.2). It is likely that the animators self-censored their work given that as early as 1964 the artistic coercion characteristic of the Cultural Revolution already had begun with the criticism of *Early Spring in*

February and other live-action feature films. Furthermore, criticism of fantasy, myth, and fairy tales intensified during the period. In January 1964, Ke Qingshi, the Party secretary for Shanghai, proposed "dramatizing the thirteen years after 1949" (*daxie shisan nian*) and "emphasizing the contemporary and slighting the ancient" (*houjin bogu*), arguing that only contemporary motifs featuring living people (*huoren*)—not ancient people (*guren*) and dead people (*siren*)—could properly disseminate socialist ideas.[32] Qian Jiajun and his colleagues began preparations for the animated film *The Story of Kitty* (*Xiaomao de gushi*) in 1964, but the project soon was suspended given the political sensitivity of the animal motif.[33] Anthropomorphism was condemned as a way of defaming workers, peasants, soldiers, and children, and was officially banned at the Shanghai Animation Film Studio in November 1965.[34] The release of *Heroic Little Sisters of the Grassland* a month later was timely. Thereafter, animated films were characterized by the absence of anthropomorphic animals.

Heroic Little Sisters of the Grassland is the only cel-animated film made during the Seventeen Years that survived artistic censorship and was continuously reproduced as a media fetish in different artistic forms during the Cultural Revolution.[35] At the height of the period, the film's realist animals disappeared. In November 1970, the Shanghai People's Press published a linked-picture (*lianhuan hua*) version directly adapted from the animated film. This version had the same title and the same plot as the animated version. The role of Chairman Mao is more prominent, however, and class struggle is more heavily emphasized. The father of the sisters is represented as an oppressed shepherd liberated by Mao. The Party

Figure 4.2. Domesticated sheep and the two Mongolian sisters of the people's commune in *Heroic Little Sisters of the Grassland,* 1965.

secretary staged "speaking bitterness" (*suku*) campaigns to publically criticize reactionary herd owners. The two sisters are little Red Guards who wear Mao badges and read Mao's little red books.[36] Because of the more prominent roles of Mao, revolution, and class struggle in the linked-picture version, animals are pushed into the background, as depicted in the cover image (see figure 4.3).

When *Heroic Little Sisters of the Grassland* was made into the ballet model performance work *Sons and Daughters of the Grassland* (*Caoyuan ernü,* 1975), animals were all but absent. The sisters are represented as brother and sister and are played by two adults. The ballet makes the story more dramatic and sensational than either the animated or linked-picture version by adding as a class enemy a reactionary herd owner who steals the sheep of the people's commune by letting them escape. When he is exposed, he attempts to kill the children, but soldiers of the People's Liberation Army appear at the critical moment to save them.[37] The drama of class struggle further marginalizes the sheep's role. The children's whips and herding gestures are the only remnants of the sheep (figure 4.4). Stage lighting, which focuses exclusively on the positive heroes, further foregrounds human protagonists and pushes animals, if any, into darkness and invisibility.

The degree to which animals are invisible or absent marks the revolution's intensity and vice versa. The disappearance of the anthropomorphic sheep in the model-animated version of *Heroic Little Sisters of the Grassland* indicates the penetration of the Cultural Revolution into animation. The absence of animals from *Sons and Daughters of the Grassland* reflects intensified revolutionary conflict. The ballet effectively transformed the animated film into a de facto Maoist model

Figure 4.3. Marginalized animals in the distant background in *Heroic Little Sisters of the Grassland* (linked-picture version), 1970.

Figure 4.4. Landscape with sheep herders but without sheep in *Sons and Daughters of the Grassland* (ballet version), 1975.

work, the most prominent and the most invisible feature of which is the absence of animals.

The official disappearance of animals also gave rise to the "fetishization" of machines—telegraph poles, power lines, ship, tractors, trains, and helicopters—as icons of socialist modernity.[38] Telegraph poles and power lines in the landscape take on prominent roles in the various versions of *Heroic Little Sisters* (figures 4.3 and 4.4), for example, to valorize socialist modernity and its industrial achievements.

The iconography of socialist machines culminated in *Trial Voyage* (*Shi hang,* 1976), which drew directly on a live-action feature film by the same title (1959). *Trial Voyage* was the first film to feature the motif of heavy industry and the struggle between the proletariat and capitalist roaders. In the animated version, the protagonist Lu Dahai and his workers build *East,* a ten-thousand-ton oceangoing cargo ship. All of the ship's parts are made in China. After the ship is completed, Lu Dahai asks for a trial voyage. Party leader Chen Zongjie argues that Chinese parts are poor quality and tells Lu Dahai to use imported parts or he will postpone the trial. Lu Dahai refuses, insisting that China can build its own ship without relying on foreign parts. After numerous rounds of political struggle, Lu Dahai takes a highly successful trial voyage, on which he and his workers even rescue a Taiwanese fishing boat. A ship was a common metaphor for China during the Cultural Revolution, in which Chairman Mao as the helmsman steered the country on its socialist course.[39] The ship in *Trial Voyage* marked the height of the fetishization of machines and the cult of Mao in animated films. Such films differed from others in using adults as protagonists, resembling live action, and appealing to a more sophisticated adult audience.

When animals did appear, they were represented as the collective property of a people's commune, such as the sheep in *Heroic Little Sisters of the Grassland,* the pigs in *The Major Course* (*Zhu ke,* 1975), and the horses in *Galloping Horses* (*Junma feiteng,* 1975).[40] To highlight human action, these domesticated animals were positioned in the background and nearly invisible. They were also depicted in clamorous herds or packs without the individuality, personality, dignity, and freedom that solitary animals in the wild had traditionally been given.

The Lamb of the Commune: Ethnicity, Femininity, and Animality

Ethnic minorities began to appear in Chinese animated film in the late 1950s. The first such film, *Golden Earrings and an Iron Hoe* (*Jin erhuan yu tie chutou,* 1956), draws on a Yao legend in which an old man faints in front of his house and is helped by a poor Yao peasant boy. Grateful for the boy's kindness, the old man's daughter gives the boy a pair of golden earrings, which turn into two golden keys. The boy uses the keys to open a treasure-filled cave, where he picks out what appear to be an ordinary millstone and iron hoe, only to discover that they magically produce grain. The greedy landlord tries to seize the treasure but ends up being killed. The boy then marries the old man's daughter and they live happily ever after. Subsequent animated films portraying ethnic minorities followed this pattern. For example, *The Girl Made of Wood* (*Mutou guniang,* 1958) draws on a Mongolian legend, *A Zhuang Brocade* (*Yifu zhuangjin,* 1959) on a Zhuang legend, *The Shepherd and the Princess* (*Mutong yu gongzhu,* 1960) on a Bai legend, *The Girl with Long Hair* (*Changfa mei,* 1963) on a Dong legend, and *Peacock Princess* (*Kongque gongzhu,* 1963) on a Dai legend. Such films incorporated fantastic elements and emphasized ethnic diversity and cultural differences.[41] They often dramatized the different costumes, food, behaviors, ways of thinking, legends, and cultures of various ethnic traditions, rendering animated film a kind of socialist salad.

Whereas minority animated films during the Seventeen Years were concerned with ethnic traditions, myths, and legends, those during the Cultural Revolution were set in the revolutionary context and depicted cultural homogeneity. Ethnic difference was subordinated to class difference, though ethnic minorities were still marked as an exotic Other relative to Han Chinese, the aim being to construct a homogeneous and monolithic national identity. The transition from the past to the present, from fantasy to revolutionary realism, and from ethnic difference to class difference began with *Heroic Little Sisters of the Grassland,* which became a model for later animated films.

Issues of ethnicity reinforced the realist orientation of the film.[42] Scholars point out the strong ties between race and realism, even proposing the concept of racial realism. According to Madhu Dubey, "political claims about African-American literature have always depended on realist aesthetics, from the documentary impulse of the slave narratives to the reflectionist principles prescribed by the cultural nationalist program."[43] In his studies of ethnic minorities in China, Dru Gladney also observes that explicit realism was used to portray the female body of ethnic minorities in contemporary Chinese arts; however, the state restricted the use of realism to portrayals of the female Han body.[44] During the Cultural Revolution, the Chinese government also appropriated ethnic minorities to present a racially authentic revolutionary narrative in the name of constructing a coherent national identity. The logic of this nationalist discourse is that even unruly "barbarians" living in borderlands embraced Chairman Mao and his socialist revolution. Ethnic revolutionary realism was prominent in the minority films produced during the period.

Issues of ethnicity, childhood, and animals are often intertwined. According to evolutionary theory, humans evolved from animals, so it is no wonder that a child usually has some atavistic animalist characteristics. Like animals, children are usually unsophisticated and suspicious of nothing; they crawl, cry, bite, eat, and excrete to their heart's content. Functioning as "a liminal figure at the discursive threshold dividing species as well as races," the child, according to Andrew Jones, is a "housed beast" that needs to be developed and civilized.[45] These ideas are also pervasive in sociology. Karl Marx once proposed a progressive stage theory of human civilizations: primitive, slavery, feudal, capitalist, socialist, and communist. In line with this social evolution, ethnic minorities and aboriginals, regarded as primitive, are positioned as the early stage, or the childhood, of human history.[46]

Imagined this way, ethnic minorities and animals often have a metonymic relationship in mainstream Chinese narratives. In real life, ethnic minorities usually make their living from and live with animals in the borderlands.[47] In the folklore, myths, and legends of many ethnic minorities, ancestors are depicted as animals or animal totems are worshipped. In the semi-autobiographical novel *Wolf Totem* (*Lang tuteng*, 2004), for example, the author Jiang Rong notes that in many Chinese classics and legends, Mongolians are descended from wolves.[48] A story from *Book of the Later Han* (*Hou Hanshu*) illustrates that a dog named Pan Hu is the ancestor of the barbarians (*manyi*) in China.[49] It is no surprise that in the traditional Chinese writing system, ethnic minorities are often classified with animals. The most popular radicals in ethnonyms were associated with a bug or beast (*chong*) and a dog (*quan*). Animal radicals for ethnic minorities were replaced with human classifiers in the mid-twentieth century, but the stereotype remains current among Han Chinese.[50]

Ethnic minorities frequently appear with animals in visual representations in China. As a transitional film between the Seventeen Years and the Cultural Revolution, *Heroic Little Sisters of the Grassland,* compared with its linked-picture and ballet versions, still has traces of earlier fantastic animated films. Although in this film the sheep stop talking and become realistic, they are portrayed as adorable and are given prominent shots throughout. Some animators criticize the rigid stylization of animation during the Cultural Revolution yet regard *Heroic Little Sisters* as a success and attribute its success to the vivid portrayal of the sheep.[51] In fact, ethnicity sanctioned the relative overrepresentation of animals. This is because, as Paul Clark points out, minority films have the propensity to "explore normally avoided subjects" in socialist China.[52] Only two animated films were named after animals at that time, *Galloping Horses* and *The Golden Wild Goose*; the former is set in Inner Mongolia and the latter in Tibet. *The Major Course* features pigs and is set in the ethnic Zhuang Autonomous Region in Guangxi province. *Two Little Peacocks* (*Liangzhi xiao kongque*, 1977) features wild peacocks and ethnic Dai children.

Han stereotypes present ethnic minorities as innocent little girls with animal companions. Paul Clark argues that ethnic minorities of northern China tend to be represented as hard, masculine, and virile, and their peers in the South as softer, more feminine, and more likely to sing and dance.[53] Rather than using gender to analyze conventions of representing ethnic minorities, I propose using the concept of animality, which encompasses both masculinity and femininity. The anthropologist Louisa Schein notes the metonymic relationship between feminized ethnic minorities and animals (and nature in general). In Chinese mass media representations, ethnic minorities are figured through an infantilized woman, who "frequently appeared communing with animals or nestled among trees and flowers."[54] Ethnic minorities are therefore associated with primitiveness, fauna, and flora.

In communing and (over)identifying with animals, the ethnic girl herself becomes an animal or an anthropomorphic animal par excellence. The metonymic relationship culminates in the film *Peacock Princess*, which is based on an ethnic Dai legend. The metamorphosis of a peacock into a princess (as in the film) or of a princess into a peacock tellingly illustrates the symbiotic relationship. *Peacock Princess* is one of the few Chinese animated films that portray such a transformation. In Chinese animation, metamorphosis—understood as the transformation of body forms between humans and animals or other nonhuman objects—is typically portrayed using ethnic minorities. For instance, *The Girl Made of Wood* deals with a tree stump's metamorphosis into a Mongolian girl. *The Girl with Long Hair* is the story of the transformation of the long hair of a Dong girl into a waterfall.[55] In *The Hunter Hailibu* (*Lieren Hailibu,* 1985), a squirrel is transformed into a Mongolian girl, who turns out to be the daughter of the Mountain God. The

Mongolian boy Hailibu understands the language of animals and is transformed into a stone. *The Cloak Made of One Hundred Birds' Feathers* (*Bainiaoyi,* 1996) is about a canary's transformation into a Miao girl. Ethnicity is associated with the transgression of categories, with feminized ethnic bodies as pliant, malleable, and subject to animated metamorphosis.

When the animals disappeared in *Heroic Little Sisters of the Grassland,* the two Mongolian sisters took their place. The girls are cute and plump with round faces and big eyes. Their femininity, infantility, and naiveté are not only patronizing and trivializing but also render them objects of intense fascination. They radiate animalistic physical strength and agility. They run, jump, and boisterously keep running for days on end in harsh weather—all to protect the sheep of the people's commune.

Ethnic bodies, especially female ones, are prone to overanimation, literally and metaphorically, and display excessive physical movement, dancing, and noisy vocalizations such as chattering, giggling, and singing.[56] In *Heroic Little Sisters,* the girls are extremely animated, become exhausted, fall into a coma, and are taken to the hospital by a rescue party led by the Party secretary.[57] This marks the turning point in their lives. When the girls wake up at the hospital, they are symbolically dead as daughters of their father because the Party secretary reanimates them, giving them a new life and a new identity as "Chairman Mao's good children." In other words, they are assimilated into the family structure of the socialist state. As Tani Barlow points out, Maoist women/*funü* "got situated first in *guojia*/state and then, through the magic of metonymy, within the modern *jiating*/family."[58]

Like the domesticated sheep of the people's commune, the Mongolian sisters become docile lambs co-opted and owned by socialist China. A childish female voice sings the theme song: "Our dearest Chairman Mao, oh Chairman Mao, our grassland is prospering under the sunshine of Mao Zedong Thought. Our dearest Party, oh Party, little shepherds are growing up under your guidance; little shepherds are growing up under your guidance." The sisters are shepherds for the people's commune, and Chairman Mao shepherds Mongolians into socialist China.[59] Ethnicity is associated with the compliance of lambs as well as the transgression of exploring taboo subjects in mainstream socialist imagination such as animals and body metamorphosis.

The Wolf in the Forest: Villains, Masculinity, and Animality

Live-action films during the Seventeen Years featured what are referred to as middle characters (*zhongjian renwu*), those ambiguously situated between heroes and villains. However, as the Cultural Revolution intensified, such characters disappeared in model performance works. Negative characters that appear include vicious landlords, traitors, and spies attempting to sabotage socialism. During the Seventeen Years, these were both male and female. During the Cultural Revolution, they were exclusively male.

Human villains were rare in animated films during the Seventeen Years, primarily because most story lines featured animals and fantastic stories, and only a few appeared in revolutionary realist films of the mid-1960s.[60] However, after the disappearance of animals in *Heroic Little Sisters of the Grassland,* human villains began to dominate the screen. Like those in model performance works, villains in animated films were exclusively male during the Cultural Revolution.[61] Their masculinity intensifies the life-or-death revolutionary struggle between rivals, because violent nationalism is usually configured in masculine terms, which is best exemplified in war.[62]

Rosemary Roberts argues that although villains in Maoist model works were male, the conventions of revolutionary aesthetics feminized them, as evidenced by dwarfed stature, high-pitched voices, and feminine movements and gestures.[63] Issues of gender were important partly because human action dominated Maoist model works. Because animation is considered an artistic form heavily populated by animals, I propose animality as a kind of third gender that blurs the binary between masculinity and femininity, and use this concept in examining animated films made during the Cultural Revolution.

The animality of the villains relates to the disappearance of anthropomorphic animals, who took metaphorical refuge in male bodies. In animated films at the time, most villains were named after animals: the Wolf in the Forest (*Shanzhong lang*) in the film *The Little Trumpeter* (*Xiao haoshou,* 1973), the Crabs with Two Legs (*Liangzhi jiao de pangxie*) in *Little Sentinels of the East Sea* (*Donghai xiao shaobing,* 1973), the Polar Bear (*Beiji xiong*) in *Arrows with Firecrackers* (*Daixiang de gongjian,* 1974), and the Stinking Pufferfish (*Chou hetun*) in *The Night of the Flooding Tide* (*Da chaoxun zhiye,* 1975). Similarly, villains in model works were named after animals: Vulture (*Zuoshan diao*) in *Taking Tiger Mountain by Strategy,* White Tiger (*Baihu*) in *Surprise Attack on the White Tiger Brigade* (*Qixi baihu tuan,* 1972), and Viper Gallbladder (*Dushedan*) in *Azalea Mountain* (*Dujuan shan,* 1974). Indeed, revolutionary language during the Cultural Revolution was replete with animal metaphors. The most frequent example is Ox Demons and Snake Spirits (*Niugui sheshen*), which was standard for so-called class enemies.[64] In chapter 1, I discuss wartime speciesism, specifically, the use of animal images to humiliate and denigrate wartime enemies in Chinese, Japanese, and American cartoons and animated films. I maintain that speciesism functioned in alternative ways when animals were visually absent from animated films during the Cultural Revolution, generating what I call a disembodied or invisible speciesism.

Exuberant with animality, animated villains can occupy only nonhuman space. Villains in live-action feature films during the Seventeen Years were not radically animalized, usually had human names, and lived like ordinary people before they were exposed and captured as enemies of the country. These villains, especially spies, lived in bourgeois wallpapered homes or seductive boudoirs away from socialist doctrine.[65] However, during the Cultural Revolution, the villains were animalized and given names of animals, were forced to leave their homes, and took shelter in caves, lairs, and dens, wandering like wild beasts in the forests and along national borders to escape revolutionary hunters.

The relocation of villains from home (humans and the built environment) to wilderness (animals and Otherness) is most clear in *The Little Trumpeter*. At the opening of the film, the major villain is a landlord who lives in a large, luxurious house and oppresses the protagonist, a young ox-herding boy (the ox is almost invisible throughout the film). The landlord's name is Wolf in the Forest, suggesting his inhumanity and cruelty. This animality is further dramatized by his appetite: he eats the gallbladder of vipers. When the Red Armies come, they oust the landlord and attach a pair of revolutionary couplets to the gate of his house. The horizontal couplet reads, "Long live the Chinese Communist Party," and the vertical one reads, "The sickle cut off the old world; the axe carves out a new world." With these couplets, the communists symbolically transform the landlord's house into a humane revolutionary headquarters. The landlord and his cohort are homeless, dubbed running dogs (*zougou*), and flee to the wilderness, where they wait for the opportunity to return and take revenge. Thus the landlord really becomes a wolf in the forest, one that ends up being tracked and killed by the ox-herding boy.

Given their animalistic instincts, such villains are capable of metamorphosis and assume malleable identities to survive in the wilderness. At the same time, they leave traces of their movement and put themselves in danger, as in *Little Sentinels of the East Sea*, which was released during a tense period of China-Taiwan relations. In this film, a group of Taiwanese spies, dubbed crabs with two legs (suggesting their movement across the Taiwan Strait), land at a coastal village and undertake acts of sabotage. The spies are exposed and attacked by the people's militia. Three of them escape and attempt to steal a boat and flee back to Taiwan. On their way to the seashore, they meet a girl and her younger brother, who herd the (almost unseen) sheep of the people's commune. To deceive the children, the spies dress in People's Liberation Army uniforms. Their identity, however, is revealed by their perception of the animals. One says flatteringly to the children, "Your family has so many sheep." Their words alert the girl to their treachery: socialist sheep belong to the people's commune, not to individual families. She then tells her brother to go back to the village for help while she follows the spies. They try to mislead her down the wrong road, but their footprints betray them and the girl tracks them down. They try to kill her but are prevented from doing so by the pursuing soldiers who have come, after hearing her brother's story, to rescue her.

Animality both joins and separates villains and ethnic minorities, creating a common yet non-unified Other for the communist state to lord over. Whereas ethnic minorities are assimilated domestic animals ready to sacrifice their lives for the Party, villains are vicious wild beasts in the forest to be tracked down and killed by revolutionary hunters. Just as ethnic minorities are excluded from the Party-state in a superficial inclusion, villains are included by virtue of their expulsion. In both cases, humans, like animals (sparrows, tigers) at that time, are reduced to "bare life" in that their lives can be taken arbitrarily in the name of the Party-state. This shared reduction, Haiyan Lee argues, is a typical feature of modernity. Bare life in this instance is associated with Giorgio Agamben's concept of exclusion: it is about unprotected human and animal life (such as Jews during World War II and wild and domestic animals in the 2003 SARS outbreak in China) excluded from the sovereign state.[66] I contend that in radical socialist modernity during the Cultural Revolution, inclusion in the sovereign state can reduce humans and animals to bare life, as the case of the animated ethnic minorities and lambs demonstrates. Such extreme circumstances offer no escape.

Ethnic minorities are children and villains are adults, usually the oldest characters in animated films. In sharp contrast to rosy-cheeked ethnic girls in their brightly colored costumes, male villains usually have dark and gloomy faces and wear dark clothes, reinforcing their affinity with nighttime and secrecy. Villains are either skinny, always dwarfed by monumental heroes, or fat, suggesting hedonistic behaviors with excessive eating and drinking. Considered both nonhuman and inhuman, these villains exude animal vitality, which justifies the relentless revolutionary violence against them. Only after villains are eliminated can socialist children (both Han and minority) and Chairman Mao (the Party) live happily ever after in these animated revolutionary fairy tales.[67]

The Fox Hunts the Hunter: The Return and Revenge of the Animal

The reappearance of animals in animated film in 1976 more or less openly declared the imminent end of the Cultural Revolution. Just as the disappearance of the animal is associated with ethnic minorities (Mongolians) in *Heroic Little Sisters of the Grassland,* its return in *The Golden Wild Goose* is again bound up with ethnic minorities (Tibetans). Ethnicity is therefore self-contradictory as a category: it is associated with both revolutionary realism (the most realist and authentic) and with revolutionary romanticism (the most unreal and fantastic, which can be turned into a transcendental truth).

Figure 4.5. Tibetan children riding on the golden wild goose to Tiananmen Square in *The Golden Wild Goose,* 1976.

Golden Wild Goose is set immediately after the 1959 Tibetan Uprising. In this film, Tibet is plagued by grasshoppers. Rumor has it that only the golden wild goose, an auspicious bird in Tibetan legend, can exterminate the grasshoppers and bring happiness to the local people. The Tibetans pray to the Buddha but in vain. Chairman Mao promises to send a helicopter to exterminate the grasshoppers. Several Tibetan children volunteer to help prepare for the helicopter's arrival and in the process successfully thwart a scheme to blow it up. The helicopter finally arrives and kills the grasshoppers. The Tibetans, who marvel at the power of the helicopter, are convinced of the superiority of socialist modernity and Mao's effective leadership.

The animal makes its appearance in the film's daydream sequence. As part of their preparation work, the children climb a snow-capped mountain in search of a snow-lotus flower, which they plan to present as tribute to the helicopter. When they find the flower, a close-up shot shows them gazing at it in ecstatic reverence. This shot is immediately followed by a sequence from the children's daydream, in which they ride the legendary golden wild goose to fly across the Great Wall that traditionally separates ethnic barbarians from the Han, and present the snow-lotus flower as a tribute to Mao in Tiananmen Square, where Mao's monumental portrait—first featured in *Heroic Little Sisters*—emerges among a sea of red banners and balloons with slogans of "Long Live Chairman Mao and the Chinese Communist Party" (figure 4.5).

The appearance of the magic wild goose—the return of the oppressed (à la Marx) and repressed (à la Freud)—foreshadowed the demise of Mao and the collapse of an ideological system (the Cultural Revolution) despite the association of the snow-lotus flower and a long life. Only several months later, Mao died and the Cultural Revolution soon came to an end. The revolutionary rhetoric, though touted as rational at the time, fell flat precisely because it was too rational.

Here the fantastic was associated with the metaphor of wings and flying. As mentioned earlier, the disappearance of the animal from children's literature began with the persecution of Chen Bochui in 1960. Chen's advocacy for fantasy was best represented by his book *Fantasy Has Colorful Wings* (*Huanxiang zhangzhe caise de chibang*). One of the stories in it tells of an ambitious cat who wants to fly. For Chen, fantasy is associated with wings and flying. The word "flying" was in fact a keyword in the movement against Chen and fantasy, which began with the essay "What Kind of Wings? Where to Fly?" ("Shenmeyang de chibang wang narfei") published in *The People's Literature* (*Renmin wenxue*) in June 1960. The essay argued that Chen's advocacy for fantasy demonstrated his bourgeois orientation; therefore his fantasy with colorful wings could not take flight in socialist China.[68] A popular slogan was coined at the time to criticize the flying animals and fantasy in children's visual culture and literature: "Ancients and animals flying all over the sky, poor those lonely workers, peasants, and soldiers" (*guren dongwu mantian fei, kelian jimo gong nong bing*).[69] As symbols of fantasy, flying animals were inimical to revolution and revolutionary realism, thus their disappearance in *Heroic Little Sisters of the Grassland* marked the start of the Cultural Revolution, and their reappearance in *Golden Wild Goose* foreshadowed its end.

The boundary between the fantastic and the realistic in *The Golden Wild Goose* is blurred by the relationship between the magic golden wild goose and the helicopter. The goose is associated with both the primitiveness of Tibet and the helicopter as an icon of socialist modernity, challenging ten years of visual dominance of machines. The goose and the helicopter are two sides of the same coin. Both kill grasshoppers and bring happiness to Tibetans. Both are associated with physical movement. The difference is that the wild goose resides in dreams and legends, and the helicopter in reality. The distinction between the fantastic and the realistic, dream and reality, organic and mechanical is ambiguous. We can even say that the real helicopter is more fantastic and the fantastic wild goose is more real. This paradox culminated in the tribute-offering daydream sequence.

The Tibetan children's longing for Chairman Mao is depicted at the moment that Tibet was trying to break away from China in 1959. Was the socialist assimilation of Tibetans merely a dream?

If the fantastic animal displaced the machine in *Golden Wild Goose,* it supplanted it in *One Night at the Art Studio* (*Hualang yiye,* 1978). Produced two years after Mao's death, this film is a reflection on children's visual arts during the Cultural Revolution. Set in a children's art studio, the film features two machine villains: an iron club with spikes like wolf fangs and a tall metallic cap. The club and cap walk into the studio at night and destroy the pictures they deem inappropriate by crossing them out: drawings of animals (rooster, elephant, giraffe) and of children's daily life activities (studying, swimming, doing good deeds, greeting their teacher), and landscapes (see figure 4.6). When the clock strikes midnight, the children and animals come to life and restore the pictures. A human villain in a picture, however, also comes to life, runs away, and asks the club and the cap to come back to the studio. When the three villains return, the children and animals launch a battle against them (and win). The relationship between animals and machines in this film is far more confrontational and violent than that between the goose and the helicopter in *Golden Wild Goose.*

In the beginning of *One Night at the Art Studio,* only the club and cap are animated; the animals and children are still inside the pictures. The cross mark the villains used on the pictures was used frequently on stills of animated films criticized and banned during the period.[70] The lines of the cross effectively bind and immobilize the animals. The animals, however, break free, come off the

Figure 4.6. Animated machine (spiked club) crosses out the inanimate drawings of animals in *One Night at the Art Studio,* 1978.

pictures, and start moving. After they win the battle, they confine the animated machines within a picture, rendering them inanimate. This scenario vividly demonstrates the power relationship between animals and machines in animated films. What could and could not be animated was not only an aesthetic issue, but also a political one.

The club and the cap represent the notions of "beating to death with a club" (*yi bangzi dasi*) and "putting on a high cap" (*dai gaomao*), metaphors for the persecution of arts and artists during the Cultural Revolution. The machines' crossing out of animals in the beginning of the film pave the way for their own destruction, because the animals come to life to resist the artistic coercion imposed on them. Artistic transformation is a self-generated process, a revolution from within. In this battle against machines, animals side with children and regain their place in children's visual arts only after defeating the machines. These animals are enlarged to the extent that the children ride a rooster like a horse (see figure 4.7). The goose is similarly enlarged. The magnification of the returned animals radically reasserts their presence and visual dominance after a decade's absence from the screen.

Speaking human language is pivotal for the returned animals. Philosophers such as Descartes have pointed out that the difference between humans and animals is language.[71] Although humans have the capacity for language, animals have only cries, grunts, or croaks. Spivak's rhetorical question "Can the subaltern speak?" is often interpreted from the perspectives of class, gender, and race.[72] It

Figure 4.7. Aggrandized rooster in *One Night at the Art Studio,* 1978.

raises the question of species as well, because animals cannot speak and are the lowest of the low among the subalterns. However, in animated film, fairy tale, apologue, parable, and fable, what Akira Lippit calls the "minor genre," animals do speak and even "speak too much."[73] The talking anthropomorphic animal is probably the most prominent feature of these minor genres, partly because of their origin in oral tradition.

During the Cultural Revolution, animals expressed themselves only indirectly. Their return in the late 1970s gave speech back to them. In *Golden Wild Goose,* the goose speaks through ventriloquism. In the daydream sequence, the goose's flight to Beijing is accompanied by an off-screen song by Tsering Dekyi, a famous Tibetan female singer.[74] This disembodied voice is thus reembodied by the wild goose. In *One Night at the Art Studio,* the rooster does not speak, but at the end of the film finally gives a triumphant pre-dawn crow—a cry that welcomes the sun rise and puts an end to the night of the Cultural Revolution.

The Fox Hunts the Hunter is the first animated film featuring a speaking animal after a decade of silence. When the fox begins to speak, it is about getting revenge.[75] Reversing the relationship between animals and machines, as in *Art Studio,* is not enough. Instead, the fox aims to subvert the power relationship between humans and animals, the hunter and the hunted, and the eater and the eaten. *The Fox Hunts the Hunter* features a clever fox who takes a gun from a young and incompetent hunter and tries to kidnap and eat him (figure 4.8). Even though an old hunter intervenes and kills the fox, the young hunter is terrified. The film's male voiceover confirms his symbolic death: "If a hunter loses his gun and trembles in front of beasts, he is already dead even if he still physically lives." The fox has triumphed in symbolic domination. In reversing the two roles, the fox reverses the power relationship between humans and animals—both biologically and representationally—that began with the decimation of sparrows in the four pests campaign years earlier. The emphasis on the powerless hunter's youthfulness subverts the socialist rhetoric through which Mao manipulated children and young people in the late 1950s into becoming the major force behind the destruction of sparrows.

At the beginning of the film, when the forest animals spread the rumor that a fox has turned into a powerful wolf, a winking owl appears. It appears again at the end of the film when the fox and the wolf kidnap the young hunter and are ready to kill and eat him. The owl is modeled on *Owl* (*maotou ying*), originally painted by Huang Yongyu for a friend in 1973. Huang's *Owl* was severely criticized for the owl's having one eye closed. Displayed in a special exhibition of blacklisted paintings at the National Art Gallery in Beijing in March 1974, the painting was identified with the caption "Huang Yongyu produced this *Owl* in 1973. With its one open eye and the other closed, the owl suggests Huang's and like-minded artists'

Figure 4.8. Fox gives the usurped gun to wolf and asks him to kidnap the young hunter in *The Fox Hunts the Hunter,* 1978.

animosity toward the Proletarian Cultural Revolution and the Socialist system."[76] In traditional Chinese culture, the nocturnal owl is an ominous creature associated with darkness, night, secret, evil, and unknown forces. Beginning in the late 1950s, however, the owl came to be regarded as an auspicious bird because it eats sparrows and rats, two of the four pests. Despite these positive associations, Huang's winking owl became one of the most politicized animals during the Cultural Revolution decade. Its reappearance in *The Fox Hunts the Hunter* underscores the film's subtle connections with the period.

A Close-Up of Revolutionary Realism: Animal and Form

Conventional scholarship on literature and arts during the Cultural Revolution has a political perspective that traces back to Mao's 1942 Yan'an talk, in which he stipulated that literature and the arts should be subordinate to politics. More recent studies are beginning to challenge this political-determinist approach by highlighting the power of the arts to transform both themselves and social realities. In so doing, these studies draw attention to the internal rupture within the arts that contributed to their decline. In a study of sun-facing courtyards and urban communal culture in Shanghai during the mid-1970s, for example, Nicole Huang argues that "the reasons for their demise need to be located within urban communal culture itself."[77] In his studies on the model opera films of the period, Paul Clark points out that because film as an art that is close to indexical realism and naturalism, the adoption of a highly theatrical and performative aesthetic inspired by Peking opera was a poor fit, an internal illogic that contributed to the implosion of the Cultural Revolution.[78] In a similar vein, Jason McGrath argues that the highly theatrical artistic form of model works used ironically to portray revolutionary realities, "must have contributed to the sudden collapse of the ideological authority of Maoism by the end of the 1970s."[79] The arts were not determined by politics and ideology; instead, they shaped themselves and even transformed the ideologies that policed them. The rupture between artistic form and revolutionary ideology was also prominent in animated films and was bound up with the disappearance of animals in the mid-1960s.

Animals, which dominate animated film, are closely associated with the formal style of animation. Thomas Lamarre points out that the force of animation—namely, its plasmatic movement—is usually channeled into animal and other nonhuman characters because the human audience pays less attention to the accuracy of animals' movement and is more tolerant of violent deformation and transformation of animal body forms than of human characters.[80] Animals therefore play a central role in defining animation as characterized by plasmaticity, movement, and fantasy.

The disappearance of animals in films thus led to a formalist rupture in animation, the embedded risks of which Chinese animators and critics pointed out. As early as 1962, Chinese animators sensed the dangers, as evident in debates over the release of *Red Cloud Cliff*. Skepticism culminated in the release of *Heroic Little Sisters of the Grassland* three years later even though that realist orientation was officially sanctioned and oppositional views stifled. Chinese animators consider it more difficult in animation to portray humans than animals, contemporary than ancient subjects, positive than negative characters, and praise than satire. *Heroic Little Sisters* violated these conventions because it had contemporary subject matter and praised a human hero in a documentary style. Although the film was a hit, even its director, Qian Yunda, insisted that animators should appreciate the difficulty inherent in a realist approach with serious political themes. He wrote in the early 1980s explaining this stance:

> In regard to the realist orientation of *Heroic Little Sisters of the Grassland*, it is fine if it is just experimentation. We should not make this kind film often. This is because animated film is not suitable for constructing positive heroes in a serious way. This is the same with crosstalk and cartoons, which are not suitable for praising heroes.[81]

Animated films gradually returned to the plasmatic and fantastic mode after Mao's death in 1976.

The rupture between artistic form and realist ideology is best exemplified in the prominent use of close-ups in Cultural Revolution films. During the Seventeen

Years, the essence of animation had been motion and movement, and close-ups tended to freeze movement and expose the artificiality and limitations of animation. In *A Zhuang Broçade*, animators used close-ups to portray the face of an elderly ethnic minority woman and were questioned by reviewers who argued that in close-ups the hand-drawn lines became more visible and thus the artificiality of the form was exposed.[82] With the disappearance of animals and the realist turn in animation in the middle 1960s, it became conventional to portray heroes using close-ups at the most revolutionary, dramatic, and revelatory moments. Use of close-ups was guided by the principle of three prominences and pushed animated film to model on live-action film.

Take *The Little Trumpeter.* The film's protagonist is an embittered herd boy named Xiaoyong whose parents are killed by their landlord. The boy joins the Red Army to avenge his parents, becomes a trumpeter, and is wounded in battle. When he regains consciousness and sees his trumpet, the camera cuts to a close-up of his longing and determined face, which is gradually superimposed with a semi-diegetic Communist flag (see figure 4.9). At this thematically revelatory moment, the plasmatic movement is suspended and the fluidity of line comes to a stop.

The use of close-ups in revolutionary animated films proved self-defeating, however. The goal was to highlight the heroes' dignity and to draw attention to their determined, piercing eyes and heavy eyebrows, a trademark of Cultural Revolution–era animated films.[83] Rather than reinforce revolutionary realism, however, the close-ups drew attention to the constructedness of the heroic face. The revolutionary eyes and faces were nothing, the close-up made clear, but drawn lines and layers of pigment. The realism revealed the unreal.

Figure 4.9. Close-up of Xiaoyong's face in *The Little Trumpeter,* 1973.

Most animated films during the Cultural Revolution were characterized by the socialist realism prominent in live-action feature films of the Seventeen Years. Thus animation lost its medium-specificity (plasmaticness and fantasy) and became more like realist live-action, and live-action lost its medium-specificity and looked more like theatrical performative operas (best exemplified in the formulaic *liangxiang* pose in model opera films), resulting in a domino chain of what Jason McGrath calls the "formalist drifts" of the Cultural Revolution.[84] Pushed to extremes, the formalist rupture within animation itself turned out to be a passing phase.

Conclusion: A Decade of Dis/appearance

Conventional studies of the Cultural Revolution typically center on presence by placing political struggle and human action in a revolutionary light. This chapter has focused on what was absent, namely, animals, which were critical to defining (socialist) modernity (in a negative way) and the medium specificity of animation. I thus reframe the Cultural Revolution as a decade of dis/appearance. Animals as both biological creatures and representations in film disappeared. Ordinary humans also disappeared to the extent that only heroes and villains and ethnic minorities inhabited the revolutionary world. In other words, humans also became an endangered species. In addition, many cultural relics, buildings, forests, and even landscapes disappeared in the political and economic campaigns launched during that time.[85] Dis/appearance here does not mean nonexistence, because what disappeared, or was forced to disappear, would return and scatter their traces, registering what Ackbar Abbas calls "a kind of pathology of presence."[86] Dramatized scenarios of dis/appearance were played out not only in material reality, but also in the realm of visual representations.

Animals disappeared not only from reality in Mao's wars against nature, but also from representation (model opera films, animated films, children's literature, visual arts) as radical artistic forms and cultural policies were adopted. I call this the double disappearance of animals, a phenomenon unique to the radical socialist modernity of the Cultural Revolution.[87] The animal is the crucial figure of fantasy and the antithesis of revolution and realism. Its disappearance marked the start of the Cultural Revolution and its return ten years later marked the end. Situated between the earth-bound sheep and the flying wild goose, the Cultural Revolution can be reframed as a decade of absent animals. They were displaced yet not completely replaced by humans and machines, however. Their visual disappearance gave rise to their spectral reappearance in language.

Animality as a category of third gender between masculinity and femininity is crucial in understanding animated films of the period. Whereas those during the Seventeen Years emphasized anthropomorphism, those during the Cultural Revolution emphasized disembodied speciesism in the form of metonymy and metaphor. Metamorphosis, or the transformation of body forms between humans and animals, no longer functioned in physical and visual terms. The fairy tale of the Seventeen Years was transformed into a revolutionary message. What made the revolution real and fantastic was not the heroes, what Ban Wang calls the "sublime figures of history," but rather the internal Other(s) exemplified by ethnic minorities and villains, who constantly disrupted the ideal of a homogeneous and monolithic national identity under the solid leadership of Mao.[88]

Epilogue

Television and Animated Encounters in Postsocialist China

Between the late 1970s and mid-1980s, after the Cultural Revolution had ended, the Shanghai Animation Film Studio saw an outburst of artistic creativity—a period regarded as the second golden age of Chinese animation.[1] Numerous animated films of great artistic merit were produced. Many of them—such as *Nezha Makes Havoc in the Sea* (*Nezha naohai,* 1979), *Three Monks* (*Sange heshang,* 1980), *Monkeys Fish the Moon* (*Houzi laoyue,* 1981), and *Feelings of Mountain and River* (*Shanshui qing,* 1988)—won national and international awards and were canonized as masterpieces. Animated filmmaking during this period continued to follow the guiding principle of national style. During the mid-1980s, however, the Shanghai Animation Film Studio and Chinese animation in general faced a crisis.

As China officially opened to the world beginning in the late 1970s, socialist collectivism, along with the unity and cohesion of the Shanghai Animation Film Studio, began to disintegrate. Experienced animators left the studio in pursuit of better opportunities abroad. Fung Yuk-sung, Xu Lianhua, Tu Jia, Wu Qiang left for Hong Kong; Ma Guoliang, Lei Yu, Wong Baoqiang, Huang Qiao, Qin Baoyi, Zhang Xiaoqi and many others left for the United States; Huang Wei and Chen Feng left for Japan; Zhu Kanglin left for Australia.[2] This tremendous loss of talent sharply contrasts with the late 1940s and early 1950s, when renowned artists and animators from around the world came to Shanghai to devote themselves to the emerging animation industry.

In addition, as China became enmeshed in the global economic network, the monopoly status of the Shanghai Animation Film Studio began to decline. Many other state-owned studios began to make animated films. The Beijing Science Education Film Studio established an animation division in 1982 and the Changchun Film Studio in 1984. Both produced many high-quality animated films. Other state-owned film studios, such as the Liaoning Science Education Film Studio, Nanjing Film Studio, Fujian Film Studio, and August First Film Studio, followed suit, all of them in competition with the Shanghai Animation Film Studio.

At the same time, the number of joint ventures and wholly foreign-owned animation studios mushroomed beginning in the mid-1980s, including Shenzhen

Jade Animation Company (1985), Pacific Rim Animation (1987), Times Animation Company in Guangzhou (1986), and Dalian Avanty International Animation (1988).[3] Between 1986 and 1989, some one hundred experienced animators resigned from the Shanghai Animation Film Studio, joined the international companies, and worked on outsourced projects from Japan and the West. This decision was understandable because the monthly salary at the Shanghai Animation Film Studio was several hundred yuan per month, but several thousand and even ten thousand at the international studios.[4] This tremendous loss of professional talent was referred to as the Great Escape and the Sinking of the Titanic. Revenues dropped from CN¥1.43 million in 1987 to CN¥0.48 million in 1988. People who stayed put were confused and no longer of one mind, draining the studio's cohesive strength and effectiveness. By 1989, the Shanghai Animation Film Studio was in crisis.[5]

Making things worse was that the multiplication of joint and foreign-owned animation studios shifted the focus of Chinese animation from creative production to outsourced projects. Facing tremendous financial pressure, the Shanghai Animation Film Studio also began to work on outsourced projects as well. As early as 1979, it had worked on a project from Tōei Animation in Japan in an experimental, small-scale collaboration that entailed inking and painting about seven thousand cels.[6] From 1985 onward, the studio worked more extensively on outsourced projects from Japan, America, Germany, France, and other countries, and on more important parts of the outsourced projects.[7] By doing so, it increased its profits from CN¥550,000 in 1984 to CN¥1.13 million in 1985, CN¥1.41 million in 1986, and CN¥1.7 million in 1987.[8] To improve its ability to work on profitable outsourced projects, the studio established the Shanghai Yilimei Animation Company in 1990 with capital support from Hong Kong Yili Development Limited Cooperation. Zhou Keqin was the company's first president, serving from 1991 to 2007. Yilimei worked on projects outsourced from abroad until it closed in 2010 because outsourcing was no longer profitable.

In the 1990s, many domestic private animation companies began to flourish, among them Sunchime Cartoon (1996), Jiang Toon Animation (2000), and Creative Power Entertaining (2001), which further eroded the Shanghai Animation Film Studio's monopoly. At the same time, independent animated filmmaking became more and more popular and numerous small studios were established, such as Liu Jian's Le Joy Animation Studio (2007). Independent animated films, such as Liu Jian's features and Ray Lei's shorts, became increasingly active at film festivals and gradually displaced national style films on the international stage.

In addition to these material sociohistorical changes in the industry, new technology and new media, such as television, became more popular and led to the unprecedented commercialization of animation. The first television station in China was in Beijing, which began broadcasting on May 1, 1958. By the end of 1960, China had twenty television stations and sixteen experimental ones.[9] During the socialist decades, animated films were released primarily in theaters, but some were also broadcast on television, which only a few privileged people were able to watch—usually high-ranking officials. On December 7, 1980, *Astro Boy* (fifty-two episodes, 1963, Japan) was released on China Central Television (CCTV), for free, under the condition that CCTV broadcast the advertisements of Casio products. *Astro Boy* was the first foreign animated film introduced in post-Mao China. After that, many foreign animated films from Japan and the West, such as *Doraemon, Kimba the White Lion, Lulu the Flower Angel, The Smart Little Monk Yixiu, Mickey Mouse,* and *Donald Duck,* flooded the Chinese market and gradually transformed the industry's structure and the aesthetic tastes of Chinese audiences. Animation franchise toys became popular with Chinese children and eventually dominated the toy market. Their infiltration into the domestic market was regarded by many Chinese as a form of cultural imperialism.

The release of *Astro Boy* had a tremendous impact on animated filmmaking. Inspired by its commercial success, the Shanghai Animation Film Studio experimented with the production of a number of its own television animation series such as *The Stories of Afanti* (*Afanti de gushi,* fifteen episodes, 1979–1988), *The Wandering Life of the Three-Haired Boy* (*Sanmao liulang ji,* five episodes, 1984), *Police Chief Black Cat* (*Heimao jingzhang,* five episodes, 1984–1987), and *The Canabash Brothers* (*Hulu xiongdi,* thirteen episodes, 1986–1987).[10] Nearly every urban household in China bought a television during the 1980s, just as those in the United States had in the 1950s. By the end of 1987, television broadcasting reached 78 percent of the Chinese population.[11] Following the example of the Shanghai Animation Film Studio, many television stations also began to produce animation series independently. Among the first were the Shanghai TV Station (1983) and China Teleplay Production Center Co. (1984). Other provincial stations soon followed suit.[12] Television animation became so popular that, for Chinese audiences, since the mid-1980s, watching animation came to mean watching television.[13] By the late 1980s, television animation dominated the market and began to displace traditional cinema animation. Most domestic television animation series made in the 1980s adopted the technology of traditional cinematic animation. That is, they were first made on film and then converted to video for television, which was a very costly process. The first animated short produced on video with television technology was *The Roundtable Meeting of Circles* (*Yuande yuanzhuo huiyi,* 1986), produced by the Youth and Children Department of Beijing Television. From then on, television-technology animation increased in popularity because of its low budget and high commercial value and during the 1990s came to dominate the animation market.[14]

Shanghai Animation Film Studio had difficulty in adapting. Still following the production pattern of socialist China, the studio needed only to fulfil the government's annual quota. If the studio produced more films than required, the government would not purchase and distribute the extras. If the studio sold the extras to television stations, it received only 2 percent or 3 percent of the total cost. Production costs were high because the studio continued to use expensive cinema animation methods.[15] It could not produce an episode every week, as foreign television animation series did at the time, nor could it produce a series with dozens or even hundreds of episodes to capture audiences along with profits from the toy market. Because of the high cost, the series it produced could not compete with imported TV animation series, which were released either for nothing or for a very low price. The challenges were immense.

With the popularization of television, audiences were individualized and diversified; they could now stay at home and watch privately. According to Neil Postman, television withholds no secrets and thus is open to all; it blurs the boundary between adults and children and contributes to the disappearance of childhood.[16] In line with this, children, as the collective audience of animated film since 1949, disappeared with the rise of television in 1980s China. Animated films could no longer easily locate its target audience, which became decentralized, diversified, and elusive. In other words, animated filmmaking at the Shanghai Animation Film Studio during the socialist decades was a centripetal force enhanced by socialist collectivism, but in postsocialist China a centrifugal one. The centrality, unity, and cohesion of the Shanghai Animation Film Studio disintegrated during the late 1970s and 1980s, until the state (China Film Distribution and Exhibition Corporation in particular) finally stepped in and abolished its monopoly for unified purchases and marketing, a change that pushed Shanghai Animation Film Studio fully into the capitalist market on January 1, 1995.

The film *Three Monks* highlights the effects of the demise of socialist collectivism on Shanghai Animation Film Studio. The film was directed by Ada (Xu Jingda, 1934–1987), whose artistic career peaked in the 1980s.[17] Water is central to this film, in which it symbolizes life, anima, and animation. The first monk arrives at the temple, carries water, and then fills the vase held by the Goddess of Mercy. The withered plant in the vase comes back to life and the Goddess of Mercy smiles. When the second and the third monks arrive, no one is willing to carry water. The plant dies and the Goddess of Mercy closes her eyes. Gradually the temple's life force ebbs away. Only when the temple catches fire do the three monks work together to carry water and extinguish the fire. From then on, they carry water together, reanimate the temple, and live happily ever after. The film suggests that only by working collectively can animators (the three monks) make masterpieces, bring about the prosperity of Chinese animation, and prevent the degeneration of Shanghai Animation Film Studio (the temple). Made at a historical threshold in 1980, *Three Monks* evokes the animators' nostalgic longing for the collectivism of socialist animated filmmaking. It can also be seen as prophetic of its imminent disintegration.

Considered from another perspective, however, the dramatic sociohistorical and technological changes of the 1980s introduced new opportunities and prospects for Chinese animation. Accelerated transnational flows of culture in the age of globalization have the potential to generate more animated interstices and contact zones that in turn may trigger new frictions, artistic creativity, and animation of cultures. Animated encounters between domestic and international others might bring challenges and threats, but also they can bring about new visions, adaptations, transformations, and even new birth. The series *Police Chief Black Cat* became a big hit in having drawing on Japanese and American animations yet keeping a Chinese identity. It is a pity that after being criticized for its departure from the spirit of national style, Dai Tielang and other animators did not finish the series and continue their experimentation. Otherwise, *Police Chief Black Cat,* both an artistic and commercial success, should have provided an alternative "national style" to Chinese animation. Perhaps it is time for the Shanghai Animation Film Studio and Chinese animation more generally to seize the opportunities of glocalization and adapt to a changing and much more diversified world of animation in their pursuit of artistic and commercial success.

Transnational flows of culture and animated encounters are more conspicuous in the context of globalization and thus can be more easily recognized and acknowledged, but transnational undercurrents predating the 1980s remain invisible in histories of Chinese animation. To foreground these hidden histories, I have therefore focused on the multidirectional movements in animated filmmaking in China between the 1940s and 1970s—specifically, between China and Japan in the 1940s and 1950s, the Sino-Soviet and Sino-West encounter in the 1950s and early 1960s, and internal border crossings (ethnic minorities and Taiwan in Greater China) during the Cultural Revolution. I demonstrate that when Chinese animation was most nationalized and centralized, transnational undercurrents challenged the notion of pure national style and national identity. Transnational movements, in fact, are what made Chinese animation Chinese.

Although I am concerned with transnational undercurrents in the formation of national cultures, it is impossible to cover all animated encounters in one monograph. This study could be expanded in many directions. For instance, an article-length study could be devoted to the Wan brothers' animated shorts in Republican China prior to the emergence of *Princess Iron Fan* (*Tieshan gongzhu)* in 1941, which would highlight the animated encounter between Chinese animation and the West (the United States in particular). Chapter 1 mentioned the introduction of Disney's *Snow White* (1937) to Shanghai in 1938. Its reception and the presence of American and European animation in Republican Shanghai deserve further study. *Princess Iron Fan*'s journey to Hong Kong and the Wan brothers' activities there (1947–1956) also call for more research.[18] The animated encounter between Chinese and Czech puppet animation during the socialist decades merits scholarly attention. A more detailed study of the Sino-Soviet encounter in the 1950s is also needed. Another article-length study could be devoted to the presence of the West in animated films in socialist China to examine how transnational movements and animated encounters are configured in imaginative and representational rather than in material and territorial terms.[19] Other potential topics for further study include music, soundscape, gender issues, screening, and audience viewing experience and reception of socialist animated films. Rather than a closure or destination, this book is an opening, a point of departure for many academic journeys ahead.

Appendix 1: Animated Films by Mochinaga Tadahito

Wartime Japan

1. *Until an Animated Film Is Made* (*Manga eiga no dekiru made* 漫画映画の出來るまで, 1938). School of Applied Arts of Japan.
2. *The Marine Corps of Ducks* (*Ahiru rikusentai* あひる陸戰隊, 1940). Art Film Company.
3. *Ant Boy* (*Ari-chan* アリチャン, 1941). Art Film Company.
4. *Momotarō's Sea Eagles* (*Momotarō no umiwashi* 桃太郎の海鷲, 1943). Art Film Company.
5. *Fuku-chan's Submarine* (*Fuku-chan no sensuikan* フクちゃんの潜水艦, 1944). Asahi Film Company.

Socialist China

1. *The Year of Liberation* (*Fanshen nian* 翻身年, puppet animation, 1947). Northeast Film Studio.
2. *Dreaming to Be Emperor* (*Huangdi meng* 皇帝夢, puppet animation, November 1947). Northeast Film Studio.
3. *Capturing the Turtle in the Jar* (*Wengzhong zhuobie* 甕中捉鱉, December 1948). Northeast Film Studio.
4. *Thank You Kitty* (*Xiexie xiao huamao* 謝謝小花貓, 1950). Shanghai Film Studio.
5. *Little Iron Pillar* (*Xiao Tiezhu* 小鐵柱, 1951). Shanghai Film Studio.
6. *Kitty Goes Fishing* (*Xiaomao diaoyu* 小貓釣魚, 1952). Shanghai Film Studio.
7. *Picking Mushrooms* (*Cai mogu* 採蘑菇, 1953). Shanghai Film Studio.
8. *Who Meowed?* (*Miaowu shi shei jiao de* 喵嗚是誰叫的? puppet animation, 1979). Shanghai Animation Film Studio.

Postwar Japan (all puppet-animated)

1. *Mr. Bitter Beer's Magician* (*Horoniga-kun no majutsushi* ほろにが君の魔術師, 1953), with Kawamoto Kihachirō. Asahi Beer Company.
2. *The Melon Princess and the Demon* (*Uriko-hime to amanojaku* 瓜子姫とあまのじゃく, 1956). Puppet Animation Film Studio.
3. *Five Little Monkeys* (*Gohiki no kozaru-tachi* 五匹の子猿たち, 1956). Puppet Animation Film Studio.
4. *Little Black Sambo Subdues the Tiger* (*Chibikuro Sanbo no tora-taiji* ちびくろサンボのとらたいじ, 1956). Puppet Animation Film Studio.
5. *Little Black Sambo and His Twin Brother* (*Chibikuro Sanbo to futago no otōto* ちびくろサンボとふたごのおとうと, 1957). Puppet Animation Film Studio.
6. *The Mysterious Drum* (*Fushigina taiko* ふしぎな太鼓, 1957), Kawamoto Kihachirō made the puppets. Puppet Animation Film Studio.
7. *Removing a Big Tumor* (*Kobutori* こぶとり, 1958), Kawamoto Kihachirō made the puppets. Puppet Animation Film Studio.
8. *Lovely Puppet Tea Kettle* (*Bunbuku-chagama* ぶんぶくちゃがま, 1958), Kawamoto Kihachirō made the puppets. Puppet Animation Film Studio.
9. *Little Boy Penguins Lulu and Kiki* (*Pengin bōya ruru to kiki* ペンギンぼうやルルとキキ, 1958). Puppet Animation Film Studio.
10. *The Fox That Became the King* (*Ōsama ni natta kitsune* 王さまになったきつね, 1959). Puppet Animation Film Studio.
11. *A Boy and a Little Racoon Dog* (*Shōnen to kodanuki* 少年と子だぬき, 1992).

Videocraft International, United States (all puppet-animated)

1. *The New Adventures of Pinocchio* (TV series, 1960).
2. *Willy McBean & His Magic Machine* (theatrical feature film, 1963).
3. *Rudolph the Red-Nosed Reindeer* (TV series, Christmas special, 1964).
4. *Andersen's Fairy Tales / The Daydreamer* (theatrical feature, puppet animation and live action, 1966).
5. *The Ballad of Smokey the Bear* (TV movie, 1966).
6. *Mad Monster Party* (theatrical feature film, Halloween special, 1967).

Appendix 2: Leaders of the Shanghai Animation Film Studio

Wan Guchan, head of the Animation Department of Star Productions, April 1922; head of the Animation Department of New China Productions, early 1940

Qian Jiajun, head of the Education Movie Picture Society, Chongqing, August 1941

Mochinaga Tadahito, head of the Animation Group at the Northeast Film Company, late 1946; head of the Animation Branch at the Northeast Film Studio, June 1948

Te Wei, head of the Animation Group at the Northeast Film Studio, Autumn 1949; head of the Animation Group at the Shanghai Film Studio, March 1950; president of the Shanghai Animation Film Studio, 1957–1984

Yan Dingxian, president of the Shanghai Animation Film Studio, 1984–1988

Zhou Keqin, president of the Shanghai Animation Film Studio, March 1989–December 1991

Chang Guangxi, president of the Shanghai Animation Film Studio, December 1991–1993

Jin Guoping, president of the Shanghai Animation Film Studio, 1994–2005

Wang Tianyun, legal representative of the Shanghai Animation Film Studio, 2004–2014

Qian Jianping, president of the Shanghai Animation Film Studio, 2010–2016; legal representative of the Shanghai Animation Film Studio, 2016–present

Appendix 3: Major Publications on Chinese Animation

South Art News (*Nanguo yixun*), Guangzhou and Hong Kong, January 1947–1949

South Art News was the first periodical on Chinese animation and cartoon in China. Founded by Luo Yiwei, a student of Qian Jiajun, it had editorial offices in Guangzhou and Hong Kong, where it introduced background information on animation and cartoons, animators and artists, and their works. It also promoted teaching and educational activities at South Animation Academy (Nanguo donghua yishu xueyuan), founded by Luo Yiwei in Guangzhou and Hong Kong in the winter of 1946. *South Art News* published approximately fifty issues, the first twenty-four printed in Guangzhou and the others in Hong Kong. The target audience included adults, professionals, and others interested in animation. Clippings of this periodical, titled *HKAA Hong Kong Art Archive Primary Source: Volume 11,* are available at Department of Fine Art's Resource Center, the University of Hong Kong, Hong Kong.

Red Guard Cinema (*Hongweibing dianying*), Shanghai, July 1967–?

Early in the Cultural Revolution, in August 1966, the Red Guards took over the Shanghai Animation Film Studio and renamed it Red Guard Film Studio. Its film magazine, titled *Red Guard Cinema,* was published in July 1967, the first and probably the last issue. The magazine criticized many of the animated films made during the Seventeen Years (1949–1966) and featured the guidelines and policies of animated filmmaking. Red Guard Film Studio also issued other publications, such as *The Ugly History of Liu Shaogou* (*Liu Shaogou choushi*) in 1967, which vehemently criticized Liu Shaoqi, then president of China, through caricature and cartoons. Both magazines are available for public access at the Library of the Hong Kong University of Science and Technology, Hong Kong.

Monkey King (*Sun Wukong*), Shanghai and Beijing, June 1980–May 1990

Its editorial office located at the Shanghai Animation Film Studio, the pictorial *Monkey King* was printed by the China Film Press in Beijing and introduced animated films made by the Shanghai Animation Film Studio as well as animated films from abroad to children. Zhang Songlin and Wang Xingguan were its first editors. Its title was provided by Song Qingling, the widow of Sun Zhongshan. The pictorial is available for public access at the National Library of China in Beijing.

Cartoon King (*Katong wang*), Shanghai, June 1993–present

On June 1, 1993, Shanghai Animation Film Studio established *Cartoon King* to continue introducing animated films and cartoons to children and teenagers. The first editors were Chang Guangxi and Yang Jinfu. Wan Laiming provided the title. The magazine's style was influenced by Japanese animation and manga. It is available at the Shanghai Library, Shanghai.

China Animation (*Zhongguo donghua*), September 2005–present

China Animation was established as the official periodical of China Animation Association, a government organization founded in Shanghai in 1985. The first chief editor was Dong Hua. The periodical is elitist, representing authoritative and official viewpoints supported by mainstream animated filmmaking and the Chinese government. It is available at the National Taiwan University Library, Taiwan.

Association for Chinese Animation Studies (*Guoji huayu donghua yanjiu xiehui*), Hong Kong, August 2015–present

The Association for Chinese Animation Studies (ACAS) is the leading scholarly and public organization dedicated to introducing and promoting Chinese animation to the English-speaking world. Founded in Hong Kong in 2015, the ACAS publishes academic and popular writing related to Chinese animation—specifically, animated films made in greater China—mainland China, Hong Kong, Taiwan, Macao, and Chinese diasporic communities worldwide. This grouping includes films made solely or partially by ethnic Chinese or Chinese-speaking animators, even if the films are not officially labeled as Chinese. ACAS publications also cover cartoons, comics, linked pictures (*lianhuan hua*), toys, and other cultural products or activities closely related to Chinese animation. Submissions are welcomed. The association's mission is to connect studios, animators, researchers, teachers, and fans around the world to increase the international presence and recognition of Chinese animation on the global stage.

Notes

Introduction

1. Greene, *From Fu Manchu*; Chung, "Kung Fu Panda."

2. Bernstein, "The Panda That Roared"; Magnier, "China's Imported Panda"; Zhu, "Gongfu xiongmao."

3. After the anti-Japanese war erupted in 1937, the fourth brother Wan Dihuan gave up his animation career and became a businessman, running a photography studio in wartime Shanghai to support the extended Wan family. Therefore, the Wan brothers usually refers to the first three, who remained active in animated filmmaking throughout their lives (Wan, *Wo yu Sun Wukong*, 78).

4. The film exhibition was held in Hong Kong between July 19 and August 1, 1962. Twelve famous local actors and actresses, including Ng Cho-fan, Hsia Moon, Kung Chiu-hsia, and Fung Lam, attended the opening ceremony. Eight Chinese animated films were screened in Hong Kong and Kowloon. Approximately one hundred thousand people visited the exhibition (Bao, *Zhongguo donghua*, 147–148).

5. *Hongweibing dianying*, 30.

6. Du, "Chinese Animation." First-generation filmmakers refers to the film directors active before the end of the 1920s, such as Zhang Shichuan and Zheng Zhengqiu, who were the pioneers of Chinese cinema. Second generation refers to those active mainly in the 1930s and 1940s, such as Cai Chusheng and Fei Mu. The third generation includes directors active roughly during the socialist decades (1949–1976), such as Xie Jin and Xie Tieli. The fourth generation includes filmmakers active after 1978, such as Huang Shuqin, Zhang Nuanxin, and Xie Fei. The mid-1980s witnessed the rise of the fifth-generation filmmakers, such as Zhang Yimou, Chen Kaige, and Tian Zhuangzhuang, who made Chinese film more visible on the global stage. The sixth generation mainly refers to independent filmmakers in contemporary China, such as Wang Xiaoshuai, Jia Zhangke, and Zhang Yuan.

7. Crofts, "Reconceptualizing National Cinema(s)"; Berry, *Postsocialist Cinema.*

8. Pu, *Donghua chuangzuo qishilu*, 118.

9. Du, interview with Zhou Keqin, former president of the Shanghai Animation Film Studio (March 1989 to December 1991), June 14, 2015. Zhou Keqin further pointed out that during the socialist decades, some senior animators like Wan Laiming, Wan Guchan, and Qian Jiajun were persecuted by the Communist Party, but mainly because of their association with the Nationalist Party before 1949, not because of their animated films per se. However, their films were used to criticize and attack their "suspicious" class backgrounds.

10. The statistics are from Zhang and Gong, *Shei chuangzao*, 105.

11. Fung, "In Full Bloom (1)," 17; Wang, *Zhengtu* vol. 3, 4; *Zhengtu* vol. 4, 17. Bao, *Zhongguo donghua*, 73–75.

12. Only three animated feature films were produced during the socialist decades: *A Zhuang Brocade* (*Yifu zhuangjin,* 1959), *Peacock Princess* (*Kongque gongzhu,* 1963), and *Uproar in Heaven* (*Danao tiangong,* 1961–1964).

13. Wang, *Zhengtu,* 2:82.

14. When Chinese animators relocated from Changchun to Shanghai in the early 1950s, some of them took part-time jobs by drawing New Year's pictures (*nianhua*) and linked pictures (*lianhuan hua*), which in turn affected their work in animated filmmaking. The Shanghai Animation Film Studio held meetings to criticize and correct them. From then on, these kinds of side part-time jobs became rare at the studio (Mochinaga, *Animēshon Nitchū kōryūki,* 217).

15. Du, interview with Zhou Keqin, August 29, 2015.

16. Condry, *Soul of Anime*, 2.

17. Zhang and Gong, *Shei chuangzao,* 65.

18. Du, interview with Duan Xiaoxuan, June 16, 2015.

19. Ibid.

20. These films include *Grandma's Jujube Tree* (*Laopopo de zaoshu,* 1958), *The Beautiful Little Goldfish* (*Meili de xiao jinyu,* 1958), *Celebrating the Harvest during the Mid-Autumn Festival* (*Bayue shiwu qing fengshou,* 1958), *The Woodcutter Maiden* (*Kanchai guniang,* 1959), *The Bee and the Earthworm* (*Mifeng yu qiuyin,* 1959), and *The Radish Comes Back* (*Luobo huilai le,* 1959).

21. Jones, *Developmental Fairy Tales,* 105–111.

22. For a critique of the demonization of Maoist era in Western scholarship, see Vukovich, "Maoist Discourse and Its Demonization," in *China and Orientalism*, 47–65. Also see Tang, *Visual Culture in Contemporary China.*

23. Donald, "Children as Political Messengers," 79–100.

24. Farquhar, *Children's Literature in China*, 10.

25. Chow, *Primitive Passions*, 113.

26. Anagnost, "Children and National Transcendence," 199.

27. Bhabha, "Of Mimicry and Man"; Irigaray, *This Sex Which.*

28. Zhong, "Meishupian de xin tiandi," 72.

29. Lu, "Kaifeng de mouxie," 34.

30. Cai, "Zuzhi ertong kanhao," 23–25.

31. Anagnost, "Children and National Transcendence," 213.

32. Du, 2010 interview with Duan Xiaoxuan, a powerful camerawoman who dominated animation technology during the socialist decades. Actually, the case of Duan Xiaoxuan, the first female camera operator in the history of Chinese animation, also demonstrates how totalitarian politics could liberate women from traditional gender roles in animated filmmaking (see Du, "Socialism").

33. Du, interview with senior animator Fung Yuk-sung.

34. According to Alex Zahlten, a similar case can be found in Japanese cinema. Although small independent ("pink film") companies made sex films in the 1970s without being censored, the major studio Nikkatsu ran into trouble when it produced exactly the same kind of film and introduced them in their public theaters. What was objectionable was not the content itself but instead how it was introduced to the mainstream culture. For a discussion of pink film, see Zahlten, *The End of Japanese Cinema.*

35. Many animators, scholars, and intellectuals regard the Seventeen Years (1949–1966), especially the years between 1955 and 1965, as the first golden age of Chinese animation. As I will demonstrate, this first golden age should also include the wartime era and the Cultural Revolution. Animated films produced during the Cultural Revolution should not be dismissed as sheer propaganda. Rather, despite their explicit ideological messages, the significance of their artistic and research value is similar to the eight model works (modernized and revolutionarized Peking opera, ballet, and symphony) produced at the same time. After the Cultural Revolution had ended, the Shanghai Animation Film Studio experienced an outburst of artistic creativity. This period, from the late 1970s to the late 1980s, is commonly regarded as the second golden age (see epilogue).

36. Chen, *Zai xuexi Sulian.*

37. Pontieri, *Soviet Animation*, 38–41.

38. MacFadyen, *Yellow Crocodiles*, 31–61. One more example of the ambiguous relationship between totalitarian politics and animation is Czech puppet animation. During Communist rule, Czech puppet animation enjoyed its golden age.

39. Macdonald, *Animation in China*; Wu, *Chinese Animation*. In addition to the two scholarly texts, Rolf Giesen's book for a popular audience, *Chinese Animation,* is a thorough collection of Chinese animated films throughout history.

40. In addition to the three books, various studies of Chinese animation are in English (for example, Leyda, *Dianying*; Bendazzi, *Cartoons*; Bao, *Fiery Cinema*; Li, "A National Cinema"; Voci, "DV and Animateur Cinema in China"; Farquhar, "Monks and Monkey"; Lent and Xu, "China's Animation Beginnings"; Lent, *Animation in Asia*; Donald, *Little Friends*; Quiquemelle, "The Wan Brothers"; Edera, "The Animated Film"; Cui, "Pursuit of a National Style"; Kang, "*Shui Mo Dong Hua*"; Yang, "Animating

Landscape"; Du, "Dis/appearance"; Guo and Li, "Animating Chinese Cinemas"). For all PhD dissertations, see http://acas.ust.hk/category/research-center/dissertation-reviews.

41. Yan and Suo, *Zhongguo donghua*; Zhang, *Ershi shiji Zhongguo*; Xu and Wang, *Du donghua*; Xiao, *Guochan donghua dianying*; Bao, *Zhongguo donghua.*

42. Quoted in Condry, *Soul of Anime*, 91–94.

43. Guo, "Jinnianlai guanyu dianying."

44. Yin, "Donghua dianying zhong."

45. Songlin, "Meishu dianying yao zou minzuhua de daolu," 50; Luo, "Dianying minzuhua lunbian," 16–17; Yin, "Donghua dianying zhong"; Songlin, "Yuyou minzu xing."

46. James Clifford proposed the concept of "routes" in *Routes: Travel and Translation in Late Twentieth Century*. For a more elaborate discussion, see Friedman, *Mappings*, 151–178.

47. Iwabuchi, *Recentering Globalization*, 24–38.

48. Napier, *Anime*, 24–26.

49. When I interviewed Duan Xiaoxuan in the summer of 2010, she was saddened by how contemporary animated films produced by the Shanghai Animation Film Studio seem to be losing their distinctly Chinese identity and increasingly resembling anime.

50. Nye, *Bound to Lead*; *Soft Power*.

51. Quoted in Bao, *Zhongguo donghua*, 225.

52. Wan, Wan, and Wan, "Xianhua katong," 1–2.

53. Yan and Suo, *Zhongguo donghua*, 36.

54. Chow, "On Chineseness," 6.

55. Songlin, "Meishu dianying yao," 50; Zhang, "Chuangzao fuyou minzu"; Xiao, *Guochan donghua dianying*.

56. Many scholars have analyzed transnational Chinese live-action film since the 1990s. Rey Chow argues that "film has always been, since its inception, a transcultural phenomenon, having as it does the capacity to transcend culture" ("Film and Cultural Identity," 174). Regarding cinema as a modern "universal language" that has the potential to unify the dialects of the world, Zhen Zhang approaches early Shanghai cinema as a "local vernacular with unabashed cosmopolitan aspirations" (*An Amorous History*, 2, 3). Sheldon Lu contends that "film in China has always been of a transnational character" (*Transnational Chinese Cinemas* 4, 25). Yingjin Zhang advocates the notion of "polylocality" and proposes the approach of "comparative film studies," which covers a larger field than transnational film studies (*Cinema, Space, and Polylocality*, 1–15). Yiman Wang discusses the transnational connections between Shanghai, Hong Kong, and Hollywood in *Remaking Chinese Cinema*.

57. Man'ei was taken over by the Communist Party and was transformed into the Northeast Film Company on October 15, 1945. Exactly one year later, on October 15,

1946, the Northeast Film Company was transformed into the Northeast Film Studio, itself renamed the Changchun Film Studio in 1955. Although the Changchun Film Studio originally evolved from Man'ei, it tried to disavow its Japanese connection by claiming that its founding date was October 15, 1946, rather than October 15, 1945 (Chen, Qi, and Zhang, *Changchun yingshi*, 211).

58. Wang, *Zhengtu,* 3:154.

59. Bao, *Zhongguo donghua,* 167.

60. Voci, "DV and Animateur Cinema in China," 265. One more example can be found in the controversy over *Fuwa* (2007), an animated television series that features the five Beijing Olympics mascots. *Fuwa* was proudly celebrated as a successful Chinese animation that dwarfed other imported products. When some sharp-eyed bloggers pointed out that the image of the five protagonists drew on an anime titled *Sergeant Frog* (*Keroro Gunsō,* 2004), the official and public discourses tried to suppress such remarks. As a result, the controversy over *Fuwa*'s Japanese connection did not escalate in China (see Voci, *China on Video,* 44).

61. Zhu, "Has Chinese Film?"

62. Manovich, "What Is Digital Cinema?" 408.

63. Eisenstein, *Eisenstein on Disney,* 21.

64. Lamarre, "Speciesism, Part I," 79.

65. Eisenstein, *Eisenstein on Disney,* 5.

66. Quoted in Solomon, "Animation," 11.

67. Lamarre, *The Anime Machine,* xxix.

68. Ibid., 7.

69. Ibid., xxiii.

70. Here I draw on Mary Louise Pratt's term "contact zone," defined by her as "social spaces where disparate cultures meet, clash, and grapple with each other, often in highly asymmetrical relations of domination and subordination—like colonialism, slavery, or their aftermaths as they are lived out across the globe today" (*Imperial Eyes*, 4).

71. Huntington, *Clash of Civilizations.*

72. Here is an example of animation crossing representational borders. When live-action films failed to represent the West in socialist China due to the limited resources (no American actors and inability to shoot on location) and Cold War ideologies (deliberate erasure of American presence), animation seized the opportunity to represent the unrepresentable and even dramatized its (over)presence on screen. Animation thus returned to its primitive role as special effects to achieve what live-action film could not in early film history because of practical reasons (Du, "International Childhood Fraternity"). Animation is also diplomatic in adapting to new media such as the television, computer, and cell phone. For an example of animation's diplomacy in adapting to new media, see Wells, "Smarter than the Average."

73. The first episode of *Uproar in Heaven* (1961) was released in Japan in 1965 (see Komatsuzawa, *Mochinaga Tadahito*, 63).

74. Pang, *Creativity and Its Discontents*, 174.

75. To animate an object, animators need to draw many slightly varied pictures, which are photographed frame by frame. When these frames are played consecutively (usually twenty-four frames per second), the illusion of movement is created and the object is animated. This is due to the "persistence of vision," namely, the lingering effect of an image on the retina after its exposure to the eye (0.1 to 0.4 seconds).

76. Appadurai, *Modernity at Large*, 27–47.

Chapter 1: An Animated Wartime Encounter

1. On animated filmmaking in Manchuria, see chapter 2.

2. For more about Mochinaga Tadahito, see chapter 2.

3. For representative studies of Sino-Japanese cultural exchanges, see Thornber, *Empire of Texts*; Baskett, *The Attractive Empire*.

4. Fu, *China Forever*, 2. For more information about Star Productions and United China Productions, see Pang, *Building a New China in Cinema*.

5. Information about Zhang Shankun is based on Fu, *Between Shanghai and Hong Kong*, 93–132. See also Fu, "Ambiguity of Entertainment."

6. Fu, *Between Shanghai and Hong Kong*, 38–48; Fu, "Ambiguity of Entertainment."

7. Bao, *Fiery Cinema*, 2.

8. For positive comments on the resistance message of this film at that time, see *Mulan Congjun*.

9. For example, the trip of the famous writer Zhou Zuoren to wartime Japan aroused widespread controversy and suspicion in China (Li, "Lun Zhou Zuoren").

10. Zhou and Li, *Zaoqi Xianggang dianyingshi*, 281, 299.

11. Yau, *Japanese and Hong Kong Film*, 36. The oldest surviving animated feature film in the world is a German stop-motion silhouette film titled *The Adventures of Prince Achmed*, directed by Lotte Reiniger. The second is Disney's *Snow White* (1937), the third is Fleischers' *Gulliver's Travels* (1939), and the fourth is Disney's *Pinocchio* (1940). Some people believe that the first animated feature film was *The Apostle* (*El Apóstol*, 1917), produced in Argentina. The film is no longer extant, so whether it was a feature film cannot be verified (see Bendazzi, *Cartoons*, 50).

12. This film was adapted from Alexandre Dumas the younger's 1848 novel *La dame aux Camélias*, which tells the story of the tragic love between a courtesan named Lady of the Camellias and Armand Duval, a young man from the bourgeois class. The story was adapted into several English films. For the adaptation of the story of Camille into Chinese literature, see Hu, *Tales of Translation*, 67–105.

13. A similar dynamic occurred in the 1980s when the feature films made by fifth-generation filmmakers were accused of pandering to the West after their success abroad. Had they not traveled outside China, it is unlikely that these films would have been accused of catering to the West. It is their travel and popularity abroad that made people reexamine these films with a suspicious and critical perspective.

14. "Mulan Congjun yun Ri kaiying," 21.

15. Yan, *Senji Nitchū*, 251.

16. Uchida, "Muran jyū gun," 26.

17. "Chūka eiga yunyū yotei."

18. Wolff, "On the Road Again"; Blunt, *Travel, Gender, and Imperialism*; Milani, *Words, Not Swords.*

19. Leed, *Mind of the Traveler,* 217.

20. A typical example was singer and actress Li Xianglan, also known as Yamaguchi Yoshiko or Ri Kōran, a Japanese woman who adopted a Chinese identity. Another wartime example was Princess Aixinjueluo Xianyu, also known as Chuandao Fangzi in Chinese and Kawashima Yoshiko in Japanese.

21. Huang, *Women, War, Domesticity,* 8.

22. Lee, *The Stranger*, 139.

23. Kandiyoti, "Identity and Its Discontents."

24. A typical example of promoting patriotic prostitutes in wartime China was Sai Jinhua (see Lee, *The Stranger,* 120–136).

25. Hung, "Female Symbols," 167. Nora is the female protagonist in *A Doll's House,* a three-act play written by Henrik Ibsen in 1879. Nora is an ideal nineteenth-century wife and mother, but ultimately leaves her family. She was celebrated as an icon of liberated women during the May Fourth Movement in China in 1919, an intellectual and cultural movement that regarded Chinese tradition as cannibalistic and oppressive.

26. Information here draws on Wan, *Wo yu Sun Wukong*; Qiuquemelle, "Wan Brothers," 175–180; Yan and Suo, *Zhongguo donghua,* 10–25; Ono, *Chūgoku no animēshon,* 5–42; Bi and Huang, *Zhongguo manhua shi,* 94, 122; Lent and Xu, "China's Animation Beginnings"; Peng, *Donghua dashi.*

27. Wan Laiming was also a papercutting silhouette artist and sculptor. He made silhouettes for famous figures such as Hu Die and Zhou Enlai. Photographs of these silhouettes were published in *The Young Companion* and other popular magazines. Wan was also one of the six most famous sculptors during this period. In 1934, Wan Laiming made a copper statue for Hu Wenhu, a patriotic oversea Chinese man known as the King of Balm Oil. The statue was later sent to Singapore (see Zhi, "Wan Laiming juezhao," 44).

28. Mei Xuechou, Cheng Peilin, Li Wenguang, Li Zeyuan, and others established the Great Wall Film Company in New York in May 1921. After the studio made two

films about Chinese costume and martial arts, it was relocated to Shanghai in 1924 (see Wang, *Zhengtu* 1:32).

29. Although the Wan brothers were the most active, productive, and persevering filmmakers of animated shorts in the early history of Chinese animation, it is risky to attribute all the "firstness" to them. Other animators were active at that time. Some scholars have traced the origins of animated film shorts to even earlier figures. They hold that *Uproar in Heaven* (*Danao tiangong*), made by Yang Zuotao in 1923, can be regarded as the earliest animated film short in China (see Fu, *Zhongguo yingpian dadian,* 2). Some people hold that the first animated short can be traced back to *The Ball Man* (*Qiuren*), which is a combination of live action and animation made by Great China-Lily Film Company in 1919 (see Ren, "Donghua yingpian," 28). Some scholars defended the Wan brothers' *Uproar in an Art Studio* as the first animated short in history because the earlier so-called shorts were not made with the frame-by-frame animation method (Bao, "Qianyan," in *Zhongguo donghua*). Unfortunately, these early animated films are no longer extant, and verifying the claims is difficult.

30. For further discussion of the series, see Maltin, *Of Mice and Magic,* 84–90.

31. Other films were *Dog Detective* (*Gou zhentan*), *The New Year Goods* (*Nianhuo*), *New Tides* (*Xinchao*), *The Year of National Goods* (*Guohuo nian*), *Loophole* (*Loudong*), *Resistance* (*Dikang*), *Bloody Money* (*Xue qian*), and *Saving the Motherland with Aviation* (*Hangkong jiuguo*).

32. The first talkie animated film in the world was *Steamboat Willie* (Disney, 1928).

33. For a detailed study of Tian Han, see Luo, *The Avant-Garde.*

34. Wan, *Wo yu Sun Wukong,* 85; Fu, *Between Shanghai and Hong Kong,* 7; Fu, *Zhongguo yingpian dadian,* 14. The third Wan brother, Wan Chaochen, probably returned from Chongqing to Shanghai later in June 1941, when the first two brothers had almost completed *Princess Iron Fan* (see Mei, "Wanshi disan xiongdi," 466).

35. Bao, *Zhongguo donghua,* 23–29.

36. Qian, *Yige donghua,* 87; Bao, *Zhongguo donghua,* 41. There were other animation activities as well. In 1943, Liang Jin produced *The Kite* (*Fengzheng*), a silent black-and-white animated short without dialogue but accompanied by music at Huabei Film Company, Beijing (discussed in chapter 2).

37. Maltin, *Of Mice and Magic,* 91.

38. Chang, "Future of Animated Cartoon," 8–10.

39. "Baixue Gongzhu," 2. It was said that Yang Zuotao, the maternal uncle of renowned anthropologist Fei Xiaotong, was involved in making *Snow White.* Of the twenty designing animators for *Snow White,* seven were Chinese, including Yang Zuotao and Chen Erzhen (Bao, *Zhongguo donghua,* 24).

40. "Baixue Gongzhu zai Zhongguo," 1204. Based on this animated film, director Wu Yonggang made a live-action feature film titled *Zhongguo Baixue Gongzhu* (1940),

starring Chen Juanjuan, the so-called Shirley Temple of the East. *Snow White* was also released in other cities in the hinterland of wartime China. Some Japanese soldiers viewed this film in wartime Hankou (Tsuji, *Chūka den'ei shiwa,* 150).

41. For more information about Zhang Shankun and his film companies in occupied Shanghai, see the works of Poshek Fu.

42. At that time, Wan Dihuan ran a family photography studio in Shanghai and Wan Chaochen was still in Chongqing ("Wan Laiming kunzhong," 1).

43. Wan, *Wo yu Sun Wukong,* 88. In 1927, Unique Film Productions had made a popular live-action feature film *Princess Iron Fan,* Hu Die playing the title role.

44. "Tieshan Gongzhu tishen," 83. Rotoscoping is an animation technique in which the movement in animated films is based on live-action films. Before making an animated film, animators use real actors to make a live-action film. Next they project frame by frame the images of this film on a glass panel. Animators then redraw these images and use them in their animated film. The projection equipment is called a rotoscope, and the technique that uses this equipment is called rotoscoping. This technique makes movement in an animation smoother and more lifelike. *Snow White* was made using rotoscoping. Marjorie Belcher, a sixteen-year-old dancer and daughter of a Hollywood dance studio owner, posed as Snow White. She also posed as the Blue Fairy in *Pinocchio* (Disney, 1940). Max Fleischer was credited as the inventor of rotoscoping. His patent application was filed on December 6, 1915, and approved on October 9, 1917. His character Betty Boop was also rotoscoped (see Barrier, *Hollywood Cartoons,* 22–23, 194–195).

45. "Tieshan Gongzhu tongxiao gongzuo," 579.

46. "Tieshan Gongzhu liang mingge," 184.

47. Wan and Wan, "Tessen Kōshu," 57.

48. "Hao Zisun: Tieshan Gongzhu," 712; "Jinshang tianhua," 70. The story was made into an animated film titled *Fighting over the Pillow* (*Qiang zhentou*) by the Shanghai Animation Film Studio in 1985.

49. Dower, *War without Mercy.*

50. Lamarre, "Speciesism, Part I," 101.

51. Dower, *Japan in War and Peace,* 39.

52. Ibid., 39–40; High, *Imperial Screen,* 473.

53. Lamarre, "Speciesism, Part I," 86.

54. Hung, *War and Popular Culture,* 106.

55. For studies of animal epithets in Republican China, see Wasserstrom and Wong, "Taunting the Turtles," 32.

56. Wan, *Wo yu Sun Wukong,* 90.

57. Ibid., 90.

58. Bao, *Fiery Cinema,* 372.

59. Wan, *Wo yu Sun Wukong,* 70–71.

60. For the life of Li Xianglan, see Yamaguchi, *Fragrant Orchid.*

61. Rubin, "The Traffic in Women," 44.

62. Lee, *The Stranger,* 80.

63. For more about travel by the elder two Wan brothers and *Princess Iron Fan* to Hong Kong, see Du, "Suspended Animation." In January 1948, the third brother, Wan Chaochen, visited Canada and the United States and brought *Princess Iron Fan* there. Walt Disney watched this film. Wan worked as an intern at United Productions, learning how to make color animated films through Technicolor (see Wan Chaochen, "Zhongguo donghua zhuanjia," 9). A recently identified document demonstrates that Wan Chaochen was sponsored by Nanjing Agriculture Education Film Company and stayed in the United States for eighteen months between July 1946 and late 1947 (see Bao, *Zhongguo donghua,* 48–49). According to a Japanese record, Wan Chaochen—supported by the Ministry of Culture of the Nationalist government—stayed in America to learn animation technology from Disney for two years between 1946 and 1948. He brought Disney's three-hole system back to Shanghai in 1948. He then accepted a job offer from the Nationalist government and designed and produced an animation camera stand in a military factory. The Nationalists tried to bring the film production facilities with them when they fled to Taiwan in 1949. Wan Chaochen already had dismantled the animation stand and hid its parts. After the Communists took power, he reassembled the animation stand and worked for the Shanghai Film Studio and later the Shanghai Animation Film Studio (see Komatsuzawa, *Mochinaga Tadahito,* 56).

64. Komatsuzawa, "Princess Iron Fan," 226.

65. Wartime Japan was characterized by limited supplies and severe shortages of basic commodities and other resources. This was the first time that the Japanese film industry was forced to adjust to any kind of restrictions. After war was declared, for example, the production of celluloid film dropped significantly. The film industry was forced to economize rather than increase production of raw film. In December 1940, the Motion Picture Raw Film Control Council implemented a quota system for raw film. In terms of distribution, a film distribution company was formed in 1942 and categorized all the movie theaters in Japan into two groups (red line and white line) to economize the limited film stock. This distribution company also issued a journal to launch campaigns to save raw film material and report projection accidents in all Japanese theaters (Okada, "Nitrate Film Production in Japan," 285).

66. Fu, "Ambiguity of Entertainment," 68.

67. Quoted in Komatsuzawa, "Princess Iron Fan," 228.

68. "Saiyūki," *Eiga junpō,* April 1, May 21, July 1, 1942.

69. Ibid., September 11, 1942.

70. Wan and Wan, "Tessen Kōshu," 56.

71. Sawada, "Chūgoku saisho no chōhen," 99; Noguchi, "Manga eiga to sono sakusha," 27.

72. Sato, *Currents in Japanese Cinema,* 101.
73. For discussion of Momotarō cartoons, see Dower, *War without Mercy.*
74. Antoni, "The Peach Boy," 180.
75. Ono, "The Long Flight."
76. Noguchi, "Manga eiga to sono sakusha."
77. Imamura, "Manga eiga hyō."
78. Noguchi, "Manga eiga to sono sakusha," 27; Seo et al., "Manga Saiyūki gappyō."
79. Noguchi, "Manga eiga to sono sakusha," 23.
80. Ueno, "Nippon eiga no jakuten."
81. Seo, "Manga eiga no gijutsu," 17.
82. Noguchi, "Manga eiga to sono sakusha," 25.
83. Seo et al., "Manga Saiyūki gappyō," 64. Seo improved the storytelling component for two of the Momotarō animated films, but they were still slow and the plots lacked the lively action of *Princess Iron Fan.* However, Tezuka Osamu learned from *Princess Iron Fan's* well constructed narrative. The international appeal of his animation *Astro Boy* is associated with its skillful storytelling and characterization rather than the animation techniques. The film used the technique of "limited" animation, which means it deviated from the "full animation" of *Princess Iron Fan* that was applauded by wartime Japanese animators and critics and resembled the Disney style with its close attention to detail.
84. Seo, "Manga eiga no gijutsu," 17.
85. Noguchi, "Manga eiga to sono sakusha," 22–27; Seo et al., "Manga Saiyūki gappyō"; Kondō, "Momotarō no umiwashi."
86. "Zadankai Nihon"; "Manga eiga hatten."
87. Yamaguchi, *Nihon animēshon eigashi,* 40.
88. Kinoshita, "Kaigun manga eiga."
89. For different versions of the story, see Antoni, "The Peach Boy."
90. Wang, "Xiyouji zai haiwai."
91. Nakata, *Nihon dōwa,* 192.
92. Tezuka, *Boku no Son Gokū,* 3–4:87, 43.
93. High, *Imperial Screen,* 265.
94. Baskett, *Attractive Empire,* 34.
95. Seo, "Manga eiga no gijutsu," 17.
96. Kinoshita, "Kaigun manga eiga."
97. Kondō, "Momotarō no umiwashi."
98. Kinoshita, "Kaigun manga eiga," 56.
99. Qin, "Shanhai sokai gekijō animēshon."
100. Tezuka, "Tōkī igo no manga eiga," 111.
101. Yamaguchi and Watanabe, *Nihon animēshon eigashi,* 43.
102. Hagiwara, *Masaoka Kenzō to sono jidai,* 138–162.

103. In many articles and posters published in *Eiga junpo* in 1943, *Momotarō's Sea Eagles* was celebrated as the first animated feature film in Japan. Some scholars still regard it as such. I consider *Momotarō's Divine Sea Warriors* to be the first, however, given that in length it is comparable to *The Adventures of Prince Achmed*, *Snow White*, *Gulliver's Travels*, *Pinocchio*, and *Princess Iron Fan,* all of which predate it.

104. Before its use in *Momotarō's Divine Sea Warriors,* the "aiueo" song in *Momotarō's Divine Sea Warriors* was used to teach the Japanese language to local people in Japan's South Sea colonies such as the Philippines and Indonesia. When the Japanese Imperial Navy subsequently used the film to teach local people Japanese, the song became even more popular in Japan's colonies (Ono, "Anime eiga jijō").

105. Hagiwara, *Masaoka Kenzō to sono jidai,* 162.

106. For these images, see Te, *Wo kongsu.*

107. Ono, *Chūgoku no animēshon,* 34.

108. Other well-known silhouette animators include Arai Kazugorō, Tobiishi Nakaya, and Takemura Takeshīji. Additional silhouette animated films include *Kaguya hime* (1942), *Ōgon no kagi* (1939), and *Jakku to mame no ki* (1941).

109. Miyao, *Aesthetics of Shadow,* 2.

110. Tezuka, "Atogaki."

111. Ohnuki-Tierney, *Monkey as Mirror.*

112. For analyses of "cuteness," see Ngai, "Cuteness of the Avant-Garde."

113. Tezuka, *Boku no Son Gokū,* vol. 2, 43.

114. Ibid., 61. This style of self-reflexivity is prominent in this Japanese manga. In the chapter "The Lion Demon with Nine Heads" ("Kokonotsu atama no shishi majin"), Tezuka even enters the story and assumes the role of Tripitaka in order to continue the journey to the west (6:8–96).

115. Leonard and Yamagata, "Hō ni aragatte no shinpo."

116. Tezuka,"Atogaki."

117. Ibid.

118. The transistor radio, the stereo phonograph, and the television all emerged in Japan in the late 1950s (see Ridgely, *Japanese Counterculture,* 35–68).

119. Shiraishi, "Doraemon Goes Abroad," 297.

120. Steinberg, *Anime's Media Mix,* 11–12.

121. Atomu first appeared as a minor character in Tezuka's manga *Atomu taishi,* which was published as a serial in a manga magazine titled *Shōnen* in April 1951. In April of the next year, Atomu became the protagonist in a manga entitled *Tetsuwan Atomu,*, which was published in *Shōnen* between 1952 and 1963.

122. In the West, limited animation can be traced to the 1930s and the early years of the *Looney Tunes* series.

123. In 1967, Tezuka and his company Bug Productions adapted *My Sun Wukong* into *The Great Adventures of Wukong* (*Gokū no dai bōken*), a serialized TV animation

running thirty-nine episodes. *The Great Adventures of Wukong's* futuristic setting is evocative of *Star Wars.* The story of Princess Iron Fan is rendered in the tenth episode, "Conquer Us with Heart" ("Hāto de itadaki," episode 10). Bull Demon King becomes a mad scientist who creates Fiery Mountain with machines and chemicals in an attempt to conquer the universe. Princess Iron Fan, the scientist's assistant, is transformed into a seductress who tries to conquer Tripitaka and his disciples with her beauty and magical banana leaf fan. Monkey steals the fan and extinguishes the fire at the end of this episode. Unlike the passive and self-sacrificing girl who waits for Monkey to return home in *Alakazam the Great,* Monkey's lover in *The Great Adventures of Wukong* becomes a mischievous fairy with her own magical powers and she accompanies him all the way to India. The influence of Tezuka's versions of the Chinese story are evident in the Hong Kong live-action feature film *A Chinese Odyssey* (*Dahua xiyou,* 1995) with Stephen Chow as Monkey, which includes Monkey's lover and a garrulous Tripitaka.

124. Schodt, *Astro Boy Essays,* 76–97.

125. Ibid. Raz Greenberg highlights the Jewish connections in Tezuka Osamu's manga (see "A Yiddish Manga").

126. Tezuka, *Boku no manga jinsei,* 110–114.

127. From Xiaoli, "Fangri sanji." *Sun Wukong* was a children's magazine established in June 1980 that introduced to children the animated films made by the Shanghai Animation Film Studio. It ceased publication in May 1990. On June 1, 1993, the magazine *King of Cartoons* (*Katong wang*) was launched to continue to introduce animated films to children, but it gradually became a magazine for girls. In September 2005, *China Animation* (*Zhongguo donghua*) was launched as the official magazine of China Animation Association, which was founded in 1985. The earliest animation magazine was *South Art News* (*Nanguo yixun*), which was founded by Luo Yiwei in January 1947 and ceased publication in 1949 (for a list of magazines and journals on Chinese animation, see appendix 3).

128. "Tezuka Osamu's Atom and Son Gokū Exhibition—Were Atom's Roots in Chinese Animation?" TezukaOsamu.net, August 29, 2006, accessed February 8, 2018, http://tezukaosamu.net/jp/iroiro/161.html.

129. This film is set in the year 3010. Tripitaka becomes a merchant who travels the universe with his adopted daughter. He outwits Monkey, Pigsy, and Sandy and takes them to his space shuttle. They travel to another planet and overcome the villains (Bull Demon King and Princess Iron Fan), thereby saving the universe from destruction. In the end, Tripitaka sacrifices his life when Fiery Mountain explodes. Monkey marries Tripitaka's adopted daughter, and Pigsy and Sandy continue their journey across the universe in Tripitaka's space shuttle.

130. The five visits took place on November 10–18, 1980; December 25–29, 1981; October 29–November 3, 1983; September 12–14, 1984; and November 8–18, 1988

(see *Tezuka Osamu Official*, http://tezukaosamu.net/jp/about/1980.html, accessed February 8, 2018).

131. Schodt, *Astro Boy Essays*, 94.

132. The film *My Sun Wukong* is a creative adaptation of *Journey to the West*. When Monkey is born from a stone, he becomes a very large monster controlled by a devil. He even tries to eat a baby monkey but stops when a female monkey cries and begs for mercy. He is then transformed into a stone monkey of normal size and later becomes king of the monkeys. The devil assails him in his dreams and urges him to grow stronger and stronger. Monkey then leaves his kingdom to learn magic powers from a Daoist master and becomes so powerful that the Jade Emperor invites him to become an official in heaven. Monkey becomes furious and wreaks havoc in heaven when he discovers that his position is nothing more than a lowly groom. Buddha subdues him and then imprisons him beneath a mountain. Five hundred years later, Tripitaka arrives and frees Monkey. They embark together on the journey and en route pick up Pigsy and Sandy. The devil then kidnaps Tripitaka and asks Monkey to join him to overthrow Buddha. To conquer the devil and save Tripitaka, Monkey exhausts all of his energy and vanishes in a final explosion. Just when Tripitaka thinks that Monkey has died, an eagle drops a walnut into Tripitaka's hand, from which Monkey is reborn. Tripitaka and his three disciples happily continue their journey to India.

133. Wan Laiming died in Shanghai on October 7, 1997 (Chen, *Zhongguo dianying biannian*, 1992).

134. Information in this section is based on "Tezuka Osamu shi to Son Gokū." See also Zhang, "Riben xinzuo fanchen."

135. Ibid.

Chapter 2: Mochinaga Tadahito and Animated Filmmaking in Early Socialist China

1. The biographical information on Mochinaga in this section draws on three sources: Mochinaga, *Animēshon Nitchū kōryūki*; Komatsuzawa, *Mochinaga Tadahito*; and Ono, "Tadahito Mochinaga."

2. Disney animator Ub Iwerks invented the multiplanar camera in the mid-1930s. Disney first used this sophisticated camera in *The Old Mill* in 1937. The camera creates three-dimensional effects in the background of animated films (Maltin, *Of Mice and Magic*, 51). For theoretical discussion of the multiplanar camera, see Lamarre, *The Anime Machine*, 2009.

3. Ono, *Chūgoku no animēshon*, 36.

4. Mochinaga, *Animēshon Nitchū kōryūki*, 95.

5. Korean animator Yong-Hwan Kim participated in the production of *Momotarō's Divine Sea Warriors*. After the end of the war he returned to Korea and established an animation studio in Seoul (Kim, "Critique of the New Historical Landscape," 65).

6. Mochinaga, *Animēshon Nitchū kōryūki,* 102.

7. Information about filmmaking in Manchuria in this section is based on Li, "Phantasmagoric Manchukuo"; Baskett, *Attractive Empire,* 28–40; Furuichi, *Manying dianying yanjiu.*

8. Zhang, "Manying," 119.

9. Mochinaga, *Animēshon Nitchū kōryūki,* 110.

10. Baskett, *Attractive Empire,* 32.

11. Mochinaga, *Animēshon Nitchū kōryūki,* 118–126.

12. Hu, *Xin Zhongguo,* 5.

13. Ibid., 8.

14. Zhang, "Dongdang niandai de huiyi," 8.

15. Ma, "Dongbei dianying gongsi," 30–34.

16. Mochinaga, *Animēshon Nitchū kōryūki,* 138.

17. Zhang, "Dongdang niandai de huiyi," 12.

18. Hu, *Xin Zhongguo,* 16.

19. Zhao, "8.15 hou de Changchun," 2.

20. Ibid., 6.

21. Hu, *Xin Zhongguo,* 23.

22. Zhang, "Dongdang niandai de huiyi," 23.

23. During their stay at Man'ei, Uchida Tomu taught courses for actors and actresses and Kimura Sotoji taught general arts and literature (Chen, Qi, and Zhang, *Changchun yingshi,* 115).

24. Mochinaga, "Renmin dianying de kaiduan," 167.

25. Mochinaga, *Animēshon Nitchū kōryūki,* 147.

26. Ono, *Chūgoku no animēshon,* 50.

27. Zhang, "Dongdang niandai de huiyi," 26. The Chinese characters (Dongbei dianying zhipianchang) on the arch of the main entrance gate of the film studio were written by a Japanese named Morikawa Kazuo, father of Morikawa Kazuyo. Adopting the Chinese name Mou Lin, Morikawa Kazuo also wrote the Chinese characters in the opening credits sequences of early socialist live-action films such as *Bridge* (*Qiao,* 1949), *The White-Haired Girl* (*Baimaonü,* 1950), and *Door No. 6* (*Liuhao men,* 1952). He also wrote the Chinese characters in the opening credits sequences of dubbed Soviet films, such as *Kuban Cossacks* (1949) and *Zoya* (1944). See Morikawa and Morikawa, *Zhongguo wode,* 29, 170.

28. Wang, *Zhengtu,* 1:140.

29. Hu and Gu, *Manying,* 221; Hu, *Dongying de Riben ren,* 24–26, 33, 41. The names of the eighty-four Japanese experts are listed in Hu's book. Records in China and Japan differ slightly (see Komatsuzawa, *Mochinaga Tadahito,* 44).

30. Hu, *Dongying de Riben ren,* 33, 41.

31. Komatsuzawa, *Mochinaga Tadahito,* 44.

32. Since 1936, especially after the eruption of the anti-Japanese war in July 1937, many Chinese intellectuals, filmmakers, actors, and actresses went to Yan'an. One of them was Jiang Qing, who later became Chairman Mao's wife. The Yan'an Film Troupe was officially established as part of the General Political Department of the Eighth Route Army in the autumn of 1938. It marked the beginning of the communist film industry in China. After it was disbanded in August 1945, its staff joined Northeast Film Company (Clark, *Chinese Cinema,* 26).

33. Hu, *Xin Zhongguo,* 37, 39, 103.

34. Morikawa and Morikawa, *Zhongguo wode dier zuguo,* 155.

35. Yan and Suo, *Zhongguo donghua dianyingshi,* 32–33.

36. Te Wei's successors as president include Yan Dingxian, Zhou Keqin, Chang Guangxi, and Jin Guoping (see appendix 2).

37. Baskett, "Goodwill Hunting," 120.

38. Hu and Gu, *Manying,* foreword.

39. Young, *Japan's Total Empire,* 33–34; Duara, *Sovereignty and Authenticity.*

40. Li, "Phantasmagoric Manchukuo."

41. Nornes, *Japanese Documentary Film,* 55–59.

42. Hu and Gu, *Manying,* 82.

43. Mochinaga, *Animēshon Nitchū kōryūki,* 123.

44. Yoshida, "Man'ei kara," 82.

45. Asada, "Manhua dianying de mimi."

46. Asada, "Manga eiga."

47. Li, "Manhua yingpian zhizuo guocheng."

48. Cong, "Yousheng huodong manhua."

49. For more discussions of *kamishibai,* see Orbaugh, *Propaganda Performed,* 2.

50. "Yousheng manhua."

51. Choe, "Manshū eiga shirami."

52. Yamaguchi, *Aishū no Manshū eiga,* 201–203.

53. Choe, "Manshū eiga shirami;" Li, "A National Cinema," 91.

54. Yamaguchi, *Aishū no Manshū eiga,* 203–208.

55. Yoshida, "Aa maboroshi no satsueijo Man'ei," 56.

56. Yan and Suo, *Zhongguo donghua,* 32.

57. High, *Imperial Screen,* 125.

58. Baskett, *Attractive Empire,* 31.

59. Mochinaga, *Animēshon Nitchū kōryūki,* 142–144.

60. Zhang, "Dongdang niandai de huiyi," 26.

61. Mochinaga, *Animēshon Nitchū kōryūki,* 177.

62. "Women he nimen jinjin woshou."

63. "Women shi buhui quxi de."
64. Dower, *Embracing Defeat,* 272.
65. *Red Flag* was renamed *Red Flag Newspaper* (*Shimbun Akahata*) in 1997.
66. Mochinaga, *Animēshon Nitchū kōryūki,* 234.
67. Du, interview with Mochinaga Noriko, March 1, 2010.
68. Zhang, "Dongdang niandai de huiyi," 27; Duan, "Yiyidaishui de nongnong qinqing," in Morikawa and Morikawa, *Zhongguo wode dier zuguo,* 184.
69. Mochinaga, "Zhongsheng nanwangde," 26.
70. Du, interview with Mochinaga Noriko, March 1, 2010.
71. Swearingen and Langer, *Red Flag in Japan,* 235.
72. Dower, *Embracing Defeat,* 273.
73. Du, "Suspended Animation."
74. Sun, "Zhongguo shouwei," 48; Qian, *Yige donghua,* 349.
75. Wan, "Zhongguo donghua," 9; Komatsuzawa, *Mochinaga Tadahito,* 56; Bao, *Zhongguo donghua,* 48–49.
76. Zhang and Gong, *Shei chuangzao,* 73.
77. Zhang, "Dongdang niandai de huiyi," 27. According to Hu Chang, the name of the coal mine was Dalianhe meikuang located in Yilan County (*Dongying de Riben ren,* 30; for the names of the forty-three Japanese who worked in the coal mine, see 110).
78. Ono, *Chūgoku no animēshon,* 54.
79. The earliest puppet-animated film in China may have been Wan Chaochen's *Go to the Frontiers* (*Shang qianxian*) in 1939. The film is no longer extant, and whether it is puppet stop-motion animation or just marionette performance is therefore difficult to verify.
80. Cheng, *Zhongguo dianying fazhanshi,* 390; Mochinaga, *Animēshon Nitchū kōryūki,* 170.
81. Ono, *Chūgoku no animēshon,* 61; Mochinaga, *Animēshon Nitchū kōryūki,* 169.
82. Mochinaga, "Zuichu de muou," 156.
83. Mochinaga, *Animēshon Nitchū kōryūki,* 76–81.
84. Ibid., 352.
85. See Morikawa and Morikawa, *Zhongguo wode dier zuguo,* 55.
86. For a discussion of mobile film projection, see Chen, "Mobile Film Projection."
87. Mochinaga, *Animēshon Nitchū kōryūki,* 196.
88. Yan and Suo, *Zhongguo donghua,* 31.
89. Mochinaga, *Animēshon Nitchū kōryūki,* 273.
90. Yan and Suo, *Zhongguo donghua,* 32–33.
91. Duan, "Chiyong Zhiren xiansheng."
92. In wartime Japanese manga, Jiang Jieshi is portrayed as an emaciated man with a bandage on his face. Mochinaga might have seen such images of Jiang during his stay in Tokyo (see Okamoto, "Images of the Enemy," 213).

93. He, "Wei ertong dianying," 14.

94. Ibid.

95. Zhang, "Manying," 120.

96. Chen, "Dressing for the Party."

97. Mori, *Teihon animēshon,* 231.

98. Mochinaga, *Animēshon Nitchū kōryūki,* 63.

99. After they joined the Shanghai Animation Film Studio, the three Wan brothers focused on different kinds of animations. Wan Laiming focused on cel animation, Wan Guchan on papercutting animation, and Wan Chaochen on puppet animation. Wan Chaochen stayed in Shanghai after he came back from the United States in 1948 (Du, "Suspended Animation").

100. Bao, *Zhongguo donghua,* 77.

101. Mochinaga, *Animēshon Nitchū kōryūki,* 225.

102. Sina Online, "Waijiaobu dang'an jiemi."

103. There was probably a Japanese animated film that included limited puppet animation before those made by Mochinaga Tadahito. This earlier film is titled *Princess Kaguya* (*Kaguya hime,* 1942). The end of the film focuses on how the girl protagonist rides in an ox carriage and flies to the moon. A puppet is used to portray the ox. However, the puppet animation sequence is brief and used as a special effect to achieve what live-action could not accomplish in this film. It was animated by Masaoka Kenzō, who was well known for his cel animation (Mori, *Teihon animēshon,* 226–227).

104. Wang, *Zhengtu,* 1:150.

105. Mochinaga, *Animēshon Nitchū kōryūki,* 241.

106. The predecessor of Tōei Animation was Japan Animated Films Studio (Nihon dōga eigasha), founded by Yamamoto Sanae and Masaoka Kenzō in 1948. From 1952, it became known as Nichidō Eigasha. Tōei purchased the studio and incorporated it into Tōei Animation in 1956. Tōei Animation was dubbed as the "Disney of the East." The first feature film produced by Tōei is *Tale of the White Serpent* (*Hakujaden,* 1958). Yamaguchi, *Riben donghua quanshi,* 53–55.

107. Mochinaga, *Animēshon Nitchū kōryūki,* 244. Upholding the ideal of art for art's sake and insisting that "animation should serve children and the people," Mochinaga might have also had reservations about the capitalist and commercial mode of production at Tōei Animation. He also disapproved of working on projects outsourced from abroad because they were overly driven by commercial and financial interests.

108. Mochinaga, "Eiga no mikata."

109. Mochinaga, "Mittsu no kuni no manga eiga o mite." Mochinaga personally liked the Soviet film *The Golden Antelope.* I found a copy of its script at his home.

110. Okamoto, "Buttai (ningyō) animēshon," 136.

111. Iizawa, "Shijō yutakana Cheko."

112. Ono, "Guranpuri."

113. Goldschmidt, *Enchanted World,* 138; *Rudolph the Red-Nosed Reindeer,* 75.

114. Mochinaga, *Animēshon Nitchū kōryūki,* 249–251.

115. In *Rudolph the Red-Nosed Reindeer,* Tad Mochinaga is the animation supervisor and Nagashima Kizo is the associate director. For a discussion of the Halloween special *Mad Monster Party,* see Goldschmidt, *Mad Monster Party.*

116. The information in this paragraph is based on Goldschmidt, *Rudolph the Red-Nosed Reindeer,* 73–93; Okamoto, "Buttai (ningyō) animēshon"; Du, interviews with Mochinaga Noriko, June 27 and July 7, 2015.

117. Ibid.

118. Goldschmidt, *Enchanted World,* vi.

119. Goldschmidt, *Rudolph the Red-Nosed Reindeer,* 10.

120. Ibid., 45–58.

121. Clements, *Anime,* 108–109; Goldschmidt, *Enchanted World.*

122. The Shanghai Animation Film Studio began to work on projects outsourced from Japan in the late 1970s.

123. Mori, *Teihon animēshon,* 226.

124. Mochinaga, *Animēshon Nitchū kōryūki,* 252–253.

125. Beginning in the mid-1980s, Chinese animators working on films outsourced from Japan imitated the anime style and were losing the Chinese national style.

126. Mochinaga, *Animēshon Nitchū kōryūki,* 282–284. Mochinaga's advice was candid and sincere at a critical time in the late 1970s when Shanghai Animation Film Studio began to work on outsourced projects from Japan. He worried that Chinese animation would have a similar fate as his Japanese studio. When he visited Shanghai Animation Film Studio in September 1987, he was disappointed and even angered by the fact that the studio was working on a large scale on projects outsourced from abroad. Mochinaga, *Animēshon Nitchū kōryūki,* 332–334.

127. Mochinaga, *Animēshon Nitchū kōryūki,* 255.

128. After Mochinaga left China, the first animated film to feature a cat was *Good Kitty Mimi* (*Haomao Mimi,* 1979), produced in the same year as Mochinaga's *Who Meowed?* In 1962, a paperfolding-animated film entitled *A Head of Cabbage* (*Yike da baicai,* 1962) only tangentially featured a cat and a rabbit, and its title did not include a feline protagonist. I asked Mochinaga Noriko the reason why Mochinaga Tadahito was so interested in animating cats. She answered that personally Mochinaga Tadahito loved dogs and had pet dogs, but it was easier to draw cats than dogs (Du, interview with Mochinaga Noriko, June 27, 2015). From the perspective of animation theories, cats are more plasmatic than dogs. Unlike the fixed meanings of dogs (loyalty) and limited movements (cannot jump high or climb trees), cats are more fluid and elusive in terms of both physical movement and personality, which make them excellent objects for animation. This was especially the case in early socialist China, when animation technology and talent were limited.

129. *Soviet Animation* (Moscow: Sovexportfilm, 1986).

130. Mochinaga, "Eiga no mikata."

131. Norman McLaren conducted the Healthy Village project for the United Nations Organization for Education, Science and Culture and published a book under that title in 1949. He lived in Chongqing between August 1949 and summer 1950. He made many educational slides and filmstrips to teach local peasants about healthful habits.

132. Ri Shunki, "Sōren monogatari."

133. The other two well-known students of Mochinaga Tadahito were Okamoto Tadanari (1932–1990) and Magari Fumiko (1936–). Mochinaga also worked as the technology supervisor for Gakken Film Bureau. Most of its animators benefited from Mochinaga's supervision.

134. Kawamoto, "Mochinaga Tadahito sensei."

Chapter 3: Inter/National Style and National Identity

1. In addition to the Japanese influence discussed in the previous chapter, there were Czech and Disney influences in the 1950s. Chinese puppet animation had connections with Czech puppet animation, an example of which is *Peacock Princess* (*Kongque gongzhu*, 1963). The cel-animated *Crossing over the Mountain of Monkeys* (*Guo houshan,* 1958) was indebted to the Disney style of animation.

2. Cheng, *Zhongguo dianying,* 2:403–405.

3. Pickowicz, "Acting like Revolutionaries"; Pickowicz, *China on Film*; Clark, *Chinese Cinema,* 37–38.

4. Clark, *Chinese Cinema,* 70–79.

5. Yang, "Socialist Realism"; Wang, "Socialist Realism."

6. Chang, *Painting,* 72.

7. Andrews, *Painters and Politics,* 168.

8. The dispute between the two parties also centered on the use of the terms *guohua* and *caimohua* (color-and-ink painting). *Guohua* was associated with national identity, and *caimohua* referred to painting media. Between 1949 and 1957, when Jiang Feng was in power, use of the term *caimohua* to replace *guohua* increased steadily. However, in 1957, Jiang Feng was denounced for his use of the term *caimohua.* After Jiang Feng was purged in 1957, *guohua* became widely used during the ensuing "elevation of standards" period. For instance, the Caimohua Department was established in the Hangzhou Art Academy in 1952. However, when Jiang Feng became unpopular, the Academy changed the name of the Caimohua Department to Guohua Department in December 1957 (Andrews, "Traditional Painting").

9. Xia, "Ba woguo dianying," 13.

10. Clark, *Chinese Cinema,* 86.

11. Ibid., 85.

12. Andrews, *Painters and Politics,* 287.

13. The co-production failed and China made the film on its own in 1979.

14. *Xiang Sulian dianying xuexi,* 55–62.

15. Zhang, *Ershi shiji Zhongguo,* 62. In the early 1950s, some Soviet, American, Germany, and other foreign animated films at the Shanghai Animation Film Studio were originally from Man'ei. Chinese animators brought these films with them when they relocated from Changchun to Shanghai in March 1950.

16. Yan and Suo, *Zhongguo donghua,* 36.

17. Qian, *Yige donghua,* 154–157.

18. Zhang and Gong, *Shei chuangzao,* 101.

19. Macdonald, *Animation in China,* 91.

20. Pu, *Donghua chuangzuo qishilu,* 265–279.

21. In 1980s China, the television animation series *Police Chief Black Cat* (*Heimao jingzhang,* 1984–1987) suffered the same fate. Although it became popular in China, its animators were forced to cease production because authorities decreed that it was not in accordance with the national style. It might not be a coincidence that the crow and the cat were black both physically and symbolically.

22. Pu, *Donghua chuangzuo qishilu,* 265–266.

23. Disney's *Snow White* and the Soviet animated film *The Tale of the Dead Princess and Seven Knights* (1951) also look similar.

24. Te, "Chuangzao minzu," 50.

25. The studio previously produced experimental shorts in preparation for *Little Tadpoles Look for Mama.*

26. Berry, "Absent American."

27. *Dreaming to Be Emperor* (*Huangdi meng,* 1947) and *Capturing the Turtle in the Jar* (*Wengzhong zhuobie,* 1948) were also made in immediate response to political events during the civil war between the Communist Party and the Nationalist Party at that time and can be regarded as the precursor to the new genre of international-motif animation (for a discussion of these two films, see chapter 2).

28. These films include *Showing True Colors* (*Yuanxing bilu,* 1960), *The Asian People Expelling the God of Plague* (*Yazhou renmin nuzhu wenshen,* 1961), *Support Dominicans' Struggle against Military Invasion* (*Zhichi Duomi'nijia renmin fandui wuqi qinlüe,* 1965), *Support Vietnamese's Struggle against American Imperialists* (*Zhichi Yuenan renmin dadao Meiguo qinlüe zhe,* 1965), *Exposing the Peace Talk Swindle of American Imperialism* (*Jiechuan Meidi hetan pianju,* 1965), and *The Great Declaration* (*Weida de shengming,* 1968).

29. The plasmatic movement characteristic of early Disney films and the Fleischers was also used in other animated films that did not fully belong to the national or international style. A typical example is *Crossing over the Mountain of Monkeys,* which

is evocative of early Disney style. Even in *Uproar in Heaven,* a leading representative of the national style, the early Disney style of plasmaticness and metamorphosis of body forms delineates the fight between Monkey King and the celestial deity Erlangshen. The national style in this film was therefore "tinged" by undercurrents of international style. A pure national style may not exist.

30. Plasmaticness and the transformation of body forms were rare in national style animated films in socialist China. The transformation of body forms usually took place between animals and ethnic girls, as I discuss in chapter 4. Sometimes gods and deities achieve bodily transformation, as demonstrated by Monkey King and Erlangshen in *Uproar in Heaven.* However, plasmaticness and the transformation of body forms were common in international style films. The transformation of body forms often took place between Western (American in particular) imperialists and metals, and the plasmatic and violent movements were frequently used on these foreigners (see Du, "Political Immediacy").

31. Wang, "Zuotan meishu dianying," 41.

32. Zhang, "Genghao de xuexi Sulian."

33. As I discuss later, the adoption of a female voiceover is associated with the intended audience of the film: children. The young female voiceover functions as a mother or teacher figure who tells bedtime stories to children. The other three ink-painting animated films did not exclusively target children as their audience.

34. Huang and Yu, *Donghua dianying tansuo,* 101–102. In China, the most influential animation photographer was Duan Xiaoxuan, who worked for the Shanghai Animation Film Studio for many decades. In an interview with Duan Xiaoxuan in August 2010, she explained politely that the technique of ink-painting animation remains a national secret (for more on Duan, see Du, "Socialism"; for a discussion of Mochinaga Tadahito, see chapter 2).

35. The younger generation of animators made a few computer-generated ink-painting animated films, but the technique and visual effects are totally different. Such films are not discussed in this volume.

36. Liang, "Weida de guanhuai," 36.

37. Lu, "Zuigao de jiangyu," 1–2.

38. Bian, *Li Keran,* 187.

39. Ibid., 35. In practice, Li Keran frequently cited a line from Mao's poem, *Jiangshan ruci duojiao* (This land is so rich in beauty) in his paintings. He also painted revolutionary sites such as Jinggangshan and Mao's childhood home in Hunan.

40. Zhou, *Wenyi zhanxian shang,* 63.

41. Andrews, *Painters and Politics,* 119.

42. From the seventeenth to the nineteenth century, Chinese art was dominated by literati painters dubbed the Four Wangs, a group advocating an eclectic style based on the imitation of great masters of the past (see Lai, *Ch'i Pai Shih,* 113).

43. Woo, *Chinese Aesthetics,* 65.

44. Quoted in Li, "Qian yan," 1.

45. Te, "Meishu dianying," 1.

46. Ibid., 1–2.

47. Although the ink-painting form of *Little Tadpoles Look for Mama* appeals to adults, the story was designed mainly for children.

48. Te, "Chuangzao minzu," 50.

49. Te, "Meishu dianying," 4.

50. Ibid.

51. Chang, *Painting,* 73.

52. In 1964 the Gang of Four criticized the subject matter of *Uproar in Heaven* because they regarded the sinister Jade Emperor as an allusion to Mao and the leaders of the Communist Party. Monkey's rebellion against the Jade Emperor is therefore interpreted as disloyalty to Mao.

53. Wu Yingju, a renowned musician, composed the flute music for this animated film as well as many other animated films in the Mao era. Wu Yingju lived a diasporic life in Vietnam. He returned to China and joined animated filmmaking in Shanghai in 1950. Lu Chunling, dubbed the magical flute master, played the flute in this film.

54. When I screened this film before Amercian undergraduate students learning Chinese at the University of Wisconsin–Madison, they said that they could not understand it.

55. Tang, "Shuimo donghua," 64.

56. Shapiro, *Mao's War,* 86.

57. Doane, "Voice in the Cinema," 42.

58. Chen, "Guanyu fengjingshi."

59. These paintings include *Ox-Herding in the Four Seasons* and *Ox-Herding in Autumn Pasture* by Yan Ciping (1164–1181), *Returning Home from Ox-Herding through Snow* and *Buffaloes and Herd Boys in Rainstorm* by Li Di (ca. 1163–1225), *Herd Boy and Buffalo beneath Bamboo* and *Landscape with Herd Boy and Oxen* by Ma Lin (ca. mid-thirteenth century), *Herd Boy with Water Buffalo and Calf* by Li Tang (ca. 1050–after 1130), and *Herd Boy Taming the Ox* by Zhi Xu (1114–1193). Scarlett Ju-yu Jang, "Ox-Herding Painting," 61.

60. Barnhart and Barnhart, "Images of Children," 53.

61. Jang, "Ox-Herding Painting," 60.

62. Ibid., 66.

63. In fact, the animation camera remains still. Because movement is relative, animators slide the landscape painting and thus create the illusion of the camera's movement.

64. Jang, "Ox-Herding Painting," 61.

65. Barnhart and Barnhart, "Images of Children," 53.

66. Jang, "Ox-Herding Painting," 64.

67. Ibid., 63.

68. Ball, *Animal Motifs,* 87.

69. Jang, "Ox-Herding Painting," 83.

70. Blumenthal, "Models in Chinese Moral Education."

71. Ibid., 64.

72. The cold colors in ink paintings were at odds with the "red" art during the Cultural Revolution. Ink paintings were labeled "black paintings" by Jiang Qing during the period. At the height of the Cultural Revolution, even *Little Tadpoles Look for Mama* was criticized for its use of anthropomorphic animals despite its politicized ending. The argument against fairy tales and talking animals was "Can cats speak? Can roosters sing?" As a result, animals disappeared in animated films. *Little Tadpoles Look for Mama* was also criticized for advocating maternal love and humanism rather than class struggle (Chen, "Tongxin yu tongxin lun"). Because of its apolitical content, *The Herd Boy's Flute* was criticized for advocating no class struggles (*jieji douzheng ximie lun*). Some people even said that the herd boy playing the flute on the water buffalo implied the notion of boasting (*chuiniu*), suggesting that the Communist Party's three flags (General Line, the Great Leap Forward, and the People's Commune) were nothing but *chuiniu* (see Yan and Suo, *Zhongguo donghua,* 94). *The Herd Boy's Flute* was also criticized for its dreamlike qualities, which were deemed useless for revolution. Some people also suggested that the herd boy should wear a red scarf, like young pioneers did (see *Hongweibing dianying,* 31).

Chapter 4: Animals, Ethnic Minorities, and Villains in Animated Film during the Cultural Revolution

An earlier version of this chapter appeared in *positions: asia critique* 24, no. 2 (2016): 435–479.

1. For an example of the negative narration of the Cultural Revolution, see Thurston, *Enemies of the People.*

2. Clark, *Chinese Cultural Revolution*; *Chinese Cinema,* 125–153; Zhang, *Chinese National Cinema,* 216–224.

3. Clark, *Chinese Cultural Revolution,* 2.

4. Clark, *Chinese Cultural Revolution; Chinese Cinema*; Zhang, *Chinese National Cinema.*

5. *The Rooster Crows at Midnight* and *Heroic Little Sisters of the Grassland* were not banned during the Cultural Revolution because of their revolutionary content.

6. Yan and Suo, *Zhongguo donghua,* 94–95. A different record demonstrates that the Shanghai Animation Film Studio was renamed Red Guard Film Studio in February

1967 and altogether nineteen animated films were produced between 1972 and 1976 (see Bao, *Zhongguo donghua,* 152, 154).

7. Lippit, *Electric Animal,* 2–3.

8. Ibid., 2, 3, 185.

9. Quoted in Shapiro, *Mao's War,* 87.

10. Shapiro, *Mao's War,* 87. A puppet-animated film, titled *Killing Sparrows* (*Da maque,* 1958), depicts the variety of methods children used to kill sparrows in the late 1950s.

11. For studies of Chinese theater, see Chen, *Acting the Right Part.*

12. Chen was not the first writer to propose the notion of "children's heart." Zhou Zuoren made a similar argument in the 1930s.

13. Chen, "Tongxin yu."

14. Quoted in Yan and Suo, *Zhongguo donghua,* 94.

15. Dorfman and Mattelart, *How to Read Donald Duck.* This book was first published in Chile in 1972.

16. Wheeler, "Children in Transition," 163.

17. For the debates over fairy tales in 1920s Soviet Union, see Zipes, *Enchanted Screen,* 323; Kelly, *Children's World,* 98.

18. For detailed discussions of fairy tales in Republican China, see Jones, *Developmental Fairy Tales.*

19. Beeck, *Suspended Animation,* 23–32.

20. Given the imminence of the Cultural Revolution, animated films produced during the Seventeen Years were severely criticized and banned. These denounced films fall into three categories: those that experimented with various artistic forms, such as ink painting; those that featured fairy tales, folklore, legends, anthropomorphic animals, gods, and spirits; and those that depicted children's daily life without overt depiction of political struggle.

21. This animated film was adapted from a long poem written by Liang Shangquan, a renowned writer of Sichuan province (for the original story, see Liang, *Hongyun ya*).

22. For discussion of love and emotion in China, see Lee, *Revolution of the Heart.*

23. Sun, "Yici chenggong," 15. For similar arguments, see Chen, "Meishupian yeneng," 4.

24. Jin, "Kuazhang yu shufu," 55.

25. Wu, "Meishu dianying," 53.

26. Ironically, the so-called revolutionary realism during the Cultural Revolution was mostly based on imagination and fantasy. During the Seventeen Years, the convention was for animators to first go out, experience life, and sketch from life before they made an animated film in the studio, a practice that began with Mochinaga's time. This was no exception for fantastic and expressionistic films like *Kitty Goes Fishing*

and *The Herd Boy's Flute.* The fantastic films during the Seventeen Years thus had a physical indexicality to reality. Chinese animators also went to Inner Mongolia before they made *Heroic Little Sisters of the Grassland.* During the height of the Cultural Revolution, however, most animators were imprisoned and could not travel freely. In some cases, they had to invent revolutionary animated films using their imagination, although sometimes they referred to live-action films. They made films that featured ethnic minorities such as *The Golden Wild Goose,* but they did not go to Tibet and other locales of minorities before making these films.

27. Other realist puppet animated films include *The Rooster Crows at Midnight* and *The Red Army Bridge.* The first film revolves around the struggle between a landlord and his tenants. The second film recounts conflicts between Nationalist armies and villagers who side with the Red Army.

28. For the two Mongolian sisters in history, see Bulag, "Models and Moralities."

29. Revolving around revolutionary legends, *Red Cloud Cliff* and other realist animated films made before *Heroic Little Sisters of the Grassland* did not directly portray and praise Mao.

30. Bian, "Shengdong de xingxiang"; "Meishu yingpian."

31. Qian, "Guanyu xiandai," 129.

32. Zhang and Gong, *Shei chuangzao,* 127.

33. Chang, "Yongyuan de laoshi," 181. Animators also wanted to make *Nezha Makes Havoc in the Sea* (*Nezha naohai,* 1979) in the early 1960s, but could not because animals, myths, and folklore were forbidden. They made the film after the Cultural Revolution was over.

34. Chen, *Zhongguo dianying* (2006), 387.

35. Some realist puppet animated films revolving around class struggle survived artistic persecution, such as *The Rooster Crows at Midnight.* Animated films made during the Seventeen Years were criticized for portraying "kings and princes, gifted scholars and beautiful ladies, little cats and dogs" (*diwang jiangxiang, caizi jiaren, shenxian guiguai, xiaomao xiaogou*). Animated films revolving around the daily life of contemporary children were also criticized for defaming children and distorting reality (*chouhua ertong, wanqu xianshi*) (see Wang, *Zhengtu,* 3:2).

36. For discussions of Mao's little red book, see Cook, *Mao's Little Red Book.*

37. Ironically, the image of this class enemy was based on Haschuluu, who in fact saved the two sisters' lives. He became an enemy in the film because he was labeled a rightist. The Party of Inner Mongolia finally issued an official document in 1985 stating that Haschuluu was the actual hero who saved the two sisters' lives (Li, "Caoyuan yingxiong").

38. The papercut animated film *The Battle Song of the 10,000-Ton Water Hydraulic Forging Press* (*Wandun shuiyaji zhange,* 1972) was an unabashed eulogy of a socialist machine.

39. The film *Night of the Flooding Tide* revolves around a fishing boat. After 1949 villagers finally complete building their own fishing boat with the help of the Party. Heroic village children thwart the scheme of saboteurs to destroy the boat.

40. The depiction of domestic animals as collective property of the commune began with *Heroic Little Sisters of the Grassland. Galloping Horses,* an animated film with a reference to animals in its title, appeared as early as 1975. Although the title suggests the importance of animals, the film was about the domesticated animals of a people's commune in Inner Mongolia. Released close to the end of the Cultural Revolution, *The Golden Wild Goose* was the first animated film whose title referred to a fantastic wild animal. *Two Little Peacock,* a story of ethnic Dai children and peacocks, was the first animated film after the Cultural Revolution to foreground wild and non-fantastic animals. Ethnic Dai children find two peacock eggs in the wilderness. They incubate the eggs and raise the peachicks. Later they present the two peacocks during a water-splashing festival to the local People's Liberation Army as tribute. The children's actions show the continued tendency to represent wild animals as domesticated and collectivized. In *The Goat Returns Home* (*Shanyang huile jia,* 1977), the animal finally belongs to a family, not to the commune. This film conveys a double message. First is a child helping a lost goat to return to its home. Second is the beginning of decollectivization and the liberation of animals who were "lost" by losing anthropomorphism and becoming collective properties of people's communes. After this film, animals gradually returned to animation. In sociohistorical reality, the collectivization in agriculture (including animals) began in the mid-1950s, but the collectivization of animals was not represented in animation until *Heroic Little Sisters of the Grassland.*

41. For studies of minority live-action films, see Clark, *Chinese Cinema,* 95–101; "Ethnic Minorities"; Zhang, "From 'Minority Film' "; Berry, "Race."

42. Chris Berry uses the term "race" for ethnic minorities in China ("Race: Chinese Film"). Yingjin Zhang questions the term "race" and advocates "ethnicity" ("From 'Minority Film' "). These terms are location specific. Whereas "race" is the convention in the West, "ethnicity" is the conventional usage in China.

43. Dubey, *Signs and Cities,* 44.

44. Gladney, "Representing Nationality," 116.

45. Jones, *Developmental Fairy Tales,* 82.

46. This kind of linear and progressive notion of history has been criticized by many scholars. In *The Savage Mind,* Claude Lévi-Strauss argues that primitive people's way of thinking is neither belated nor inferior to that of modern people. Rather, they just have a different and parallel mode of thinking (15).

47. For issues of ethnic minorities in real life, see Dreyer, *China's Political System,* 299–326.

48. Jiang, *Wolf Totem.*

49. White, *Myths of the Dog-Man,* 141–142. For detailed discussions of the dog-man, see Lee, *The Stranger,* 77.

50. Fiskesjö, "Animal Other."

51. Qian, "Guanyu xiandai," 130.

52. Clark, "Ethnic Minorities," 20.

53. Clark, *Chinese Cinema,* 96.

54. Schein, "Gender," 75.

55. In the animated film *The Golden Conch* (*Jinse de hailuo,* 1963), a conch transforms into a pretty Han girl. However, in this case, the conch is not a marker of the Han ethnicity.

56. *Five Golden Flowers* (*Wuduo jinhua,* 1959), a live-action film that features ethnic Bai girls, is another example.

57. The film demonstrates that the two girls are fully recovered. In real life, however, they were paralyzed due to frostbite.

58. Barlow, "Theorizing Woman," 174.

59. Lu Xun once made an analogy between training animals and ruling the people: "The way of training wild animals is much like the shepherding of the people, which is why our ancients referred to great men as 'herders.' And yet animals such as cattle and sheep who allow themselves to be herded are more fearful than wild animals, which is why the ancients weren't always able to depend on 'trust' alone, and had to resort to the fist as well, or what is also known more grandly as 'legitimacy' " (quoted in Jones, *Developmental Fairy Tales,* 149).

60. The evil and exploitative landlord in the puppet animated film *The Rooster Crows at Midnight* is one example. *The Red Signal* (*Hongse de xinhao,* 1959) is one animated film during the Seventeen Years that featured a human villain in the role of a spy. This spy disguises himself as a bear (probably alluding to the Soviet Union) living in the forest before he is exposed and captured by revolutionary children.

61. The heroes in model works and animated films are both male and female, partly because of Jiang Qing's rise to power.

62. Mosse, *Nationalism and Sexuality,* 67.

63. Roberts, *Maoist Model Theatre,* 223.

64. For the use of animals in language during the Cultural Revolution, see Ji, *Linguistic Engineering,* 193.

65. Wang, "Those Who Lived."

66. Lee, *The Stranger,* 84; Agamben, *Homo Sacer.*

67. The hostile relationship between wolves and sheep changed in post-Mao China: wolves and sheep began to fall in love with each other. For the representations of wolves and sheep in contemporary popular culture, see Chen, "Wolf Comes!"

68. He, "Shenmeyang," 128.

69. Quoted in Farquhar, *Children's Literature,* 280.

70. For cross mark used as a signature for the banned animated films during the Cultural Revolution, see *Hongweibing dianying,* 25, 27. *Red Guard Cinema* was affiliated with the Shanghai Animation Film Studio during the Cultural Revolution.

71. Descartes, *Discourse,* 32.

72. Spivak and Morris, *Can the Subaltern Speak?* 1.

73. Lippit, "Parable of Animals."

74. The theme song of *Heroic Little Sisters of the Grassland* was rendered in a childish female voice, reinforcing the feminized and thus subordinate position of ethnic minorities.

75. Language, animals, and ethnic minorities are closely related with each other. The puppet animated film *Songs Fly over the Five-Finger Mountain* (*Gesheng feichu Wuzhishan,* 1978) portrays an ethnic Li girl, who becomes mute in the oppressive "old" society. She becomes able to speak and sing beautiful songs for the people in socialist China only after her village is liberated by the CCP.

76. Quoted in Wang, "Winking Owl," 436.

77. Huang, "Sun-Facing Courtyards," 163.

78. Clark, *Chinese Cultural Revolution,* 111.

79. McGrath, "Cultural Revolution," 372.

80. Lamarre, "Speciesism, Part III."

81. Qian, "Guanyu xiandai," 132.

82. Yu, "Zuotan meishu dianying," 37.

83. Ono, *Chūgoku no animēshon,* 128.

84. For detailed analyses of the "formalist drifts" in live-action films during the Cultural Revolution, see McGrath, "Cultural Revolution Model."

85. The representations of ruins in arts also disappeared from the 1950s onward and did not resurface until the late 1970s (see Wu, *Story of Ruins,* 186–187).

86. Abbas, *Hong Kong,* 8.

87. Landscape and bird-and-flower paintings were banned during the Cultural Revolution. As a result, animals also disappeared systematically in paintings. To present a more positive and elegant image to foreign visitors at hotels and railway stations, Zhou Enlai helped loosen the control on arts, and in the early 1970s the animal motif reemerged. These paintings were later criticized by Jiang Qing and displayed at the Black Painting Exhibitions, including Chen Dayu's *Welcoming Spring* (1973) that features an angry rooster, Huang Yongyu's *Winking Owl* (1973), and Cheng Shifa's *Girl and Deer* (1973) (see Andrews, *Painters and Politics,* 369–377). The disappearance of animals in Chinese paintings and other artistic forms calls for more research but is not the primary focus here.

88. Wang, *Sublime Figure.*

Epilogue

1. The period between 1956 and 1965, the era of national style, conventionally is regarded by Chinese animators, scholars, and intellectuals as the first golden age.

2. Zhang Qin left for Hong Kong and Zheng Shaoru and Chen Yuguang left for Malaysia as early as in the 1960s (Fung, "In Full Bloom (2)").

3. Zhongguo, "Zhongguo donghuaye."

4. Du, interview with Xu Zuming.

5. Zhou, "Meiying," 117.

6. Bao, *Zhongguo donghua,* 165.

7. Du, interview with Zhou Keqin, June 14, 2015.

8. Bao, *Zhongguo donghua,* 166.

9. Huang and Xu, "Broadcasting and Politics."

10. Other animated television series include *Golden Monkey Conquers the Demon* (*Jinhou xiangyao,* five episodes, 1985), *The Adventures of a Slovenly Boy* (*Lata dawang qiyuji,* thirteen episodes, 1986–1987), *The Stories of Pipi the Boy* (*Pipi de gushi,* ten episodes, 1988), *Shuke and Beita the Mice* (*Shuke yu Beita,* thirteen episodes, 1989–1992), *The Diamond Canabash Brother* (*Hulu xiao jingang,* six episodes, 1989–1991), and *The Magic Mongolian Horse* (*Qiyi de Menggu ma,* two episodes, 1989–1990).

11. Hong, "China's TV Program Import."

12. Zhongguo, "Zhongguo donghuaye," 92.

13. Zhang, *Ershi shiji Zhongguo,* 158.

14. Wu, "Animation," 89.

15. Zhang, *Ershi shiji Zhongguo,* 135.

16. Postman, *Disappearance of Childhood,* 80.

17. For discussions of this film, see Bao, *Cong sanju hua.*

18. Du, "Suspended Animation."

19. Du, "International Childhood Fraternity."

Bibliography

Abbas, Ackbar. *Hong Kong: Culture and the Politics of Disappearance.* Minneapolis: University of Minnesota Press, 1997.

Agamben, Giorgio. *Homo Sacer: Sovereign Power and Bare Life.* Stanford, CA: Stanford University Press, 1998.

Anagnost, Ann. "Children and National Transcendence in China." In *Constructing China: The Interaction of Culture and Economics,* edited by Kenneth G. Lieberthal, Shuen-fu Lin, and Ernest P. Young, 195–221. Ann Arbor: University of Michigan Press, 1997.

Andrews, Julia. *Painters and Politics in the People's Republic of China: 1949–1979.* Berkeley: University of California Press, 1994.

———. "Traditional Painting in New China: *Guohua* and the Anti-Rightist Campaign." *Journal of Asian Studies* 49 (August 1990): 555–585.

Antoni, Klaus. "The Peach Boy (Momotarō) and the Spirit of Japan: Concerning the Function of a Fairy Tale in Japanese Nationalism of the Early Showa Age." *Asian Folklore Studies* 50, no. 1 (1991): 155–188.

Appadurai, Arjun. *Modernity at Large: Cultural Dimensions of Globalization.* Minneapolis: University of Minnesota Press, 1996.

Asada Isamu 浅田勇. "Manga eiga wa dōshite dekiruka: Chikaku dekiru Man'ei manga eiga ni gokitai kudasai" 漫画映画はどうして出来るか 近く出来る満映漫画映画に御期待下さい [Why can animated films be made: Please expect the answer from Manchukuo Film Association's forthcoming animated films]. *Manzhou dianying* 滿洲電影 [Manchuria film] 3, no. 12 (December 1939): 26–27.

———. "Manhua dianying de mimi" 漫畫電影的秘密 [The secret of animated film]. *Manzhou dianying* 滿洲電影 [Manchuria film] 3, no. 12 (December 1939): 26–27.

"Baixue Gongzhu" 白雪公主 [*Snow White*]. *Nanhai yinxing* 南海銀星 [Silver star in southern sea] 1, no. 7 (1938): 2.

"Baixue Gongzhu zai Zhongguo guanzhong sishi yuwan tupo jilu" 白雪公主在中國觀眾四十餘萬突破記錄 [*Snow White* in China: Audience exceeded 400,000, breaking record]. *Diansheng zhoukan* 電聲週刊 [Voice of cinema weekly] 8, no. 29 (1939): 1204.

Ball, Katherine M. *Animal Motifs in Asian Art: An Illustrated Guide to Their Meanings and Aesthetics.* Mineola, NY: Dover Publications, 2004.

Bao Jigui 鮑濟貴. *Zhongguo donghua dianying tongshi* 中國動畫電影通史 [History of Chinese animation]. Beijing: Lianhuanhua chubanshe, 2010.

Bao Lei 包蕾. *Cong sanju hua dao yibu donghuapian: Sange Heshang* 從三句話到一部動畫片 三個和尚 [From three sentences to an animated film: *Three Monks*]. Beijing: Zhongguo dianying chubanshe, 1984.

Bao, Weihong. *Fiery Cinema: The Emergence of an Affective Medium in China, 1915–1945.* Minneapolis: University of Minnesota Press, 2015.

Barlow, Tani. "Theorizing Woman: Funü, Guojia, Jiating (Chinese Women, Chinese State, Chinese Family)." In *Scattered Hegemonies: Postmodernity and Transnational Feminist Practices,* edited by Inderpal Grewal and Caren Kaplan, 173–196. Minneapolis: University of Minnesota Press, 2006.

Barnhart, Richard, and Catherine Barnhart. "Images of Children in Song Painting and Poetry." In *Children in Chinese Art,* edited by Ann Barrott Wicks, 31–56. Honolulu: University of Hawai'i Press, 2002.

Barrier, Michael. *Hollywood Cartoons: American Animation in Its Golden Age.* New York: Oxford University Press, 1999.

Baskett, Michael. *The Attractive Empire: Transnational Film Culture in Imperial Japan.* Honolulu: University of Hawai'i Press, 2008.

———. "Goodwill Hunting: Rediscovering and Remembering Manchukuo in Japanese 'Goodwill Films.'" In *Crossed Histories: Manchuria in the Age of Empire,* edited by Mariko Asano Tamanoi, 120–149. Honolulu: Association for Asian Studies and University of Hawai'i Press, 2005.

Beeck, Nathalie op de. *Suspended Animation: Children's Picture Books and the Fairy Tale of Modernity.* Minneapolis: University of Minnesota Press, 2010.

Bendazzi, Giannalberto. *Cartoons: One Hundred Years of Cinema Animation.* Bloomington: Indiana University Press, 1994.

Bernstein, Richard. "The Panda That Roared." *New York Times,* July 20, 2008. Accessed August 1, 2015. http://www.nytimes.com/2008/07/20/weekinreview/20bernstein.html.

Berry, Chris. *Postsocialist Cinema in Post-Mao China: The Cultural Revolution after the Cultural Revolution.* New York: Routledge, 2004.

———. "Race: Chinese Film and the Politics of Nationalism." *Cinema Journal* 31, no. 2 (Winter 1992): 45–58.

Berry, Michael. "The Absent American: Figuring the United States in Chinese Cinema of the Reform Era." In *A Companion to Chinese Cinema,* edited by Yingjin Zhang, 552–574. Malden, MA: Wiley-Blackwell, 2012.

Bhabha, Homi. "Of Mimicry and Man: The Ambivalence of Colonial Discourse." *Discipleship: A Special Issue on Psychoanalysis* 28 (Spring 1984): 125–133.

Bi Keguan 畢克官 and Huang Yuanlin 黃遠林. *Zhongguo manhua shi* 中國漫畫史 [The history of Chinese cartoons]. Beijing: Wenhua yishu chubanshe, 1986.

Bian Pingshu 邊平恕. *Li Keran* 李可染. Beijing: Zhongguo renmin daxue chubanshe, 2003.

Bian Shanji 邊善基. "Meishu yingpian de liangduo xinhua" 美術影片的兩朵新花 [Two new flowers of animation]. *Wenhui bao* 文匯報 [Wenhui daily] (October 19, 1973).

———. "Shengdong de xingxiang, ganren de yishu" 生動的形象 感人的藝術 [Vivid images, touching arts]. *Renmin ribao* 人民日報 [People's daily] (March 11, 1966).

Blumenthal, Eileen Polley. "Models in Chinese Moral Education: Perspectives from Children's Books." PhD diss., University of Michigan, Ann Arbor, 1977.

Blunt, Alison. *Travel, Gender, and Imperialism: Mary Kingsley and West Africa.* New York: Guilford Press, 1994.

Bulag, Uradyn E. "Models and Moralities: The Parable of the Two 'Heroic Little Sisters of the Grassland.'" *China Journal* 42 (July 1999): 21–41.

Cai Tingxuan 蔡廷軒. "Zuzhi ertong kanhao geming dianying" 組織兒童看好革命電影. *Dianying yishu* 電影藝術 [Film art] 3 (1965): 23–25.

Chang, Arnold. *Painting in the People's Republic of China: The Politics of Style.* Boulder, CO: Westview Press, 1980.

Chang, Eileen. "Lun katonghua zhi qiantu" 論卡通畫之前途 [On the future of animated cartoon]. In *Zhang Ailing wenji* 張愛玲文集 [Anthology of Eileen Chang], 8–10. Hefei: Anhui wenyi chubanshe, 1992.

Chang Guangxi 常光希. "Yongyuan de laoshi" 永遠的老師 [Forever teacher]. In *Yige donghua zhe de zuji* 一個動畫者的足跡 [The footprints of an animator], edited by Qian Shanzhu 錢珊朱, 181–182. Hong Kong: Long donghua, 2014.

Chen Bo 陳播. *Zhongguo dianying biannian jishi: Zong gang juan xia* 中國電影編年紀事 總綱卷 下 [A chronology of Chinese film: The outline, vol. 2]. Beijing: Zhongyang wenxian chubanshe, 1992.

———. *Zhongguo dianying biannian jishi: Zonghe juan* 中國電影編年紀事 綜合卷 [A chronology of Chinese film: Comprehensive volume]. Beijing: Zhongyang wenxian chubanshe, 2006.

Chen Bochui 陳伯吹. "Tongxin yu tongxin lun" 童心與童心論 [Children's heart and the theory of children's heart]. *Ertong wenxue yanjiu* 兒童文學研究 [Studies of children's literature] 3, no. 4 (1980): 1–20.

———. *Zai xuexi Sulian ertong wenxue de daolu shang* 在學習蘇聯兒童文學的道路上 [On the road of learning Soviet children's literature]. Beijing: Shaonian ertong chubanshe, 1958.

Chen Jianhua. "Wolf Comes! Change of Values in Twenty-First Century China." *Twenty-First Century Bimonthly* 121 (October 2010): 44–48.

Chen Mo 陳墨, Qi Zhi 啟之, and Zhang Jin 張錦 ed. *Changchun yingshi: Dongbei juan* 長春影事 東北卷 [Oral histories of cinema in Changchun: Northeast]. Beijing: Minzu chubanshe, 2011.

Chen, Tina Mai. "Dressing for the Party: Clothing, Citizenship, and Gender-Formation in Mao's China." *Fashion Theory* 5, no. 2 (2001): 143–171.

———. "Mobile Film Projection in Socialist and Post-Socialist China." *China Policy Institute Analysis.* University of Nottingham, UK. Accessed August 1, 2015. https://blogs.nottingham.ac.uk/chinapolicyinstitute/2015/05/08/enduring-themes-of-propaganda-mobile-film-projection-in-socialist-and-post-socialist-china.

Chen Yude 陳育德. "Guanyu fengjingshi, shanshui huaniaohua de jiejixing wenti" 關於風景詩 山水花鳥畫的階級性問題 [On the issue of class in landscape poetry, landscape painting, and bird-and-flower painting]. *Wenyi bao* 文藝報 [Literature and art newspaper] 10 (1960): 33–43.

Chen Weibo 陳維博. "Meishupian yeneng fanying xianshi shenghuo: Kan muoupian Hongyunya yougan" 美術片也能反映現實生活 看木偶片紅雲崖有感 [Animated film can also reflect real life: On the puppet animated film *Red Cloud Cliff*]. *Jiefang ribao* 解放日報 [Liberation daily] 10, no. 8 (1963): 4.

Chen, Xiaomei. *Acting the Right Part: Political Theater and Popular Drama in Contemporary China.* Honolulu: University of Hawai'i Press, 2002.

Cheng Jihua 程季華. *Zhongguo dianying fazhan shi* 中國電影發展史 [History of Chinese cinema]. Beijing: Zhongguo dianying chubanshe, 1963.

———. *Zhongguo dianying fazhan shi: Di er juan* 中國電影發展史 第二卷 [History of Chinese cinema, vol. 2]. Beijing: Zhongguo dianying chubanshe, 1998.

Choe Kilsung 崔吉城. "Manshū eiga Shirami wa Kowai kō" 満州映画虱はこわい考 [On the Manchurian animated film *Terrible Lice*]. *Ajia shakai bunka-kenkyu* [Journal of social and cultural studies on Asia], no. 6 (March 31, 2005): 121–136.

Chow, Rey. "Film and Cultural Identity." In *The Oxford Guide to Film Studies,* edited by John Hill and Pamela Church Gibson, 169–175. New York: Oxford University Press, 1998.

———. "On Chineseness as a Theoretical Problem." *Boundary 2* 25, no. 3 (Fall 1998): 1–24.

———. *Primitive Passions: Visuality, Sexuality, Ethnography, and Contemporary Chinese Cinema.* New York: Columbia University Press, 1995.

"Chūka eiga yunyū yotei no shin Chūgoku eiga" 中華映画輸入予定の新中国映画 [New Chinese films scheduled to be imported]. *Eiga junpō* 映画旬報 [Movie times]).

Chung, Hye Jean. "Kung Fu Panda: Animated Animal Bodies as Layered Sites of (Trans) National Identities." *Velvet Light Trap* 69 (Spring 2012): 27–37.

Clark, Paul. *Chinese Cinema: Culture and Politics since 1949.* Cambridge: Cambridge University Press, 1987.

———. *The Chinese Cultural Revolution: A History.* Cambridge: Cambridge University Press, 2008.

———. "Ethnic Minorities in Chinese Films: Cinema and the Exotic." *East-West Film Journal* 1, no. 2 (1987): 15–32.

Clements, Jonathan. *Anime: A History.* London: Palgrave Macmillan, 2013.

Clifford, James. *Routes: Travel and Translation in Late Twentieth Century.* Cambridge, MA: Harvard University Press, 1997.

Condry, Ian. *The Soul of Anime: Collaborative Creativity and Japan's Media Success Story.* Durham, NC: Duke University Press, 2013.

Cong Xian 從賢. "Yousheng huodong manhua shi zheyang zhizao de" 有聲活動漫畫是這様製造的 [Sound animated films were made this way]. *Kexue zhishi* 科學知識 [Scientific knowledge] 1, no. 8 (1933): 49–51.

Cook, Alexander C. *Mao's Little Red Book: A Global History.* New York: Cambridge University Press, 2014.

Crofts, Stephen. "Reconceptualizing National Cinema(s)." *Quarterly Review of Film and Video* 14, no. 3 (1993): 49–67.

Cui, Jian. "The Pursuit of a National Style of Chinese Animation." *Animation Journal* 14 (2006): 44–62.

Descartes, René. *Discourse on the Method for Conducting One's Reason Well and for Seeking Truth in the Sciences.* Indianapolis, IN: Hackett, 1998.

Doane, Mary Ann. "The Voice in the Cinema: The Articulation of Body and Space." *Yale French Studies,* no. 60 (1980): 33–50.

Donald, Stephanie. "Children as Political Messengers: Art, Childhood, and Continuity." In *Picturing Power in the People's Republic of China,* edited by Harriet Evans and Stephanie Donald, 79–100. Lanham, MD: Rowman & Littlefield, 1999.

———. *Little Friends: Children's Film and Media Culture in China.* Lanham, MD: Rowman & Littlefield, 2005.

Dorfman, Ariel, and Armand Mattelart. *How to Read Donald Duck: Imperialist Ideology in the Disney Comic.* New York: International General, 1984.

Dower, John W. *Embracing Defeat: Japan in the Wake of World War II.* New York: W. W. Norton, 1999.

———. *Japan in War and Peace: Selected Essays.* New York: New Press, 1993.

———. *War without Mercy: Race and Power in the Pacific War.* New York: Pantheon Books, 1986.

Dreyer, June. *China's Political System: Modernization and Tradition.* New York: Longman, 2010.

Du, Daisy Yan. "Chinese Animation at International Film Festivals." Association for Chinese Animation Studies, February 16, 2016. Accessed February 8, 2018. http://acas.ust.hk/2016/02/16/chinese-animation-at-international-film-festivals-a-report-from-the-19th-seoul-international-cartoon-animation-festival-south-korea-2015-2.

———. "The Dis/appearance of Animals in Animated Film during the Chinese Cultural Revolution, 1966–1976." *positions: asia critique* 24, no. 2 (2016): 435–479.

———. "International Childhood Fraternity: Imagining the West in Animated Film in Socialist China." Paper presented at the annual conference of Society for Cinema and Media Studies (SCMS), Atlanta, GA. March 30–April 3, 2016.

———. Interview with senior animator Fung Yuk-sung (1940–), Hong Kong, August 11, 2015.

———. Interview with Xu Zuming, Shanghai, June 15, 2015.

———. Interviews with Mochinaga Noriko, daughter of Mochinaga Tadahito. March 1, 2010; June 27 and July 7, 2015.

———. Interviews with senior animator Duan Xiaoxuan (1934–), Shanghai, August 1, 2010; June 16, 2015.

———. Interviews with senior animator Zhou Keqin (1942–), Shanghai, June 14, 2015; Hong Kong, August 29, 2015.

———. "Political Immediacy, Metal-morphosis, and the Caricatured Western Leaders in Agitprop Animation in Socialist China, 1949–1965." Paper presented at the Conference of Comparative Perspectives on Sense, Sensibility, and Sentimentality, Hong Kong University of Science and Technology, May 2016.

———. "Socialism and the Rise of the First Camerawoman in History of Chinese Animation." *Gender and Animation: Animation Studies 2.0,* Society for Animation Studies (SAS) Blog, December 3, 2014. Accessed February 8, 2018. http://blog.animationstudies.org/?p=977.

———. "Suspended Animation: The Wan Brothers and the (In)Animate Mainland-Hong Kong Encounter, 1947–1956." *Journal of Chinese Cinemas* 11, no. 2 (2017): 140–158.

Duan Xiaoxuan 段孝萱. "Chiyong Zhiren xiansheng yu xin Zhongguo meishu dianying" 持永只仁先生與新中國美術電影 [Mr. Mochinaga Tadahito and animation in socialist new China]. Paper presented at the Mochinaga Tadahito Symposium, Saga City, Japan, February 5–7, 2010.

———. "Yiyidaishui de nongnong qinqing" 一衣帶水的濃濃親情 [Kinship across a narrow strip of water]. In *Zhongguo wode dier zuguo* 中國我的第二祖國, 183-187 [China: My second motherland], by Morikawa Kazuyo 森川和代 and Morikawa Shinobu 森川忍. Translated by Wang Xiaozhi. Beijing: Zhongguo guangbo dianshi chubanshe, 2009.

Duara, Prasenjit. *Sovereignty and Authenticity: Manchukuo and the East Asian Modern.* Lanham, MD: Rowman & Littlefield, 2003.

Dubey, Madhu. *Signs and Cities: Black Literary Postmodernism.* Chicago: University of Chicago Press, 2003.

Edera, Bruno. "The Animated Film in the People's Republic of China." *ASIFA Animafilm* (Spring 1980): 35–39.

Eisenstein, Sergei. *Eisenstein on Disney,* edited by Jay Leyda. London: Methuen, 1988.

Farquhar, Mary Ann. *Children's Literature in China: From Lu Xun to Mao Zedong.* London: M. E. Sharpe, 1999.

———. "Monks and Monkey: A Study of 'National Style' in Chinese Animation." *Animation Journal* 1, no. 2 (Spring 1993): 5–27.

Fiskesjö, Magnus. "The Animal Other: China's Barbarians and Their Renaming in the Twentieth Century." *Social Text* 29, no. 4 (Winter 2012): 57–79.

Friedman, Susan Stanford. *Mappings: Feminism and the Cultural Geographies of Encounter.* Princeton, NJ: Princeton University Press, 1998.

Fu Hongxing 傅紅星. *Zhongguo yingpian dadian: Donghuapian juan* 中國影片大典動畫片卷 [Catalogue of Chinese film: Animation]. Beijing: China Radio and Television Publishing House, 2012.

Fu, Poshek. "The Ambiguity of Entertainment: Chinese Cinema in Japanese-Occupied Shanghai, 1941–1945." *Cinema Journal,* no. 1 (Autumn 1997): 66–84.

———. *Between Shanghai and Hong Kong: The Politics of Chinese Cinemas.* Stanford, CA: Stanford University Press, 2003.

———. *China Forever: The Shaw Brothers and Diasporic Cinema.* Urbana: University of Illinois Press, 2008.

Fung, Yuk-sung. "In Full Bloom: The Development of Contemporary Chinese Animation (1)." *Hong Kong Film Archive Newsletter* 68 (May 2014): 14–17. Accessed April 16, 2018. https://www.lcsd.gov.hk/CE/CulturalService/HKFA/archive/newsletters/68/68_news_e.pdf.

———. "In Full Bloom: The Development of Contemporary Chinese Animation (2)." In *Hong Kong Film Archive Newsletter* 69 (August 2014): 2–14. Accessed February 8, 2018. https://www.lcsd.gov.hk/CE/CulturalService/HKFA/archive/newsletters/69/69_more_c.pdf.

Furuichi Masako 古市雅子. *Manying dianying yanjiu* 滿映電影研究 [Studies of Manchukuo Film Association cinema]. Beijing: Jiuzhou, 2010.

Giesen, Rolf. *Chinese Animation: A History and Filmography 1922–2012.* Jefferson, NC: McFarland, 2014.

Gladney, Dru C. "Representing Nationality in China: Refiguring Majority/Minority Identities." *Journal of Asian Studies* 53, no. 1 (February 1994): 92–123.

Goldschmidt, Rick. *The Enchanted World of Rankin/Bass.* Buena Park, CA: Miser Bros Press, 2014.

———. *Mad Monster Party.* Buena Park, CA: Miser Bros. Press, 2011.

———. *Rudolph the Red-Nosed Reindeer.* Buena Park, CA: Miser Bros Press, 2014.

Greenberg, Raz. "A Yiddish Manga: The Creative Jewish Roots of Japan's God of Comics." *Innovative Research in Japanese Studies* (May 24, 2014): 89–111. Accessed February 8, 2018. https://www.h-net.org/announce/show.cgi?ID=213982.

Greene, Naomi. *From Fu Manchu to Kung Fu Panda: Images of China in American Film.* Honolulu: University of Hawai'i Press, 2014.

Guo, Li, and Jinying Li, eds. "Animating Chinese Cinemas." Special issue, *Journal of Chinese Cinemas* 11, no. 2 (2017).

Guo Qing 郭青. "Jinnianlai guanyu dianying minzuhua de tantao yu zhenglun" 近年來關於電影民族化的探討與爭論 [The debates over the nationalization of films in recent years]. *Dianying yishu* 電影藝術 [Film art] 11 (1985): 35–41.

Hagiwara Yukari 萩原由加里. *Masaoka Kenzō to sono jidai 'Nihon animēshon no chichi' no senzen to sengo* 政岡憲三とその時代「日本アニメーションの父」の戦前と戦後 [Masaoka Kenzō and his era: The prewar and postwar years of the father of Japanese animation]. Tōkyō: Seikyūsha, 2015.

"Hao Zisun: Tieshan Gongzhu qian jiaying duanpian" 好子孫 鐵扇公主前加映短片 [*Filial Children*: A short film screened before *Princess Iron Fan*]. *Zhongguo yingxun* 中國影訊 [News of Chinese cinema] 2, no. 37 (1941): 712.

He Si 何思. "Shenmeyang de chibang wang narfei" 什麼樣的翅膀往哪兒飛 [What kind of wings? Where to fly?]. *Renmin wenxue* 人民文學 [The people's literature] 6 (1960): 124–128.

He Yi 賀宜. "Wei ertong dianying shiye de fazhan er nuli" 為兒童電影事業的發展而努力 [Working hard to develop children's cinema]. *Dazhong dianying* 大眾電影 [Popular cinema], no. 22 (1954): 14.

High, Peter. *The Imperial Screen: Japanese Film Culture in the Fifteen Years' War: 1931–1945.* Madison: University of Wisconsin Press, 2003.

Hong, Junhao. "China's TV Program Import 1958–1988: Towards the Internationalization of Television." *Gazette* 52 (1993): 1–23.

Hongweibing dianying 紅衛兵電影 [Red Guard cinema]. Shanghai, July 1967.

Hu Chang 胡昶. *Dongying de Riben ren* 東映的日本人 [The Japanese staff at the Northeast Film Studio]. Changchun: Changchun shi zhengxie wenshi ziliao weiyuanhui, 2005.

———. *Xin Zhongguo dianying de yaolan* 新中國電影的搖籃 [The cradle of the cinema in socialist new China]. Changchun: Jilin wenshi chubanshe, 1986.

Hu Chang 胡昶 and Gu Quan 古泉. *Manying: Guoce dianying mianmian guan* 滿映國策電影面面觀 [Manchukuo Film Association: Aspects of national policy film]. Beijing: Zhonghua shuju, 1990.

Hu, Ying. *Tales of Translation: Composing the New Woman in China, 1899–1918.* Stanford, CA: Stanford University Press, 2000.

Huang, Nicole. "Sun-Facing Courtyards: Urban Communal Culture in Mid-1970s' Shanghai." *East Asian History* 25/26 (June/December 2003): 161–182.

———. *Women, War, Domesticity: Shanghai Literature and Popular Culture of the 1940s.* Boston: Brill, 2005.

Huang, Yu, and Xu Yu. "Broadcasting and Politics: Chinese Television in the Mao Era, 1958–1976." *Historical Journal of Film, Radio, and Television* 17, no. 4 (October 1997): 563–574.

Huang Yushan 黃玉珊 and Yu Weizheng 余爲政. *Donghua dianying tansuo* 動畫電影探索 [Exploring animated film]. Taipei: Beishitu, 2004.

Hung, Chang-Tai. "Female Symbols of Resistance in Chinese Wartime Spoken Drama." *Modern China* 15, no. 2 (April 1989): 149–177.

———. *War and Popular Culture: Resistance in Modern China, 1937–1945.* Berkeley: University of California Press, 1994.

Huntington, Samuel. *The Clash of Civilizations and the Remaking of World Order.* New York: Simon & Schuster, 1996.

Iizawa Tadashi 飯澤匡. "Shijō yutakana Cheko no ningyō no eiga" 詩情豊かな チェコの人形の映画 [Poetic Czech puppet animation]. *Josei no tomodachi* 婦人之友 [Women's friends] 53, no. 4 (1959): 146–150.

Imamura Taihei 今村太平. "Manga eiga hyō 漫画映画評 [Comments on animated films]. *Eiga junpō* 映画旬報 [Movie times] (October 1, 1942): 39–40.

Irigaray, Luce. *This Sex Which Is Not One.* Translated by Catherine Porter with Carolyn Burke. Ithaca, NY: Cornell University Press, 1985.

Iwabuchi, Koichi. *Recentering Globalization: Popular Culture and Japanese Transnationalism.* Durham, NC: Duke University Press, 2002.

Jang, Scarlett Ju-yu. "Ox-Herding Painting in the Sung Dynasty." *Artibus Asiae* 52, no. ½ (1992): 60–61.

Ji, Fengyuan. *Linguistic Engineering: Language and Politics in Mao's China.* Honolulu: University of Hawai'i Press, 2004.

Jiang, Rong. *Wolf Totem: A Novel.* Translated by Howard Goldblatt. New York: Penguin, 2008.

Jin Xi 靳夕. "Kuazhang yu shufu: Meishupian chuangzuo wenti suibi" 誇張與舒服 美術片創作問題隨筆 [Exaggeration and moderation: Random thoughts on animated filmmaking]. *Dianying yishu* 電影藝術 [Film art] 1 (1963): 55.

"Jinshang tianhua: Tieshan Gongzhu qian jiaying huaji duanpian" 錦上添花 鐵扇公主前加映滑稽短片 [Icing on the cake: A comical short film to be screened before *Princess Iron Fan*]. *Guolian yingxun* 國聯影訊 [News from China United Film Company] 1, no. 9 (1941): 70.

Jones, Andrew. *Developmental Fairy Tales: Evolutionary Thinking and Modern Chinese Culture.* Cambridge, MA: Harvard University Press, 2011.

Kandiyoti, Denize. "Identity and Its Discontents: Women and the Nation." In *Colonial Discourse and Post-Colonial Theory: A Reader,* edited by Patrick Williams and Laura Chrisman, 376-391. New York: Columbia University Press, 1994.

Kang, Helen. "*Shui Mo Dong Hua:* The History of Brush Painting Animation." *Animation Journal* 14 (2006): 63–75.

Kawamoto Kihachirō 川本喜八郎. "Mochinaga Tadahito sensei no omoide" 持永只仁先生の思い出. In *Animēshon Nitchū kōryūki: Mochinaga Tadahito jiden* アニメーション 日中交流記: 持永只仁自伝 [Sino-Japanese cultural exchange in animated filmmaking: Autobiography of Mochinaga Tadahito], 339–341. Tōkyō: Tōhō shoten, 2006.

Kelly, Catriona. *Children's World: Growing Up in Russia, 1890–1991.* New Haven, CT: Yale University Press, 2007.

Kim, Joon-Yang. "Critique of the New Historical Landscape of South Korean Animation." *Animation: An Interdisciplinary Journal,* no. 1 (July 2006): 61–81.

Kinoshita Takeo 木下武男. "Kaigun manga eiga no shin sakuhin" 海軍漫畫映画の新作品 [New animated film by the Navy]. *Shin eiga* 新映画 [New cinema] 3, no. 5 (May 1, 1943): 56–57.

Komatsuzawa Hajime 小松沢甫. *Mochinaga Tadahito no ashiato: Unmei o kirihiraita animēshon sakka* 持永只仁の足跡: 運命をきりひらいたアニメーション作家 [The footprints of Mochinaga Tadahito: The animator who controlled his fate]. Tōkyō: Rekishi bukai ban, 2000.

———. "Princess Iron Fan." In *The Japan/America Film Wars: WWII Propaganda and Its Cultural Contexts,* edited by Abe Mark Nornes and Fukushima Yukio, 225–229. Chur, Switzerland: Harwood Academic Publishers, 1994.

Kondō Hidezō 近藤日出造. "Momotarō no Umiwashi o mite 桃太郎の海鷲を観て" [Watching *Momotarō's Sea Eagles*]. *Shin eiga* 新映画 [New cinema] 3, no. 5 (May 1, 1943): 46–47.

Lai, T. C. *Ch'i Pai Shih.* Seattle: University of Washington Press, 1973.

Lamarre, Thomas, *The Anime Machine: A Media Theory of Animation.* Minneapolis: University of Minnesota Press, 2009.

———. "Speciesism, Part I: Translating Races into Animals in Wartime Animation." *Mechademia* 3 (2009): 75–95.

———. "Speciesism, Part III: Neoteny and the Politics of Life." *Mechademia* 6 (2011): 112–114.

Lee, Haiyan. *Revolution of the Heart: A Genealogy of Love in China 1900–1950.* Stanford, CA: Stanford University Press, 2007.

———. *The Stranger and the Chinese Moral Imagination.* Stanford, CA: Stanford University Press, 2014.

Leed, Eric. *The Mind of the Traveler: From Gilgamesh to Global Tourism.* New York: Basic Books, 1991.

Lent, John. *Animation in Asia and the Pacific.* Bloomington: Indiana University Press, 2001.

Lent, John, and Ying Xu. "China's Animation Beginnings: The Roles of the Wan Brothers and Others." *Asian Cinema* 14, no. 1 (2003): 56–69.

Leonard, Sean, and Yamagata Hiroo. "Hō ni aragatte no shinpo: Amerika ni okeru Nihon anime no bakuhatsu-teki seichō to fan ryūtsū, chosakuken" 法に抗っての進歩: アメリカにおける日本アニメの爆発的成長とファン流通、著作権 [Progress against the law: The explosive growth of Japanese animation in the United States, fan distribution, and copyright]. Accessed February 7, 2018. http://cruel.org/other/animeprogress.html.

Leyda, Jay. *Dianying: Electric Shadows*. Cambridge, MA: MIT Press, 1972.

Li Fu 李甫. "Lun Zhou Zuoren de zuoguan yu dongdu" 論周作人的做官與東渡 [On Zhou Zuoren's officialdom and his travel to Japan]. *Yuzhou feng* 宇宙風 [Cosmic wind], no. 120 (1941): 16–18.

Li, Jie. "A National Cinema for a Puppet State: The Manchurian Motion Picture Association." In *The Oxford Handbook of Chinese Cinemas*, edited by Carlos Rojas, 79-97. New York: Oxford University Press, 2013.

———. "Phantasmagoric Manchukuo: Documentaries Produced by the South Manchurian Railway Company, 1932–1940." *positions: asia critique* 22, no. 2 (2014): 329–369.

Li Lei 李蕾. "Manhua yingpian zhizuo guocheng" 漫畫影片製作過程 [The process of making an animated film]. *Manzhou dianying* 滿洲電影 [Manchuria film] 4, no. 4 (April 1940): 33–35.

Li Qun 力群. "Qianyan" 前言 [Preface]. In *Qi Baishi yanjiu* 齊白石研究 [Studies of Qi Baishi], edited by Li Qun 力群, 1–2. Shanghai: Shanghai renmin meishu chubanshe, 1959.

Li Xinyu 李新宇. "Caoyuan Yingxiong xiao jiemei ji ta beihou de gushi" 草原英雄小姐妹及它背後的故事 [*Heroic Little Sisters of the Grassland* and its secret stories]. In *Zhongguo wenshi jinghua nianxuan* 中國文史精華年選 [Annual collection of prime Chinese literature and history], 187–191. Guangzhou: Huacheng chubanshe, 2008.

Liang Ping 梁蘋. "Weida de guanhuai: Ji Zhou Enlai he Chen Yi guanxin meishu dianying de jijian shi" 偉大的關懷 記周恩來和陳毅關心美術電影的幾件事 [Great care: Several examples that show Zhou Enlai's and Chen Yi's care for animated films]. In *Huihuang yu fenjin Shanghai dianshitai sishi zhounian wenji donghua shaoerjuan* 輝煌與奮進 上海電視臺四十周年文集 動畫少兒卷 [Glory and progress: Anthology of the 40th anniversary of Shanghai TV: Volume of animation and children], 32–38. Shanghai: Shanghai renming chubanshe, 1998.

Liang Shangquan 梁上泉. *Hongyun ya* 红雲崖 [*Red Cloud Cliff*]. Beijing: Zhongguo qingnian chubanshe, 1959.

Lippit, Akira Mizuta. *Electric Animal: Toward a Rhetoric of Wildlife*. Minneapolis: University of Minnesota Press, 2000.

———. "The Parable of Animals: Animated Language." In *Tiere im Film: Eine Menschheitsgeschichte der Moderne,* edited by Maren Möhring, Massimo Perinelli, and Olaf Stieglitz, 11–26. Köln: Böhlau Verlag, 2009.

Lu Guangda 盧光大. "Kaifeng de mouxie yingyuan dui ertong zhuanchang zuzhi de hen buhao" 開封的某些影院對兒童專場組織得很不好 [Some cinemas in Kaifeng did not do a good job in organizing special screenings for children]. *Dazhong dianying* 大眾電影 [Popular cinema] 3 (February 11, 1955): 34.

Lu, Sheldon. "Chinese Cinemas and Transnational Film Studies." In *Transnational Chinese Cinemas: Identity, Nationhood, Gender,* edited by Sheldon Lu, 1–34. Honolulu: University of Hawai'i Press, 1997.

Lu Yihao 盧怡浩. "Zuigao de jiangyu: Huiyi Chen Yi tongzhi canguan meishu dianying zhanlanhui" 最高的獎譽 回憶陳毅同誌參觀美術電影展覽會 [The highest award:

In memory of Comrade Chen Yi's visit of the animation film exhibition]. *Dazhong dianying* 大眾電影 [Popular cinema] 5 (1979): 1–2.

Luo, Liang. *The Avant-Garde and the Popular in Modern China: Tian Han and the Intersection of Performance and Politics.* Ann Arbor: University of Michigan, 2014.

Luo Yijun 羅藝軍. "Dianying minzuhua lunbian" 電影民族化論辯 [Debates on the nationalization of films]. *Dianying yishu* 電影藝術 [Film art] 4 (1985): 16–17.

Ma Shouqing 馬守清. "Dongbei dianying gongsi chengli qianhou" 東北電影公司成立前後 [Before and after the establishment of the Northeast Film Studio]. In *Yi Dongying* 憶東影 [In memory of the Northeast Film Studio]. Changchun: Jilin wenshi chubanshe, 1986.

Macdonald, Sean. *Animation in China: History, Aesthetics, Media.* New York: Routledge, 2016.

MacFadyen, David. *Yellow Crocodiles and Blue Oranges: Russian Animated Film since World War Two.* Montreal: McGill-Queen's University Press, 2005.

Magnier, Mark. "China's Imported Panda." *Los Angeles Times.* July 28, 2008.

Maltin, Leonard. *Of Mice and Magic: A History of American Animated Cartoons.* New York: McGraw-Hill, 1987.

"Manga eiga hatten no tame no shomondai" 漫画映画發展のための諸問題 [Problems for the development of animated film]. *Eiga hyōron* 映画評論 [Magazine of film review] (September 1944): 37–41.

Manovich, Lev. "What Is Digital Cinema?" In *The Visual Culture Reader,* edited by Nicholas Mirzoeff, 405–416. New York: Routledge, 2002.

McGrath, Jason. "Cultural Revolution Model Opera Films and the Realist Tradition in Chinese Cinema." *Opera Quarterly* 26, no. 2–3 (2010): 343–376.

McLaren, Norman. *The Healthy Village: An Experiment in Visual Education in Western China.* Paris: UNESCO, 1949.

Mei Yu 梅御. "Wanshi disan xiongdi Wan Chaochen yijiang jiaru katongbu" 萬氏第三兄弟萬超塵亦將加入卡通部 [The third Wan brother, Wan Chaochen, is going to join the animation department]. *Dazhong yingxun* 大眾影訊 [Popular film news] 2, no. 7 (1941): 466.

Milani, Farzaneh. *Words, Not Swords: Iranian Women Writers and the Freedom of Movement.* Syracuse, NY: Syracuse University Press, 2011.

Miyao, Daisuke. *The Aesthetics of Shadow: Lighting and Japanese Cinema.* Durham, NC: Duke University Press, 2013.

Mochinaga Tadahito 持永只仁. *Animēshon Nitchū kōryūki: Mochinaga Tadahito jiden* アニメーション日中交流記: 持永只仁自伝 [Sino-Japanese cultural exchange in animated filmmaking: Autobiography of Mochinaga Tadahito]. Tōkyō: Tōhō shoten, 2006.

———. "Eiga no mikata" 映画の見方 [Film review]. *Shin josei* 新女性 [New women] 51 (April 1955): 61–63.

———. "Mittsu no kuni no manga eiga o mite" 三つの国の漫画映画を見て [Watching animated films from three countries]. *Shin josei* 新女性 [New women] 52 (May 1955): 86–89.

———. "Renmin dianying de kaiduan" 人民電影的開端 [The beginning of the people's cinema]. In *Yi Dongying* 憶東影 [In memory of the Northeast Film Studio], 165–167. Changchun: Jilin wenshi chubanshe, 1986.

———. "Zhongsheng nanwangde meihao huiyi: Yuan Dongying Riben youren fanghua hou de yifeng laixin" 終生難忘的美好回憶 原東影日本友人訪華後的一封來信 [Unforgettable memories: A letter from the former Japanese staff of the Northeast Film Studio after visiting China]. *Dazhong dianying* 大眾電影 [Popular cinema], no. 2 (1979): 26.

———. "Zuichu de muou" 最初的木偶 [The beginning of puppet animation]. In *Yi Dongying* 憶東影 [In memory of the Northeast Film Studio], 156–164. Changchun: Jilin wenshi chubanshe, 1986.

Mori Takuya 森卓也. *Teihon animēshon no gyagu sekai* 定本アニメーションのギャグ世界 [The world of gags in animated film]. Tōkyō: Asupekuto, 2009.

Morikawa Kazuyo 森川和代 and Morikawa Shinobu 森川忍. *Zhongguo wode dier zuguo* 中國我的第二祖國 [China: My second motherland]. Translated by Wang Xiaozhi. Beijing: Zhongguo guangbo dianshi chubanshe, 2009.

Mosse, George. *Nationalism and Sexuality: Middle-Class Morality and Sexual Norms in Modern Europe.* Madison: University of Wisconsin Press, 1985.

Mulan Congjun: Shanghai gebao jiaping ji 木蘭從軍: 上海各報佳評集 [*Mulan Joins the Army*: A collection of positive newspaper criticism]. Hong Kong, 1939.

"Mulan Congjun yun Ri kaiying" 木蘭從軍 運日開映 [*Mulan Joins the Army*: To be released in Japan]. *Diansheng zhoukan* 電聲週刊 [Movie tone weekly] 10, no. 3 (1940): 21.

Nakata Senpo 中田千畝. *Nihon dōwa no shin kenkyū* 日本童話の新研究 [New studies of Japanese fairy tales]. Tōkyō: Muratashoten, 1980.

Napier, Susan J. *Anime: From Akira to Howl's Moving Castle.* New York: Palgrave Macmillan, 2005.

Ngai, Sianne. "The Cuteness of the Avant-Garde." *Critical Inquiry* 31, no. 4 (Summer 2005): 811–847.

Noguchi Hisamitsu 野口久光. "Manga eiga to sono sakusha 漫画映画とその作者" [Animated films and their authors]. *Eiga no gijutsu* 映画の技術 [Cinema technology] (September 1942): 22–27.

Nornes, Abé Mark. *Japanese Documentary Film: The Meiji Era through Hiroshima.* Minneapolis: University of Minnesota Press, 2003.

Nye, Joseph. *Bound to Lead: The Changing Nature of American Power.* New York: Basic Books, 1990.

———. *Soft Power: The Means to Success in World Politics.* New York: Public Affairs, 2004.

Ohnuki-Tierney, Emiko. *The Monkey as Mirror: Symbolic Transformations in Japanese History and Ritual.* Princeton, NJ: Princeton University Press, 1987.

Okada, Hidenori. "Nitrate Film Production in Japan: A Historical Background of the Early Days." *The Oxford Handbook of Japanese Cinema,* edited by Daisuke Miyao, 265–287. Oxford: Oxford University Press, 2014.

Okamoto, Rei. "Images of the Enemy in the Wartime Manga Magazine, 1941–1945." In *Illustrating Asia: Comics, Humor Magazines, and Picture Books,* edited by John Lent, 204–220. Honolulu: University of Hawai'i Press, 2001.

Okamoto Tadanari 岡本忠成. "Buttai (ningyō) animēshon——sono hitotsu no sokumen" 物体（人形）アニメーション——そのひとつの側面 [Puppet animation: One aspect]. In *Sekai no sakka-tachi kōza animēshon* 世界の作家たち 講座アニメーション [Authors in the world: Lectures on animation], edited by Noborikawa Naoki 登川直樹, 132–137. Tōkyō: Bijutsu shuppansha, 1987.

Ono Kōsei 小野耕世. "Anime eiga jijō" アニメ映画事情 [The state of animated film]. *Shio* 潮 [Tides] (September 1984): 152–159.

———. *Chūgoku no animēshon* 中国のアニメーション [Chinese animation]. Tōkyō: Heibonsha, 1987.

———. "Guranpuri wa hai tekunikku no ningyō eiga sa" グランプリは ハイテクニックの人形映画さ [Grand prize: High-technique puppet animation]. *Kinema junpo* キネマ旬報 [Movie times] (September 1978): 110–112.

———. "The Long Flight of Manga and Anime: The History of Comics and Animation in Japan." In *The Illusion of Life 2: More Essays on Animation*, 99–118. Australia: Power Publications, 2007.

———. "Tadahito Mochinaga: The Japanese Animator Who Lived in Two Worlds." *Animation World Magazine* 4, no. 9 (December 1999).

Orbaugh, Sharalyn. *Propaganda Performed: Kamishibai in Japan's Fifteen-Year War*. Boston: Brill, 2015.

Pang, Laikwan. *Building a New China in Cinema: The Chinese Left-Wing Cinema Movement, 1932–1937*. Lanham, MD: Rowman & Littlefield, 2002.

———. *Creativity and Its Discontents: China's Creative Industries and Intellectual Property Rights Offenses*. Durham, NC: Duke University Press, 2012.

Peng Xinqi 彭新琪. *Donghua dashi Wan Laiming* 動畫大師萬籟鳴 [The animation master Wan Laiming]. Zhengzhou: Haiyan chubanshe, 1988.

Pickowicz, Paul. "Acting like Revolutionaries: Shi Hui, the Wenhua Studio, and Private-Sector Filmmaking, 1949–52." In *Dilemmas of Victory: The Early Years of the People's Republic of China*, edited by Jeremy Brown and Paul Pickowicz, 256–287. Cambridge, MA: Harvard University Press, 2010.

———. *China on Film: A Century of Exploration, Confrontation, and Controversy*. Lanham, MD: Rowman & Littlefield, 2012.

Pontieri, Laura. *Soviet Animation and the Thaw of the 1960s: Not Only for Children*. New Barnet, UK: John Libbey, 2012.

Postman, Neil. *The Disappearance of Childhood*. New York: Vintage Books, 1994.

Pratt, Mary Louise. *Imperial Eyes: Travel Writing and Transculturation*. New York: Routledge, 1992.

Pu Jiaxiang 浦稼祥. *Donghua chuangzuo qishilu* 動畫創作啓示錄 [Revelation on animated filmmaking]. Beijing: Beijing lianhe chuban gongsi, 2014.

Qian Shanzhu 錢珊朱. *Yige donghua zhe de zuji* 一個動畫者的足跡 [The footprints of an animator]. Hong Kong: Long donghua, 2014.

Qian Yunda 錢運達. "Guanyu xiandai ticai wenti: Shezhi donghuapian Caoyuan Yingxiong Xiaojiemei de tihui" 關於現代題材問題 攝制動畫片草原英雄小姐妹的體會 [On contemporary subject matter: Reflections on making the animated film *Heroic Little*

Sisters of the Grassland]. In *Meishu dianying chuangzuo yanjiu* 美術電影創作研究 [Studies on animated filmmaking]. Beijing: Zhongguo dianying chubanshe, 1984.

Qin Gang 秦剛. "Shanhai sokai gekijō animēshon hōei-shi kō" 上海租界劇場アニメーション放映史考 [On the screening of animated films in the theaters of Shanghai International Settlement]. In *Shanhai sokai no gekijō bunka* 上海租界の劇場文化 [The theater culture of Shanghai International Settlement], edited by Ōhashi Takehiko, Sekine Maho and Fujita Hiroyuki, 204–221.Tōkyō: Bensei, 2015.

Qiuquemelle, Marie-Claire. "The Wan Brothers and Sixty Years of Animated Film in China." *Perspectives on Chinese Cinema,* edited by Chris Berry, 175–186. London: British Film Institute, 1991.

Ren Shuang 任霜. "Donghua yingpian de shezhi guocheng" 動畫影片的攝製過程 [The process of making an animated film]. *Changcheng huabao* 長城畫報 [Great Wall pictorial] 23 (1952): 28.

Ri Shunki 李舜姫. "Sōren monogatari 双蓮物語" [Twin lotuses]. In *Sekai to jinkō* 世界と人口 [The world and the population] (March 1993): 18–25.

Ridgely, Steven. *Japanese Counterculture: The Antiestablishment Art of Terayama Shuji.* Minneapolis: University of Minnesota Press, 2011.

Roberts, Rosemary A. *Maoist Model Theatre: The Semiotics of Gender and Sexuality in the Chinese Cultural Revolution.* Boston: Brill, 2010.

Rubin, Gayle. "The Traffic in Women: Notes on the Political Economy of Sex." In *Deviations: A Gayle Rubin Reader,* 33–65. Durham, NC: Duke University Press, 2011.

"Saiyūki" 西遊記 [*Journey to the West*]. *Eiga junpō* 映画旬報 [Movie times]. April 1, May 21, July 1, September 11, 1942.

Sato, Tadao. *Currents in Japanese Cinema.* New York: Harper & Row, 1982.

Sawada Minoru 澤田稔. "Chūgoku saisho no chōhen manga eiga Tessen Kōshu o megutte" 中國最初の長篇漫畫映画 鐵扇公主 をめぐって [On China's first animated feature film, *Princess Iron Fan*]. *Eiga hyōron* 映画評論 [Magazine of film review] (April 1942): 96–99.

Schein, Louisa. "Gender and Internal Orientalism in China." *Modern China* 23, no. 1 (January 1997): 69–98.

Schodt, Frederik. *The Astro Boy Essays.* Berkeley, CA: Stone Bridge Press, 2007.

Seo Mitsuyo 瀬尾光世. "Manga eiga no gijutsu" 漫畫映画の技術 [The technology of animated film]. *Eiga no gijutsu* 映画の技術 [Cinema technology] (September, 1942): 15–17.

Seo Mitsuyo 瀬尾光世, Tamura Kiyoshi 田村潔, et al. "Manga Saiyūki gappyō" 漫画西遊記合評 [Collective criticism of the animated film *Journey to the West*]. *Eiga no gijutsu* 映画の技術 [Cinema technology] (September, 1942): 64–66.

Shapiro, Judith. *Mao's War against Nature: Politics and the Environment in Revolutionary China.* Cambridge: Cambridge University Press, 2001.

Shiraishi, Saya. "Doraemon Goes Abroad." In *Japan Pop! Inside the World of Japanese Popular Culture,* edited by Timothy J. Craig, 287–308. London: M. E. Sharpe, 2000.

Sina Online. "Waijiaobu dang'an jiemi pilu zhuduo neimu" 外交部檔案揭秘披露諸多內幕 [Documents of Ministry of Foreign Affairs revealing hidden histories]. *Dahua-*

Shantou Special Economic Zone Evening News, October 2, 2004. Accessed March 14, 2018. http://news.sina.com.cn/c/2004-10-02/14133824995s.shtml.

Solomon, Charles. "Animation: Notes on a Definition." In *The Art of the Animated Image: An Anthology,* edited by Charles Solomon, 9–12. Los Angeles: American Film Institute, 1987.

Songlin 松林. "Meishu dianying yao zou minzuhua de daolu" 美術電影要走民族化的道路 [Animated film should walk on the path of nationalization]. *Dianying yishu* 電影藝術 [Film art] 2 (1979): 49–50.

———. "Yuyou minzu xing, yuyou guojixing: Meishu dianying minzu fengge de xingcheng he fazhan" 愈有民族性 愈有國際性 美術電影民族風格的形成和發展 [The more national, the more international: The formation and development of the national style]. *Dangdai dianying* 當代電影 [Contemporary cinema] 2 (1985): 99–103.

Soviet Animation. Moscow: Sovexportfilm, 1986.

Spivak, Gayatri Chakravorty. "Can the Subaltern Speak?" In *Can the Subaltern Speak? Reflections on the History of an Idea,* edited by Rosalind C. Morris, 21–78. New York: Columbia University Press, 2010.

Steinberg, Marc. *Anime's Media Mix: Franchising Toys and Characters in Japan.* Minneapolis: University of Minnesota Press, 2012.

Strauss, Claude Lévi. *The Savage Mind.* Chicago: University of Chicago Press, 1966.

Sun Huijia 孫慧佳. "Zhongguo shouwei donghua jiaoshou: Qian Jiajun pingzhuan" 中國首位動畫教授 錢家俊評傳 [The first animator professor: A biography of Qian Jiajun]. *Jilin yishu xueyuan xuebao*吉林藝術學院學報 [Journal of Jilin College of the Arts] 75, no. 2 (2006): 48–53.

Sun Yi 孫毅. "Yici chenggong de changshi: Kan meishupian Hongyunya" 一次成功的嘗試 看美術片紅雲崖 [A successful experiment: On the animated film *Red Cloud Cliff*]. *Dazhong dianying* 大眾電影 [Popular cinema] 10 (1963): 15.

Swearingen, Rodger, and Paul Langer. *Red Flag in Japan: International Communism in Action 1919–1951.* Cambridge, MA: Harvard University Press, 1952.

Takatsuna Hirofumi 高綱博文. *Senji Shanhai 1937–45 nen* 戦時上海 1937–45 年 [Wartime Shanghai: 1937–1945].Tōkyō: Kenbunshuppan, 2009.

Tang Cheng 唐澄. "Shuimo donghua yinggai fazhan" 水墨動畫應該發展 [Ink-painting animation should be developed]. *Meishu dianying chuangzuo yanjiu* 美術電影創作研究 [Studies on animated filmmaking]. Beijing: Zhongguo dianying chubanshe, 1984.

Tang, Xiaobing. *Visual Culture in Contemporary China: Paradigms and Shifts.* Cambridge: Cambridge University Press, 2015.

Te Wei 特偉. "Chuangzao minzu de meishu dianying" 創造民族的美術電影 [Creating a national fine arts film]. *Meishu* 美術 [Fine arts] 10, no. 11 (1960): 50–52.

———. "Meishu dianying chuangzuo fangtan" 美術電影創作放談. *Meishu dianying chuangzuo yanjiu* 美術電影創作研究 [Studies on animated filmmaking], 1–11. Beijing: Zhongguo dianying chubanshe, 1984.

———. *Wo kongsu* 我控訴 [I accuse]. Shanghai: Yiqun chubanshe, 1941.

Tezuka Osamu 手塚治虫. "Atogaki" あとがき [Afterword]. In *Boku no Son Gokū* ぼくの孫悟空 [My Sun Wukong]. In *Tezuka Osamu manga zenshū* 手塚治虫漫画全集 [A complete collection of Tezuka Osamu's manga], vol. 8. Tōkyō: Kōdansha, 1997.

———. *Boku no manga jinsei* ぼくのマンガ人生 [My manga life]. Tōkyō: Iwanami shoten, 1997.

———. *Boku no Son Gokū* ぼくの孫悟空 [My Sun Wukong]. In *Tezuka Osamu manga zenshū* 手塚治虫漫画全集 [A complete collection of Tezuka Osamu's manga], vols. 2–4 and 6. Tōkyō: Kōdansha, 1997.

———. "Tōkī igo no manga eiga" トーキー以後の漫画映画 [Animated film after talkies]. In *Sekai no sakka-tachi kōza animēshon* 世界の作家たち 講座アニメーション [Authors in the world: Lectures on animation], edited by Noborikawa Naoki 登川直樹, 106–131. Tōkyō: Bijutsu shuppansha, 1987.

"Tezuka Osamu shi to Son Gokū" 手塚治虫氏と孫悟空 [Tezuka Osamu and Sun Wukong]. Accessed February 8, 2018. http://japanese.china.org.cn/jp/archive/zryhhj/node_2185493.htm.

Thornber, Karen Laura. *Empire of Texts in Motion: Chinese, Korean, and Taiwanese Transculturations of Japanese Literature.* Cambridge, MA: Harvard University Asia Center, 2009.

Thurston, Anne F. *Enemies of the People: The Ordeal of Intellectuals in China's Great Cultural Revolution.* Cambridge, MA: Harvard University Press, 1988.

"Tieshan Gongzhu liang mingge Debaoge yu Jixiangyamei" 鐵扇公主兩名歌 得寶歌與雞香鴨美 [Two famous songs from *Princess Iron Fan:* "Obtaining a Treasure" and "Delicious Chicken and Duck Meat"]. *Dianying xinwen* 電影新聞 [News of cinema], no. 37 (1941): 184.

"Tieshan Gongzhu tishen yanyuan jueding" 鐵扇公主替身演員決定 [The stuntmen for *Princess Iron Fan* were decided]. *Zhongguo yingxun* 中國影訊 [News of Chinese cinema] 1, no. 11 (1940): 83.

"Tieshan Gongzhu tongxiao gongzuo you Guoli Yinzhuan peiyin" 鐵扇公主通宵工作由國立音專配音 [Working overnight for *Princess Iron Fan*: Dubbing by National Music Institute]. *Dianying xinwen* 電影新聞 [News of cinema], no. 145 (1941): 579.

Tsuji Hisakazu 辻久一. *Chūka den'ei shiwa: Ippeisotsu no nitchū eiga kaisō-ki* 中華電影史話: 一兵卒の日中映画回想記 1939–1945 [Historical anecdotes of Chinese cinema: The memoir of a Japanese soldier on Sino-Japanese film].Tōkyō: Gaifūsha, 1998.

Uchida Kimio 内田岐三雄. "Muran jyū gun" 木蘭従軍 [Mulan joins the army]. *Eiga junpō* 映画旬報 [Movie times] (July 11, 1942): 26.

Ueno Kōzō 上野耕三. "Nippon eiga no jakuten" 日本映画の弱点 [The weakness of Japanese cinema]. *Nippon eiga* 日本映画 [Japan cinema] 11 (1942): 11–19.

Voci, Paola. *China on Video: Smaller-Screen Realities.* London: Routledge, 2010.

———. "DV and Animateur Cinema in China." In *DV-Made China: Digital Subjects and Social Transformations after Independent Film,* edited by Zhen Zhang, 260–288. Honolulu: University of Hawai'i Press, 2015.

Vukovich, Daniel. *China and Orientalism: Western Knowledge Production and the P.R.C.* New York: Routledge, 2012.

Wan Chaochen 萬超塵. "Zhongguo donghua zhuanjia zai Mei kaocha" 中國動畫專家在美考察 [Chinese animators were studying in the United States]. *Yingyin* 影音 [Voice of cinema] 6, no. 9–10 (1948): 9.

Wan Laiming 萬籟鳴. *Wo yu Sun Wukong* 我與孫悟空 [Sun Wukong and I]. Taiyuan: Beiyue wenyi, 1986.

Wan Laiming 萬籟鳴 and Wan Guchan 萬古蟾. "Tessen Kōshu seisaku hōkoku" 鐵扇公主製作報告 [A report on the making of *Princess Iron Fan*]. *Eiga hyōron* 映画評論 [Magazine of film review] (December 1942): 55–57.

Wan Laiming 萬籟鳴, Wan Guchan 萬古蟾, and Wan Chaochen 萬超塵. "Xianhua katong" 閑話卡通 [Random thoughts on cartoons]. *Mingxing* 明星 [Stars] 5, no. 1 (1936): 1–2.

"Wan Laiming kunzhong shoupin Guolian huishe Tieshan Gongzhu" 萬籟鳴昆仲受聘國聯繪攝鐵扇公主 [The twin Wan Brothers were hired by China United Film Company to make *Princess Iron Fan*]. *Zhongguo yingxun* 中國影訊 [News of Chinese cinema] 1, no. 5 (April 19, 1940): 1.

Wang, Ban. "Socialist Realism." In *Words and Their Stories: Essays on the Language of the Chinese Revolution*, edited by Ban Wang, 101–118. Boston: Brill, 2011.

———. *The Sublime Figure of History: Aesthetics and Politics in Twentieth-Century China.* Stanford, CA: Stanford University Press, 1997.

Wang, Eugene. "The Winking Owl: Visual Effect and Its Art Historical Thick Description." *Critical Inquiry* 26, no. 3 (Spring 2000): 435–473.

Wang Lina 王麗娜. "Xiyouji zai haiwai" 西遊記在海外 [*Journey to the West* abroad]. *Gudian wenxue zhishi* 古典文學知識 [Knowledge of classical literature] 4, (1999): 117–126.

Wang Liuyi 王六一. *Zhengtu: Zouxiang bainian de Zhongguo donghua* 征途 走向百年的中國動畫 [Long march: Toward a hundred years of Chinese animation], vols. 1–4. Guizhou: Guizhou renmin chubanshe, 2012.

Wang, Qi. "Those Who Lived in a Wallpapered Home: The Historical Space of the Socialist Chinese Counter-Espionage Film." *Journal of Chinese Cinemas* 5, no. 1 (2011): 55–71.

Wang, Yiman. *Remaking Chinese Cinema: Through the Prism of Shanghai, Hong Kong, and Hollywood*. Honolulu: University of Hawai'i Press, 2013.

Wang Zhaowen 王朝聞. "Zuotan meishu dianying" 座談美術電影 [On fine arts film]. *Dianying yishu* 電影藝術 [Film art], no. 2 (1960): 38–42.

Wasserstrom, Jeffrey, and Sin-kiong Wong. "Taunting the Turtles and Damning the Dogs: Animal Epithets and Political Conflict in Modern China." *Indiana East Asian Working Paper Series on Language and Politics in Modern China* no. 9. Bloomington: Indiana University, 1996. Accessed February 9, 2018. http://www.indiana.edu/~easc/publications/doc/working_papers/Issue%209%201996%20Summer%20IUEAWPS%20Wang,%20Wasserstrom%20and%20Wong.pdf.

Wells, Paul. "Smarter than the Average Art Form: Animation in the Television Era." In *Prime Time Animation: Television Animation and American Culture,* edited by Carol Stabile and Mark Harrison, 15–32. London: Routledge, 2003.

Wheeler, Lora D'Anne. "Children in Transition: Popular Children's Magazines in Late Imperial and Early Soviet Russia." PhD diss., University of Southern California, Los Angeles, 2001.

White, David Gordon. *Myths of the Dog-Man*. Chicago: University of Chicago Press, 1991.

Wolff, Janet. "On the Road Again: Metaphors of Travel in Cultural Criticism." *Cultural Studies* 7, no. 2 (1993): 224–239.

"Women he nimen jinjin woshou, gongtong wei fandui Meidi er douzheng ba" 我們和你們緊緊握手 共同爲反對美帝而鬥爭吧 [Let us clasp hands and fight against American imperialism]. *Dazhong dianying* 大眾電影 [Popular cinema], no. 19 (1951): 2–3.

"Women shi buhui quxi de" 我們是不會屈膝的 [We will never bend our knees]. *Dazhong dianying* 大眾電影 [Popular cinema] no. 19 (1951): 2–3.

Woo, Catherine Yi-yu Cho. *Chinese Aesthetics and Ch'I Pai-shih.* Hong Kong: Joint Publishing Co., 1986.

Wu, Hung. *A Story of Ruins: Presence and Absence in Chinese Art and Visual Culture.* Princeton, NJ: Princeton University Press, 2012.

Wu Lun 武倫. "Meishu dianying fanying dangdai shenghuo wenti" 美術電影反映當代生活問題 [View on animated film's capacity of reflecting contemporary life]. *Dianying yishu* 電影藝術 [Film art] 4 (1963): 53–54.

Wu, Weihua. "Animation in Postsocialist China: Visual Narrative, Modernity, and Digital Culture." PhD diss., City University of Hong Kong, 2006.

———. *Chinese Animation, Creative Industries and Digital Culture.* New York: Routledge, 2017.

Xia Yan 夏衍. "Ba woguo dianying yishu tigao dao yige gengxin de shuiping" 把我國電影藝術提高到一個更新的水平 [Raising the standard of our country's film art]. *Hongqi* 紅旗 [Red flag], no. 19 (1961): 5–17.

Xiang Sulian dianying xuexi 向蘇聯電影學習 [Learn from Soviet film]. Hankou: Zhongnan renmin wenxue yishu chubanshe, 1952.

Xiao Lu 肖路. *Guochan donghua dianying chuantong meixue tezheng jiqi wenhua tanyuan* 國產動畫電影傳統美學特徵及其文化探源 [Traditional aesthetics in Chinese animated films and their cultural origins]. Shanghai: Shanghai shiji chuban jituan, 2008.

Xiaoli 小力. "Fangri sanji" 訪日散記 [Notes on the journey to Japan]. *Sun Wukong* 孫悟空 [Monkey King] vol. 4, 1981.

Xu Jing 許婧 and Wang Yang 汪煬. *Du donghua: Zhongguo donghua huangjin bashi nian* 讀動畫 中國動畫黃金八十年 [Eighty years of Chinese animation]. Beijing: Chaohua chubanshe, 2005.

Yamaguchi Katsunori 山口且訓 and Watanabe Yasushi 渡辺泰. *Nihon animēshon eigashi* 日本アニメーション映画史 [History of Japanese animation]. Osaka-shi: Yūbunsha, 1977.

Yamaguchi Takeshi 山口猛. *Aishū no Manshū eiga* 哀愁の満州映画 [Melancholic Manchurian cinema]. Tōkyō: Santen shobō, 2000.

Yamaguchi Yasuo 山口康男. *Riben donghua quanshi: Riben donghua lingxian shijiede qiji* 日本動畫全史: 日本動畫領先世界的奇跡 [A complete history of Japanese animation: The miracle of Japanese animation leading the world]. Beijing: Zhongguo kexue jishu chubanshe, 2008.

Yamaguchi, Yoshiko. *Fragrant Orchid: The Story of My Early Life.* Translated by Chia-ning Chang. Honolulu: University of Hawai'i Press, 2015.

Yan Hui 嚴慧 and Suo Yabin 索亞斌. *Zhongguo donghua dianying shi* 中國動畫電影史 [History of Chinese animation]. Beijing: Zhongguo dianying chubanshe, 2005.

Yan Ni 晏妮. *Senji Nitchū eiga kōshōshi* 戦時日中映画交渉史 [Sino-Japanese cinematic exchanges during World War II]. Tōkyō: Iwanami shoten, 2010.

Yang, Lan. "Socialist Realism versus Revolutionary Realism plus Revolutionary Romanticism." In *The Party Spirit: Socialist Realism and Literary Practice in the Soviet Union, East Germany and China*, edited by Hilary Chung, Michael Falchikov, Bonnie S. McDougall, and Karin McPherson, 88–105. Amsterdam: Rodopi, 1996.

Yang, Panpan. "Animating Landscape: Chinese Ink-and-Wash Animation, 1960–2013." *International Journal of Comic Art* 16, no. 2 Fall/Winter (2014): 380–397.

Yau, Kinnia. *Japanese and Hong Kong Film Industries: Understanding the Origins of East Asian Film Networks*. New York: Routledge, 2010.

Yin Yan 尹巖. "Donghua dianying zhong de Zhongguo xuepai" 動畫電影中的中國學派 [The Chinese school of animation]. *Dangdai dianying* 當代電影 [Contemporary cinema] 6 (1988): 71–79.

Yoshida Sadaji 吉田貞次. "Aa maboroshi no satsueijo Man'ei: Nihon no eigajin ga nokoshita sono mijikai inochi ああ幻の撮影所満映: 日本の映画人が遺したその短かい命 [The phantasmagoric Manchukuo Film Association: The short life of a film studio left behind by Japanese filmmakers]. *Eiga satsuei* 映画撮影 [Cinematography], no. 71 (June 1980): 53–58.

———. "Man'ei kara Jinginakitatakai made" 満映から『仁義なき戦い』まで [From Man'ei to the film *Battles without Honor and Humanity*]. *FB: Eiga kenkyū-shi* FB: 映画研究誌 [FB: Film research magazine], no. 3 (August 1994): 59–97.

Young, Louise. *Japan's Total Empire: Manchuria and the Culture of Wartime Imperialism*. Berkeley: University of California Press, 1998.

"Yousheng manhua: Maiyou" 有聲漫畫 買油 [Sound cartoon: *Purchasing Oil*]. *Manzhou dianying* 滿洲電影 [Manchuria film] 4, no. 4 (April 1940): 70–73.

Yu Feng 郁風. "Zuotan meishu dianying" 座談美術電影 [On Chinese animated film]. *Dianying yishu* 電影藝術 [Film art] 2 (1960), 37–38.

"Zadankai Nihon manga eiga no kōryū" 座談会 日本漫画映画の興隆 [Roundtable forum: The prosperity of Japanese animated film]. *Eiga hyōron* 映画評論 [Magazine of film review] (May 1943): 12–19.

Zahlten, Alex. *The End of Japanese Cinema: Industrial Genres, National Times, and Media Ecologies*. Durham, NC: Duke University Press, 2017.

Zhang Haowen 張皓雯. "Riben xinzuo fanchen Zhongguo donghua luomo" 日本新作 反襯中國動畫落寞 [New work by Japan: Contrast to the decline of Chinese animation]. *Guoji xianqu daobao* 國際先驅導報 [International herald leader], November 5, 2004. Accessed February 8, 2018. http://japan.people.com.cn/GB/35468/35500/2968620.html.

Zhang Huilin 張慧臨. *Ershi shiji Zhongguo donghua yishushi* 二十世紀中國動畫藝術史 [History of the art of Chinese animation in twentieth century]. Xi'an: Shanxi renmin chubanshe, 2002.

Zhang Junxiang 張駿祥. "Genghao de xuexi Sulian, baowei shehui zhuyi de dianying shiye" 更好地學習蘇聯 保衛社會主義的電影事業 [Better learn from the Soviet

Union: Protect socialist cinema]. *Zhongguo dianying* 中國電影 [Chinese cinema], no. 11 (1957): 8–14.

Zhang Songlin 張松林. "Chuangzao fuyou minzu fengge de Zhongguo meishu dianying" 創造富有民族風格的中國美術電影 [Producing Chinese animated films with national style]. In *Zhongguo dianying nianjian* 中國電影年鑒 [China film yearbook], 174-183. Beijing: Zhongguo dianying chubanshe, 1981.

Zhang Songlin 張松林 and Gong Jianying 貢建英. *Shei chuangzao le Xiao Kedou Zhao Mama Te Wei he Zhongguo donghua* 誰創造了小蝌蚪找媽媽 特偉和中國動畫 [Who created *Little Tadpoles Look for Mama*: Te Wei and Chinese animation]. Shanghai: Shanghai renmin chubanshe, 2010.

Zhang Xinshi 張辛實. "Dongdang niandai de huiyi" 動盪年代的回憶 [Memories of the chaotic years]. In *Yi Dongying* 憶東影 [In memory of the Northeast Film Studio], 7–27. Changchun: Jilin wenshi chubanshe, 1986.

Zhang Xuezhi 張學智. "Manying: Riben duihua wenhua qinlüe de tiezheng" 滿映 日本對華文化侵略的鐵證 [Manchukuo Film Association: Hard evidence of Japan's cultural imperialism in China]. *Dianying yishu* 電影藝術 [Film art], no. 2 (2003): 118–119.

Zhang, Yingjin. *Chinese National Cinema.* New York: Routledge, 2004.

———. *Cinema, Space, and Polylocality in a Globalizing China.* Honolulu: University of Hawai'i Press, 2010.

———. "From 'Minority Film' to 'Minority Discourse' Questions of Nationhood and Ethnicity in Chinese Cinema." In *Transnational Chinese Cinemas: Identity, Nationhood, Gender,* edited by Sheldon Lu, 81–104. Honolulu: University of Hawai'i Press, 1997.

Zhang, Zhen. *An Amorous History of the Silver Screen: Shanghai Cinema 1896–1937.* Chicago: University of Chicago Press, 2005.

Zhao Dongli 趙東黎. "8.15 hou de Changchun xingshi he dui yuan Manying de gongzuo" 8.15後的長春形勢和對原滿映的工作 [Changchun after August 15 and the takeover of Manchukuo Film Association]. In *Yi Dongying* 憶東影 [In memory of the Northeast Film Studio]. Changchun: Jilin wenshi chubanshe, 1986.

Zhi Qiu 知秋. "Wan Laiming juezhao: Yingxing jianying" 萬籟鳴絕招 影星剪影 [Wan Laiming's feat: Paper cutout silhouettes for film stars]. *Dazhong dianying* 大眾電影 [Popular cinema] 21 (2003).

Zhong Ling 鐘靈. "Meishupian de xin tiandi: Jianping Lubian Xinshi, Sidianban, Banye Jijiao, Hongjun Qiao" 美術片的新天地 簡評路邊新事 四點半 半夜雞叫 紅軍橋 [The new territory of animation: Comments on *New Deeds on the Roadside*, *Four and a Half O'Clock*, *The Rooster Crows at Midnight*, *The Red Army Bridge*], *Dianying yishu* 電影藝術 [Film art] 3 (1965): 70–72.

Zhongguo Donghua Xuehui 中國動畫學會. "Zhongguo donghuaye zai qianjin zhong de kunnan he xiwang" 中國動畫業在前進中的困難和希望 [The difficulties and hopes of Chinese animation industry on its way to development]. *Zhongguo dianying nianjian* 中國電影年鑒 [Yearbook of Chinese cinema], 92–93. Beijing: Zhongguo dianying chubanshe, 1989.

Zhou Chengren 周承人 and Li Yizhuang 李以莊. *Zaoqi Xianggang dianyingshi* 早期香港電影史 [History of early Hong Kong cinema]. Hong Kong: Sanlian shudian, 2005.

Zhou Keqin 周克勤. "Meiying: Nanwang de 1989" 美影：難忘的1989 [Shanghai Animation Film Studio: The unforgettable year of 1989]. In *Zhongguo dianying nianjian* 中國電影年鑒 [Yearbook of Chinese cinema], 117–118. Beijing: Zhongguo dianying chubanshe, 1990.

Zhou Yang 周揚. *Wenyi zhanxian shang de yichang da bianlun* 文藝戰綫上的一場大辯論 [A great debate in literature and art]. Beijing: Zuojia chubanshe, 1958.

Zhu Jidong 朱繼東. "Gongfu xiongmao weihe mofang Zhongguo gongfu ye rang Zhongguo yingren wangchen moji?" 功夫熊貓為何模仿中國功夫也讓中國影人望塵莫及 [How did *Kung Fu Panda* awe and shame Chinese filmmakers by imitating Chinese kung fu?]. *Zhu Jidong blog*, 2008.

Zhu, Ying. "Has Chinese Film Finally Produced a Real Hero?" *ChinaFile*, August 18, 2015. Accessed February 8, 2018. http://www.chinafile.com/reporting-opinion/culture/has-chinese-film-finally-produced-real-hero.

Zipes, Jack. *The Enchanted Screen: The Unknown History of Fairy-Tale Films*. New York: Routledge, 2011.

Index

Bold page numbers refer to figures.

About the Author

Daisy Yan Du is an associate professor in the Division of Humanities at the Hong Kong University of Science and Technology, Clear Water Bay. She has published articles on animation, film, gender, and popular culture in numerous journals and is founder of the Association for Chinese Animation Studies (http://acas.ust.hk), the leading scholarly and public organization dedicated to introducing and promoting Chinese animation to the English-speaking world.